Education in South-E

Education in South-East Asia

Edited by
Colin Brock & Lorraine Pe Symaco

Oxford Studies in Comparative Education
Series Editor: David Phillips

SYMPOSIUM
BOOKS

Symposium Books
PO Box 204, Didcot, Oxford OX11 9ZQ, United Kingdom
www.symposium-books.co.uk

Published in the United Kingdom, 2011

ISBN 978-1-873927-56-4

This publication is also available on a subscription basis
as Volume 21 Number 2 of *Oxford Studies in Comparative Education*
(ISSN 0961-2149)

Printed and bound in the United Kingdom by Hobbs the Printers, Southampton
www.hobbs.uk.com

Contents

CHAPTER 1

Introduction

COLIN BROCK & LORRAINE PE SYMACO

We would like to thank all those who have contributed chapters, whether nation-specific or thematic. They have all made a useful contribution to the literature in the field of comparative and international education as well as that of South-East Asian Studies. Indeed this is the first volume in the longstanding series *Oxford Studies in Comparative Education* to be devoted to this region, and the academic literature on this area is in general rather thin. This may be because conventional images of nations tend to place them either in the 'developed and industrialised' category or in the 'underdeveloped and rural' category. With the exception of Singapore and Brunei Darussalam, none of the countries in the region are in the High Income Countries Category, while at most three – Cambodia, Lao PDR and Myanmar [1] – are regarded as Low Income Countries. Countries in the region are mostly Lower Middle Income Countries, with the exception of Malaysia being a High Middle Income Country, according to the World Bank (2010).

All but Timor-Leste are members of the Association of Southeast Asian Nations (ASEAN), which has its headquarters in Jakarta. This city is the location for the regional offices for the wider Asia/Pacific region recognised by many international organisations such as UNESCO. Such organisations tend to operate on a parameter of Asia/Pacific or East Asia/Pacific, which means that on the major databases such as the Global Monitoring Reviews, South-East Asia as a region of its own may not have data at that level to illustrate its overall distinctive nature within the range of developing countries in the world. The region is also unusual in that between a quarter and a third of its area is open water with its two largest and most populous countries, Indonesia and the Philippines, being major archipelagos. This, together with a great deal of mountainous territory, including active volcanoes and structural instability, means that they have to cope with a difficult geographical environment. In addition to the massive Indian Ocean tsunami of 2004, and subsequent smaller ones, there has been devastation of schooling from ash clouds and mud slides.

Culturally too, the region is diverse, deriving from a wide range of indigenous cultures on top of which there are overlays of colonial legacy. These vary from British in Brunei Darussalam, Myanmar, Malaysia and Singapore, to Dutch in Indonesia, Portuguese in Timor-Leste, French in Cambodia, Lao PDR and Vietnam, and Spanish and American in the Philippines. In Thailand, the region has one of the very few developing countries in the world that was not colonised by the West. The result is a remarkable kaleidoscope of local languages, the survival of metropolitan languages with different degrees of influence on educational policy and practice, and a few lingua francas. Language is one of the two key identifiers of culture, the other being religion. Here again the region is distinctive in ways that have fundamental influences on all forms of education. Indonesia is the most populous Islamic nation in the world, while Islam is very influential in Malaysia in that it is the religion of the politically dominant culture – the same being the case in Brunei Darussalam. Christianity is dominant in the Philippines, except for some parts of the region of Mindanao, which makes for internal tensions affecting education. Timor-Leste is the other country that is dominantly Christian in the region aside from the Philippines.

Although, as indicated, most countries are middle income or better in economic terms, there is a great deal of disparity in this respect also. Urban–rural disparities of economy and wealth make for fundamental differences in educational chances despite generally positive efforts by all governments to support schooling for all. Rural areas exhibit a range of economies from traditional gathering, to survival subsistence farming to massive plantations. Within some of the larger urban areas are among the largest and most poverty-stricken slum communities alongside business districts of world class.

All these wide disparities must be borne in mind when discussing education on a national scale. In some nations of the region, sub-national political units may have considerable influences on educational policy, funding and provision which, again, may not be easily evident when painting the broad brush. Necessarily the majority of the chapters that follow cover the 10 nation-states in ASEAN, plus Timor-Leste, but there are also a number of thematic chapters in order to highlight issues that are of regional significance, such as gender, higher education, language policy, quality assurance at tertiary level, and sustainable development. Each of these chapters will now be introduced briefly.

The chapter on Brunei Darussalam by Omar Haji Khalid focuses on the education system of the country along with some of the policy directions set for education by the government. Notable in his chapter is the increasing focus of Brunei Darussalam on using the education sector as means to promote and sustain competitive manpower especially relevant in this time of globalisation. Important issues such as the country's language policy and English serving as a 'language for development' are also discussed.

The role of education in post-conflict states as relevant to Cambodia and Timor-Leste is also tackled in this book. The chapter by Martin Hayden & Richard Martin on Cambodia mentions that despite the country's increasing participation rates at the primary level, there seems to be a concern about the sharp decrease beyond this level (i.e. secondary, higher education and technical vocational). Limited resources along with a socio-political culture that is portrayed to be 'hierarchical and bureaucratic' also prove to be serious barriers in utilising the education system for development. Bob Boughton examines the educational development of Timor-Leste through five periods of Portuguese colonial rule, decolonisation, Indonesian military occupation and the Resistance, and under United Nations administration. He also mentions a critical factor of employing education as a means of constructing a 'national identity and culture' along with the overriding identification of education for economic advancement – an essential challenge especially relevant to post-conflict nations of heavy colonial influence.

The chapter on Indonesia by Assad Baunto similarly discusses the country's educational development through phases of the pre-colonial period (Islamisation), the colonial period under the Dutch, the post-colonial period (*Orde Lama* and *Orde Baru*), and post-Soeharto (Decentralisation). Issues relevant to the country's system such as education quality, the trade-off of prioritising basic education over other levels, mismatch of graduate skills with the labour market, and insufficiencies of the decentralisation reform are also discussed.

Socialist Republics Lao PDR and Vietnam are covered by Richard Noonan (Lao PDR) and Pham Lan Huong & Gerald Fry (Vietnam). The chapter on Lao PDR gives a historical context of the educational development in the country from the Classical Period of 1353-1895 through to the Revolution of 1975-86. Current challenges and issues faced by Lao PDR as similar to other developing countries in the region are also reviewed, which among others include limited resources and financing, repetition and drop-out rates (though rates have fallen in recent years), and teacher deployment. The chapter on Vietnam tackles various issues surrounding its education system, including those relating to the policy of social mobilisation for education (which served in the expansion of Vietnam's education capacity); educational disparities; quality of education as a reflection of its teachers, teaching methods, and educational programmes; and the crisis in higher education. The imminent role of education in propelling Vietnam into one of the most competitive countries in the region is also highlighted.

Historically associated countries Malaysia and Singapore are also reviewed in this book. Siow Heng Loke & Chang Lee Hoon describe the priority laid by the government on education and training in terms of developing and advancing the human capital of Malaysia. The empowering force of education in terms of promoting national unity, given the three main racial groups in the country (*Bumiputras*, Chinese and Indians), is also addressed. Critical education reforms since independence such as early childhood, teacher and tertiary education are discussed. The chapter on Singapore by Jason Tan highlights data on the different levels of schooling in the country, along with themes of marketisation of education, promoting social cohesion through National Education policy, and the promotion of 'thinking schools'. Given the more advanced status of Singapore's economic condition and education system, issues still continue to persist in the education sector such as disparities in terms of educational attainment and the need to focus on approaches that cater to 'creative and critical thinking' more than rote 'drilling and coaching practices'.

Country case studies also include the politically diverse orientations of governments from the more subdued Myanmar to the liberally democratic Philippines. The chapter on Myanmar by Richard Martin addresses the needs of the current education system. It also suggests alternative ways on how the education sector can improve given the restrictions placed by the government in some aspects. The role of international organisations and the call for a more engaging role in the country are also highlighted. A more active role played by private organisations in terms of education and training is also sought in relation to the growing private sector in Myanmar. Lorraine Symaco provides the chapter on the Philippines and gives an overview of some of the more pressing problems in the Philippine education system. Insufficient resources coupled with policies that do not readily and effectively address the concerns of the sector are highlighted. Despite the increasing expansion of the education sector in terms of enrolment, problems such as corruption, lack of access and equity, and the dismal overall quality of education prevent the education sector from fully optimising its expected role for development.

The unique characteristic of Thailand being the only country in the region that has never been colonised by foreign powers shows its impact and influence on the teaching and learning process of the country. Natthapoj Vincent Trakulphadetkrai further explores this idea through the comparative use of frameworks on cultural dimensions. Comparative analyses between Thailand and other countries in the region in terms of the 'Education for All' goals are also presented. Chapters on gender and language policy as relevant to education form part of the five thematic chapters included in this book. The chapter on gender by Colin Brock & Pei-Tseng Jenny Hsieh gives a comparative perspective of gender and the education sector in South-East Asia. The link between gender, education and development is also highlighted. Factors affecting female participation in any form of education, such as situations of conflict and work (child labour, migrant workers) among others, are discussed. Keith Watson writes about education and language policies in South-East Asia. He stresses the significance of language and discusses further the ethnic and linguistic diversity as relevant to the region. Dilemmas faced by governments in the region in terms of balancing national unity and linguistic rights of certain groups are also examined.

The thematic chapters also include discussions by Anthony Welch on higher education and Somwung Pitiyanuwat on quality assurance in higher education. The higher education chapter provides a comparative overview of the higher education sector of five ASEAN member-states (Indonesia, Malaysia, the Philippines, Thailand and Vietnam). Issues relating to the extent of privatisation in these countries are reviewed along with similarly significant issues on globalisation, internationalisation and regionalisation. The chapter on quality assurance gives a comparative overview of the quality assurance mechanisms and practices of the 11 countries included in this book. Challenges and issues in quality assurance are considered along with the different quality assurance bodies relevant to the region's education quality review.

The chapter on sustainable development and education completes the five thematic chapters of this book. Mikko Cantell & Derek Elias discuss the significance of advocating education for sustainable development. They highlight the role of education in development and the need to define what type of education enables sustainable development. Policy reorientations of international organisations in this regard are also emphasised.

Note

[1] It is the editors' decision to use Myanmar instead of Burma, adhering to the official name of the country as at present. Given the focus of this book on South-East Asia, it is also important to note that ASEAN also uses the current official name of Myanmar to refer to the country.

Reference

World Bank (2010) World Development Indicators.
http://worldbank.org/data-catalog/world-development-indicators/wdi-2010 (accessed 15 November, 2010).

12

CHAPTER 2

The Education System of Brunei Darussalam

OMAR HAJI KHALID

SUMMARY This chapter provides a brief overview of Brunei Darussalam, its education system and history. It provides a brief description of the national education vision, goals and strategies, and their alignment with the National Development Plan. It describes the policy directions for education for the next 10 years, and recent development, especially with a new education system (SPN21) based on a bilingual (English and Malay language) policy and reforms in higher education.

Introduction

Brunei Darussalam, a sovereign nation, is situated at the heart of South-East Asia. Bandar Seri Begawan, the capital, is the seat of the government of Sultan Sir Hassanal Bolkiah, the ruler of the sultanate – a Muslim monarchy. The size of the country is roughly 5760 square kilometres with 70% of its area covered with tropical forest and swamp. It is situated on the north-west end of the island of Borneo. It has about 160 kilometres of coastline, facing the South China Sea. The country is divided into four districts, namely Belait, Tutong, Brunei-Muara and Temburong. The district of Temburong is separated from the other districts by Limbang, a district in Sabah which is part of Malaysia. The principal means of communication between Temburong and other districts of Brunei Darussalam is by river or overland via Limbang. The country is surrounded by Malaysian states Sabah and Sarawak.

Brunei Darussalam became a British protectorate in 1888. In 1906, a British resident was nominated as representative of the British government. His role was to advise the Sultan in all matters except Malay customs, traditions and Islam. With the establishment of the Resident System, the British then set up government departments, beginning with customs, and begun to take charge of executive and administrative responsibilities. The 1959 Agreement established a written constitution which gave Brunei internal self-government. In 1971, the agreement was amended and revised to assert full internal independence except for defence and external matters.

Prior to 1984, the country was known as Brunei. The longer name was adopted at the time of independence, and means 'abode of Peace'. Brunei Darussalam became independent on 1 January 1984.

Brunei Darussalam became a member of the Association of Southeast Asian Nations in 1984 as well as its sister organisation, the South-East Asian Ministers of Education Organisation (SEAMEO). SEAMEO is a collaborative organisation in the field of education and training with full membership comprising of 11 nations, namely Brunei Darussalam, Singapore, Malaysia, the Philippines, Thailand, Indonesia, Myanmar, Vietnam, Timor-Leste, Cambodia and Laos. Brunei Darussalam hosts the specialist regional centre for technical/vocational education.

As of 2008, Brunei Darussalam has a population of 396,692 (World Bank, 2010). The population is predominantly Malay (about 74%), of which the majority are Muslims. Chinese and other races constitute about 16% and 10% respectively. Approximately 45.8% (114,100) of the population are below the age of 20 years (World Health Organization, 2004). Table I shows the make-up of the country's population.

	2001	%	2005	%	2010	%	Average annual growth rate	
							RKN8	RKN9
Total population	322,800		370,100		410,600		2.7	2.2
Age structure								
0-14	100,900	30.3	111,000	30.0	115,000	28.0	2.4	2.0
15-64	222,600	66.9	248,400	67.1	283,300	69.0	2.7	2.9
65 and above	9,300	2.8	10,700	2.9	12,300	3.0	3.5	3.7

Note: RKN8 = 8th National Development Plan (2000-2005); RKN9 = 9th National Development Plan (2007-11).

Table I. Population size (estimated) and age structure, 2001-10.
Source: Population Census 2001 and Department of Statistics (JPKE, 2001).

National Vision and Goals

In 2007, the government of Brunei Darussalam introduced a National Development Policy and Strategy. In its publication *Outline of Strategies and Policies for Development*, the Brunei Darussalam national vision, there are three long-range goals that it hopes to achieve by 2035 (JPKE, 2007). They are:

1. for Brunei Darussalam to have an accomplished and well-educated people brought about by an education system that is comparable to the highest international standards;
2. for its citizens to achieve a high quality of life that is among the top 10 nations in the world; and
3. to have a dynamic and sustainable economy that would place the country among the top 10 nations in the world in terms of income per capita.

The national vision requires that the National Development Plan of eight integrated and well-coordinated national strategies be implemented by the relevant stakeholders along four themes, namely:

1. Investing in Human Capital;
2. Accelerating the Pace of Social Progress and Maintaining Political Stability;
3. Widening the Economic Base and Strengthening the Foundation for a Knowledge-based Economy; and
4. Strengthening the Institutional Capacity.

The purpose of the *Outline of Strategies and Policies for Development* is to provide a framework for the implementation of the national vision by stating clearly the directions each strategy (which includes education) should take in the next 10 years (2007-17) (JPKE, 2007, Part 1).

The main thrust of the education strategy for the next 10 years (2007 to 2017) will focus on:

- investing in early childhood development;
- strengthening secondary and tertiary education as well as vocational schools;
- improving the quality of teaching and learning;
- widening participation in learning;
- investing in research, development and innovation; and
- improving the management of educational institutions.

Below are the policy directions for education as developed by the Ministry of Education.

Policy Directions for Education in the Next 10 Years

- *Education sector road map*: A master plan for the education sector will be developed which will be formulated and implemented within the next five years with the primary aim of integrating plans and requirements of all the relevant stakeholders. The master plan will take into account future demographic changes, long-term economic growth targets, among other things, and will cover all levels of education from pre-school to tertiary.

- *Development of school functions*: Decentralisation of some of the management (including financial) and administration of schools will be integrated in the system resulting in a more competitive and accountable school system. A blueprint for a mandatory ICT training scheme for teachers, school administrators and education officers will also be prepared.
- *Promotion of lifelong learning*: Efforts shall focus on reviewing all aspects of the lifelong learning culture, including international best practices. Institutional mechanisms will be established to develop a lifelong learning culture. Programmes to develop the local pool of experts will be launched, and various appropriate modalities (including the provision of an appropriate scheme of service that enables workers to take up in-service training throughout their working life) will be utilised. A relevant incentive structure will be built into the policy to deepen the culture of lifelong learning among Bruneians. Measures will also be taken to continuously upgrade and strengthen the skills and professionalism of the existing local workforce.
- *Strong link between educational institutions and industry*: Policy measures will be introduced to build some flexibility in the educational system in order for it to be more responsive to the demands of the industry. Partnership mechanisms will be further developed to include consultation with the public and the private sectors. On a wider scope, the government will facilitate and strengthen its cooperation with institutions in other countries as well as explore similar opportunities with multinational corporations in developing industrial training and research and development (R&D).
- *Innovative ways of providing education*: Innovative delivery of education through distance learning, open learning and the use of technologies will be explored. Innovative approaches to education by using technologies will be further explored to reduce costs, increase access to education, expand the range and training options, and increase the quality of education.
- *International dimension in the country's education system*: To improve the standard and quality of education, policies will be introduced to facilitate the adoption of international best practices in education, and international partnerships in research and teaching. In 2007, the Ministry of Education engaged the Australian Council of Educational Research to conduct a study on students' achievement in mathematics and reading and writing in English. The result was presented to the Ministry of Education in December 2008 with a number of recommendations for raising standards, and further improvements in teaching and learning. An early step that the Ministry has taken was to recruit more specialist teachers of English to teach at primary and secondary levels. The Ministry also recruited native English speakers through the Centre for British Teachers and this has produced

significant result in raising the standard of spoken language among school leavers.

- Enhanced knowledge infrastructure: Universities and other higher learning and research institutions, and other elements of the knowledge infrastructure will be utilised to support the knowledge transfer between organisations. Efforts will be made to strengthen networks among researchers and R&D institutions, locally and abroad.

Other policies that can be derived from the other strategies are:

- *High labour productivity and competitiveness*: Owing to the constraint of having a small population, Brunei Darussalam needs to increase its labour productivity and competitiveness. These will be increased through education, adoption of appropriate and advanced technology, increased dynamism in the labour market, and institutional rearrangements in the public sector in order to ensure smoother flows of work. The female labour force participation rate is to be increased so that the chronic dependence on skilled foreign labour can be reduced.
- *Expanded knowledge-based activities*: There is a need to shift the emphasis from production-based activities to knowledge-based activities. An important ingredient in these knowledge-based activities is the R&D capacity of the nation. This requires strengthening of science and technology and R&D policies, improvement in institutional and human capacity, focusing on main research thrusts and provision of sufficient and timely funding. Activities on R&D have always been low or minimal (JPKE, 2007). It has been acknowledged that the absence of a central agency to champion the science, technology and innovation (STI) development in the country 'has led to a poorly coordinated and integrated STI policy with no specific objectives' and 'led to failure to explicitly outline and execute strategies that will enable the country to capitalize fully the benefits of STI in national development' (JPKE, 2007, p. 171). Table II is a comparison of STI indicators (for 2002-03) showing that Brunei Darussalam is far below those of several major industrial countries in the region.

	Brunei Darussalam	Singapore	Malaysia	Korea	Japan
R&D personnel per million people	282	4352	294	2979	5085
Expenditure of R&D as % of GDP	0.03	2.2	0.7	2.9	3.1

Table II. Comparison of STI indicators (2002-03).
Source: Department of Economic Planning (2007, p. 171).

* *Enhanced role of women in development*: The strategic direction in the next 10 years is to significantly increase the participation rate of women in the workforce to 75%. Along this line, the government will formulate national policy to ensure more opportunities for women to participate directly in nation building as well as the decision-making process. To facilitate this, appropriate support services including childcare, crèche centres, flexible terms and conditions, and working hours will be provided to advance women's participation in business and in public services.

Education in Brunei Darussalam

The school system in the country has essentially been inherited from the British system. The first Malay-vernacular school was established in 1912, with a total enrolment of 53 boys. Between the periods of 1912 and 1929, the enrolment increased to 756 (boys). The first Chinese-medium school was opened in 1916, and then an English school and an Anglican Mission school in 1931. A Malay school for girls was established in 1930. Prior to 1975, a large number of students were sent abroad by the government, the majority to British schools, to study Advanced-level (A level) courses leading to higher education. In 1975 the Sixth Form Center was opened with an enrolment of 501 students. Upon successful completion of their A levels, many proceeded to higher institutions in the United Kingdom (UK). A few took courses in Australia, New Zealand, Malaysia or Singapore. In 1985, Universiti Brunei Darussalam (University of Brunei Darussalam) was established, with an initial enrolment of about 185 students.

A bilingual system of education was introduced in 1985 in all government-run schools in Brunei Darussalam under the Ministry of Education. The schools were integrated from two separate systems into a single system. Before 1985, the Ministry of Education had a Malay-medium and an English-medium system. Malay-medium students were required to learn English as a foreign language and the medium of instruction was Malay for all subjects. For the English-medium students, Malay language was a compulsory subject among the core subjects of English, mathematics and science at both primary and secondary levels. Malay-medium students who had completed their secondary education were then required to sit the Singapore Cambridge General Certificate of Education (SGCE) examinations at Ordinary then Advanced level while English-medium students were required to sit the Brunei Cambridge General Certificate of Education (BGCE) examinations. The SGCE were set and marked in Singapore and the BGCE in the UK. The SGCE, for Malay-medium students in Singapore, was already being phased out by that time and a special arrangement had been made to enable Brunei Darussalam continued use of the facilities of the SGCE Examination Board for the Malay-medium examination.

In 1985, the mandated change affected only government-run schools. The privately funded Chinese school system and the Arabic-medium system (which includes all religious schools), which came under the jurisdiction of the Ministry of Religious Affairs, were not required to, and nor did they, switch to a bilingual mode. It should be noted here that a few non-government schools adopted the change voluntarily. The Arabic-medium system, which also used the SGCE Examination Board, was similar to the Malay-medium system except that Arabic was taught as students' second language. Students who successfully completed the Arabic-medium system would either continue on to a Middle Eastern country or would enter the Malay-medium stream, at the Sixth Form Center, for advanced courses.

The Outcome of the Mandated Change

The purpose of educational change, presumably, is to help schools accomplish their goals more effectively by replacing some structures, programs and/or practices with better ones.
(Fullan, 1982, p. 15)

The Ministry of Education mandated that, as from 1 January 1992, all non-government schools must follow the National Education System. Before this mandated change, students at non-government, English-medium schools completed their primary education in six years. On the other hand, students at government schools would initially attend Malay-medium schools for the first four years and then become eligible for transfer to English-medium schools for the remaining three years of primary education. Students at non-government, English-medium schools could however apply to transfer to government English-medium schools after completing year 3, in effect gaining one year.

The new policy, requiring the first three years of education to be delivered in a Malay medium and thereafter in English, resulted in fewer problems for the English government schools than for the Malay government schools. The English schools merely recruited extra Malay-medium staff to cover the first three years while the Malay schools faced a severe shortage of English-medium teachers and a large surplus of Malay-medium teachers.

The mandated change in the English-medium schools involved only the first three years of primary education. The long-term implication for these schools is that some students now have a lower command of the English language in year 4, compared to when English was the medium of instruction from year 1. Repeatedly, the Primary School Certificate Examination (PCE), which all students sit at the end of their primary education, indicated that the English-medium schools had a better track record than the bilingual schools. The examination is in English, with the exception of the Malay-language paper, and this would indicate that English-medium students, who had a three-year lead (i.e. more contact hours) in the English language, were indeed at an advantage over the bilingual students. Parents who saw this advantage began to register their children with non-government schools and waiting lists were often as long as three years. Even between government-run schools, a discrepancy was noticed between the PCE results of rural and urban schools. The rural schools generally had significantly lower pass rates than the urban schools and the majority of those students who failed, did so in either English or mathematics. Some rural schools in the 1991 PCE had a pass rate as low as 13%. In those schools, 30% to 80% of the final-year primary students had to repeat another year. Clearly for students in these groups, the system has failed to adequately motivate them. What could have caused this poor performance? Is it because the better teachers are in urban schools, or could it be that motivated teachers who are moved into rural settings become less motivated as a consequence of poor support and limited resources (difficulty in getting textbooks, teaching materials, chalk and photocopiers, no electricity, poor housing, among others)? Could it be that rural students have lower self-esteem or is it merely that they cannot relate their school work to the local environment? These discrepancies certainly merit some form of study. Is there a significant primary school dropout rate between urban and rural schools and between genders? Data of this kind needs to be collected and brought to the attention of policy makers, administrators, teachers and the community, as an indicator of the effectiveness of schools. A combination of several factors may have contributed to the poor achievements of those students, among which, I suspect, are included leadership, teachers' attitude and competence, the remoteness of the schools and the associated communication problems and resources.

As mentioned, the Malay-medium schools had to make the biggest adjustment when adopting the National Education System, although the transformation was done in stages beginning with the year 1 intake of students in 1985 and following it through to 1997. Many of the Malay-medium teachers, who had taught general subjects with the exception of English as a subject, were not able to switch their medium of instruction from Malay to English. As civil servants, they were permanently employed by the government. Therefore, some were sent for inservice/upgrading courses and some assigned to non-teaching duties.

The switch to the National Education System was not totally accepted by all quarters of the population. Parents who had registered or enrolled their children in the English-medium schools saw the bilingual mode as eroding further the school system in the state and taking away the element of choice. Many felt that their children, with six years of English-medium instruction, would have a head start over those with only three years of English-medium instruction. Contrary to this belief, studies have shown that in some cases, second-language learning of English appears to be remarkably successful when students are initially instructed in and gain their first literacy in their native language, with later introduction of systematic English as a second language (Rosier & Holm, in Toohey, 1985, p. 289). Rosier & Holm report that a bilingual programme of this kind promotes more successful second-language learning than a programme which utilises only English as a medium of instruction. Before the change-over to the new system, students from the Malay-medium schools were assessed and the high achievers selected for transfer to English-medium schools. With the introduction of the bilingual system, some English-medium schools were concerned about overall achievement if they were required to take in academically low achievers who would normally have remained in the Malay-medium system. The Malay-medium advocates saw this as an erosion of Malay values and a threat to their sovereignty. Teachers in the Chinese school system, which was already switching to a somewhat trilingual system (Chinese and English with Malay as a subject), were concerned at not being able to teach the Chinese language within the new curriculum. One possible objective of the government, when the National Education System was imposed on all schools in the state, was an attempt to bring all the communities closer to the mainstream of Bruneian society through one common language, that is, Malay as the national language and a medium of communication among all races.

The bilingual system of education has continued to this day even with the introduction of the new education system (SPN21) in 2009. Both languages were equally emphasised and English is widely used in most major commercial establishments and large corporations. In the new education system, the use of English as medium of instruction was further expanded in the primary curriculum. Prior to SPN21, children were taught in English only after year 3 at primary school with English as a subject taught from year 1. However, in 2007, English-medium instruction in mathematics began from year 1 instead of year 3 and was followed by science in 2009. The introduction of English-medium instruction at that early stage in the two subjects received mixed reactions among teachers. However, preliminary feedback from teachers is encouraging but more studies need to be done to show the outcome of this early introduction of English-language instruction for the two subjects. It is too early to tell whether this will result in more children taking mathematics and science in later years, particularly at secondary and tertiary levels. It is generally perceived that most government schools in Brunei Darussalam have not served learners well. However, to improve the standard of education in government schools the government has introduced several programmes which include the following:

- recruitment of better qualified English language teachers;
- providing frequent in-service training for teachers and administrators;
- encouraging teachers to upgrade their academic qualifications to degree level;
- conducting workshops, by subject specialists, for practising teachers;
- implementing a new reading scheme through the Reading and Language Acquisition project in 1989. The aims of this project are to raise children's proficiency in English and to foster their interest in

books. The project, using big books (large print), has been mainstreamed and become a core feature in both English and Malay language teaching in schools.

English has always been the traditional second language. It is a legacy from a former colonial period. It is considered as a language that acts as a 'bridge' to higher learning, and better access to institutions of higher learning within the Commonwealth and the English-speaking world. By narrowing it down to just the Malay language, access to higher education for Bruneians would be limited to only the Malay-speaking world such as Malaysia and Indonesia. English is perceived as the language of 'development':

> Taking into account that the present state of our development requires knowledge and that the sources of knowledge are not readily available in books written in Malay ... If the foreign language [English] is not mastered, and if the condition is allowed to continue, then our knowledge of a subject, as we continue to teach them in the Malay language, cannot expand.
> (Al Sufri, 1982, p. 16, translated from Malay)

Basic Education Statistics

Brunei Darussalam provides free education from kindergarten, including university training abroad for its citizens. Education is compulsory between the ages of 5 and 16. Six years of primary education are followed by seven years of secondary education. As of 2005, the net enrolment ratio in primary schools was 93.4 % and 83.7% for secondary schools. In 2009, 99,153 students were enrolled in government and non-government institutions from primary to tertiary levels (Department of Planning, Research & Development, 2009). The survival rate in the primary cycle was 99.2% in 2004, while 68% of those eligible attended secondary school. There were about 160 primary schools, with 44,681 pupils. The pupil–teacher ratio at the primary level was about 12 to 1 in 2009. In 1989, there were approximately 20,000 secondary school students. The enrolment more than doubled in 2009, with 44,906 students.

In 2008, Brunei Darussalam introduced nine-year compulsory education. The official policy is to promote bilingual education, Malay and English, in all schools under the Ministry of Education. As of 2000, public expenditure on education was estimated at 5.2% of GDP. From 2000 to 2007 about 9% of total government expenditure was spent on education (United Nations Development Programme, 2009).

In enrolment at primary level, the ratio of males and females is roughly equal. Female enrolment is 48%, 48.7% and 56.8% at primary, secondary and tertiary levels respectively. More females entered tertiary education than males. However, a larger percentage of male students (61.2% in 2009) take the vocational and technical route. At the pre-university level, 58.4% of the enrolment is female. The trend is that more female students continue on to higher education. At Universiti Brunei Darussalam, females now comprise two thirds of the student population (see Table IIIa).

In terms of the total teaching workforce, 68.8% of the 9574 teachers at primary, secondary and tertiary institutions are female (Minister of Education, 2009). However, the predominance of female teachers tends to be at primary and secondary levels (75.8% and 65.3% respectively) while a higher percentage of male teachers/lecturers is found in technical/vocational and higher education institutions (53.4% and 57.4% respectively) (see Table IIIb).

Recent Developments

In line with the National Development Plan, the Ministry of Education has developed goals to: (a) raise students' achievement in the three core subjects of English, mathematics and science; (b) increase the percentage of student cohort enrolment into higher education from 14% to 30% by 2012; (c) provide alternative pathways to tertiary education for up to another 50% of student cohorts, especially in technical and vocational education; and (d) strengthen proficiency in the national language (Bahasa Melayu).

In 2009, the government of Brunei Darussalam embarked on a number of major educational reforms. The Ministry of Education introduced *Sistem Pendidikan Negara Abad 21* (National Education System for the Twenty-first Century). It is a far-reaching reform that requires change at several levels and is designed to provide greater access to all learners, and transform teaching and learning.

The Brunei government also engaged the Australian Council for Educational Research (ACER) in 2007 to conduct a study of numeracy and English reading and writing standards in Brunei. The collaboration between ACER and the Bruneian Ministry of Education also aims to build Brunei's capacity in test development and psychometrics. The project is the first stage of establishing a system to monitor the development of literacy and numeracy in primary and secondary schools. ACER's main role is in the examination of the Bruneian curriculum, development of assessment instruments in line with the curriculum, construction of reporting scales, and training of staff in item writing, test administration, interpretation of results and use of data analysis software.

District	Primary			Secondary			Pre-university			Technical/vocational			Higher institution			Total		
	M	F	T	M	F	T	M	F	T	M	F	T	M	F	T	M	F	T
Government																		
Brunei Muara	10,067	9136	19,203	12,276	11,260	23,536	1526	2169	3695	922	604	1526	2714	3563	6277	27,505	26,732	54,237
Tutong	1774	1720	3494	2196	2026	4222	142	278	420	-	-	0	-	-	0	4112	4024	8136
Belait	2106	1756	3862	2133	1861	3994	294	407	701	461	261	722	-	-	0	4994	4285	9279
Temburong	531	443	974	545	516	1061	-	-	0	-	-	0	-	-	0	1076	959	2035
Total	14,478	13,055	27,533	17,150	15,663	32,813	1962	2854	4816	1383	865	2248	2714	3563	6277	37,687	36,000	73,687
Arabic schools																		
Brunei Muara	177	406	583	214	483	697	161	122	283			0	190	261	451	742	1272	2014
Tutong	82	-	82	456	-	456	-	-	0	-	-	0	-	-	0	538	-	538
Belait	25	31	56	-	-	0	-	-	0	-	-	0	-	-	0	25	31	56
Temburong	10	16	26	-	-	0	-	-	0	-	-	0	-	-	0	10	16	26
Total	294	453	747	670	483	1153	161	122	283	0	0	0	190	261	451	1315	1319	2634
Non-government																		
Brunei Muara	6284	5878	12,162	2312	1970	4282	-	-	0	323	215	538	26	26	52	8945	8089	17,034
Tutong	609	578	1187	-	-	0	-	-	0	-	-	0	-	-	0	609	578	1187
Belait	1474	1465	2939	787	772	1559	-	-	0	-	-	0	-	-	0	2261	2237	4498
Temburong	51	62	113	-	-	0	-	-	0	-	-	0	-	-	0	51	62	113
Total	8418	7983	16,401	3099	2742	5841	0	0	0	323	215	538	26	26	52	11,866	10,966	22,832
Grand total	23,190	21,491	44,681	20,919	18,888	39,807	2123	2976	5099	1706	1080	2786	2930	3850	6780	50,868	48,285	99,153

Note: M = male, F = female, T = total.

Table IIIa. Number of students by level and district, 2009.
Source: Department of Planning, Research & Development (2010).

Ministry	Sector													
	Pre-Primary		Primary		Secondary³		Post-Secondary		Technical/Vocational		Tertiary Education		Total	
	T	F	T	F	T	F	T	F	T	F	T	F	T	F
Total	596	596	3739	2836	3740	2445	304	195	506	236	638	270	9574	6590
Education	256	239	2448	1765	3018	2009	742	391	478	218	583	243	7047	4647
Religious Affairs	0	0	100	76	231	144	51	32	0	0	45	24	427	276
Culture, Youth & Sports	0	0	0	0	0	0	22	10	0	0	0	0	22	10
Prime Minister's Office	0	0	0	0	0	0	18	12	0	0	0	0	18	12
Private	340	337	1191	995	491	292	0	0	28	18	10	3	2060	1645

Note:
School levels are categorized as follows:
Pre-primary: Pre-School (for government schools) and Kindergarten (for private schools); Primary: Year 1 to Year 6.; Secondary: Year 7 to Year 8 and Secondary 3 to Secondary 5; Post-Secondary: Sixth Form; VTE: Vocational and Technical Education; Tertiary: Universities, Institut Teknologi Brunei.
Sixteen private schools offered both primary and secondary education.
Three government schools offered secondary education up to sixth form level which are clustered into the total number of secondary schools.
T – Total, F – Female.

Table IIIb. Number of teachers by level and ministry, 2009.
Source: Education Statistics March 2009
(Department of Planning, Development & Research).

Following a trial of assessment instruments in November 2007, population testing of numeracy and English reading and writing skills took place in May 2008 of all students in government-funded schools under the Ministry of Education in each of years 4, 6 and 8. The test scores are spread over eight band scales with band 1 as the lowest and band 8 the highest score. A report was completed later that year and the main findings of the report (Anderson, 2008a, b) are as follows.

A. English Language Writing

Table IV shows the number of students in each of the bands for each year level.

1. Students with scale scores in bands 1, 2 and 3 were still learning how to write a few common, recognisable words and put them into simple sentences. About 40% of students in year 4, 15% in year 6 and 3% in year 8 were still in this band. In year 4, students switched from mainly a Malay-medium curriculum to an English-medium curriculum. A large

number of them are not well prepared for an English-medium curriculum.
2. The majority of students have not acquired the necessary writing skills and competence in their year group. For example, in secondary 2, more than 50% of students are still in bands 1 to 5. Required competence for secondary 2 should be from band 6 and above.
3. The majority of secondary 2 students, 87%, had sufficient vocabulary and understanding of sentence structure to write a coherent story. Approximately 13% required teacher support to learn basic writing skills. Of these, 3% required intensive, remedial support, but the other 10% were almost at the stage of writing coherent text independently.

Bands	Primary 4 (year 4) n	P4 %	Primary 6 (year 6) n	P6 %	Secondary 2 (year 8) n	S2 %
8			6	0.1	185	2.9
7	1	0.0	51	1.1	345	5.5
6	200	4.3	989	21.2	2391	38.0
5	1180	25.1	2066	44.2	2509	39.8
4	1259	26.8	835	17.9	627	10.0
3	982	20.9	372	8.0	126	2.0
2	731	15.6	232	5.0	51	0.8
1	194	4.1	78	1.7	5	0.1

Table IV. Distribution of students across bands by year level.

B. Reading

Reading skill	Band	P4 %	Primary 4 (year 4) n	P6 %	Primary 6 (year 6) n	S2 %	Secondary 2 (year 8) n
Independent	8	0.4	21	0.4	20	2	98
readers	7	0.5	24	2	85	8	476
	6	3	120	8	358	21	1335
Emerging	5	5	234	20	920	29	1790
independent	4	16	728	27	1260	25	1572
readers							
Basic literacy	3	34	1562	26	1197	14	848
skills	2	27	1243	16	724	2	143
	1	15	707	2	79	0.4	26

Note: Percentages may not total 100 due to rounding.

Table V. Percentage distribution of primary 4 (year 4), primary 6 (year 6) and secondary 2 (year 8) students across reading bands.

C. Mathematics

Band	% P4	n P4	% P6	n P6	% S2	n S2
8	0.1	3	2.3	106	5.3	333
7	0.3	12	7.0	322	12.6	787
6	1.7	79	17.6	811	25.4	1584
5	7.0	322	30.5	1406	37.9	2365
4	23.6	1084	25.4	1170	16.3	1016
3	35.0	1610	13.1	603	2.4	147
2	22.9	1050	3.5	161	0.1	7
1	9.4	434	0.7	32	0.0	

Table VI. Distribution of P4, P6 and S2 students over mathematics bands.
Source: Data from the report by Butler & Anderson (2008).

Table VI shows that:

1. By the time pupils complete their primary schooling, about 50% have reached band 5 and above. Less than 1% have reached bands 7 and 8.
2. By the time they complete year 8, about 87% of them will have achieved band 5 and above.
3. Students fared better in mathematics than in reading and writing.

Tertiary Education Reform

One of the main long-term objectives of the National Development Plan is to 'accelerate human resource development to meet the country's demand of an increasingly sophisticated economy' (BDSNDP, 1993, p. 18). Therefore, great emphasis is placed upon education, particularly post-secondary education. The government of Brunei realises that an appropriately trained, skilled and educated workforce in adequate numbers is a necessary co-requisite for growth and development. The importance of technical and vocational education as a means of assisting in economic and social objectives is similarly recognised in the National Development Plan. Through its Plan, the Brunei government has given considerable priority to the improvement and expansion of technical and vocational education and training in order to respond to the economic challenges of the future (BDENDP, 2000).

The government realises the need to develop its infrastructure in order to significantly increase its citizens' access to higher education and greater levels of training. Currently, the number of students entering vocational education (2.8% of the total student population) or university is small. Estimated figures indicate that in 2009, the number of students entering higher education was only 13% (Department of Planning, Research & Development, 2009). In 2001, the figure was 4.1% (Economic Planning Unit, 2007). The Ministry of Education also plans to increase the number of vocational schools and to expand existing schools to accommodate 15,000 more students in the next five years. Currently, there are three technical schools and five vocational technical schools, including the recently completed Wasan Vocational (agricultural) School.

Further reforms were implemented or in the pipeline. In late 2007, the Government of Brunei engaged Professor Graham Upton, a former Vice-Chancellor of Oxford Brookes University (UK), to make a study of the higher education needs of Brunei. Based on his recommendations (Upton, 2008), Institut Teknologi Brunei (ITB), which was established in 1987, was then upgraded to university status in October 2008. A polytechnic was also planned and due to begin operation sometime in the second half of 2011. Brunei currently has three universities (under the Ministry of Education) and one university college (Islamic Religious Teacher Training University College under the Ministry of Religious Affairs). Universiti Brunei Darussalam, the first national university, was established in 1985, Universiti Sultan Shariff Ali in January 2007, and then ITB.

Conclusion

Many challenges lie ahead for education reform in Brunei Darussalam. Key to the success are many factors, including the readiness of teachers to support the education reform. For the percentage of higher education entry to increase from its present 13% – in order to support the country's aim to effectively respond to the knowledge economy – students' success rates at Ordinary and Advanced levels need to improve significantly. It will also be critical for students to reach a high level of attainment in reading, writing and mathematics at primary level if they are to progress to tertiary education. The major demands are for transparency, clarity, more training for teachers and dialogue between policy makers and implementers. The major areas of development that are currently being fiercely debated and can bring about significant progress are issues of corporate governance, autonomy, finance, research and academic numeration.

References

Al-Sufri, M.J. (1982) Chorak Pendidikan Di-Brunei Pada Masa Hadapan. Paper presented at Brunei Malay Teacher Association Seminar. Bandar Seri Begawan: Majlis Pelajaran Brunei. LC Classification: LA1281.M64 1982.

Anderson, P. (2008a) Report to Brunei Darussalam Ministry of Education: National Study of Student Competencies in Mathematics and English (NSSCME) – interpreting the English language writing data. Australian Council for Educational Research unpublished report.

Anderson, P. (2008b) Report to Brunei Darussalam Ministry of Education: National Study of Student Competencies in Mathematics and English (NSSCME) – interpreting the English reading data. Australian Council for Educational Research unpublished report.

BDENDP (2000) Brunei Darussalam: eighth National Development Plan. Jabatan Percetakan Kerajaan, Kementerian Undang-Undang, Negara Brunei Darussalam.

BDSNDP (1993) Brunei Darussalam: sixth National Development Plan (1991-1995). Jabatan Percetakan Kerajaan, Kementerian Undang-Undang, Negara Brunei Darussalam.

Butler, M. & Anderson, P. (2008) Report to Brunei Darussalam Ministry of Education: National Study of Student Competencies in Mathematics and English (NSSCME) – interpreting the mathematics data. Australian Council for Educational Research unpublished report.

Department of Economic Development Planning, Prime Minister's Office (2007) Brunei Darussalam Long-Term Development Plan: Wawasan Brunei 2035, Outline of Strategies and Policies for Development (OSPD) 2007–2017; National Development Plan (RKN) 2007–2012

Department of Planning, Development & Research, Ministry of Education (2009) Education Statistics March 2009.

Department of Planning, Development & Research, Ministry of Education (2010) 2010 Education Statistics.

Fullan, M. (1982) *The Meaning of Educational Change.* Toronto: Ontario Institute for Studies in Education Press.

JPKE (2001) Population Census 2001 and Department of Statistics.

JPKE (2007) Brunei Darussalam Long-term Development Plan, Wawasan Brunei 2035, Outline of Strategies and Policies for Development (OSPD) 2007-2017, National Development Plan (RKN) 2007-2012. Government Printing Department, Prime Minister's Office, Brunei Darussalam.

Ministry of Education (2009) The National Education System for the 21st Century (SPN21), Negara Brunei Darussalam.

Toohey, K. (1985) English as a Second Language for Native Canadians, *Canadian Journal of Education*, 10(3), 275-293.

United Nations Development Programme (2009) UNDP Living Up To Its Commitments. http://www.gm.undp.org/documents/UNDP_ANNUAL_REPORT_EN_FINAL.pdf

Upton, G. (2008) Higher Education in Brunei Darussalam (1st, 2nd and 3rd Consultative Reports). Unpublished report submitted to the Higher Education Review Committee.

World Bank (2010) World Development Indicators, 3 February.

World Health Organization (2004) Brunei Darussalam Environmental Health Country Profile, 19 November.

CHAPTER 3

The Education System in Cambodia: making progress under difficult circumstances

MARTIN HAYDEN & RICHARD MARTIN

SUMMARY This chapter documents the rapid development of the education system in Cambodia since the late 1990s, when peace was finally restored. Cambodia now has an education participation rate of over 90% for children aged 6-11 years, but only one-third of young people aged 12-14 years take part in lower-secondary schooling. Cambodia's poverty is an overriding influence, affecting the availability of schools and teachers, the ability to manage curriculum quality, and the adequacy of provisions made for the education of children with particular forms of disadvantage. A policy of decentralising management and administration of the education system is officially supported, but its implementation is impeded by the need for more capacity building, especially concerning management and budgeting skills. Corruption and a traditional socio-political culture that is hierarchical, bureaucratic and centralised are impediments to community-based decision-making processes about education.

Introduction

Cambodia is one of the poorest countries in Southeast Asia. Despite impressive annual economic growth rates since the mid-1990s that have helped to raise living standards and enable the more rapid development of infrastructure (roads, clean water, electricity, schools, hospitals, clinics), Cambodia's gross national income per capita in 2008 was only US$600, below that of its nearest neighbours, Laos (US$740), Vietnam (US$890) and Thailand (US$2840) (World Bank, 2009). One third of its population, which in 2009 was estimated to be 14.5 million people, lives in a state of absolute poverty, the incidence of which is higher outside the main urban centres –

only 22% of the population is urbanised (Central Intelligence Agency [CIA], 2009).

Cambodia is also one of the most youthful countries in Southeast Asia. In 2009 its median age was only 22.1 years, above that for Laos (19.3 years), but below that for Vietnam (27.4 years) and Thailand (33.3 years) (CIA, 2009). Not surprisingly, therefore, education is a high national priority. Cambodia's immediate goal is to have all young people completing at least nine years of schooling.

Cambodia shares with Laos and Vietnam a recent history of warfare. In Cambodia's case, it was a prolonged and destructive civil war that erupted in 1970 and did not properly conclude until the late 1990s. The effect of warfare on Cambodia's education system was devastating.

This chapter addresses the contemporary state of the education system in Cambodia. It reports on the system's recent history and current status, and it documents the pressing challenges being faced. Cambodia is making a huge effort to rebuild and improve its education system. It has had remarkable recent success in lifting participation rates at the primary school level. With only about 30% of young people currently completing the first nine years of schooling, however, there is clearly a great deal more progress to be made.

The Setting

Cambodia's recent history has been dominated by warfare and political instability. Following independence from France in 1953, Cambodia's head of state, King Norodom Sihanouk, instigated a process of social and economic modernisation, against a background of limited economic resources and an escalating war in neighbouring Vietnam. As the impact of the war in Vietnam spread to Cambodia, Sihanouk aligned Cambodia politically with North Vietnam and China, setting the scene for a pro-Western coup d'état in 1970 that was led by General Lon Nol. In the civil war that followed, the Khmer Rouge, a Cambodian guerrilla movement, initially loyal to Sihanouk, assumed control of large parts of the countryside. In 1975, the Khmer Rouge took control of Phnom Penh. A brutal restructuring of Cambodian society ensued in which as many as two million Cambodians, or about one quarter of the population, were sent to their deaths, whether by execution, starvation or illness. The victims were disproportionately from the urbanised and educated classes. Vietnamese forces removed the Khmer Rouge from power in 1979, but warfare continued. The Vietnamese departed from Cambodia in 1989, leaving behind a sympathetic government with Mr Hun Sen as the prime minister. Peace accords intended to end conflict between warring factions in Cambodia were signed in 1991. The first-ever democratic elections followed, in 1993. Political instability continued, however, and it was not until the late

1990s, when Hun Sen finally achieved a clear mandate as leader, and when the Khmer Rouge had finally capitulated, that peace was fully restored.

Cambodia is an extremely poor country, heavily reliant on agriculture. In 2007, 59% of the population relied on agriculture and fisheries for a livelihood (World Bank, 2007, p. 6). An industrial sector based on garment manufacturing and construction has developed, and tourism is steadily becoming an important source of foreign income. These industries are fragile, however, because of their vulnerability to global economic conditions, and, in any case, their impact in terms of wealth creation tends to be confined to urban areas. Cambodia does have valuable reserves of offshore oil and gas, as well as significant deposits of bauxite and gold, and these resources will make an important contribution to national wealth over coming years. There is concern, though, about the extent to which much of this additional wealth could be concentrated in the hands of those who are already quite rich. Commenting on the economic condition of the country, the World Bank (2007, p. iii) has observed that: 'In 2004, the living standards of the poorest fifth of the population were only 8 percent higher than they were a decade earlier; over this same period, the living standards of the richest fifth rose five times as fast (45 percent).' Regarding the political condition of the country, USAID (2008, p. 1) has observed that: 'The government is hampered by weak institutions, lack of transparency, and an entrenched system of patronage. Although recent and upcoming elections hold promise for a more open political environment, power remains concentrated in the executive branch, and opposition parties are disorganized and divided.' The point is that, though resource-based wealth has the potential to contribute to long-term social and economic development, whether or not it does so will depend to a large extent on there being a political will to use this wealth to raise the living standards of those who are least well-off (World Bank, 2007, p. 168; Sothearith, 2009).

The recent history of Cambodia's education system mirrors the nation's recent political history. When Cambodia became a French protectorate in 1863, a traditional model of education based upon boys (almost exclusively) going to the local temple, or *wat*, to be taught Buddhist doctrine and history, as well as basic literacy and practical skills for rural life, began to be displaced by a Western model. In 1917, when the first Law on Education was adopted, primary and secondary levels of education, comparable to those existing in France, were formally established. The French did not invest heavily in the education of young people (especially girls) in Cambodia, however, and it was not until the early 1930s that the first high school diplomas, based upon the French *baccalauréat*, were awarded (Sopheak & Clayton, 2007). After independence from France, the education system began to expand at a faster rate, with a significant burst of growth occurring during the late 1960s (Ayres, 2000, p. 449). The coup in 1970 brought this phase of expansion to an end, and the period from 1975 to 1979 saw the complete destruction of the system. Before being removed in 1979, the Khmer Rouge had closed down the education system, abandoning schools for use as 'prisons, pigsties, or storage sheds' (Ayres, 2000, p. 450). During the 1980s, the Vietnamese, working with local authorities, sought to rebuild the system along Soviet lines, but progress was hampered by the lack of teachers and infrastructure. Another phase of reconstruction began in the mid-1990s, assisted by a large infusion of funds and technical support from international aid agencies. In the late 1990s, the current phase of redevelopment began. This phase is proving to be sustained and has been characterised by an increasing emphasis on decentralisation, involving provincial, district and local authorities. There has also been a growing acceptance of the value of private-sector investment, especially in the higher education sector.

The Legislative and Regulatory Framework

The Education Law of 2007 provides a legal framework for the education system. This Law aims to 'determine the national measures and criteria for establishing the completely comprehensive and uniform education system ensuring the principles of freedoms of studies in compliance with the Constitution of the Kingdom of Cambodia' (Kingdom of Cambodia, 2007, Article 1). The National Supreme Council of Education, chaired by the prime minister, has responsibility for developing policy proposals and long-term strategies. This Council is also required to evaluate the system's performance and determine its resource requirements. The Ministry of Education, Youth and Sport (MoEYS) is given responsibility for issuing relevant regulations. It is also instructed to develop, review and modify education policies, principles, plans and strategies, in accordance with national strategies and strategic development plans.

Planning for the education system takes place within the framework of a National Strategic Development Plan (NSDP). The NSDP for 2006-10 focuses on poverty reduction, gender equity, increased real investment, institutional and human capacity building, economic reform and the attainment of economic growth. Within this framework, a five-yearly Education Strategic Plan (ESP) guides the development of the education system. The ESP for 2006-10 identifies three priority areas: ensuring equitable access to education, increasing the quality and efficiency of education services, and institutional development and capacity building for decentralisation (MoEYS, 2005a). Specific targets for each of these priority areas include, respectively:

- expanded access to early childhood education programs; specific new measures to ensure that all six-year-olds commence primary education; reduced parental cost barriers to attendance at primary school; lower repetition and drop-out rates at all grade levels; additional new schools and facilities; and increased enrolment rates in the lower-secondary and upper-secondary levels;

- increased salaries and allowances for teachers; improved implementation of child-friendly school policies; the implementation of a plan to train 5000 new teachers each year for five years; the development of a revised teacher demand and supply strategy; an increase in the level of operational autonomy and accountability of schools for budgetary matters and decisions about programs; implementation of pre-service and in-service teacher development programs; the conduct of training programs for teachers in the use of information and communications technologies in the classroom; the implementation of minimum standards of student achievement for grades 3, 6 and 9; and the introduction of performance monitoring systems for teachers; and
- adoption of a new Education Law; the development and implementation of capacity-building programs in the areas of program and financial planning, monitoring and audit skills, for provincial, district and school levels of management as well as across all budget management centres; adoption of a management information system across the education system; and the development of a strategic plan for the higher education sector.

Supporting the ESP is an Education Sector Support Program (ESSP) that sets out how priorities identified in the ESP will be achieved and funded (MoEYS, 2005b). The ESSP also takes account of program activities and priorities required for the purposes of achieving Cambodia's National Education For All Plan 2003-15 (MoEYS, 2003). In the case of lower-secondary enrolments, for example, the ESSP for 2006-10 proposed that there should be an increase from 26.1% in 2005 to 39% in 2008 in the net enrolment rate (the proportion of the relevant age group participating in a particular level of education) in grades 7 to 9. Strategies for achieving this target were identified as: increasing the operational budgets for schools serving poorer communities; providing poverty-targeted scholarships for students in grades 7 to 9; expanding the provision of lower-secondary classes; and ensuring the supply of a sufficient number of qualified teachers. The ESSP then proposed programs to be developed to enable these strategies to be implemented. One program was the nationwide provision of scholarships for poor students and girls. Responsibility for implementing these programs was assigned. Finally, the ESSP documented relevant needs for capacity building, including, for example, the need to 'support the strengthening of school directors and teachers' performance, focusing particularly on strengthening of school management, teaching-learning methodology and school development planning' (MoEYS, 2005b, p. 9).

A positive feature of the planning cycle for education is the conduct of mid-term reviews. A mid-term review of the ESP and the ESSP for 2006-10 was undertaken in 2008 (MoEYS, 2009a). Of note from this document is the fact that the target set of a 39% net enrolment rate in lower-secondary schooling by 2008 was not met. The actual net enrolment rate in 2008 was

34.8% – a significant improvement on the rate of 26.1% for 2005, but not as high a rate as had been targeted. In fact, this pattern was evident across many of the targets set for 2006-10. They were generally much too ambitious. The mid-term review provides a revealing account of the kinds of obstacles encountered by provincial authorities in trying to achieve the national targets. These included: '1) lack of facilities/equipment including new schools and teacher houses, 2) low inspection capacity including lack of professional inspectors, 3) low budget management capacity including lack of trained accountants, 4) late disbursement of PB [program-based budgets], 5) frequent migration, 6) poor living standard, 7) teachers not following pedagogy, 8) limited understanding on CFS [child-friendly school policies], and 9) inaccurate population statistics' (MoEYS, 2009a, p. 11). In other words, the attainment of national targets was constrained by the limitations of physical capital, human resources and administrative systems. These limitations derive in large part, but not entirely, from national poverty.

MoEYS is also responsible for the development of education policies. Important among these are policies for curriculum development (MoEYS, 2004a), non-formal education (MoEYS, 2004b), information and communications technologies in schools (MoEYS, 2007a), child-friendly schools (MoEYS, 2007b), education for children with disabilities (MoEYS, 2008a), and education in the context of HIV/AIDS (MoEYS, 2008b). There is not, however, much information available about the effectiveness of the implementation of these policies.

The Ministry itself has seven departments, one of which has responsibility for all of the early childhood and school education sectors, and one of which has responsibility for higher education. Consistent with a national commitment to decentralising management and administration, provincial education offices, of which there are 24, are largely responsible for the implementation of national programs and policies. Provincial education offices then rely on district education offices and local school management committees to give effect to the delivery and monitoring of programs.

Over one quarter of all expenditure on education is channelled through program-based budget areas, of which there are 12 – formerly known as Priority Action Programs. Important among these are 'education service efficiency', 'early childhood education', 'primary education quality and efficiency', 'lower secondary education access, quality and efficiency', 'upper secondary education access and equity' and 'scholarships and incentives'. The focus of program-based budgeting is on reducing the household costs of education. Some budget areas have been integrated with donor-funded initiatives (World Bank, 2005).

Data Sources

The various planning documents produced by MoEYS are an important source of information about the education system in Cambodia. These are available from the MoEYS website. Also available from this website are policy statements regarding curriculum development, non-formal education, child-friendly schools, and so on. A recent summary report by MoEYS (2009b) of the Ministry's performance in 2008 is of special note for the richness of the performance-related data it provides.

Reports from international agencies, including UNESCO, the United Nations International Children's Fund (UNICEF), the Asian Development Bank, the World Bank and the World Food Programme, are additional sources of information. Important among these is a recent World Bank report on equity and development in Cambodia (World Bank, 2007).

There is a sparse but developing academic literature on Cambodia's education system. The system is developing so rapidly, though, that only those documents written within the past five years are of much relevance. Recent papers by Dy (2004), Pellini (2005), Tan (2007), and Marshall et al (2009) are of note. A valuable account of the historical development of the system is provided by Ayres (2000).

Interviews conducted in 2009 and early in 2010 with senior managers from MoEYS, and with school and university leaders from around Phnom Penh, also inform this chapter. The purpose of these interviews was to check assumptions and conclusions based on documentary sources. No attempt is made here, however, to analyse the interview data systematically, and so there are no explicit references in this chapter to comments made in the interviews.

The Education Sectors

Cambodia's education system is structured as follows: pre-primary (ages 3 to 5 years), primary (ages 6 to 11 years), lower secondary (ages 12 to 14 years), upper secondary (ages 15 to 17 years), and higher education (ages 18 and above). There is, in addition, a technical and vocational education and training (TVET) sector (ages 15 and above).

Some indication of the relative size of these sectors is provided by results reported from the *Cambodian Socio-economic Survey* of 2007 (Ministry of Planning, 2009). Of all young people aged 5 to 24 years currently attending school, 67% reported being enrolled in primary, 20% in lower secondary, 9% in upper secondary, 0% in TVET, and 2% in higher education. Interestingly, for respondents from Phnom Penh, the proportions for upper secondary, TVET and higher education were 22%, 2% and 14% respectively, reflecting the different educational profile of urban centres in Cambodia.

Pre-primary education is a relatively small sector, with only about 15% of all children aged three to five years attending a formal or community-based pre-school program (MoEYS, 2009b). This sector is, however, rapidly expanding, with most of the growth occurring in Phnom Penh and other urban centres, where there is a higher probability of both parents being in employment. The sector includes a variety of types of institutions: public pre-schools, private pre-schools, community-based pre-schools and home-based child education. Of these, the largest enrolment numbers are in public pre-schools. Public pre-schools often charge a small fee for attendance. Fees to attend private pre-school institutions are invariably much higher. Attendance at pre-schools organised by local communities in rural areas is generally free.

A significant constraint on growth in this sector is the limited availability of trained early-childhood teachers. This shortage impacts especially on the availability of pre-school education in rural and remote areas. It also impacts adversely on the availability of pre-school education for children with disabilities and for children from ethnic minority groups.

Primary education is the largest sector, with as many as 93% of all children aged 6 to 11 years attending a primary school (MoEYS, 2009b). The retention rate from grade 1 to grade 5 is 60% (meaning that 60% of commencers in grade 1 eventually completed grade 5). The retention rate from grade 1 to grade 6 is 52.5%. The transition rate from primary school to lower-secondary school is 78.5% (MoEYS, 2009b).

Cambodia has made remarkable progress over recent years in expanding the provision of primary education. As recently as 2005, for example, only 81% of all children aged 6 to 11 years were attending a primary school. The growth has been most striking in the more remote parts of the country, where new primary schools have been built and existing ones extended. There has also been significant progress in terms of improving the participation rates of girls – these are now almost as high as for boys.

There are, though, some persistent problems. One is that children do not always commence primary school at the age of six. Though there have been recent improvements, about 10% of all children entering school for the first time are older than six years of age (MoEYS, 2009b). Another problem is that there is a relatively high incidence, estimated currently to be about 10%, of children in the primary school years having to repeat year levels. A contributing factor here is the need for many children in rural areas to have to interrupt their schooling in order to help their parents with farming. Yet another problem is the poor retention rate to grade 6. The retention rate to grade 6 is strongly affected by poverty. As in many parts of Southeast Asia, parents may not be able to afford to keep sending their children to school, or the children, once they are aged 10 or 11 years, may be required to stay at home or go to work to help contribute to the family livelihood. The abolition in 2001 of primary school fees greatly increased school attendance, but other financial obstacles remain. Finally, there is a problem of standards. Marshall and colleagues (2009) raise the possibility that a majority of grade 3 children may be 'non-proficient' on assessment tasks in Khmer language and mathematics, that is, their performance is below expected benchmarks for their age group. Assuming that this pattern is widespread, then it is a matter of grave concern.

Lower-secondary education is the second-largest sector, with 34.8% of all children aged 12 to 14 years attending a lower-secondary school in 2008 (MoEYS, 2009b). Though never managing to keep up with ambitious national targets, the recent expansion of participation in lower-secondary schooling has been significant. It is in rural areas that the participation rates are lagging behind. Many rural and remote parts of Cambodia do not yet have a lower-secondary school. Successive scholarship schemes for girls and for young people from very poor backgrounds have had a positive impact on lower-secondary participation rates, but achieving the goal of universal participation in lower-secondary schooling, which is supposed to be achieved by 2015, may take more than five years to achieve. No fees are charged for attendance at public-sector lower-secondary schools – and the vast majority of them are public-sector schools.

Upper-secondary education is a smaller sector, with only 14.8% of all young people aged 15 to 18 years attending an upper-secondary school (MoEYS, 2009b). Participation by girls in upper-secondary schooling is improving (41% of all students in 2008 were female), but it lags behind participation by boys. Admission to upper-secondary schooling is determined on the basis of performance in a compulsory examination completed at the end of grade 9. Though the pass rate (94.8%) in this examination in 2008 was high, the proportion of grade 9 students proceeding to grade 10 was only 71.5% (MoEYS, 2009b). Young people from rural and remote parts of the country were less likely to proceed to upper-secondary education.

TVET is a relatively new and relatively small sector within the education system. Since 2006, it has been governed by a National Training Board, chaired by a deputy prime minister, and structured to give representation to a variety of employer, labour and governmental interests. This Board gives direction to the director general of TVET in the Ministry of Labour and Vocational Training.

It is estimated that there may be as many as 12,000-14,000 equivalent full-time students enrolled in TVET colleges, but statistics about TVET enrolments are not all that reliable, and, in any case, are clouded by the plethora of long-course/short-course and formal/non-formal course programs available. In 2008, for example, almost 80,000 students were enrolled in short-course programs (Association of Canadian Community Colleges, 2009, p. 90). There may, in addition, be a very large number of students engaged informally in TVET-type programs conducted by private providers, including non-government organisations.

Generally, students completing lower-secondary education would prefer to proceed to an upper-secondary school, and then to higher education, rather than obtain a TVET qualification. This situation, which is not uncommon in many countries, is of great concern to employers. According to a recent survey of employers (Cambodia Development Resource Institute, 2009), the current output of TVET graduates, estimated at 4400 in 2007 (presumably long-course graduates), is well below requirements for the future – it was estimated that about 19,000 TVET graduates per annum are needed by 2015. There is also a perception that the sector needs to focus more on the development of 'soft' skills (the ability to make decisions, solve problems, have a positive attitude to work), and that training should focus on new areas of skill development, rather than on areas that are already saturated (hairdressing, tailoring, mechanics). The Asian Development Bank has recently approved a US$24.5 million grant for a project to improve the TVET sector. This project is expected to achieve an expanded and more integrated training system. The project will focus initially on three industry sectors – mechanics, construction, and business services and information and communication technology.

Higher education is a rapidly expanding sector, especially in terms of number of institutions. In 2008, there were 63 higher education institutions in Cambodia (18 public and 45 private), providing for somewhere between 50,000 and 100,000 higher education students. The actual number of students is difficult to determine with any precision because of discrepancies in statistical reporting and the fact that students may enrol concurrently at several institutions (Chealy, 2006). Twice as many higher education students are enrolled in private higher education institutions as in public ones. Indeed, the higher education sector is beginning to rely very heavily on the private sector. The government appears to accept that there is a need for even more private-sector higher education institutions. In 2008, it licensed an additional seven new private higher education institutions. A curious aspect of private-sector higher education institutions in Cambodia is that prominent public officials are permitted to invest in them.

One of the priorities in the ESP for 2006-10 was that there should be a higher education access and equity program to enable increased participation in higher education by targeted groups: 'Priority target groups will be poor students graduating from the model and rural secondary schools qualifying for admission into Phnom Penh-based universities. Some priorities will be given to students enrolling for less market oriented and more socially beneficial programs, especially education, health, agriculture, science and mathematics education' (MoEYS, 2005a, p. 23). There was also reference to the development of a higher education student loan scheme. These developments appear to have been delayed. One possible reason is that a government vision statement for the sector is imminent. This statement is intended to provide a strategic plan for the sector up to 2020. In doing so, it will need to address problems associated with the lack of employment opportunities for graduates, even in areas of pressing national importance, including science, technology, mathematics, agriculture and health. There are also difficult issues to be resolved regarding ongoing curriculum inflexibilities (despite the official adoption of a national credit transfer system), the shortage of well-trained lecturers and research support staff, insufficient resources for English language training, an extreme shortage of library materials, inadequacies of the computing infrastructure, deficiencies in the quality of higher education management, uneven quality standards across the system, a lack of sufficient transparency in the management of budgets, and the general social exclusiveness of the higher education system.

Teacher education, though conducted mainly outside universities, may be regarded as forming part of the higher education system. Provincial and regional Teacher Training Centres are responsible for training primary and lower-secondary teachers. The National Institute of Education is responsible for training upper-secondary teachers. In the ESP for 2005-06, the following statement is made (MoEYS, 2005a, p. 23):

> The teacher development program objective will be to ensure an efficient supply of basic cycle and upper secondary school teachers for system expansion and to upgrade TTC [Teacher Training Centre] trainers, school directors and other key MoEYS personnel. A second objective will be ensuring that TTC intakes and subsequent trained teacher deployment respond to growing demands in rural/remote and disadvantaged areas, especially by recruiting teacher trainees from remote and ethnic minority areas. A third objective will be to provide in-service teacher training.

Subsequently, in the ESSP for 2006-10 (MoEYS, 2005b, p. 2), targets for teacher education were set as follows:

> (a) 95% of new graduates from TTCs will be assigned to work in disadvantage and remote areas by 2008, (b) from the beginning of 2006 onward, 1,500 student teachers will be recruited from the remote areas sources and then assigned back to work at the source areas after they finish at teacher training, and (c) based on present projections from 2006 onwards MoEYS needs to recruit 5,000 new teachers per annum for 5 years.

The addition of 5000 new teachers per annum for five years would add significantly to the size of the national teaching labour force – in 2006, there were approximately 45,000 primary and 17,500 secondary teachers. If a significant proportion of them came from the remote areas of the country, then opportunities for developing the education system in remote areas would be greatly enhanced. By 2009, however, the target of 5000 additional new teachers each year was not quite being achieved, and MoEYS was continuing to express concern that there were insufficient teachers in rural and remote areas, which was undermining the quality of education and learning in these areas (MoEYS, 2009b).

Finances

Cambodia's budgetary commitment to education has not until recently compared well with that of its nearest neighbours. Over the period from 2002 to 2007, for example, public expenditure on education as a percentage of total government expenditure averaged 12.4% for Cambodia, compared with 14% for Laos and 25% for Thailand (United Nations Development Programme, 2009). From 2002 to 2005, public expenditure on education as a percentage of GDP averaged 1.9% for Cambodia, compared with 2.3% for Laos and 4.2% for Thailand (World Bank, 2007). Comparable figures for Vietnam are not readily available, but Vietnam's public expenditure commitment to education has certainly been considerably higher than Cambodia's (Ministry of Planning and Investment, 2006, p. 15).

A contributing factor has been Cambodia's unusually low revenue-to-GDP ratio. From 1995 to 2004, this ratio averaged 6.8%, compared with an average of 14.2% for 50 other low-income countries (World Bank, 2007, pp. 156-157). In short, Cambodia was not collecting as much revenue through its taxation system as it could have been, thus restricting its capacity to spend on areas of social need, including its education system (World Bank, 2009, p. 87).

Over recent years, there has been a steady increase in public expenditure on education (Benveniste et al, 2008, p. 60). The ESP for 2006-10 projected that education's share of the total government recurrent budget would be 20% by 2009. Even allowing for some shortfall in reaching this target, the trend in public expenditure on education over recent years has been strongly positive. Late in 2009, for example, the National Assembly approved a budget allocation for MoEYS in 2010 that is almost 50% higher than the budget allocation approved in 2007 (Sakada, 2009).

For much of the past decade, a policy of increasing public expenditure on demand-side interventions has been followed (Tan, 2007, p. 17). The focus of this kind of expenditure is on increasing demand for education by reducing its cost to households. Examples include the removal of tuition fees for primary and lower-secondary schooling, and the provision of scholarship support for particular categories of students. At the same time, however, supply-side interventions, in the form of building more schools, providing teaching materials and training more teachers, have had to be maintained, though there is a recent concern expressed in documents from MoEYS (see, for example, MoEYS, 2009a) that plans for public expenditure on capital items need to be renewed. Official donor assistance, which continues to be a very important element in Cambodia, accounting for as much as one fifth of all educational expenditure, has traditionally focused on addressing supply-side needs.

Education continues to represent an appreciable cost for Cambodian households. According to the *Cambodian Socio-economic Survey* of 2007 (Ministry of Planning, 2009), the average household expense per child for education was equivalent to US$42 per school year. There were, of course, large differences by level of education. For pre-primary schooling, the average annual expense was US$14; for primary schooling, it was US$15; for lower-secondary schooling, it was US$45; for upper-secondary schooling, it was US$105; for TVET, it was US$350; and for higher education, it was

US$463. What is evident here is the extent to which the size of the financial burden for households increases when children progress beyond the primary level of schooling.

Levels of expenditure on education are, of course, not uniform across all Cambodian households. There is a huge gap between the expenditure patterns of the rich and the poor (and, by implication, urban and rural communities) – in 2004, for example, household educational expenditure per child was found to be 25 times greater among the richest 20% of households than it was amongst the poorest 20% (World Bank, 2007, p. 127).

Challenges

The education system in Cambodia faces enormous challenges. In many respects, these relate directly to the fact that Cambodia is a very poor country. There are, however, some striking inequities in educational provision that, left unchecked, could have catastrophic consequences for the social and political stability of the country.

Urban–rural differences in educational outcomes are especially striking. In 2008, for example, the proportion of the relevant age group participating in lower-secondary schooling in urban areas was 55.9%, while in rural areas it was 31.5%, and in remote areas it was only 11.1% (MoEYS, 2009b). Each year, these rates improve marginally, but the urban–rural gap is not closing. At the upper-secondary level, the gap is even wider, and, though relevant statistics are not readily available, the gap is likely to be at its widest in the higher education sector. A potent factor contributing to the gap is the intergenerational transmission of educational disadvantage. In Cambodia, a child whose father has had no schooling is likely to complete only 3.7 years of schooling, whereas a child whose parent has a university qualification is likely to complete 13.1 years of schooling (World Bank, 2007, p. 133). Parents in rural areas are less likely to have completed many years of schooling (World Bank, 2007, p. 125), and they are also much more likely to be living in absolute poverty. Addressing the challenge of raising educational outcomes in rural areas requires a significant and sustained effort, and hence a great deal of financial commitment. The problem will not be resolved simply by ensuring that rural areas have the same level of provision of teachers and schools as is available in urban areas.

It is in rural and remote areas that remaining gender differences in educational outcomes are also most in evidence. Cambodia has made remarkable progress in closing gender gaps in school participation at the primary and lower-secondary levels. In 2007-08, for example, the proportion of the relevant age group participating in primary schooling was 93.2% for boys and 93.3% for girls. The proportion of the relevant age group participating in lower-secondary schooling was 33.7% for boys and 35.9% for girls (MoEYS, 2009b). Beyond lower-secondary schooling, however, the gender gap widens, with only 41% of upper-secondary students being female, and with boys outnumbering girls by a factor of 3 to 1 in higher education (World Bank, 2007, p. 143). It is in rural areas that girls face more obstacles to continuing their schooling beyond the lower-secondary level (MoEYS/UNICEF, 2005, pp. 10-11).

The differences in educational outcomes between urban and rural areas are related to an extent to the fact that young Cambodians who are of Chinese descent are more likely to be living in urban areas. It is widely accepted in Cambodia, though relevant data are difficult to locate, that levels of educational attainment for young people of Chinese descent are significantly better than those for other young people. Cambodia is much more ethnically homogeneous than other countries in its region. About 90% of all Cambodians are Khmer, and only small percentages of the population are Vietnamese (5%), *Khmer Loeu* (indigenous peoples living in isolated mountainous areas) (4%) or Chinese (1%). These figures understate, however, the proportion of the population that is second-, third- or fourth-generation Chinese. While there is no overt discrimination against minority ethnic groups, neither is there much official willingness to tolerate non-Khmer festivities (for example, the Lunar New Year) in terms of their impact on school attendance. There are noteworthy relationships between socioeconomic status and ethnic background. The urban-based Chinese community is generally of high socioeconomic status, while the rural-based Vietnamese and indigenous communities are generally of low socioeconomic status.

Another very significant challenge concerns the quantity and quality of teaching services. Class sizes in Cambodian schools are high – indeed, they are considerably higher than in Laos, Vietnam or Thailand (Benveniste et al, 2008, p. 39). Estimates of the average number of pupils per teacher in primary schools range between 40 and 50. One reason for this situation is that, ever since the Khmer Rouge period, trained teachers have been in short supply in Cambodia. Over the period from 1993 to 2005, for example, the number of primary student enrolments increased by 67%, but the number of primary teachers increased by only 7% (World Food Programme, 2009). The problem also has some contemporary origins, though. Reviewing the performance of the education system in 2007-08, MoEYS (2009b, p. 17) observed that there was a 'shortage of teachers in all levels; especially in remote and disadvantaged area[s]'. The government has not, until recently, been investing sufficiently in expanding the number of teachers. In the ESP for 2006-10, it signalled an intention to recruit 5000 new teachers per annum for five years. It does not seem to be achieving that target. One obvious reason for this situation is that the salary levels of teachers are woefully low.

Various reports document the fact that teachers in Cambodia are poorly qualified – in 2006, for example, 34.5% of teachers in remote areas, 6.4% in rural areas, and 4.2% in urban areas had not themselves studied beyond the primary level (UNESCO, 2006; Benveniste et al, 2008, p. iii). Teachers are also not all that strongly motivated by their pay (Benveniste et al, 2008,

p. 47). Teachers receive lower-than-average incomes when considered across all economic sectors. They are not even as well rewarded as other civil servants. It has been observed that 'teachers who are sole income earners and sustain a family with children are likely to live in poverty if they were to rely only on their earnings from teaching, particularly in urban areas' (Benveniste et al, 2008, p. v). To supplement their income, second jobs are important. Private tutoring is particularly common, especially at the lower- and upper-secondary levels. The *Cambodian Socio-economic Survey* of 2007 (Ministry of Planning, 2009) found that 21% of 10-to-14 year-olds and 45% of 15-to-19 year-olds took private lessons after school. These lessons often take place in class sizes of 15 or so students at a teacher's home. Teachers may also conduct additional classes at their schools, charging unofficial fees for this service, though this practice is now banned by MoEYS (however policing of the ban has to date been weak). In the process of increasing their incomes by these means, teachers have lost community respect in terms of their willingness to treat equally rich and poor alike (World Bank, 2007, p. vii). The trust traditionally placed in them by the community has also been diminished by practices that include making attendance at private tutorial classes the only way of acquiring knowledge that is essential for passing examinations. Teachers' costs have become an additional burden on household expenses: 'Supplementary tutoring, which operates as a sort of shadow system alongside the mainstream, consumes considerable household resources, especially in urban areas and in key final grades' (World Bank, 2007, p. vii).

The government is well aware of the need to address problems related to the teaching profession. In the ESP for 2006-10, it signalled an intention to develop performance-based pay reforms. It also declared an intention to abolish all unofficial payments by parents for grade 1 to 9 students by the end of 2008. There has also been a pledge to provide for an across-the-board salary increase of up to 20% for all teachers (Benveniste et al, 2008, p. 62). In the mid-term review report of the ESP, however, there is no mention of the salary increase for teachers, though there is reference to increasing gradually the value of school budgets, and there is also a reference to the introduction of incentives for teachers willing to work in schools in remote and ethnic minority areas (MoEYS, 2009a).

Decentralisation is a national policy goal in terms of the management and administration of the education system. The ESP for 2006-10 provides ample evidence of the government's commitment to the importance of delegating responsibilities to the provincial, district, communal and school levels. On balance, the government is making steady progress in terms of decentralising system management to the provincial level, though there are some significant impediments to effective decentralisation to the communal and school levels, and there has also been some reluctance regarding the possibility of schools having autonomy for finances and the control of resources (Shoraku, 2008, p. 4). Pellini (2005, p. 214) reports that:

'Cambodian communities have shown a deep understanding of the importance of education and, though government spending on education is increasing, they provide substantial material contributions for the improvement of schools.' At the same time, however, he observes that: 'Despite the amount of support and resources provided, communities seem to be excluded from schools' educational decision-making processes. The school cluster design includes committees at various levels that aim to promote community participation, but they do not seem to work.' Tan (2007, p. 22) develops this theme, reporting how planning for decentralisation has mostly taken place 'in a top-down and centralised manner, and Ministry staff at lower levels have been implementing reform initiatives without full awareness of the rationale for reforms – particularly at districts, communes, school clusters and schools' (cited from MoEYS/UNICEF, 2005, p. 17). Commenting on the prospects of achieving a climate of accountability at the local school management level, she observes that the traditional sociopolitical culture of Cambodia is one that is 'hierarchical, bureaucratic and centralised'. There are, in other words, cultural obstacles to the development of community-based decision-making processes about educational matters. As Shoraku (2008, p. 25) has observed in relation to school-based management: 'authority given to schools is exercised only by a few people who have been influential; many others are excluded from the decision-making process, and they are not given a platform nor encouraged to voice their opinions'.

A second impediment is corruption. Tan (2007, p. 22) refers to the tradition of patronage that exists in Cambodian culture, resting on a notion of 'the-winner-takes-all'. Individuals with a 'strong back' (*khnorng thom*), that is, having the ability to buy connections and control access to resources and decision making, are permitted to enjoy more opportunity within Cambodian society (World Bank, 2007, p. 39). The NSDP 2006-10 (para. 4.11) states that: 'A variety of actions, in many areas including reforms and behavioural changes, are needed to combat corruption and instill a *'culture of service'* whereby public administration acts truly as an instrument of efficient, effective, speedy and impartial service to all Cambodians' (Kingdom of Cambodia, 2006). Yet corruption remains rife. Transparency International (2009) ranks Cambodia as 158th (equal to Laos) out of 180 countries in terms of perceived public-sector corruption – behind Vietnam (120th) and Thailand (84th). Even the teaching profession is not universally regarded as being honest (World Bank, 2007, p. vii; Saw, 2009). Decentralisation, particularly if accompanied by more robust accountability measures, is, therefore, approached cautiously – though there is no sign to date that corruption is giving rise to pressure to return to more centralised control. Program-based budget procedures are expected to raise progressively the level of accountability in the education system, but, as noted by Benveniste and colleagues (2008, p. 82), the Cambodian education system, especially at the level of schools, has a 'low stakes' accountability mechanism, that is, breaches in accountability do not carry heavy consequences.

Linkages between the needs of the labour market and planning for the education system are not especially well developed. The Ministry of Labour and Vocational Training has responsibility for collecting, analysing and reporting on labour market information, but the relevant department within the Ministry is not regarded as having the expertise, resources or level of connectedness with other key agencies sufficient to enable it to have an impact on educational planning (Association of Canadian Community Colleges, 2009, p. ix). The government looks after its own needs by selecting the most capable university graduates to join the public bureaucracy. Banks are a second major employer of graduates. Beyond that, better-paid employment opportunities for graduates are relatively scarce. Structures to assist them to find employment that builds on their advanced knowledge and skills are weak. It has been estimated that only 10% of higher education graduates find employment in their first year after graduation (Association of Canadian Community Colleges, 2009, p. 121). The TVET sector focuses mainly on the provision of informal, short courses. There is little evidence to date to suggest that the output of graduates from this sector is either adequate to the needs of a growing economy, or focused sufficiently on areas of future strategic need for skilled labour (for example, in areas related to tourism) (Association of Canadian Community Colleges, 2009, p. 123). Participation in the upper-secondary level of schooling is based largely on aspirations to proceed to higher education, rather than on perceptions of a greater likelihood of obtaining a better job.

A great many additional challenges could also be discussed. These are officially documented, whether in the ESP for 2006-10 (MoEYS, 2005a), the ESSP for 2006-10 (MoEYS, 2005b), the mid-term review of the ESP and ESSP for 2009 (MoEYS, 2009a) or the report by MoEYS to the National Education Congress (MoEYS, 2009b). They include:

- re-establishing and monitoring effectively a national public capital expenditure program for the education system;
- providing far more training for teachers in terms of how to deliver a curriculum – with particular but not exclusive attention given to the child-friendly school curriculum initiative;
- evaluating the effectiveness of the utilisation of donor aid for the education system, and harmonising the application of this aid with national priorities and commitments;
- introducing a rigorous quality assurance and quality accreditation system for the higher education system;
- extending the teaching of foreign languages (especially English) beyond Phnom Penh and other large urban centres;
- introducing standard testing of literacy and numeracy skills for children in grades 3, 6 and 9 to assist in ensuring the universal attainment of agreed national benchmarks; and

- improving dramatically provisions made for the education of children from ethnic minorities, children with disabilities, and children with, or living in homes affected by, HIV/AIDS.

Conclusion

Poverty is pervasive as an influence on Cambodia's education system. The question arises, then, as to whether having access to more public funds would dramatically improve the quality and effectiveness of the education system. The answer has to be that it would. With more public spending, it would, for example, be possible to train and employ more teachers, improve their commitment by paying them properly, provide more support for household educational budgets in rural and remote areas, provide more scholarships for disadvantaged ethnic minority groups, make special provisions for children with disabilities and for children whose lives have been affected directly or indirectly by HIV/AIDS, build a TVET system that is properly geared to meet Cambodia's future need for trained skilled labour, and introduce rigorous quality assurance and quality accreditation processes in the higher education sector.

Some problems might not, however, be affected by more public spending. Corruption might simply get worse, while systems of patronage at local and district levels that make transparency and accountability more difficult to achieve might simply become more embedded.

The education system in Cambodia is, therefore, trying to make progress under difficult circumstances. It is very short of money. It is also trying to modernise in the context of social and political circumstances that tend to reinforce the negative aspects of traditional approaches to the preservation of social order. The way ahead for Cambodia's education system will be interesting.

Acknowledgement

The authors wish to acknowledge the valuable assistance provided by Nici Burger in the preparation of this chapter.

References

Association of Canadian Community Colleges (2009) Preparing the Strengthening Technical and Vocational Education and Training Project. A Technical Assistance Consultant's Report to the Asian Development Bank, Project Number: 40555 (TA 7116).

Ayres, D.M. (2000) Tradition, Modernity, and the Development of Education in Cambodia, *Comparative Education Review*, 44(4), 440-463.

Benveniste, L., Marshall, J. & Caridad Araujo, C. (2008) *Teaching in Cambodia*. Washington, DC: The World Bank & Ministry of Education, Youth and Sport.

Cambodia Development Resource Institute (2009). *Cambodia Outlook Brief.* Phnom Penh: CDRI. http://www.cdri.org.kh/webdata/download/ocbrief09/ocb2e.pdf (accessed 28 December 2009).

Central Intelligence Agency (2009) Cambodia. https://www.cia.gov/library/publications/the-world-factbook/geos/cb.html (accessed 12 December 2009).

Chealy, C. (2006) Cambodia, in *Higher Education in South-East Asia*, pp. 13-33. Bangkok: UNESCO Asia.

Dy, S.S. (2004) Strategies and Policies for Basic Education in Cambodia: historical perspectives, *International Education Journal*, 5(1), 90-97.

Kingdom of Cambodia (2006) *National Strategic Development Plan 2006-2010 (NSDP).* Approved January 27, 2006.

Kingdom of Cambodia (2007) Education Law.

Marshall, J., Chinna, U., Nessay, P., Hok, U.N., Savoeun, V., Tinon, S. & Veasna, M. (2009) Student Achievement and Education Policy in a Period of Rapid Expansion: assessment data evidence from Cambodia, *International Review of Education*, 55, 393-413.

Ministry of Education, Youth and Sport (2003) *Education for All 2003-2015.* Phnom Penh: MoEYS.

Ministry of Education, Youth and Sport (2004a) *Policy for Curriculum Development 2005-2009.* Phnom Penh: MoEYS.

Ministry of Education, Youth and Sport (2004b) *Policy of Non-formal Education.* Phnom Penh: MoEYS.

Ministry of Education, Youth and Sport (2005a) *Education Strategic Plan 2006-2010.* Phnom Penh: MoEYS.

Ministry of Education, Youth and Sport (2005b) *Education Sector Support Program 2006-2010.* Phnom Penh: MoEYS.

Ministry of Education, Youth and Sport (2007a) *Policy and Strategies on Information and Communication Technology in Education in Cambodia.* Phnom Penh: MoEYS.

Ministry of Education, Youth and Sport (2007b) *Child Friendly School Policy.* Phnom Penh: MoEYS.

Ministry of Education, Youth and Sport (2008a) *Policy on Children with Disabilities.* Phnom Penh: MoEYS.

Ministry of Education, Youth and Sport (2008b) *Workplace Policy on HIV and AIDS.* Phnom Penh: MoEYS.

Ministry of Education, Youth and Sport (2009a) *Mid-term Review Report – Education Strategic Plan and Education Sector Support Program 2006-2010 implementation.* Phnom Penh: MoEYS.

Ministry of Education, Youth and Sport (2009b) *National Education Congress Summary Report on the Education, Youth and Sport Performance for the Academic Year 2007-08 and the Academic Year 2008-2009 Goals.* Phnom Penh: MoEYS.

Ministry of Education, Youth and Sport & United Nations International Children's Fund (2005) *Expanded Basic Education Programme (EBEP) (Phase II) 2006-2010:*

a joint MoEYS/UNICEF proposal submitted to Sida. Phnom Penh: MoEYS & UNICEF.

Ministry of Planning (2009) *Education 2007: report based on the Cambodia Socio-economic Survey.* Phnom Penh: MoP.

Ministry of Planning and Investment (2006) *The Five-year Socio-economic Development Plan 2006-2010.* Hanoi: Ministry of Planning and Investment.

Pellini, A. (2005) Decentralisation of Education in Cambodia: searching for spaces of participation between traditions and modernity, *Compare*, 35(2), 205-216.

Sakada, C. (2009) 2010 Sees Budget Increases in Key Sectors, *VOA News.com*, 1 December. http://khmernz.blogspot.com/2009/12/2010-budget-sees-increases-in-key.html (accessed 4 January 2010).

Saw, D. (2009) Challenges Crippling Cambodian Education, *The Phnom Penh Post*, 14 October. http://www.phnompenhpost.com/index.php/2009101428937/Education-and-Career/challenges-crippling-cambodian-education.html (accessed 4 January 2010).

Shoraku, A. (2008) Educational Movement Toward School-based Management in East Asia: Cambodia, Indonesia and Thailand. Background paper prepared for the Education for All Global Monitoring Report 2009.

Sopheak, K.C. & Clayton, T. (2007) Schooling in Cambodia, in G. Postiglione & J. Tan (Eds) *Going to School in East Asia*, pp. 41-60. Westport, CT: Greenwood Press.

Sothearith. I. (2009) Cambodia Lacks Clear Spending of Resource Money, *VOA News.com*, 15 December. http://www.voanews.com/khmer/2009-12-14-voa3.cfm (accessed 4 January 2010).

Tan, C. (2007) Education Reforms in Cambodia: issues and concerns, *Educational Research and Policy Practice*, 6, 15-64.

Transparency International (2009) Corruption Perceptions Index 2009. http://www.transparency.org/policy_research/surveys_indices/cpi/2009/cpi_2009_table (accessed 3 January 2010).

UNESCO (2006) State of Teacher Education in the Asia-Pacific Region. http://www.unescobkk.org/fileadmin/template2/apeid/Documents/status_of_teachers/Cambodia.pdf (accessed 4 January 2010).

United Nations Development Programme (2009) Human Development Report 2009. http://hdrstats.undp.org/en/indicators/165.html (accessed 4 January 2010).

USAID (2008) USAID/Cambodia – country profile. http://www.usaid.gov/kh/USAID_Cambodia_overview.htm (accessed 12 December 2009).

World Bank (2005) *Cambodia: quality basic education for all.* Washington, DC: World Bank.

World Bank (2007) *Sharing Growth: equity and development in Cambodia. Equity Report 2007 (Report no. 39809-KH).* Washington, DC: World Bank.

World Bank (2009) Gross National Income Per Capita 2008, Atlas Method and PPP. http://siteresources.worldbank.org/DATASTATISTICS/Resources/GNIPC.pdf (accessed 12 December 2009).

World Food Programme (2009) Education. http://www.foodsecurityatlas.org/khm/country/education (accessed 16 December 2009).

CHAPTER 4

Education Reforms in Indonesia

ASSAD L. BAUNTO

SUMMARY This chapter provides the historical context of education reforms in Indonesia and documents the changes in its education objectives as the country traversed political upheavals, from the pre-colonial period, marked by full autonomy of education, through the colonial period of failed liberal education to post-independence characterised by consolidation of the education sector under the revolutionary government of Soekarno, centralisation under the authoritative government of Soeharto and decentralisation under democracy. The chapter highlights recent trends and challenges faced by the decentralised education reform which, if unaddressed, will lead to the disappearance of the initial gains and progress made towards universal education.

Introduction

The Republic of Indonesia is lauded as one of the few countries in South-East Asia to have achieved nearly universal basic education (World Bank, 2007). What underlies this success is the dramatic transformation the education sector has undergone through – from a less structured fully autonomous arrangement to a centralised and formal setup, and to a decentralised (and school-based management) governance system. The changes in the political and governance system in Indonesia have substantially altered the objectives of Indonesian education. Notably, the provision for universal access to education is a relatively recent phenomenon and can be traced to the period of political consolidation. The main task left in the period of decentralised governance is not only to sustain gains from universal access but also to ensure that education objectives translate to equipping Indonesian citizens with the skills and knowledge needed to be truly Indonesians as defined by the five pillars of *Pancasila* (quality). This chapter provides the historical context of education reforms in Indonesia and documents the changes in its education objectives as the country traversed political upheavals: (i) pre-colonial marked by full autonomy of education (section II), (ii) colonial period of failed liberal education (section III) and (iii) post-independence characterised by consolidation of the education sector under the revolutionary government of Soekarno, centralisation under the authoritative government of Soeharto and decentralisation under democracy (section IV). The chapter highlights recent trends and challenges faced by the decentralised education reform (section V) which, if unaddressed, will lead to the disappearance of the initial gains and progress made towards universal education.

Pre-colonial Period (pre-1800): Islamisation and full autonomy of schools

The early period of education in Indonesia was characterised as Islamic, non-formal and less structured. Education instruction and school management were highly autonomous which resulted in the marginalisation of some local communities who lacked enough local capacity to finance and operate schools. Uneven access to education is mirrored in the concentration of schools in central Java (Buchori & Malik, 2004). Instruction and school management responsibility were provided by *pesantren* (or Islamic boarding learning centres), most often conducted in mosques. *Pesantren* were administered by a cleric or *kiyai* who was both a teacher and an administrator of the learning centre. In those days, no formal curriculum was followed by the learning centres. The absence of centralised authority to establish and enforce education and instruction standards left the *pesantren* autonomous in terms of curriculum development. Teaching style and learning process varied across schools depending on the inclination or expertise of a *kiyai*. For some classes, the learning technique required the students to sit around the *kiyai*, known as the *halaqa* system. And for most classes at the mosques, no specific timetable was required for students to finish the course; education at the mosque was considered done once students were, for example, able to complete reciting the *Qur'an* (Ruswan, 1997). The learning system in *pesantren* typically revolved around students learning the basic understanding of Islamic doctrines and religious obligations, such as studying the *Qur'an*, theology, *syariah* (rules and regulations) pertaining to *ibadah* (worshiping Allah) and the Arabic language. Upon mastering the basics, students were then allowed to take advanced courses including *fiqh* (law), *tarikh* (history), *hadith* (traditions of the prophet Mohammad) and, further, a more specialised course in Islamic studies in an individualised teaching session from a *kiyai*. Individual tutoring was commonly referred to as *ngaji sorogan* (see Buchori & Malik, 2004).

Colonial Period by the Dutch (*c.*1800-1942): centralisation and failed liberal education

The idea of centralised control of education started when the Netherlands introduced liberal education in Indonesia as embodied in the colonial government's 'Ethical Policy' (*Ethische Politiek*) in September 1901. The 'Ethical Policy' was established in the context of the particular obligation on the part of the Dutch to improve the welfare of the people in the East Indies of whom the Dutch colonisers had taken much advantage. The real intention of this policy was to introduce Western education including sciences to Indonesians, which would be related to local cultures and traditions. The real intention, though noble, was never achieved in practice (Aritonang, 1994).

Three levels of education were established during the Dutch rule: primary, middle and college (independent colleges that offer a particular field). While this provided the impetus to formalise the system of education in Indonesia, the education policy during this period was nonetheless highly discriminating in favour of advancing the interests of the colonisers.

Segmentation by race and social status was apparent even as early as the primary level. The *Europeesche Lagere Scholen* exclusively served children of European descent and *Hollandsch Chineesche Scholen* catered to children of either Chinese or East Asian (but non-Indonesian) origin. The native Indonesians, on the other hand, were further segregated according to social standing. Those from the aristocracy were sent to *Hollandsch Inlandsche Scholen* while native commoners attended *Standaardschool*. Educating the Indonesian elite was part of a strategy to secure a supply of civil servants for the bureaucracy who would then serve the interests of the colonisers. Western education effectively became an extended machinery of the bureaucracy to fill in administrative needs (Aritonang, 1994).

As a result of the 'Ethical Policy', the number of schools in Indonesia rapidly expanded. Most of these schools were privately owned, typically run by religious missionaries, thanks to the subsidies that they received from the Dutch East Indies government.

Concurrently, a new policy embodied in *Staatsblad 1906* was pursued in the organisation of village schools, which became precursors of public education in the archipelago. The domain of village schools was no more than to promote basic literacy and numeracy to native commoners. This move hinted at an element of decentralisation efforts by the Dutch East Indies government to expand education in rural areas. The regulation encouraged cost-sharing arrangements so that the Dutch East Indies government shouldered operational expenditures such as teachers' salaries and villages provided capital expenditures such as school buildings and facilities. Later, this proved to be unsustainable since villages had limited financial capacity to finance capital expenditures on education. Questions were also raised as to the relevance or irrelevance of the education instruction and materials with respect to village cultures and the ability of middle and tertiary schools to absorb successful graduates of village schools (Aritonang, 1994).

Segregation of education at the primary level effectively created multiple structures of education. Each evolved with different numbers of years of study to complete the course and with different instructional materials. The *Hollandsch Inlandsche Scholen*, for example, had a seven-year period of study and adopted Dutch as medium of instruction while *Standaardschool* had a five-year period of study. Even then, this situation was already an improvement on the education policy during the period of the Dutch East Indies Company, i.e. the period prior to the formation of the Dutch colonial government, when there was no thought of providing education to native Indonesians.

Despite these efforts, the education policy to promote liberal education did not really become effective at generating an improvement in quantity and quality and only led to a widening gap of education between indigenous Indonesians and non-indigenous Indonesians and Europeans, on the one hand, and between noble and ordinary indigenous Indonesians, on the other. An account by Mestoko et al (1954) cited by Ruswan (1997) on expenditure allocation on education by the Dutch East Indies government suggests biased treatment on the part of the colonial government concerning the demand for education. As an example, education expenditure for European schools in Indonesia in 1909 was twice the amount of expenditure for schools for indigenous Indonesians even if the latter had 162,000 students. European schools in that year had only 25,000 students. This translated to education expenditures of f107.1 per student in European schools in Indonesia as opposed to f8.4 per student in indigenous schools. In 1915, when the number of students in indigenous schools almost doubled, the education expenditure was posted at f4.7 per student. In contrast, for the same year when the number of students in European schools increased by only 28%, the education expenditure in European schools was f206.3 per student, or 44 times that of indigenous schools.

In terms of supply, a sufficiently good number of subjects were taught to schoolchildren in *Hollandsch Inlandsche Scholen* even if some of the subjects offered were judged irrelevant to their needs. Village schools, on the other hand, saw provision of basic literacy and numeracy as more than sufficient to ordinary indigenous Indonesians. However, successful graduates of village schools had difficulty competing with students who completed elementary education at *Standaardschool* or *Hollandsch Inlandsche Scholen* which provided better instructional materials, in case they decided to pursue higher learning.

Fortunately, a continuing education, middle school (*Vervolgschool*), was given to graduates of village schools to address learning inadequacies. Teaching provided by middle schools was considered comparable to what was offered in *Standaardschool*. Upon completion, students of middle school or *Standaardschool* were given the opportunity to attend further studies in 'connecting schools'. Tertiary schooling was normally exclusively open to successful elementary students of *Hollandsch Inlandsche Scholen* and *Europeesche Lagere Scholen*. In later years, the colonial government established several (i) senior high schools which were open to graduates of connecting schools in case they decided to pursue higher learning, (ii) vocational schools and (iii) technical and medical colleges. No university – consisting of several faculties or colleges – existed during the period (Atmakusuma et al, 1974). There were six institutions (colleges or faculties) of higher learning offering courses in agriculture (which was attached to the college of medicine), arts, dentistry, engineering, law and medicine – all located on the island of Java. These colleges were meant to provide professional training rather than creating an environment for research or sheer pursuit of knowledge in the academe (Wicaksono & Friawan, 2007). Economies of scale were absent therefore an inter-disciplinary approach to education at the tertiary level was highly prohibitive.

Overall, the education policy of the Dutch East Indies government was not effective in raising quantity improvments and in being inclusive. By 1936, there were 585 mission schools and 159 government schools at the elementary level (Aritonang, 1994). But this distinction between private and public education becomes blurred as mission schools received subsidies from the government (i.e. the Dutch East Indies government). Meanwhile, it was estimated that only 200 students were enrolled in higher learning institutions during the colonial period (Wicaksono & Friawan, 2007). Up until the 1940s, less than 10% of Indonesian school-age children had actually received formal education (Aritonang, 1994), which provided a basis for doubting the effectiveness of the 'Ethical Policy' of the colonial government. Several measures were instituted including decentralising education financing and administration of schools, lowering subsidies received by private schools, increasing tuition fees and, to an extreme extent, reducing the number of schools and abolishing *Standaardschool* during the global depression in 1929 (Aritonang, 1994). But these were not well received and only fanned the flames of nationalist movements already flickering among the educated Indonesian elite.

Post-colonial Period (1945-present)

Education reform in Indonesia happened very swiftly after the end of the Dutch East Indies government in 1942. It coincided with the period of revolution and consolidation of power during the Soekarno rule (a period in Indonesian history aptly referred to as the Old Order or *Orde Lama*, 1942-65)[1], the throes of development during the authoritative government of Soeharto (New Order or *Orde Baru*, 1966-98) and democratic government since 1998.

Orde Lama (1942-65): national consciousness and consolidating the national education system

The national leadership of Soekarno significantly influenced education reform in Indonesia. The main objective of the leadership was the creation of an independent Indonesian state and this was embodied in the *Pancasila* (or 'five principles') which became the political foundation of the Indonesian state. Reflecting these principles, particularly concerning social justice for all Indonesian citizens, the first basic education act was ratified in 1950, which committed the government to providing six years of universal education at the primary level and to providing financial assistance to both public and private education. Also, because of the prevailing consciousness on nation building, the education reform, which was crystallised in the first education act (Law No. 15) in 1961, focused primarily on establishing a national education system including curriculum development as well as development of a national language, Bahasa Indonesia. Providing education opportunities for people living in rural areas became the priority of the reform and this was affirmed in upgrading vocational skills and continuing education. In addition, the education act of 1961 standardised the academic structure of both private and public higher education where universities consisted of faculties and divisions. Under the law, higher institutions were mandated to commit to the pursuit of learning, research and community service. The first university of the republic was established in 1949 in Jakarta, the Gajah Mada University consisting of faculties of agriculture and veterinary medicine, dentistry, engineering, law and literature, and medicine. Another one, the Universitas Indonesia, established in 1950, offered courses in sciences and liberal arts such as law and economics. Soekarno's education reform efforts only came into a halt when the struggle for power and military coup staged by the Communist Party in 1965 brought the economy to the brink of collapse.

Orde Baru (1966-98): accelerated expansion of the education sector

The priority of education changed under the new authoritarian government of Soeharto starting in 1966. The emphasis of education was on ensuring a stream of graduates to support the process of development. The national curriculum was amended in 1975 to suit the demands of economic recovery and progress. As a consequence, the 1975 curriculum became 'most overloaded and overdosed' (Yulaelawati, 2001, p. 2) and laid particular emphasis on objective examinations. Cognitive attainment by students was the emphasis of learning objectives, which, in most cases, departed from the practical application of the knowledge learnt (Raihani, 2007).

Around this period, Indonesia saw dramatic improvements in education investments since the post-independence era, especially during the period when the economy witnessed large windfall oil revenues from oil price booms. With resources at hand, the government, through presidential instruction, launched a massive school construction programme (*Sekolah*

Dasar INPRES) in every village, abolished school fees at the primary level, and organised non-formal education equivalency programmes for adults (*Kejar Paket A*), in response to government's sustained drive for equity in the provision of basic education across provinces. Provision of universal primary education (six years), which effectively aimed to increase access to elementary education to all Indonesian citizens, was a government policy spelled out in its First Long Term Development Plan 1969-94. The programmes were paralleled by recruitment and training of teachers through the establishment by the government of a School for Teacher Education. Enrolment rates among school-age children at primary level increased from 69% in 1973 to 83% in 1978 as a result of 61,807 elementary schools constructed between 1973 and 1979. The programme was successful in raising the average years (ranging from 0.25 to 0.40) of schooling of primary students and in achieving an increase of economic returns from 6.8% to 10.6% among the first cohort who were fully exposed to the programme (Duflo, 2001). The number of institutions offering higher education rose from 10 in 1950 to 317 (counting both private and state universities) by the mid-1970s (Atmakusuma et al, 1974). Despite the remarkable achievements in producing huge numbers of educated young cohorts, there was a growing apprehension as to whether the programme had generated expansion of human capital, which should include both quantity and quality expansion. For instance, the drastic implementation of the school construction programmes in villages had forced the government to appoint under-qualified staff – sometimes graduates of junior secondary schools – to fill the posts of teachers in the newly constructed primary schools whilst waiting for teachers trained at the School for Teacher Education to graduate. This move had a significant impact on the learning environment of elementary school children. Mismatched appointments were also observed in some villages where teaching posts in public education at primary level were occupied by teachers trained at religious schools, e.g. *madrasah*, who were poorly equipped to handle secular education (Hadi, 2009). Questions remained that the quality of education might have deteriorated to offset the gains made from the expansion in quantity of education (Duflo, 2001).

The seeming success of *Sekolah Dasar* and the growing demand for secondary schooling encouraged the government to pass into law the expansion of universal basic education to nine years (The Education Act of 1989), which covered junior secondary level (*Sekolah Menengah Pertanga*, or *SMP*). The government constructed at least one junior secondary-level school in every sub-district, abolished the junior secondary school fees, and launched open junior secondary education (*SMP Terbuka*), which was a distance education delivery of junior secondary education to disadvantaged students (Sadiman & Rahardjo, 1997). The same opportunities and failures observed in the *Sekolah Dasar* programme were repeated in the implementation of *SMPs*, i.e. rapid expansion of schools left government no choice but to recruit under-qualified teachers even if training initiatives for secondary school teachers were underway. Recognising the gaps in the implementation of universal education at primary level and its extension to junior secondary level, the new act redefined the minimum standards or requirements for school teachers. The Education Act of 1989 was a call from the government expressing its desire to develop the manpower needed for an industrialising economy to meet the demands of the global market.

In expanding education, the government actively involved the participation of the private sector by providing subsidies to private schools to cover part of the construction and maintenance costs and by assigning some teachers in public schools to teach in private schools (King & Orazen, 1999).

Higher education underwent a major turnaround. In 1975, the Ministry of Education issued a directive that redefined the role of higher education institutions in society. It linked the critical role of higher education institutions in the national and regional development context, i.e. need to create skilled workers and to respond to the labour market (Wicaksono & Friawan, 2007).

Meanwhile, it was only in 1975 that the government formally recognised Islamic education given the latter's significant contribution to society especially in the history of Islamisation in Indonesia and given its invaluable role in educating the indigenous population especially those living in rural areas. By then, three types of Islamic education existed in the country: *pesantren*, the *madrasah* (or religious day school) and the *Sekolah Islam* (day school that combines secular education and Islamic teachings). The Education Act of 1989 was the first national legislation to refer to *madrasah* as part of Indonesia's national education system. Islamic education has been under the supervision of the Ministry of Religious Affairs instead of the Ministry of Education. Previously, efforts to standardise and improve the *madrasah* system throughout Indonesia started as early as Soekarno's rule but were hampered by the limited financial and human resources of the Ministry of Religious Affairs, which effectively meant the Ministry had to maintain a dual education system. Under the dual education system, the *madrasah* focused on religious instruction. Fortunately, this failure was addressed when the government later initiated a model *madrasah negeri*, or state-sponsored *madrasah*, with hope that it would be replicated in the future. (Until then, the supply of *madrasah* used to be in the domain of the private sector.) By 2002, 17% (or more than 37,362 schools) of the total number of primary and secondary schools in the country were *madaris* (*madaris* is the Arabic plural of *madrasah*) (Zuhdi, 2006). *Madrasah negeri* followed the structure of secular education: *Madrasah Ibtidaiyah Negeri* (elementary), *Madrasah Tsanawiyah Negeri* (junior secondary) and *Madrasah Aliyah Negeri* (secondary). Later, the curriculum governing the *madrasah* system was redesigned in 1976, in a joint decree involving three ministries – Ministry of Education, Ministry of Religious Affairs and Ministry of Internal Affairs – to accommodate secular subjects. This positive move paved the way for empowering Indonesian Muslim schoolchildren to pursue knowledge beyond the confines of religion.

The learning objectives among Muslim students were effectively broadened from producing Islamic clerics to creating a mass of Indonesian Muslims who are not only committed to Islamic ideals but also to scientific advancement (Zuhdi, 2006).

It is also worth mentioning that around this period (in 1975), Indonesia invaded East Timor. During its 23-year occupation, Indonesia's assimilationist approach to East Timor was pronounced in its education policy. This included (i) banning the use of Tetum and Portuguese, which are the lingua franca in East Timor, and encouraging the use of Bahasa Indonesia, (ii) construction of primary schools in every village, considered to be a massive school construction programme in East Timor's history (Arenas, 1998), and (iii) deployment of teachers. While this increased the time young children spent at school, the ratio of enrolees at primary level for the East Timorese remained low relative to those enrolled children of Indonesian descent whose families had migrated to East Timor (Jones, 2001). The main reasons for the low enrolment among the East Timorese include their 'resistance' to embracing Indonesian identity (Arenas, 1998), culture shock, families' preference for East Timorese culture, among others.

Post-Soeharto (1998–present): decentralisation of education in full force

After the resignation of Soeharto as president at the height of the Asian financial crisis in 1998, Indonesia underwent a dramatic political upheaval as it adopted the democratic system of government. Education was significantly impacted so that not only the learning environment and learning processes had to accommodate democratic ideals and values, but also educational management had to be effected through the decentralised governance processes. The decentralisation efforts that were sweeping the governance structure in Indonesia introduced, in 1999, the school autonomy reform (e.g. school-based management or *Manajemen Berbasis Sekolah*) at primary and secondary levels. (The present education system in Indonesia is of two streams: secular, which is under the Ministry of National Education and Islamic, which is under the Ministry of Religious Affairs. Both streams are structured to have primary, secondary and higher education.) The decentralisation reform delineated the responsibilities of central government and local governments and shifted the responsibility of management and resources to schools and away from central authority. Under the reform, the central government is responsible for setting (i) standards for student achievement, (ii) the national curriculum, (iii) the national assessment system, (iv) standards for learning materials, (v) requirements for achievement, (vi) grading standards, (vii) requirements for admission, transfer and certification, and (viii) the development of higher education, distance education and international schools. The provincial government, on the other hand, has the primary tasks of (i) determining policy on selection and acceptance of students in relation to equity issues, (ii) providing educational materials for basic education and special education, (iii) assisting the management of higher education and (iv) managing special schools and training centres (Jalal et al, 2003). Advocates of decentralisation saw that the school autonomy reform would bring better quality of education and efficiency of allocation and use of resources (Behrman et al, 2002), and effectiveness in instructing students would create accountability of teachers and school managers to students, parents and communities, and sensitivity to local needs (Cheng, 1996; King & Orazen, 1999; Raihani, 2007). School-based management also aims to transform educators, especially school teachers, to be more innovative, pro-active and, at the same time, responsive to the needs of local communities as opposed to mechanically implementing directives of superiors. Initial steps to improve the capacity of local actors in implementing the decentralised education management were undertaken, e.g. 'learning and teaching processes, school program[me] planning and evaluation, curriculum development, staff management and recruitment, resources and facilities and maintenance, finance management, student services, school–community partnership, and school culture development' (Raihani, 2007, p. 175). But, whether these have indeed significantly influenced outcomes is yet to be empirically justified.

It would be unfair to claim that decentralisation was never thought of earlier on. In fact, the Soeharto government had, to a certain extent, implemented decentralisation in the education sector but it was only limited to physical infrastructure development and maintenance of schools. The scope for fundamental aspects of education management such as curriculum and instruction development, recruitment of teachers and budgeting responsibilities was always limited by political realities and lack of political will. Prior to the implementation of the school autonomy reform, the education sector experienced limited accountability among government agencies and ministries for education outcomes, ineffective school management, rigid budgeting processes, and uneven allocation of qualified teachers owing to poor civil service incentive structures (Raihani, 2007).

To effectively achieve the desired outcomes of the school-based management reform, the revised education authority, the Ministry of National Education, changed the education curriculum and adopted a competency-based curriculum (*Kurikulum Berbasis Kompetensi*) in 2003. The new curriculum, which was officially implemented the following year, also underscored greater involvement of school stakeholders in curriculum development. Subsequently, the national legislation governing the national education system was modified to accommodate the decentralisation trends in education management. The National Education System Act of 2003 was adopted and explicitly called for commitment to expansion and equity through compulsory and free-of-charge basic education for children of 7-15 years of age, improvements in quality and relevance, 'the implementation of principles of democracy, autonomy, decentralisation and public accountability' (Act of the Republic of Indonesia No. 20, 2003, p. 2), and autonomy of higher education. Under the law, formal education begins with kindergarten (comprised of two years) followed by primary school (six years), junior secondary (three years) and senior secondary (three years), and either a university degree from an academic or professional programme or a diploma from a polytechnic or vocational higher education programme.

The decentralised arrangement for education management was heralded as an innovation for improvements in the whole school system and for creation of local incentives to better address needs of local communities while promoting the 'unity in diversity' (*Bhinneka Tunggal Ika*) principle enshrined in the *Pancasila*. However, the decentralised setup stirred public controversy in relation to provision of religious education in that the state is strongly interfering in school management when it comes to religious instruction. The National Education Act of 2003 is, effectively, defeating the object of promoting decentralisation and autonomy since the same law requires private schools to ask permission and secure approval from the education authority with regard to recruitment of teachers who will handle religious courses (Zuhdi, 2006).

Latest Trends and Challenges

Indonesia is lauded as the model country in the South-East Asian region to have attained near-universal primary education with, by 2005, 93% of school-age children enrolled in both public and private primary schools, 65% enrolled in junior secondary schools and 42% in senior secondary schools (World Bank, 2007).[2] Indonesia aims to achieve 100% and 96% gross enrolment rates at elementary school and junior secondary school level, respectively, by 2009. At the tertiary level, as of 2005, more than 3.5 million students were enrolled in some 2300 higher education institutions, a remarkable achievement from only 200,000 students in 1975 (Wicaksono & Friawan, 2007). Despite this progress, several constraints were documented that, if unaddressed, might offset the gains achieved from the quantity expansion achieved since the government resolutely embarked on the massive school construction programme in the mid to late 1970s and the decentralisation efforts beginning in the late 1990s.

First, the most immediate challenge faced by the education sector is not the need to increase government spending on supply-side factors – in fact, the government has made considerable efforts in increasing public allotment to the education sector, but rather the need to raise the quality of education services (Arze del Granado et al, 2007; World Bank, 2007). The quality of schooling in Indonesia is, on average, low based on the results of national achievement tests, *Ebtanas* (Behrman et al, 2002). Increasing the quality of education entails improving the quality of teachers to boost student achievement, increasing students' learning time by reducing the high incidence of absenteeism and increasing the number of full-time teachers, improving teacher educational attainment and freeing certain resources such as qualified teachers to achieve efficiency goals. The latter can be achieved by changing the efficiency mix of qualified teachers through their reallocation to undersupplied districts. In a survey of 276 primary schools in Indonesia, 34% of these schools have an undersupply of teachers (World Bank, 2007). However, how teachers respond to this arrangement depends on the elasticity of supply of teachers to move to the target areas. This, in turn, requires addressing the need to have better teacher incentive structures and better teacher performance control mechanisms. Without teacher performance control, problems of moral hazard (i.e. when a teacher does not fully bear the cost of their action but is likely to take such action, such as in the case of unrecorded absenteeism or some unobservable teacher characteristics that undermine a good learning environment) can render allocation of resources inefficient. The teacher incentive arrangement may consist of a fixed wage and a proportional rule (Fabella, 2004). Other determinants of quality are qualification standards for teachers, teacher attendance and class-size ratio. The low student–teacher ratio at primary and secondary levels (Behrman et al, 2002) and tertiary education (Wicaksono & Friawan, 2007) need not necessarily imply better quality since it may be a reflection of internal inefficiency or high incidence of part-time school teachers. Currently, some 45% of school teachers at primary schools and another 17% of teachers at junior secondary schools do not have the minimum qualification set by the Ministry of National Education (World Bank, 2007). To effectively implement the mechanism for upgrading quality in education, accountability is required. The decentralised, or school-based, setup of education management provides a suitable environment for a two-pronged approach to public accountability to minimise and avoid corruption and the inefficient features of decentralised systems often characterised in developing countries. Public accountability is achieved by making sure that: (i) school district supervisors, school principals and teachers, parents and local communities enforce teacher performance control and classroom quality assurance, and (ii) the Ministry of National Education enforces the required standards, e.g. teacher and classroom quality certifications. Instituting accountability may require a performance indicator system that measures the types of skills demanded by society and local communities and that maximises social value. This measure could be accomplished by adopting a more revolutionary and systematic approach to evaluating student performance – a shift from achievement examinations to assessment of relative gains (e.g. value-added indicators). The goal is to have an evaluation system that gauges student achievement by isolating family, neighbourhood and community effects from school characteristics, which all provide variances in explaining student performance (Meyer, 1996; McCaffrey et al, 2003).

Second, there is a growing trade-off between prioritising basic education, and senior secondary and tertiary education. For instance, the participation rate at the tertiary level is low due to both supply-side (relatively few higher education institutions) and demand-side factors (low participation rates at secondary level and low continuation rates among students to pursue higher education after graduation from secondary school) (Wicaksono & Friawan, 2007).

Third, a mismatch exists between recent graduates and the job demands of productive sectors in the economy that have high potential growth, e.g. the export-orientated industrial sector (Arze del Granado et al, 2007). This points to the need to have a learning environment that fosters development of skills beyond basic competencies, e.g. problem solving, entrepreneurial and creative. This, further, highlights the need to link education objectives with national, regional and district-level development planning.

And, fourth, the decentralisation reform has not sufficiently leveraged the district government in budgeting responsibility in the education sector. Since 2001 the central government has financed a large part (more than 50% of the total) of development expenditures, covering physical education infrastructures, while the district government allocates much of its budget to routine expenditures, particularly salary payments for civil servants including public school teachers (World Bank, 2007). This trend clearly contradicts the stipulations of the decentralisation laws (Law No. 22 of 1999 and Law No. 25 of 1999), where financing for education including those areas that affect key decision variables will be the primary responsibility of the district government under the new revenue-sharing arrangements between the central and regional governments. Under the same laws, the priority of the central government in investment in education will be confined to setting policy guidelines that govern the national education system including setting criteria and minimum standards.

Conclusion

The chapter presents how education reforms evolved in Indonesia and how political realities influenced the objectives of the education reforms. It shows how universal access to education has become the dominating education objective of the country since independence in 1945 in response to widespread education deprivation that most Indonesians experienced during the colonial period. Today, Indonesia boasts to have attained nearly universal access to education at primary and junior secondary levels. However, this progress in universal education is bereft of long-term planning. Whether Indonesia can sustain its success depends on how it can respond to current challenges and broaden its education objectives to accommodate the challenges. The current education system suffers from inefficiencies that exact a toll on the quality of education as well as the seeming lack of relevance and responsiveness to the demands of the labour market.

The introduction of school-based management reform in Indonesia in 1999 provides an opportunity to address these challenges. Among the salient features of the reform are improving quality, relevance, efficiency and accountability. However, the main issue that the education sector in Indonesia faces is the low capacity – financial, institutional or otherwise – of local actors to effectively implement the reform. Initial efforts were initiated to this end, but it might take a deal of time and resources before we can judge the reform a success.

Notes

[1] Between 1942 and 1945, Imperial Japan occupied Indonesia during the Second World War. During the period, the Japanese shut down all formal education in Indonesia (Thomas, 1973).

[2] Enrolment rate figures refer to *net* enrolment rates.

References

Act of the Republic of Indonesia No. 20 (2003) National Education System.

Arenas, A. (1998) Education and Nationalism in East Timor, *Social Justice*, 25(2), 131-148.

Aritonang, J.S. (1994) *Mission Schools in Batakland (Indonesia), 1861-1940*. Leiden: E.J. Brill.

Arze del Granado, J., Fengler, W., Ragatz, A. & Yavuz, E. (2007) Investing in Indonesia's Education: allocation, equity, and efficiency of public expenditures, Munich Personal RePEc Archive Paper No. 4372. http://mpra.ub.uni-muenchen.de/4372/.

Atmakusuma, A., Teken, I.G.B., Soeharjo, A. & Asngari, P.S. (1974) *The Role of Provincial Universities in Regional Development in Indonesia: an assessment*. Singapore: Regional Institute of Higher Education and Development.

Behrman, J., Deolalikar, A. & Soon, L. (2002) *Promoting Effective Schooling through Education Decentralization in Bangladesh, Indonesia, and Philippines*. ERD Working Paper Series No. 23. Manila: Asian Development Bank.

Buchori, M. & Malik, A. (2004) The Evolution of Higher Education in Indonesia, in P. Altbach & T. Umakoshi (Eds) *Asian Universities: historical perspectives and contemporary perspectives*. Baltimore, MD: Johns Hopkins University Press.

Cheng, Y.C. (1996) *School Effectiveness and School-based Management*. London: Falmer Press.

Duflo, E. (2001) School and Labor Market Consequences of School Construction in Indonesia: evidence from an unusual policy experiment, *American Economic Review*, 91(4), 795-813.

Fabella, R. (2004) Generalized Sharing, Membership Size and Pareto Efficiency in Teams, *Theory and Decision*, 48(1), 47-60.

Hadi, Y. (2009) Innovative In-service Teacher Training for Basic Education in Indonesia. http://www.yusufhadi.net.

Jalal, F., Sardjunani, N. & Purwadi, A. (2003) General Condition of Education Sector Development in Indonesia, in F. Jalal, N. Sardjunani, B. Musthafa &

Suharti (Eds) *National Plan of Action: Indonesia's Education for All 2003-2015.* Jakarta: National Education For All Coordination Forum.

Jones, G.W. (2001) Social Policy Issues in East Timor: education and health, in H. Hill & J.M. Saldanha (Eds) *East Timor – development challenges for the world's newest nation.* Singapore: Institute of Southeast Asian Studies.

King, E. & Orazen, P. (1999) Evaluating Education Reforms: four cases in developing countries, *The World Bank Economic Review*, 13(3), 409-413.

McCaffrey, D.F., Lockwood, J.R., Koretz, D.M. & Hamilton, L.S. (2003) *Evaluating Value-Added Models for Teacher Accountability.* Santa Monica, CA: RAND Corporation.

Meyer, R.H. (1996) Value-Added Indicators of School Performance, in E.A. Hanushek & D.W. Jorgenson (Eds) *Improving America's Schools – the role of incentives.* Washington, DC: National Academy Press.

Raihani (2007) Education Reforms in Indonesia in the Twenty-First Century, *International Education Journal*, 8(1), 172-183.

Ruswan (1997) Colonial Experience and Muslim Educational Reforms: a comparison of the Aligarh and the Muhammadiyah movements. Master's thesis, Institute of Islamic Studies, McGill University, Montreal. http://digitool.library.mcgill.ca:80/R/?func=dbin-jump-full&object_id=27968&local_base=GEN01-MCG02.

Sadiman, A. & Rahardjo, R. (1997) Contribution of SMP Terbuka toward Lifelong Learning in Indonesia, in M.J. Hatton (Ed.) *Lifelong Learning: policies, practices, and programs.* Toronto: School of Media Studies, Humber College.

Thomas, R.M. (1973) *A Chronicle of Indonesian Higher Education: the first half century 1920-1970.* Singapore: Chopmen Enterprises.

Wicaksono, T.Y. & Friawan, D. (2007) Recent Development of Higher Education in Indonesia: issues and challenges. East Asian Bureau of Economic Research Working Paper Series No. 45.

World Bank (2007) Spending for Development: making the most of Indonesia's new opportunities. Indonesia's Public Expenditure Review 2007. http://siteresources.worldbank.org/INTINDONESIA/Resources/Publication/280 016-1168483675167/PEReport.pdf

Yulaelawati, E. (2001) National Education Reform in Indonesia: milestones and strategies for the reform process, paper presented at The First International Forum on Education Reform: Experiences of Selected Countries, at Office of the National Education Commission, Bangkok, 30 July-2 August.

Zuhdi, M. (2006) Modernization of Indonesian Islamic Schools' Curricula, 1945-2003, *International Journal of Inclusive Education*, 10(4-5), 415-427.

CHAPTER 5

Education in the Lao People's Democratic Republic: confluence of history and vision

RICHARD NOONAN

SUMMARY Laos is the only Southeast Asian country without a sea coast. Mountain ranges and the Mekong River provide both protection and isolation. Traditionally literacy was the preserve of the aristocracy, their administrators, some merchants, and the monks. The French never supported education in Laos as much as in Vietnam. The secular schools followed the French system, with French as the language of instruction. Following independence in 1954, UNESCO and USAID supported the 1962 reform to create a Lao system. Higher education began gradually in the late 1950s, leading to the establishment of a university in the early 1970s. Meanwhile in the 'Liberated' zone under the *Pathet Lao*, education developed separately, including a teacher training college. In the turmoil and aftermath of the Revolution in 1975, the education system was severely damaged, and recovery was slow until the economic reforms of 1986. Today education is a leading sector for the national policy of leaving 'least developed country' status by 2020.

Introduction

This chapter provides an overview of the education system in Laos today in the context of its demographic, cultural, political, and economic history. The education system in Laos is significantly different from that of other countries in the South-East Asian region. These differences are rooted in the very different historical context.

Laos, officially the Lao People's Democratic Republic (Lao PDR), is a landlocked country in South-East Asia bordered by Myanmar and China to the north west, Vietnam to the east, Cambodia to the south, and Thailand to the west. The Annamite mountains form most of the border between Laos and Vietnam. For the most part, the Mekong River separates Laos from both Thailand and Myanmar. The Mekong River is navigable in most places, but two sets of rapids, one between Luangprabang and Vientiane and another between Vientiane and Champasack, result in three navigable stretches corresponding to three historically distinct regions. The terrain is mostly mountainous, with some plains and plateaus. The most densely populated areas lie in the Mekong river basin.

History

Pre-history

The pre-history of present-day Laos is based largely on stories passed from generation to generation, sometimes corroborated by linguistic and anthropological evidence. The people of present-day Laos migrated from the mountains and valleys of southern China between the eighth and thirteenth centuries (Stuart-Fox, 1998, pp. 1-29). Theravada Buddhism is the main religion in Laos and has become one of the primary unifying features of Lao culture.

The Classical Period (1353-1895)

Political development. Lao historiography usually traces the history of present-day Laos to the Kingdom of Lan Xang or 'Land of a Million Elephants', established by Fa Ngum (1316-93). Lan Xang was one of the largest kingdoms in South-East Asia and lasted for nearly 350 years, until a royal succession dispute led to the division of the kingdom in 1720 into three principalities: Luangprabang in the north, Vientiane in the centre, and Champasack in the south. In this weakened condition, the principalities were unable to resist the growing power of the Kingdom of Siam (present-day Thailand). By the mid-nineteenth century Laos risked absorption into Siam (Stuart-Fox, 1998, pp. 100-127).

Education development. The cultural centre of Lao society has traditionally been the temple (*wat*). Although there was no 'mass education', the monks were respected sources of higher learning. Most people were peasant farmers, and literacy was neither needed nor valued as a source of social mobility, in contrast to the neighbouring Confucian societies of China and Vietnam. Literacy was higher among the aristocracy, the small corps of administrators, and urban merchants, many of whom were Chinese or Vietnamese. In the villages, a rich oral tradition was the bearer of morals and culture (Evans, 1998, p. 154).

Most youth spent several months or years as temple novices (Koret, 1999, p. 226). Temple education was free and served all people, rich and poor, both monks and the general population (males only). Monk education was divided into several levels (Somlith, 1996, pp. 13-15). At the first level, novices learned reading, writing, arithmetic, and basic morals. At the second level, monks continued to learn and copied manuscripts. At the third level, higher ranking monks continued to study the holy texts, to copy manuscripts, and to learn the grammar of the Pali language in which the earliest Theravada Buddhist texts were written. The highest ranking monk became the teacher of the king (Somlith, 1996, pp. 15-17).

Temple education for the general population included a wide range of general and vocational subjects, including mathematics, Lao language, literature, art, medical science, and fortune-telling (Somlith, 1996, p. 17).

The French Colonial Period (1895-1945)

Political development (1895-1940). The Siamese sacked Luangprabang, Vientiane, and Champasack in 1779 and sacked Vientiane again in 1828 (Stuart-Fox, 1998, pp. 111-127), bringing the Lao kingdoms under Siamese suzerainty.

In the 1860s the French obtained from Vietnam a treaty ceding Cochin China and the right to navigate the Mekong River. The right to navigate the Mekong was fateful, because it contributed ultimately to the colonisation of both Cambodia and Laos (SarDesai, 1997, pp. 126-128).

In 1887 Luangprabang was again sacked, and the King requested French protection (Stuart-Fox, 1998, p. 141). In 1893, conflict with Siam led to a French ultimatum demanding that all Lao territory east of the Mekong be ceded to France. The King of Luangprabang signed several treaties with the French, none of which was ratified by France, so the exact status of Laos remained unclear until 1941.

The French never saw Laos as a core political entity but simply as an extension of Vietnam. Luangprabang was under the Protectorate, and the King had limited powers over northern Laos, but central and southern Laos were under the colonial system administered directly by the French (Stuart-Fox, 2002, pp. 25-30).

Education development (1895-1945). The French never invested as much in education in Laos as elsewhere in French Indochina, and the budget was only for building up a corps of Lao civil servants. In 1902 a budget for secular schooling was provided for the first time. Two schools were constructed, one in Vientiane and one in Luangprabang. Although it was not the policy of the French to replace temple education with secular education, the establishment of secular schools in 1902 was the beginning of a gradual movement of education from the temples to secular schools. The French solved the lack of qualified teachers by assigning translators in government offices to teach schools part time (Khamphao Phonekeo, 1996, p. 46). Education in all of French Indochina was managed from Hanoi.

There were two separate education systems in French Indochina, namely the *French system*, which was compatible with the school system in

France, and the *Indochina system*, with a slightly different curriculum, although students were taught French from grade 1. Most French schools were located in Vietnam. The Indochina system was itself divided into two systems, namely general and vocational education (Khamphao Phonekeo, 1996, pp. 27-32).

General education was organised into 12, later 13, academic years leading to the *Baccalauréat*. Primary schooling initially comprised five academic years, but because of the problem of second language learning, it was extended to six years (Khamphao Phonekeo, 1996, pp. 26-27). Following the establishment of the Department of Indochina Education in 1920, primary school enrolments grew at a rate of well over 10% per year until 1944, as shown in Table I and Figure 1.

Year	Schools	Students
1915	10	260
1920	28	931
1925	39	1585
1932	70	7035
1935	84	6537
1939	92	7026
1942	121	7901
1944	163	11401

Table I. Secular primary schools and students in Laos 1915-44.
Source: Manynooch (2007, p. 174).

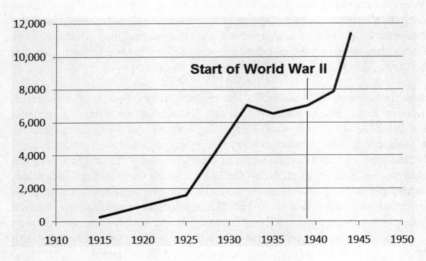

Figure 1. Primary school students in Laos 1915-44.

Growth in enrolments between 1915 and 1944 was erratic. The major jumps, 1925-32 and 1942-44, were due to the establishment of the Department of Indochina Education in 1920 and to the fear in the 1940s of losing control of Indochina. Most of the primary schools were incomplete, offering less than the full six years of schooling (Khamphao Phonekeo, 1996, p. 49). The largest lower secondary school was the Pavie School (*collége*) in Vientiane, built in 1922 with four classrooms to accommodate 120 students and a dormitory with 40 beds (Khamphao Phonekeo, 1996, pp. 26-37). There were no upper secondary schools until the Pavie School was upgraded to upper level in 1947. Students sat exams in Hanoi until 1950 (Khamphao Phonekeo, 1996, pp. 26-27).

A Master Plan for education in Indochina was developed in 1917 and remained in effect until 1945. Primary education was to be provided in the native languages and cultural identity of each region. The young were to be encouraged to complete primary and secondary education to suit local conditions and then to study at university. Schools for vocational training and handicrafts and art were to be developed in each region (Khamphao Phonekeo, 1996, pp. 27-29).

The Lao elite received a French education in Hanoi, Saigon, or France, where they were influenced by contemporary French nationalism and developed a special affinity for France (Evans, 2002, p. 73). French schools were established only in the big cities – only one in each city. They served the French students who accompanied their parents who worked in Laos and a few Lao students whose parents worked closely with French officials (Khamphao Phonekeo, 1996, p. 30).

The Indochinese schools at primary level were intended to be aligned with the local culture, traditions, and language. In 1937 over a third of primary school teachers were Vietnamese (Gunn, 2003, p. 50). At secondary level, the schools were aligned with the French system, and teachers were mainly Vietnamese (Khamphao Phonekeo, 1996, p. 30).

Buddhist education. In addition to the French schools in the urban areas, there were some rural village schools, temple schools, and schools for ethnic minorities (Khamphao Phonekeo, 1996, p. 29). The land was sparsely populated, and provision of secular education services in the more remote upland and mountainous areas was virtually impossible. Even in the rural lowland areas, it was difficult to gather enough children in one place for schooling, and older children had to contribute to their families' subsistence. Children would inherit the properties and continue the traditional way of life.

Temple schools enrolled many more students than secular public schools. In 1935 there were 387 temple schools with 7500 students (compare with figures for secular schooling, Table I). The French aim was to improve the temple schools and update the curriculum to include Western science and mathematics (Manynooch, 2007, p. 173).

School enrolments. Although enrolment rates in secular education rose gradually, as the Second World War approached, fewer than 5% of school-age children in Laos were enrolled in primary schooling, as shown in Table II, and many of the students were from Vietnamese families working with the French administration (Khamphao Phonekeo, 1996, p. 29). In 1935, Vietnamese students accounted for 21% of students in lower primary (grades 1-3), 44% in upper primary (grades 4-6), and 68% in lower secondary (Gunn, 2003, p. 54).

Year	Total pop. (000s)	Year	Students	GER (%)
1915	701	1915	260	0.2
1920	799	1920	931	0.7
1936	1184	1935	6537	3.4
1940	1350	1939	7026	3.2
1944	1539	1945	11401	4.6

Table II. Estimated primary gross enrolment ratio (GER) 1910-36.
Sources: Population, Lahmyer (2002); Students, Table I above; GER, author estimate.

There was hardly any teacher training in Laos prior to the Second World War. Most qualified primary teachers were Vietnamese trained in Hanoi. In 1942 the National Education Centre (founded in 1922) became the Teacher Training School for primary and lower secondary teachers (Ogawa, 2009, p. 288).

Political developments during the Second World War (1940-45). On 28 July 1941, Japanese troops entered Saigon. The French were allowed to administer the colony while Japan was preoccupied elsewhere. Fearful of losing its hold on the colony, France hurriedly ratified a treaty governing the colonial status of Laos.

In March 1945, Japanese forces deposed the French in Indochina. French officials fled to Laos, chased by the Japanese, who encouraged the liberation struggle against the French. Ordered by the Japanese, King Sisavangvong declared independence of the Kingdom of Luangprabang in April. Japan surrendered to the Allies on 15 August. The King seemed prepared to accept the return of French hegemony, but Prince Phetsarat declared the unification and independence of the Lao Kingdom. For that the King dismissed him as prime minister, and Phetsarat formed the Provisional Lao Issara (Free Lao) government together with his youngest half-brother, Prince Suphanuvong (Stuart-Fox, 1997, p. 63).

Renovation (1940-45). France feared Siam, especially the Pan-Thai movement launched in the 1930s (Gunn, 2005, p. 97). To strengthen their position, the French initiated the Lao Renovation Movement with the publication of *Lao Nyai* (Great Laos) and increased the education budget. The goal of the Renovation Movement was to 'provide Laos with its own personality with respect to its neighbours and to inculcate the sense of homeland' (Gunn, 2005, pp. 100-101), i.e. a sense of nationhood (under French hegemony). A School of Arts was established, and the School of Law and Administration was reorganised to speed up the replacement of Vietnamese administrators with Lao. More schools were built in 1940-45 than over the whole period 1893-1940 (Stuart-Fox, 1997, p. 55). By the end of the Second World War, a Lao nationalist intelligentsia had begun to form, with a vision of independence from France, but in Laos there was no nationwide nationalist organisation like the Viet Minh in Vietnam. Laos was deeply divided by regional antagonisms (Stuart-Fox, 1997, p. 60).

Independence Struggle (1946-54)

Political developments. In 1946 a Franco-Lao commission produced a Modus Vivendi confirming a unified Laos under the King of Luangprabang, but with major political, military, and economic powers in the hands of the French. The Modus Vivendi was considered a sham by the Lao Issara (Stuart-Fox, 2002, p. 54). In 1949 the Lao People's Liberation Army (LPLA) was established under the command of Kaison Phomvihan. The real locus of power in the communist movement Pathet Lao was in the LPLA, not the Lao Issara (Gunn, 2005, p. 280), and Suphanuvong left Lao Issara and joined forces with the Viet Minh (Stuart-Fox, 2002, p. 54, passim). The Viet Minh, seeing the struggle against the French as a 'single battlefield', provided essential inspiration and military support to the Pathet Lao in the following years.

In 1949 the General Convention, signed by France and the Royal Lao Government (RLG), gave Laos quasi-independence within the French Union. It gave the RLG control of most functions except monetary policy and customs, where Indochina-wide agreements were still in force, and limited control in defence, justice, and foreign affairs, but this was an improvement over the Modus Vivendi (Stuart-Fox, 1997, p. 70). With departure of Suphanuvong and the signing of the General Convention, the weakened moderate Issara disbanded in October 1949. In August the following year, the Pathet Lao formed a 'Resistance Government'.

The fall of Dien Bien Phu on 7 May 1954 brought a definite end to French colonialism in South-East Asia. The 1954 Geneva Agreement guaranteed Laos freedom and neutrality and the withdrawal of all foreign forces (Stuart-Fox, 1997, p. 87). A vision of independence was thus achieved, although another vision could be seen on the horizon.

Education development (1946-54). Under the Modus Vivendi, the Lao had responsibility for the Ministry of Education, although in practice it was in the hands of the French (Khamphao Phonekeo, 1996, pp. 57-58). The events of 1945 and 1946 seriously affected education in Laos. From March 1945, most schools were either abandoned or destroyed, and textbooks scattered. French teachers were tortured and became prisoners of war, and Vietnamese students and teachers were evacuated from Laos. As part of their post-war effort to strengthen their position, the French invested more in education (Evans, 1988, p. 51). Enrolments increased, but growth was not sustained, as shown in Table III and Figure 2.

Year	Schools	Students
1945	187	11,401
1947	383	23,110
1950	581	38,333
1951	609	33,552
1952	648	35,252
1953	673	41,412
1954	679	33,357
1955	972	48,798
1956	1111	63,950

Table III. Primary schools and students in Laos 1945-56.
Source: Khamphao Phonekeo (1996, p. 62).

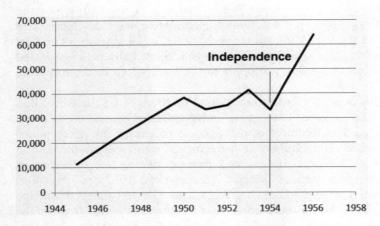

Figure 2. Primary school students in Laos 1945-56.

In addition to government schools, there were vernacular or Lao schools managed by local communities or temples. These were generally of lower quality than the schools administered by the French. Some communities petitioned to have the schools brought under French administration, but others preferred to keep the schools out of the French system because they did not want their children to attend schools far away. Temple schools were also widespread (Khamphao Phonekeo, 1996, p. 69).

With the disappearance of large numbers of French and Vietnamese teachers, filling the requirement for teachers was a major problem. One solution was the recruitment of advanced primary school students to serve as 'practice teachers' at lower primary level after a training programme lasting three to six months (Khamphao Phonekeo, 1996, p. 60).

Education in the Liberated Zone. The Resistance Government included a Ministry of Education, and a new form of primary education was established, namely mass education focusing on primary schooling and community-based literacy programmes. Primary schools were built where possible, the Lao script was simplified, some primary school textbooks were edited, and short-term teacher training programmes were organised. Education was organised mainly as community-based learning. In villages with no teachers, monks were asked to teach in the temples. Teachers were called upon to teach school during the day and adult literacy classes in the evening. The Pathet Lao sent some children to attend primary school in Vietnam (Oudom Chaleunsin, 1996, pp. 91-92).

Revolutionary Struggle (1954-75)

Political development. The 1954 Geneva Agreement did not bring true independence. The period 1954-75 involved a struggle within the context of the Cold War, for both independence and choice of political-economic system. The period was characterised by formations and dissolutions of governments, coups d'état, assassinations, establishment of competing capitals, and power struggles within coalition governments comprising royalists, rightists, right-leaning neutralists, left-leaning neutralists, nationalists, and communists (Stuart-Fox, 2002; Gunn, 2005). China, the Soviet Union, and Vietnam favoured Lao neutrality, but the USA saw coalition governments as expansion of 'international communism'.

By 1955 the USA was financing a substantial proportion of the RLG budget, including the total cost of the army and police. It pressured the RLG to suppress the 'communists within' and expanded military assistance and the presence of the US Central Intelligence Agency (CIA). American support to the RLG was massive compared with previous French support or with American support elsewhere in the region. It took the form of cash grants, commodity imports, and road, transport, and communication projects, all of which had direct military value (Stuart-Fox, 1997, pp. 89-91, passim). All this cash led to corruption, inflation, and distortions in political decision making.

The French were responsible for training the Royal Lao Army (RLA), and French advisors were attached to key ministries. They funded construction of roads, bridges, hospitals, and schools and provided hundreds of engineers, technicians, doctors, and teachers. The Democratic Republic of

(North) Vietnam (DRV) was the sole source of military assistance for the Pathet Lao fighting units (Stuart-Fox, 1997, pp. 89-93).

In November 1957 the First Coalition government was formed, led by Suvanna Phuma and including two Pathet Lao ministers. At last the country was both independent and unified, if only for a brief moment. In the National Assembly election of May 1958 the Lao Patriot Front (LPF), the best organised party and the only party reaching down to the village level, failed to win sufficient seats to gain control, although Suphanuvong was elected president of the Assembly. The only certain outcome was political instability (Stuart-Fox, 1997, pp. 100-104).

Despite a determination to compromise, in July 1958 the eight-month-old government collapsed. A financial crisis, precipitated in part by the USA, had brought about a new government, markedly right wing and anti-communist, under Phoui Sananikone. No Pathet Lao held minister posts (Stuart-Fox, 1997, pp. 94-105).

The RLA operated virtually independently of the government, and repression began, forcing the LPF underground. Suphanuvong and other high Pathet Lao officials were arrested, and reconciliation ended. In 1959 fighting broke out and the DRV began supporting renewed Pathet Lao insurgency (Stuart-Fox, 1997, pp. 104-109). Laos was drawn inescapably into the maelstrom of the Cold War, with the struggle in Vietnam driving events in Vientiane.

In October 1959 both Phetsarat and King Sisavangvong died, and Savangvatthana took over the throne. In August 1960, a coup d'état in Vientiane toppled the government, and Suvanna Phuma formed a government opposed to Phoui Sananikone's pro-Western and militant anti-communist orientation.

By 1961, Laos had descended into a three-way civil war. The Pathet Lao were backed by the DRV and the Soviet Union. Suvanna Phuma's neutralist government *at times* enjoyed the support of the Soviet Union, the People's Republic of China, and the USA. The Revolutionary Committee headed by General Phoumi Nosavan received covert support from the CIA.

In 1962 a second Geneva conference called for a peaceful, neutral, independent, and democratic Laos and for the removal of foreign military forces. The DRV signed the Agreement but never withdrew its troops. The Viet Minh were a strong military support to the Pathet Lao, and together they controlled areas in north and central Laos (Cheng, 2002, pp. 76-77). The DRV had two strategic aims in Laos – to prevent northern Laos from being used to threaten North Vietnam, and to keep the Ho Chih Minh Trail open.

The 1962 Geneva Agreement could not prevent the use of Lao territory in the conflict emerging in Vietnam. The DRV used the Ho Chih Minh Trail to infiltrate troops and materiel into South Vietnam. The USA concentrated its efforts in Vietnam but used a covert CIA-led 'secret army' in Laos to harass the North Vietnamese infiltrators (Stuart-Fox, 1997, p. 119).

In June 1962 the Second Coalition government was formed, but a series of assassinations led to its collapse in April 1963. In 1964 the Pathet Lao drove the Neutralist forces from the Plain of Jars. The covert American air war began in 1964, and by 1973 more than two million tons of bombs had been dropped on Laos. Up to a third of the devices failed to detonate, lying in the ground waiting, killing and maiming well into the twenty-first century (Stuart-Fox, 1997, p. 138).

The RLG and Pathet Lao signed a ceasefire agreement in 1973, and the US bombing ended. The Third Coalition government took office in 1974. The fighting resumed, however, and in early 1975 the National Assembly was dissolved, and rightist leaders fled to Thailand. In August 1975 Vientiane was 'liberated', and hundreds of senior bureaucrats and army officers were sent to remote 're-education camps'. By October many of the country's top bureaucrats and technicians, including half of all doctors in Laos, had fled. King Savangvatthana abdicated on 1 December, and the Lao People's Democratic Republic was proclaimed on 2 December, with Suphanuvong as president and Kaison Phomvihan as prime minister (Stuart-Fox, 2002, pp. 82-83).

Education development 1954-75 under the RLG. Between Independence and the Revolution, although Lao education developed in two different zones (the RLG Zone and the 'Liberated' Zone), progress was made because of the common understanding that education and preservation of Lao culture and traditions were important for the future development of Laos. The separate education reform programmes of the RLG and the Pathet Lao were therefore allowed to proceed undisturbed by the political instability (Khamphao Phonekeo, 1996, pp. 87-88).

After 1955 the RLG began constructing primary and secondary schools in major urban areas with American aid. By the late 1950s, however, only a third of school-age children were enrolled, and of those, only one fifth completed the full six-year primary school programme, few proceeded to secondary school, and most of those attended private schools (Stuart-Fox, 1997, p. 100).

Following Independence, one of the first reforms was the use of Lao as a medium of instruction at all levels. Laos joined UNESCO in 1951, and in 1957 a review team recommended three main objectives: (a) educational opportunities for all children, in both urban and rural areas; (b) further education and training for youth to enable them to have occupations based on their preferences and potentials; and (c) adult literacy in order to improve health and reduce poverty (Khamphao Phonekeo, 1996, pp. 75-76). UNESCO supported the 1962 education reform from the French colonial system to a 'Lao system' covering primary, secondary, and tertiary education, and introducing vocational subjects. USAID supported development of the education system at all levels (Khamphao Phonekeo, 1996, pp. 85-88).

In 1955 there were 944 public primary schools, but by 1969-70 there were more than 3000, with a combined enrolment of 199,000 students. USAID financed the writing, printing, and distribution of 84 primary school textbook titles in the Lao language in a total of three million copies. General secondary education was offered in a seven-year programme. By 1971 there were 20 public secondary schools, of which six *lycées* offered the full seven years of instruction. All *lycée* graduates were offered scholarships for advanced study in France (Whitaker et al, 1972, p. 79).

In 1966 USAID began supporting the development of a system of 'Fa Ngum Comprehensive High Schools' in the major urban centres around the country. The language of instruction was Lao. The lower secondary level comprised four years, and the upper secondary comprised three years. The curriculum was modelled after the American system but based mainly on the 1962 reform, including the introduction of practical subjects. Subjects were common at the lower secondary level but choice of specialisation was offered at upper secondary level (Khamphao Phonekeo, 1996, pp. 84-87).

Higher education began in Laos in the late 1950s with the establishment of the Institute of Law and Administration, the National School of Fine Arts (now the National Faculty of Fine Arts), the National School of Music and Dance, and the Teacher Training School, which in 1964 became the National Institute of Pedagogy (Ogawa, 2009, p. 288). The School of Medicine was added in 1969. The Institute of Law and Administration, the School of Medicine and the Pedagogical Institute were merged in the early 1970s to become Sisavangvong University, using the French language and mainly French faculty. Regional technical colleges were established in Luangprabang, Pakse, and Savannakhet.

Teacher training colleges were also established in Luangprabang, Pakse, and Savannakhet. Initially, primary teachers became qualified after completion of primary school plus one year of training at a teacher training college (6+1), and the requirements were successively upgraded to allow teaching at upper secondary level (Khamphao Phonekeo, 1966, p. 83).

It was widely agreed that the quality of Lao education was low. In the 1962-63 school year, 5759 students completed the final year of primary school (grade 6), but of these, only 3130 were entitled to take the secondary school entry exams, and only 645 passed (11% of those completing primary school). Only 205 were from state schools; the remainder were from private schools (Khamphao Phonekeo, 1996, p. 82).

In 1960, temple schools made up approximately 25% of all schools. By the time of the Pathet Lao victory in 1975 there were only a few vernacular secondary schools. The French had never cut the ties between the royalty and the *sangha* (community of Buddhists), and the ties remained relatively strong until the mid-1970s (Tarling, 2000, p. 223). In 1964 fewer than 50,000 children attended public (RLG) schools, but by 1970 the number had risen to over 210,000, as shown in Table IV (Whitaker et al, 1972, pp. 67, 76).

Secondary and tertiary education were conducted in French. By the early 1970s, the RLG had initiated plans to replace French with Lao, and teacher training materials and secondary school textbooks were beginning to appear (Evans, 1998, pp. 156-157).

Level	Schools	Students	Teachers
Primary	3068	199,111	5723
Secondary	18	6352	307
Teacher training	9	3036	448
Higher education	3	517	51
Fine arts	2	180	87
Technical	3	1172	211

Table IV. Education enrolments 1969-70 under the RLG.
Source: Whitaker et al (1972, p. 76).

Education development 1954-75 in the Liberated Zone. In 1954, predating the Geneva Agreement of 1954, the Pathet Lao had achieved controlling positions in the Liberated Zone, mainly in the northern provinces. In these areas education development was one of the priorities, and mass general education was widely developed (Oudom Chaleunsin, 1996, pp. 92-94).

By 1971 a government apparatus had emerged in the Liberated Zone, with its own administrative structure and social and economic policies. While the French influence continued in education under the RLG, Vietnamese educational philosophy and instructors influenced education in the Liberated Zone. All higher education for students from the Liberated Zones took place in Vietnamese institutions and in the Vietnamese language (Evans, 1998, p. 157, footnote). Some indication of the development of the education system in the Liberated Zone in the 1960s is shown in Table V.

	1962-63	1963-64	1964-65	1965-66	1966-67
Teachers	1200	n.a.	n.a.	n.a.	1700
Teacher training schools	1	1	1	4	8
Teacher trainees	59	96	34	261	271
Primary school students (4 years)	32,000	n.a.	n.a.	n.a.	36,000
Lower secondary students (estimate)	500	n.a.	n.a.	n.a.	400
Upper school students	47	n.a.	n.a.	n.a.	264

Notes: n.a. = not available. Primary school in the Liberated Zone comprised only four years, and lower secondary comprised two years, constituting a 4+2 system. There is considerable uncertainty about the number of students in lower secondary school.

Table V. Education development in the liberated zone, 1962-63 to 1966-67.
Source: Oudom Chaleunsin (1996, p. 99).

The Pathet Lao government in the Liberated Zone also published school textbooks. Some 57 titles were 're-edited and re-printed', including 16 for primary school, 32 for lower secondary school, and seven for the non-formal system (Oudom Chaleunsin, 1996, pp. 105).

In July 1967 the Pathet Lao government issued a three-year education plan, which included expansion of primary schooling and adult literacy. Every two villages were to have one 'complete primary school' (i.e. grades 1-4), and every province was to have a lower secondary school. By 1970 there were 45 non-formal learning centres for providing primary schooling to some 2160 adults (Oudom Chaleunsin, 1996, pp. 102-103).

The second three-year plan for education covered the period 1971-73 and focused on the continued expansion of primary education, especially grades 3 and 4, lower secondary school, and teacher training. Community support was mobilised for schools, teachers, and instructional materials. Half of the teachers were volunteers (Oudom Chaleunsin, 1996, pp. 105-106). Enrolments in the Liberated Zone in 1973-74 to 1974-75 are shown in Table VI (Oudom Chaleunsin, 1996, pp. 112).

Level	1973-74	1974-75
Primary	89,899	104,786
Lower secondary	3762	4179
Upper secondary	668	868

Table VI. School enrolment in the liberated zone, 1973-74 to 1974-75.
Source: Oudom Chaleunsin (1996, p. 112).

The Pathet Lao government in Huaphanh Province upgraded the Teacher Training School in Viengsay to higher education status with the establishment in 1974 of a section for training upper secondary teachers (Ogawa, 2009, p. 284).

Implementing the Revolution (1975-86)

Turmoil, catharsis, and fear. The final months of the revolutionary struggle saw great turbulence and upheaval, and events in Laos were charged by events in the revolutionary struggles in Cambodia and Vietnam. Phnom Penh fell on 17 April and Saigon fell on 30 April 1974. Verbal attacks by Pathet Lao Radio and demonstrations by students and workers targeted the political right wing and US presence. USAID offices were occupied and the US staff were placed under house arrest. Fearing for their lives, many of the country's educated elite and others (including many Vietnamese and Chinese) fled across the Mekong into Thailand (Stuart-Fox, 1997, pp. 160-161).

In the run-up to final victory and the immediate aftermath of wars, cathartic excesses often take place. This happened also in Laos. The command structure of the LPLA was necessarily decentralised, with initiative left to local field commanders. As if to change the course not only of the future but also the past, there were spontaneous cases of burning books and memorabilia from the old regime; in some cases it was due to fear (Evans, 1998, p. 6). Burning the books was probably not explicit Pathet Lao policy, and the story is told of Kaison Phomvihan, later prime minister, who, while travelling in a convoy, saw a group of villagers and soldiers burning a pile of books. Furious, Kaison stopped the convoy, leapt out, and instructed the assemblage: 'We do not burn books!' Nevertheless, the damage was done, and many books, especially in French and English, and especially history books, were destroyed. Most books in English, no matter what subject, were withdrawn from libraries, even at the university college at Dong Dok.

More damaging were the 're-education camps'. A decision was made to incarcerate all military and police officers and most high-ranking civil servants in re-education camps for an indefinite period. Even monks were sent to re-education camps if they were reluctant to perform their assigned roles of spreading the Party line (Stuart-Fox, 2002, p. 231). The re-education camps caused both bitterness and fear, especially as the period of re-education was prolonged and more were arrested and sent for re-education. It is estimated that at least 30,000 persons were held in the re-education camps for much of 1976 and 1977 (Stuart-Fox, 1997, p. 227, note 17).

Still more damaging was the large-scale emigration of the educated elite. It has been estimated that Laos had lost up to 90% of its small educated population as refugees. Teachers who had served under the RLG feared that they would be singled out for 're-education', and many fled to Thailand (Evans, 1998, p. 158). Most damaging of all was that those who left constituted by far the majority of all educated Lao. 'The effect on the country was catastrophic, setting back development by at least a generation' (Stuart-Fox, 2002, p. 233).

Economic reform and revision. The new government imposed a disciplined command economy. The goal, following Vietnamese Marxism, was to achieve socialism without going through the stage of capitalist development (Stuart-Fox, 1997, p. 169). The private sector was replaced with cooperatives and state enterprises. Investment, production, trade, and pricing were centralised, and barriers to internal and foreign trade were implemented. Nationalisation of commerce and industry, and tight controls and nationalisation of transportation and retailing led to shortages of goods (Stuart-Fox, 1997, p. 174). As a consequence of economic controls, the introduction of a progressive tax on rice production, and the destruction of market price incentives, farmers reverted to a subsistence economy, planting only enough for their personal needs (Stuart-Fox, 1997, p. 232).

The government soon realised its economic policies were hindering, rather than stimulating, growth and development, but no substantive reforms were introduced for almost a decade. In December 1979 it was acknowledged that it was necessary to stimulate private production for personal gain as well as capitalist production, together with collectives, the state enterprise, and joint ventures. The progressive agricultural taxes were abolished. Within a year the reforms were having an effect.

Education development in the command economy. One consequence of the RLG's efforts to modernise the education system was that the temples, which had previously served as centres of learning, were gradually marginalised by the growing corps of professional teachers. After the revolution, however, so many teachers fled that the government had to rely again on monks (Evans, 1998, pp. 56-63).

In 1975 the Lao education system was weak. There was no possibility of providing a six-year primary school education for all children, so primary schooling covered only five years (Khamphao Phonekeo, 1975, p. 89). Considerable efforts were made after 1975 to extend primary education to all ethnic groups, and an adult literacy campaign was launched, but these efforts were hampered by the exodus of qualified teachers.

The government was determined to place a primary school in every village, but the necessary teachers and instructional materials were not available. 'Skeleton schools' began to appear in order to formally fulfil the commands from above. Many of the 'teachers' had only a few years of primary schooling (Evans, 1998, pp. 157-158). The shortage of teachers was due not only to the emigration of large numbers of teachers but also to the absorption of teachers into government and business enterprises (Khamy Bouasengthong, 1996, pp. 123-124). Few books were available to students, because most of the books from the old regime had been destroyed or dispersed, and foreign books were no longer available (Evans, 1998, pp. 160-161). Despite these problems, however, there was substantial progress over the period 1975-85, as can be seen in Table VII.

Year	Primary		Lower secondary		Upper secondary	
	Schools	Students	Schools	Students	Schools	Students
1975	4444	317,126	72	26,628	11	2517
1985	7470	495,375	495	69,226	68	20,093

Table VII. General school enrolments, 1975 and 1985.
Source: Khamy Bouasengthong (1996, p. 126).

In 1978 a decree on education in the revolutionary era was issued, clarifying that: (a) schools were the tools and the responsibility of the working class; (b) education must meet the policies of the Party, and teachers worked for the Party; and (c) education must meet the requirements of production. The school system envisaged included pre-school, general education, vocational and higher education, and 'community' or non-formal education and training. Communities were mobilised to participate in construction of their schools (Khamy Bouasengthong, 1996, pp. 115-118).

In 1976, the general education system comprising 11 years (5+3+3) was established, and all schools followed the 1976 curriculum of the Ministry of Education (MOE). Many primary schools were 'incomplete'. Dropout and repetition rates were high, especially at primary level. Few students from ethnic minority communities could continue their studies beyond primary level. In addition to government schools, there were also temple schools, with teaching provided by monks. Instruction in the temple schools followed the national curriculum (Khamy Bouasengthong, 1996, pp. 121-122).

No vocational training was provided in the general education schools. MOE organised vocational training in a few provinces. Other ministries also organised vocational training in fields for which they were responsible. Study abroad was another possibility. Students selected for study abroad completed preparatory studies in science and foreign languages before they left (Khamy Bouasengthong, 1996, pp. 122-123).

At Sisavangvong University the expatriate and Lao staff fled for fear of being 're-schooled'. The University was dissolved into separate institutes, leaving the country with no degree-awarding institution. In the 1970s and 1980s many graduates from upper secondary schools could pursue higher education in the USSR and Eastern European countries.

The Pedagogical Institute at Dong Dok and the Viengsay Teacher Training College were merged into the Higher Institute of Pedagogy located in Dong Dok, the only teacher training college in the whole country.

The New Economic Mechanism: change and stabilisation. Laos initiated market economy reforms in 1986 with the New Economic Mechanism. Private business, free-market competition, market pricing, and foreign investment were allowed. Farmers were permitted to own land and sell crops on the open market. These and other forms led to increased availability of goods and services and to economic growth, and Laos achieved impressive growth over the next 10 years.

The Asian economic crisis began in July 1997. In 1998 inflation rose sharply and the value of the Kip fell perilously. The fiscal deficit widened and foreign investment fell, and the education sector was not protected (Noonan, 2001, pp. 2-4). GDP per capita fell by over 17% between 1997 and 2000. By the end of 2000, however, stabilisation was achieved, and continued structural reform led to relatively stable economic growth and a significant decline in poverty.

Education Today

Economic Growth, Poverty Reduction, and Education for All

General education. In 1990, Laos signed the Jomtien Declaration on Education for All (EFA). In 1991 the Fifth Party Congress established the education development policy for 1991-96 as enforcement of free and compulsory education, promotion of private initiative in both general and vocational education, expansion to reach remote, isolated, and mountainous areas, construction of ethnic boarding schools, reorganisation of secondary general and vocational education and training, improvement of the quality of education to international standards, and establishment of policies for the system of monks' education. On another note, concerning Buddhist education, only primary schooling (five years) is compulsory, although some 10% of children in fact never enter school and fewer than 60% complete primary school. Buddhist education is an alternative to mainstream with its combination of secular and religious teachings, both usually only at a basic level. Those wishing to continue with the religious training under this alternative can do so, which involves levels and stages, corresponding more or less to those in secular/mainstream education.

Since 1990 the Government of Laos (GOL) has promulgated laws, decrees, and recommendations to facilitate EFA implementation. The 1996 Compulsory Education Decree provides for free and compulsory primary education and recognises the need to expand education in ethnic communities and improve the quality of education through teacher training. In 2000 GOL promulgated the Education Law, which introduced inclusive education and education for children with special needs. MOE published the 'Education Strategic Vision up to the Year 2020' in 2000 and 'Education Strategic Planning (2001-2020)' the following year. These policies set the general course for development work by MOE for years to come. The EFA National Plan of Action, published in 2004, extended the concept of 'basic education' to include lower secondary schooling and also focused on non-formal and adult education. The development of general schooling from 1986-87 to 2007-08 is shown in Table VIII.

Post-secondary education and training. Post-secondary education in Laos, as in other countries, shows considerable variation. Technical, vocational, or professional schools and colleges typically offer individual courses and one-, two-, or three-year certificate and diploma programmes. There are 21 technical and vocational education and training institutions and eight teacher education institutions under MOE or the Provincial Education Services. The Ministry of Labour and Social Welfare is responsible for employment-related skill development programmes. MOE also provides non-formal programmes for basic education, literacy, and life-skills. Other ministries provide specialised training for their respective fields of authority.

The National Council for TVET and skills development (NCTS) was established in 2002 to advise on strategies, regulations, and guidelines for development of technical and vocational education and training (TVET).[1] In 2007 the TVET Master Plan (2008-15) and the TVET Strategic Plan (2006-20) were promulgated.

A growing number of private post-secondary institutions offer a range of short courses, especially in English, business, and computer applications. Some vocational training schools award one-, two-, or three-year post-secondary level certificates and diplomas. Some teacher education institutions also offer post-secondary education and training in various areas, including English language and computer skills.

	1986-87	1991-92	1995-96
Primary enrolment	560,406	581,900	757,508
Percentage female (%)	46	44	44
Gross enrolment rate (%)	-	97	-
Net enrolment rate (%)	-	59	-
Lower secondary enrolment	82,320	88,447	119,771
Percentage female (%)	43	40	40
Gross enrolment rate (%)	-	-	-
Net enrolment rate (%)	-	-	-
Upper secondary enrolment	27,681	31,826	42,163
Percentage female (%)	43	36	38
Gross enrolment rate (%)	-	-	-
Net enrolment rate (%)	-	-	-

	2000-01	2005-06	2007-08
Primary enrolment	828,113	891,881	873,759
Percentage female (%)	45	46	45
Gross enrolment rate (%)	110	116	-
Net enrolment rate (%)	80	84	-
Lower secondary enrolment	195,845	243,131	248,920
Percentage female (%)	42	44	44
Gross enrolment rate (%)	47	52	-
Net enrolment rate (%)	23	28	-
Upper secondary enrolment	88,525	147,510	153,684
Percentage female (%)	40	42	42
Gross enrolment rate (%)	23	35	-
Net enrolment rate (%)	9	16	-

Note: - = not available.

Table VIII. School enrolments, 1986-97 to 2007-08.
Source: MOE, Annual Bulletin, 1986-87, 1991-92, 1995-96, 2000-01, 2005-06.

Tertiary education typically comprises a three- or four-year higher diploma programme or a degree programme of four or more years. There is one national university, the National University of Laos, and two provincial universities – Champasack University, established in 2002, and Suphanuvong University in Luangprabang, established in 2003. Plans are currently underway for the establishment of a university in Savannakhet.

By the mid-2000s, Laos had achieved a sustained period of strong growth, but poverty persisted, especially in remote upland areas. In 2004, GOL published the National Growth and Poverty Eradication Strategy. Education was identified as a priority sector for meeting the goals of poverty eradication. In 2008 the National Education System Reform Strategy (NESRS) for 2006-15 established the overall goals, directions, and strategies for development of the education sector. The NESRS and the revised Education Law (amended in 2007) extend lower secondary schooling from three to four years, beginning in 2009-10, bringing the Lao school system up to the regional 12-year standard, as shown in Figure 3.

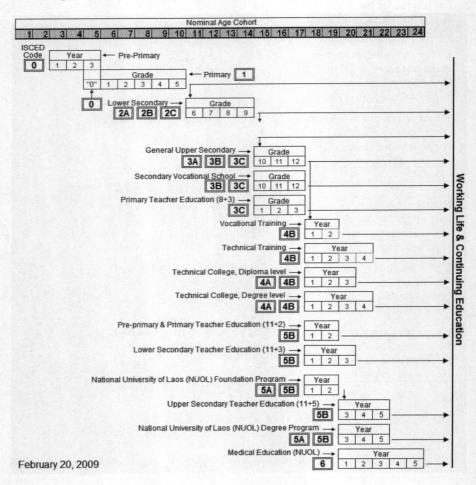

Figure 3. Lao formal education system as of 2009-10.

Challenges and Issues

Financing. Although substantial progress has been made, especially over the past two decades, considerable challenges remain. These can be seen from both an economic perspective and a pedagogical perspective. From an economic perspective, there are both supply-side and demand-side problems.

The pedagogical and economic issues are intertwined. A fundamental problem on the supply side is the level of public finance of the education sector, as suggested by Table IX. The Education Sector Development Framework (ESDF) targets 18% of the total GOL budget for the education sector by 2015 – higher than ever before – there is no stable trend to suggest that the goal will be achieved. Moreover, the budget allocations approved by the National Assembly are *provincial, not inter-sectoral*. Thus at the provincial level, inter-sectoral allocations of discretionary funds (i.e. not including salaries of civil servants) are decided by the provincial governor and the provincial financial services.

	90-91	94-95	99-00	04-05	06-07	08-09
Education budget as % of GDP	1.9	3.6	1.4	2.3	3.1	2.5
Education as % total GOL	7.2	13.9	7.2	11.0	15.7	12.8

Table IX. Public expenditure on education 1990-91 to 2008-09 (%).
Sources: Data for 1990-91 to 1999-2000 are from Noonan (2001). Data for 2004-05 and later are from MOE, Department of Finance. NSEDP6 MTR, p. 108.

This relatively low level of public sector financing of education has widespread supply-side ramifications. First and foremost, the low recurrent budget results in low teacher salaries, low budgets for instructional materials, and low operating budgets. Low teacher salaries have the result that many teachers are compelled to have other sources of income, which can result in reduced classroom time. This in turn impacts on the quality of schooling, which in turn impacts on the demand side. If the learning outcomes of schooling are too low, children and their parents see little point in schooling.

Repetition. Some evidence of the quality problem can be seen in the repetition rates shown in Table X and the dropout rates shown in Table XI. In 2005-06, nearly one third of all primary school students repeated grade 1, and nearly one fifth repeated grade 2. Repetition rates have fallen considerably in recent years, and the ESDF introduces 'phased introduction of progressive promotion', together with improved access to instructional materials and better quality schooling. It may be seen in Table X that girls are less likely than boys to repeat a grade.

Dropout. Dropout rates have also fallen in recent years, as seen in Table XI, but still today approximately one in eight drop out after grade 1. It can also be seen that although girls are less likely to *repeat* a grade than boys, they have also been *more likely to drop out* than boys, although this gender difference has declined in recent years. Analysis has shown that approximately one third of all students enrolled in grade 1 repeat at least once.[2]

Year		Grade				
		1	2	3	4	5
1991-92	F	41.4	24.6	17.2	12.7	16.9
	M	43.8	28.2	20.6	16.3	20.8
1995-96	F	37.5	20.1	12.2	8.3	12.3
	M	39.4	23.5	15.7	11.7	16.9
2000-01	F	33.5	17.9	9.8	5.5	3.7
	M	35.0	21.5	13.6	9.2	6.7
2005-06	F	31.9	16.5	10.4	6.3	3.3
	M	33.7	19.3	13.6	9.0	5.5

Table X. Repetition rates, grades 1-5, 1991-92 to 2005-06.
Source: MOE/Educational Statistics and Information Technology Center.

Year		Grade				
		1	2	3	4	5
1991-92	F	14.8	9.6	10.5	11.1	12.3
	M	13.1	8.4	7.4	7.4	11.1
1995-96	F	14.0	8.6	9.4	11.9	13.6
	M	13.3	7.9	7.6	9.0	13.2
2000-01	F	16.0	9.7	9.0	9.7	2.8
	M	16.9	10.1	8.3	8.2	4.4
2005-06	F	13.2	6.9	7.7	8.0	6.0
	M	12.7	6.7	7.8	6.5	7.4

Table XI. Dropout rates, grades 1-5, 1991-92 to 2005-06.
Source: MOE/Educational Statistics and Information Technology Center.

Grade 5 completion. From the national census data (2005) it can be found that some 10% of an age cohort of children by the age of 16 have never entered school. This evidence can be combined with what is known about dropout rates, rate of survival to grade 5, the proportion of grade 5 students sitting the exams, and the grade 5 pass rate, as shown in Table XII.

Ethnicity. Laos is a multi-ethnic, multi-linguistic country. Ethnographers and linguists distinguish over 100 ethno-linguistic groups, but the national census of 2005 distinguished 47 groups in the four families listed in Table XIII. Education participation rates for non-Lao ethnic groups are substantially lower than those for ethnic Lao for a variety of reasons related mainly to culture and geography. The ethnic Lao tend to live in the lowlands of the Mekong basin. Non-Lao ethnic communities tend to live in the less accessible and more remote hills and mountains.

Language is also a barrier, since according to the Education Law, all instruction in public schools is in the Lao language, and the language families are not mutually interpretable. In addition, children from non-Lao ethnic communities are less likely to meet a teacher from their own ethnic group than ethnic Lao children.

Proportion	Individual probability	Probability chain
Proportion of children who 'never attended school'	10	0.10
Proportion of children who attended school	90	0.90
Total age group	100	1.00
(Entered school)/(Total age group)	90	0.90
(Survival rate to grade 5)/(Entered school)	60	0.54
(Sat for exams)/(Survived to grade 5)	95	0.51
(Passed)/(Sat for exams)	93	0.48

Table XII. Proportion of children graduating from grade 5 (%).
Source: (Entered school)/(Total age group) is taken from the 2005 census (tabulated in Noonan & Xaiyasensouk, 2007, Appendix 3, Table 9). All other figures come from the 2004-05 and 2005-06 annual school survey provided by MOE/Educational Statistics and Information Technology Center.

Ethnicity	Total population		Children aged 11-16			
	Total	% total	Total cohort	% cohort	Never attended	% never attended
Lao-Tai	3,646,838	64.9	577,909	59.8	33,792	5.8
Mon-Khmer	1,269,276	22.6	187,081	25.1	40,918	21.9
Tibeto-Burman	159,298	2.8	24,374	3.0	10,063	41.3
Hmong Yao	479,395	8.5	76,988	10.7	15,434	20.0

Table XIII. Children aged 11-16 who have never attended school, by ethnicity.
Source: 2005 National Census, author tabulation.

Teacher deployment. A related problem is the allocation of teacher training positions and scholarships, the mismatch between teacher training and career intentions, employment of teacher training graduates, and the deployment of teachers. For a variety of reasons, many teacher training candidates have no intention of entering the teaching profession, and many of those who do intend to enter the teaching profession have no interest in teaching in rural or remote schools. As a result there is an imbalance between urban, rural, and remote communities, in terms of both numbers of teachers and the level of qualifications.

Technical and vocational education and training. There is a demand on the labour market for skilled workers, and there are public TVET institutions, programmes, and teachers and instructors. These institutions and programmes, however, are not well oriented toward labour market demand, with the result, for example, that there is an over-supply at the diploma and higher diploma level and an under-supply at the certificate level.

Education Sector Development Framework

In the first years of the twenty-first century, the development partners and GOL began to discuss the transition from a project-based approach to an MOE-led, programme-based, sector-wide approach with improved coordination among the development partners, within MOE, and between MOE and the development partners. In 2002, the World Bank, together with development partners, launched the EFA Fast Track Initiative to help low-income countries meet the EFA goal that all children complete a full cycle of primary education by 2015.

In November 2006, the Vientiane Declaration on Aid Effectiveness was adopted, aiming at increased country ownership, aid coordination, improved alignment of development partner support to national policies and plans, increased use of government management and reporting systems, harmonisation and simplification of development partners' procedures and activities, more effective use of resources, and the recognition that implementation and reporting are responsibilities of all signatories.

In 2007, the National Education System Reform Strategy was approved, and the ESDF, which operationalises the NESRS, was finalised in 2009. The Education Sector Working Group is the main forum for dialogue and oversight between MOE and the development partners. Thematic focal groups are to be established to facilitate technical and policy discussions between MOE and the development partners. Key to the success of the ESDF will be MOE's capacity to improve policy making, planning, budgeting, and performance assessment, to create strong linkages between them, and ultimately to achieve the ESDF targets. With the completion of the National Growth and Poverty Eradication Strategy and the ESDF, Laos became eligible in 2009 for participation in the Fast Track Initiative.

As of this writing (mid-December 2009), the establishment of the focal groups is in the final stages of preparation. When these are in place, the real work of the stakeholders in support of the implementation of the ESDF will begin.

Notes

[1] Originally established in 2002 as the National Training Council, it now covers TVET and skills development.

[2] This does not imply that one third of all individuals repeat, since some students can repeat a given grade several times.

References

Cheng Guan Ang (2002) *The Vietnam War from the Other Side: the Vietnamese Communists' perspective.* Oxford: Routledge.

Evans, Grant (1998) *The Politics of Ritual and Remembrance: Laos since 1975.* Chiang Mai: Silkworm Books.

Evans, Grant (2002) *A Short History of Laos: the land in between.* Chiang Mai: Silkworm Books.

Gunn, Geoffrey C. (2003) *Rebellion in Laos: peasant and politics in a colonial backwater.* Bangkok: White Lotus Press.

Gunn, Geoffrey C. (2005) *Political Struggles in Laos (1930-1954).* Bangkok: White Lotus.

Khamphao Phonekeo (1975) The Laotian Challenge: a 'non-polluting education system', *Prospects,* V(1), 87-95.

Khamphao Phonekeo (1996) Education during 1893-1975, Part II, in Somlith Bouasivath, Khampao Phonekeo, Oudom Chaleunsin & Khamy Bouasengthong, *History of Lao Education,* pp. 20-89. Vientiane: Toyota Foundation.

Khamy Bouasengthong (1996) Education in the Period 2 December 1975 to 1985, Part IV, in Somlith Bouasivath, Phonekeo, Oudom Chaleunsin & Khamy Bouasengthong, *History of Lao Education,* pp. 114-129. Vientiane: Toyota Foundation.

Koret, Peter (1999) Books of Search: the invention of traditional Lao literature as a subject of study, in Grant Evans (Ed.) *Laos: culture and society,* pp. 226-257. Bangkok: Silkworm Books.

Lahmeyer, Jan (2002) Laos: historical demographical data of the whole country. http://www.populstat.info/Asia/laosc.htm (accessed 23 June 2009).

Manynooch Faming (2007) Schooling in the Lao People's Democratic Republic, in G.A. Postiglione & J. Tan, *Going to School in East Asia,* pp. 170-206. Westport, CT: Greenwood Publishing Group.

Noonan, Richard (2001) *Education Financing in Lao PDR, 1990-2000: a turbulent decade of transition.* Vientiane: Sida/World Bank.

Noonan, Richard & Xaiyasensouk, Visiene (2007) *Alternative Models of Teacher Training for Remote Areas.* Vientiane: Sida.

Ogawa, Keiichi (2009) Higher Education in Lao PDR, in Yasushi Hirosato & Yuto Kitamura (Eds) *The Political Economy of Educational Reforms and Capacity Development in Southeast Asia,* pp. 283-302. Berlin: Springer.

Oudom Chaleunsin (1996) Education in the Liberated Zone, Part III, in Somlith Bouasivath, Khampao Phonekeo, Oudom Chaleunsin & Khamy Bouasengthong, *History of Lao Education,* pp. 90-113. Vientiane: Toyota Foundation.

SarDesai, R.R. (1997) *Southeast Asia: past and present,* 4th edn. Chiang Mai: Silkworm Books.

Savada, Andrea Matles (Ed.) (1994) *Laos: a country study.* Washington: Library of Congress. http://countrystudies.us/laos/.

Somlith Bouasivath (1996) Lao Education in the Early Years, Part I, in Somlith Bouasivath, Khampao Phonekeo, Oudom Chaleunsin & Khamy Bouasengthong, *History of Lao Education*, pp. 1-19. Vientiane: Toyota Foundation.

Stuart-Fox, Martin (1997) *A History of Laos*. Cambridge: Cambridge University Press.

Stuart-Fox, Martin (1998) *The Lao Kingdom of Lan Xang: rise and decline*. Bangkok: White Lotus.

Stuart-Fox, Martin (2002) *Buddhist Kingdom, Marxist State: the making of modern Laos*, 2nd edn. Bangkok: White Lotus.

Tarling, Nicholas (Ed.) (2000) *The Cambridge History of Southeast Asia. Volume Four: From World War II to the Present*. Cambridge: Cambridge University Press.

Whitaker, Donald P. et al (1972) *Area Handbook for Laos*. Washington, DC: The American University.

CHAPTER 6

Education in Malaysia: development and transformations

SIOW HENG LOKE & CHANG LEE HOON

SUMMARY Education and training have been given priority as part of the preparation for independence as well as in all Malaysia's five-year plans. This chapter reaffirms that education and skills training have been the major instruments for developing the nation's human capital and unifying the various racial groups in nation building through education. This chapter explores the role of education in addressing the development of human capital and national unity in Malaysia as spurred by the Razak Report in 1956. It also traces the key education reforms since Independence in 1957 and critically reviews the impact of these reforms and their implementation, particularly in the area of early childhood, teacher and tertiary education. It is also noted that the last two decades have been marked by the acceleration in the pace of globalisation and liberalisation of the world economy, and the impact of these trends on the educational development is further discussed.

Socio-economic Background

Malaysia is located in South-East Asia and shares its national border with neighbouring countries Thailand, Singapore, Indonesia and Brunei. It is a developing nation of about 330,000 square kilometres and in 2008, a total population of about 27.7 million with 33.9% aged below 15 years, and 4.4% aged 65 years or older (Malaysia, 2008a), with a sex ratio [1] of males to females of 104. It is characterised by a multiracial and multilingual society. The proportions of citizens are about 67% Bumiputera [2], 24.3% Chinese, 7.4% Indians and the remaining 0.35% 'others'.[3] The labour force increased by 2.1% from 2007 to 2008, those with tertiary education from 20.0% in 2005 to 22.5% in 2007 while those with secondary-level education increased from 57.6% to 58.6% (Malaysia, 2008b). The official language is

Bahasa Melayu (Malay Language) while the second official language is English.

Historically, the British had been in control of Malaysia since the late nineteenth century. Today, the Malaysian government is based on a constitutional monarchy system headed by a paramount ruler and a bicameral Parliament consisting of a non-elected upper house and an elected lower house. Emerging from British rule, Malaysia's social-economic activities have been transformed from a producer of raw materials, mainly natural rubber, tin and timber, into an emerging multi-sector economy exporting electrical, electronic, and other manufactured goods, in addition to petroleum and agricultural raw materials and products. Malaysia has entered into an era of rapid industrialisation and modernisation which have been boosted in recent years by intensive efforts in the application of science and technology in most of her economic activities. Since Independence, education too has undergone tremendous development and transformations emerging from the British educational system to one that 'must bring together the children of all races under a national educational system' (*Razak Report*, 1956, para. 12).

Malaysian Educational Structure

Initially, education in Malaysia, as a whole, is under the jurisdiction of the Ministry of Education (thereafter referred to as MOE). The MOE is responsible for managing a comprehensive school system ranging from preschool, primary, secondary, upper secondary (Form Six) and matriculation education, regulating syllabi, controlling national examinations, and supervising the development of education in the country. Malaysia's education system is based on the National Ideology or *Rukunegara*. The *Rukunegara* pledges the united efforts of Malaysians to practise the five principles: (i) Belief in God, (ii) Loyalty to King and Country, (iii) Upholding the Constitution, (iv) Rule of Law, and (v) Good Behaviour and Morality. The aspirations and principles of the *Rukunegara* are manifested in the National Philosophy of Education, which forms the policy of the Malaysian education system (Ministry of Education Malaysia, 1997).

The restructuring of the Cabinet on 27 March 2004 resulted in the division of MOE into two ministries: Ministry of Education (MOE) and Ministry of Higher Education (MOHE). The MOE is still responsible for administration of school education and teacher education institutions whilst MOHE is responsible for the administration of higher education.

Formal school education in Malaysia is provided at four levels – primary (6-12 years old), lower secondary (13-14 years old), upper secondary (15-16 years old) and post-secondary (17-18 years old). The six years of primary education aim to bring about the overall development of the child through acquisition of reading, writing, and arithmetic skills as well as the inculcation of thinking skills and values. There are two types of national primary schools based on the medium of instruction, the national primary schools in which Malay is the medium of instruction, and the national-type primary school that uses either Mandarin or Tamil as medium of instruction. After completing primary education, pupils from the vernacular (Chinese and Tamil national-type primary) schools continue their education at national secondary school, in which Malay is the medium of instruction. Depending on their performance in the Primary School Achievement Test (UPSR) the pupils from the vernacular schools are required to attend a transitional class (Remove class) at the national secondary school before entering Form One. The main objective of the Remove class is to improve the pupils' Malay language proficiency.

Secondary school education covers seven years and is divided into three main levels, lower secondary (Forms 1-3), upper secondary (Forms 4-5) and post-secondary or pre-university level (Form 6 or Matriculation). After completing three years in the lower secondary level, students sit for a public examination, the Lower Secondary Assessment (PMR). Students' performance in this examination determines their academic streaming in the upper secondary level. On completion of the two-year period at the upper secondary level, students sit for another public examination, the Malaysian Certificate of Education (SPM).

After SPM, if students want to further their studies, they can choose to do either MOE programmes or enrol in higher educational institutions (HEIs). The MOE offers two types of programmes, namely sixth form and matriculation and they prepare students for entry into HEIs. Entry into these MOE programmes is based on students' performance in the SPM examination. The sixth form takes one and a half years and prepares students for the Malaysian Higher School Certificate Examination (STPM), which is equivalent to GCE A levels in the United Kingdom. The matriculation study programme is a university-preparatory programme which is specially designed to enable students to meet the entry requirements of the public universities (Ministry of Education Malaysia, 1997).

Higher education in Malaysia is provided by HEIs comprising public and private universities, university colleges, polytechnics, colleges, and community colleges. Depending on the types of HEIs, most universities or university colleges offer programmes from certificates and diplomas to degrees while the colleges, polytechnics, and community colleges are mostly non-degree-granting HEIs. The duration for certificate-level courses is normally one year, the diplomas between two to three years, while the basic degree programmes are between three to five years, depending on specialisations.

National Leaderships and the
Development of Education in Malaysia

In tracing the development of the role of education in Malaysia since Independence, the authors took a retrospective position by tracing the visions of the current Prime Minister to past Prime Ministers so as to bring the future to the past. The purpose is to consolidate the national leaders' vision into a common chord in the development of education in Malaysia and the subsequent transformations under their leaderships.

The current and sixth Prime Minister of Malaysia, Mohd Najib bin Tun Hj Abd Razak, emphasises 'a united, peaceful and prosperous Malaysia, with abundant opportunities for all citizens' (Mohd Najib bin Tun Hj Abd Razak, 2009a). He introduces the 1Malaysia concept with the goal 'to preserve and enhance this unity in diversity which has always been our strength and remains our best hope for the future'. Since taking office in April 2008, he believes that the root of the 1Malaysia philosophy is 'predicated on mutual trust and respect between all communities; my clarion call for Malaysia is 1 dream, 1 people, and 1 nation' (Mohd Najib bin Tun Hj Abdul Razak, 2009b).

The fifth Prime Minister of Malaysia, Abdullah bin Haji Ahmad Badawi, acknowledged that Malaysia needed to deal with great changes in the global environment, while improving and upgrading the country's domestic conditions. He pointed out that 'the most important factor in becoming a developed nation is the capability and character of the country's people. Malaysia will need to move away from the notion that it is a nation with first class infrastructure, but third class mentality' (Malaysia, 2006a, pp. v-vi).

Mahathir Mohamad, the fourth Prime Minister, served Malaysia from 1981 to 2003. During his term of office, numerous national policies including education were implemented and had great impact on the growth and development of Malaysia. The Vision 2020 policy, launched in 1991 to promote Malaysia in becoming a developed country and an ethical society by the year 2020 (Mahathir, 1991), became the underlying impetus for many other policies under his leadership. In the context of education, two notable outcomes are: the 1996 Education Act to replace the 1961 Education Act to include preschool education in the National Education System; and the enactment of the 1996 Private Education Act, which was amended to allow the establishment of more private HEIs (Malaysia, 2008c).

The third Prime Minister, Hussein Onn (1976-81), was renowned for stressing the issue of unity through policies aimed at rectifying economic imbalances between communities such as the National Unit Trust Scheme and federation of cooperative societies (Koperasi Usaha Bersatu) (Hussein Onn, 2009). On the other hand, Abdul Razak Hussein, the second Prime Minister of Malaysia, was renowned for the enactment of the Malaysian New Economic Policy (NEP) in 1971, with two basic goals: to reduce and eventually eradicate poverty; and to reduce and eventually eradicate identification of economic function with race (Abdul Razak Hussein, 2009). Tunku Abdul Rahman Putra Al-Haj ibni Almarhum Sultan Abdul Hamid Halim Shah ('Tunku') was the first Prime Minister of Malaysia since the Independence of the Federation of Malaya in 1957 and the formation of Malaysia (which includes Sabah and Sarawak) in 1963. It was during Tunku's term that the foundation for a national educational system was set.

Connecting the present to the past, the visions of the first three Prime Ministers set the stage for the development of education by their successors. Their visions, reflecting the focus of education in Malaysia until the present day, are towards building a united, disciplined and trained society. However, each Prime Minister, due to the demands of political, economic and social needs at both the national (mostly experienced by the first to fourth Prime Ministers) and global arenas (as encountered by the fourth to sixth Prime Ministers), the modus operandi of these emphases have developed in many forms that led to several transformations, particularly in the education sector.

Significant Developmental Transformations in Education

The developmental transformations in education in Malaysia could be traced in several significant educational reports and policies. The initial stage in the transformation of education in Malaysia is reflected in the 1956 *Razak Report*. This report set the foundation for national education policy, that is,

> to establish a national system of education acceptable to the
> people of the Federation as a whole which will satisfy their needs
> and promote their cultural, social, economic and political
> development as a nation, having regard to the intention of making
> Malay Language as the national language of the country whilst
> preserving and sustaining the growth of the languages and culture
> of other communities living in the country. (Razak Report, 1956,
> para. 1(a))

In short, the crux of the national educational system, that is still prevalent in the present day, is the use of Malay as medium of instruction at all national secondary school levels, a centralised or national school curriculum and common public examinations.

The implementation of the national education system as outlined in the *Razak Report* was reviewed in 1960 and recommended that primary education in all fully assisted schools should be free to all, and a comprehensive education of three years' duration was to be provided at the lower secondary level (*Rahman Talib Report*, 1960). In 1964, primary school pupils were automatically promoted to the secondary level for the first time, thus enabling them to complete a minimum of nine years in school. The changes made to the national education system due to the *Rahman Talib Report* spurred the need to develop the nation's human capital in meeting the developmental needs of the country by exposing young people to vocational subjects, namely agricultural science, industrial arts and commerce. At the primary level, enrolment increased significantly from 1.14 million at the beginning of 1963 to 1.36 million in January 1968 (Wong & Ee, 1971).

Although there was an increase in students' enrolment and the duration of school education, there prevailed social and economic imbalances in Malaysian society that led to the outbreak of racial riots on 13 May 1969. The racial riots shook the nation and led to intensified efforts by the government to attain more equitable distribution of wealth among the different races through NEP and the proclamation of *Rukunegara* which marked an important milestone in the history of educational development in Malaysia.

In September 1974, a Cabinet Committee was established to review the implementation of the national education system with the aim 'of ensuring the short term as well as the long term national manpower needs are met and furthermore to ensure that this education system fulfils the national objective towards creating a united, disciplined and trained society' (Malaysia, 1985, p. 1). The outcome of the report was the formulation and implementation of the Integrated Primary School Curriculum (KBSR) in 1983, and the New Integrated Secondary Curriculum (KBSM) in 1989. The National Philosophy of Education was also formulated in 1988 to guide and strengthen the nation's education system.

The National Philosophy of Education is expressed as follows:

> Education in Malaysia is an ongoing effort towards further developing the potential of individuals in a holistic and integrated manner so as to produce individuals who are intellectually, spiritually, emotionally and physically balanced and harmonious, based on a firm belief in and devotion to God. Such an effort is designed to produce Malaysian citizens who are knowledgeable and competent, who possess high moral standards, and who are responsible and capable of achieving a high level of personal well-being as well as being able to contribute to the betterment of the family, the society and the nation at large. (Education Act, 1996, pp. 9-10)

The Vision 2020 policy plays a pivotal role in setting the stages for several education reforms in Malaysia. In order to achieve Malaysia's aspiration to become a fully developed country by 2020, the government has embarked on the educational policy to increase science and technology manpower supply to 60% versus 40% non-science manpower production. This is to ensure the creation of a critical mass of science and technology personnel to meet the demands of a knowledge-based economy (Malaysia, 2001a). In fulfilling these goals, several initiatives were undertaken by MOE such as the use of information and communication technologies (ICT) in teaching and learning via the Computer in Education programme and the Smart School programme. The purpose of the former programme was to expose pupils to basic computer literacy whilst the latter programme was one of the flagship applications of Multimedia Super Corridor, a national ICT initiative, with the purpose of equipping Smart Schools with computers and multimedia equipment to enhance teaching and learning. In addition, to encourage more students to be interested in science and technology, science as a subject was made compulsory in 1998 for all students starting at Year Four in KBSR, subsequently extended up to Form Five in KBSM.

From 1999 to 2000, the KBSR and KBSM were revised and implemented in 2004. The revision was conducted to ensure that the content and the teaching and learning approaches in schools were more relevant to the current and future needs of the nation in order to be competitive globally. The revised KBSR and KBSM focused on mastery of knowledge, skills and inculcation of noble values. Among the skills that were emphasised were critical and creative thinking, and ICT (Sharifah, 2003).

One of the significant transformations with the revision of KBSR and KBSM was the decision by the government in 2002 to change the medium of instruction from Bahasa Melayu to English for Science and Mathematics (PPSMI) beginning in 2003 in Year One, Form One and Lower (Form) Six levels. The rationale for this decision was that as most science-based courses at HEIs were dependent on reference materials that are published in English, for students to be equipped to study these subjects it would be better if a change in the medium of instruction was effected. According to the then Director of the Curriculum Development Centre, Sharifah (2003), the implications of switching the medium of instruction for science and mathematics involved 33,901 primary school teachers and 22,997 secondary school teachers, not all of whom were fluent in English. The full implementation of conversion from Bahasa Melayu to English was completed by 2008. In the transitional period between the years 2003 to 2007, questions for the public examinations, namely UPSR, PMR, SPM and STPM, were given in both Bahasa Melayu and English and students were allowed to answer part of or the whole paper in Bahasa Melayu or English. PMR and SPM were conducted fully in English from 2008 (Sharifah, 2003).

On 8 July 2009, the Malaysian government decided to revert to the teaching of the two subjects from English to Bahasa Melayu in all national schools and the mother-tongue languages in national-type schools starting from 2012. The Deputy Prime Minister and Minister of Education, Muhyiddin Yassin (2009), explained that the decision was based on a study which found 'the gap between rural and urban students has widened since PPSMI started' and 'only 19.2% of secondary school teachers and 9.96% of primary school teachers were sufficiently proficient in English'. The Minister of Education further added that there would be greater emphasis on learning the English language such as the reintroduction of English literature, increase in the duration period of English in the school timetable and increase in the number of teachers of English. As reported in the local media, the issue of the switch resulted in mixed reactions from various stakeholders, including students, parents, educationists, and entrepreneurs.

Another significant transformational change in the Malaysian education system was the enactment of the Compulsory Education Act on 1 January 2003. It was in tandem with the universal Education for All policy and compelled every Malaysian child who has reached the age of six in January of the current year to be enrolled in school and receive formal primary school education (Malaysia, 2002). This Act also intends to reduce illiteracy and dropout rates among Malaysian children especially in the rural areas as MOE data have indicated that the attrition rate was 3.1% from 1995 to 2000 in the Year 1 to Year 6 primary school enrolment in the public educational system. The main reasons cited were natural causes such as death, plus poverty and inaccessibility of schools (Malaysia, 2006b).

To generate educational excellence through collaborative planning, on 16 January 2007 MOE launched the Education Development Master Plan (EDMP) (2006-10) to promote the education agenda under the Ninth Malaysia Plan. By taking cognisance of the goals and aspirations of the Vision 2020 policy, the EDMP was based on three main aspects, namely infrastructure, content and human structure in six thrust areas (Malaysia, 2008c, pp. 19-23):

> (i) Nation Building which intends to produce citizens who possess local, global and patriotic outlook, who value and treasure the cultural heritage and arts in the formative years of schooling;
> (ii) Developing Human Capital focuses in the development of positive value systems, discipline and character building of students;
> (iii) Strengthening the National Schools so that national primary and secondary schools are the 'schools of choice';
> (iv) Bridging the Education Gap which aims to bridge the education disparities in terms of the provision of physical and non-physical amenities, students' achievements and drop-out rate.
> (v) Elevating the Teaching Profession, and
> (vi) Accelerating Excellence of Educational Institutions in which efforts are undertaken to accelerate excellences in educational institutions through the establishment of cluster schools based on their niche in academic, co-curricular and sport activities.

The MOE further announced that an educational transformation of the new curriculum and assessment would be introduced in phases, starting at preschool and Year One from 2010 (*New Straits Times*, 2009). According to the Minister of Education, the educational planning for 2010 and in the 10th Malaysia Plan (2011-15) will encompass the implementation of four educational sub-National Key Result Areas (NKRA), namely the widening and strengthening of preschool education, raising the literacy and numeracy rate, creating high-performance schools and giving recognition to outstanding principals and headmasters. The aspect of human capital development would continue to be the main thrust in planning for educational development throughout the 10th Malaysia Plan period, focusing on increasing the level of knowledge and skills, developing individuals with intellect in the fields of science and technology, and nurturing positive attitudes, values and ethics.[4]

As a summary, as Malaysia progresses from an era of nation building (1950s-70s), to an era of rapid development (1980s-beyond) due to globalisation, liberalisation and the vast development of ICT, it could be seen that the transformations that have taken place in the education arena are influenced by economic, social and political changes that occur both locally and globally. However, the challenge for Malaysia as espoused by all the Prime Ministers of Malaysia by and large still remains the same as in the early days of Independence and that is to produce a united, disciplined and trained society. Nevertheless, unlike the 1960s, the human capital that the education system produces must now be able to compete globally. The following sub-sections discuss three major issues as highlighted in the EDMP in greater detail, namely the need for quality early childhood education, teacher education and higher education. These three issues cut across the entire spectrum of the Malaysian education structure.

Quality Early Childhood Education

The early childhood education (also known as early childcare and education or ECCE) in Malaysia comprises early childcare education (for children under age 4) under the 1984 Childcare Act (308 Act), and preschool education or kindergarten (3+ to 5+ years old) under the Education Act (1996). Unlike the primary and secondary school education which fall under the sole jurisdiction of the Ministry of Education, the official bodies in charge of the supervision of ECCE are from various ministries. Early childhood care and family development is under the jurisdiction of the Ministry of Women, Family and Community Development (MWFCD). The MWFCD coordinates the national programmes on the growth and development of children and through its Social Welfare Department, the MWFCD registers all childcare centres for children in the age group 0-4 years.

The ECCE (for children age 4-6 years) falls under the responsibilities of three ministries, that is, MOE, the Ministry of Rural and Regional Development (MRRD), as well as the Department of National Unity and Integration under the Prime Minister's Department. MRRD sets up *KEMAS* (Department of Social Welfare) preschools in rural or suburban areas, the Department of National Unity and Integration establishes the *PERPADUAN* (Unity) preschools in urban areas, and MOE sets up preschools as an annex to existing primary schools. Apart from the public agencies, the other providers of preschool education include State Religious Departments (JAIN), the Malaysian Islamic Youth Movement (ABIM) and the private sector. In terms of percentage of preschool classes (Figure 1) and children enrolled in the various types of preschools (Figure 2), the largest providing agency is from the private sector, consisting of about 42% of the total preschool classes and 40% of preschool children in 2007. This was followed by the public preschool provider, KEMAS, with 31% of total preschool classes and 30% of total preschool children in Malaysia.

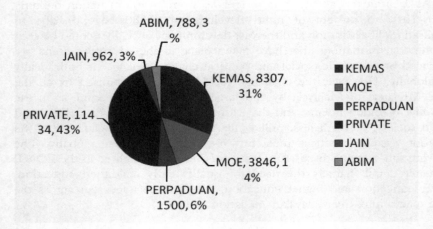

Figure 1. Number of preschool classes according to providing agencies in 2007. Source: Educational Planning and Research Division study in Curriculum Development Centre (2007).

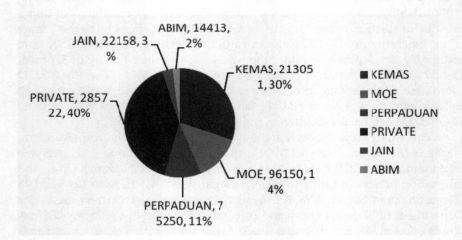

Figure 2. Number of preschool students in the various providing agencies in 2007. Source: Educational Planning and Research Division study in Curriculum Development Centre (2007).

In regulating preschools in Malaysia, the MOE had drafted several legal documents in 1972 relating to procedures on the registration of kindergartens, teachers and boards of governors, and the ECCE curriculum in 1986 and 1993. As preschool education is part of the national educational system under the Education Act 1996, all preschools, both public and private, are required by law to follow the National Preschool Curriculum (NPC) beginning in 2003. The aim of NPC is to enrich the potential of children in all aspects of development, master basic skills and have a positive attitude as well as to prepare them for a smooth transition to primary school education. The NPC is built upon six components, namely language and communication, cognitive development, spiritual and moral development, socio-emotional development, physical development, and aesthetics and creativity. Nonetheless, private preschools are permitted to offer additional programmes upon approval from MOE. In 2003, MOE approved the conversion of early intervention programmes in 28 special schools to preschool programmes for special needs children whilst those run by NGOs were given a special government grant. Public preschool programmes are free to parents and funded by government agencies. Private preschool programmes charge fees that vary from RM10-RM1000 per month (Curriculum Development Centre, 2007).

In 1984, the Childcare Centre's Act was implemented to maintain the required minimum standards for childcare centres and to resolve issues regarding registration, monitoring and inspection of the childcare centres. Under this Act, every childcare centre is required to register with the Social Welfare Department. The review of the 1984 Act led to the Care Centres (Amendment) Act 2007. Like preschools, there are various categories of childcare centres in Malaysia, namely the government-owned childcare centre, workplace childcare centre, institutional childcare centre, plantation childcare centre and home-based childcare centre. The childcare centres in Malaysia are mainly run by the private sector and the biggest government sector providing childcare centres is the MRRD, specifically KEMAS.

The latest entry to the childcare centres of Malaysia is Permata Early Childhood Education and Care (ECEC). In 2006, the Cabinet approved the programme 'Every Child is a Jewel' (Setiap Anak Permata) under the purview of the Deputy Primary Minister's Office. Permata ECEC aims to provide integrated quality care and early education services based on the needs of the local community to children under the age of 5 and their families. Pertama ECEC adopted the community-based integrated approach practised by Pen Green Centre (Corby, United Kingdom) under the SureStart Programme. These centres also prepare outreach programmes, parenting courses, counselling, and healthcare services to help local communities to build healthy and safe lifestyles. Community resource centres, libraries, speech therapy and a nutritionist's service are also provided by the Permata centres (Curriculum Development Centre, 2007).

The increasing emphasis on ECCE in Malaysia was further acknowledged under the Education Development Master Plan and National Key Result Areas. Under the EDMP, the MOE intends to increase the number of preschools to all national (public) schools especially those in rural and interior areas, provide special needs children with opportunities for education, and to have sufficient teachers as well as teacher assistants in the MOE preschools. According to Muhyiddin Yassin, under the NKRA, the government intended to increase the enrolment of preschool children of five years old by another 20% from 67% (342,706 children) in 2009 to 87% (about 440,000 children) by the year 2012 (http://www.bernama.com/bernama/v5/newsgeneral.php?id=452204, 3 November 2009).

Nonetheless, the current ECCE policies and practices raised several concerns that could hinder positive transformational changes arising from ECCE in Malaysia. As shown in Table I, only 1.31% and 1.22% of the total public expenditure on education was spent on early childhood education in 2005 and 2006 respectively. This is in comparison with 41.60% of total public expenditure on education spent on primary education and 37.07% spent on secondary education for 2005 and subsequently in 2006, 42.66% on primary education and 38.16% on secondary education. Although the figures in Table I do not include public expenditure on ECCE from other ministries such as MRRD, the minimal allocation by the government on ECCE should be of serious concern if Malaysia intends to fulfil the first goal of the Declaration of Education for All, which is the expansion of early childcare and education.

Level of education	2005	2006
Preschool	178,061,000 (1.31%)	173,528,500 (1.22%)
Primary	5,674,836,800 (41.60%)	6,060,289,900 (42.66%)
Secondary	5,057,590,900 (37.07%)	5,421,272,800 (38.16%)
Fully residential school education (secondary)	216,535,700 (1.59%)	262,630,900 (1.85%)

Table I. Estimated recurrent expenditure for MOE preschool, primary and secondary education. Source: Curriculum Development Centre (2007).

It was reported by the Curriculum Development Centre (2007) that in 2005 only 1.82% of the total population of the age group 0-4 years attended childcare centres and only 67.38% of children in the age group 4-6 years attended preschool education. Furthermore, as shown in Table II, the number of registered institution-based childcare centres not only dropped from 446 in 2004 to 306 in 2007, the Social Welfare Department reported that on record, 2176 centres (this figure includes the 306 childcare centres that registered in 2007) had at one time or another registered with the Department (Chiam, 2008).

Year	Number of registered childcare centres
2004	446
2005	311
2006	371
2007	306

Table II. Number of registered childcare centres (institution) by year.
Source: Social Welfare Department (2008, October) in Chiam (2008).

However, the above figures did not reflect the actual numbers as many home-based and institutional childcare centres were not required to register with the Social Welfare Department. The law states that if there are fewer than 10 children, premises need not be registered. Similarly, it was also reported by the Curriculum Development Centre (2007) that many preschools did not register with MOE. The non-registration of childcare centres and preschools would have long-term implications on the quality of ECCE for it is widely acknowledged that providing a healthy and positive environment is critical during the early years and a vital condition for lifelong learning (Chiam, 2008; UNESCO, 2009).

Any transformational change in the provision of quality ECCE would require quality childminders and preschool teachers in terms of professional training. In the case of Malaysia, there are marked variations in terms of duration of training and qualifications of childminders and preschool teachers. All teachers teaching in MOE preschools are trained and certified with at least a diploma in teaching. A significant number of them have a Bachelor's degree and Master's degree in ECCE. However, teachers teaching in KEMAS preschools receive six months' training whereas PERPADUAN preschool teachers receive only three weeks' training by their respective ministries. The MWFCD only require both childcare providers and childminders to attend a 10-day basic childcare course. Both public and private HEIs also offer various programmes in early childhood education, ranging from certificates to post-graduate degrees. The Malaysian Association of Kindergartens also conducts modular courses for private preschool teachers. The National Occupational Skill Standard with the collaboration of the Department of Skill Development in the Ministry of Human Resources has also offered a certificate in childcare programme since 2007. According to Chiam (2008), the marked differences in the duration of training and qualifications of ECCE teachers are indications that as long as they are not required to have high academic and professional qualifications, the status of ECCE will remain low in Malaysia.

In conclusion, there are numerous national legislations and policies in Malaysia on ECCE such as the Child Act, Education Act, Childcare Centre Act, Convention on Rights of Children, the Malaysian Plan, EDMP, and

The National Action Plan of Children. The reality still remains that the current policies and practices could undermine the quality of ECCE for all in Malaysia. Failure to address these issues would, according to the Curriculum Development Centre (2007), seem to be 'fragmented', in the eyes of the general public of Malaysia as well as a wastage of manpower and resources. Nonetheless, it is noted that of late the government has taken positive and encouraging steps towards high-quality preschool provision and care, in line with UNESCO's universal Education for All.

Teacher Education and Teaching Profession

Teacher education is under the jurisdiction of two ministries, MOE and MOHE. Teacher training colleges, or Institutes of Teacher Education Malaysia (ITEMs) as they are currently known, are under the purview of the Teacher Education Department, MOE while universities, both public and private, that offer teacher education programmes are under the purview of MOHE. Prior to the establishment of MOHE on 27 March 2004, teacher education and training in Malaysia was entirely under MOE. This section reviews teacher education at both ITEMs and HEIs.

The history of teacher education in Malaysia started with the establishment of Singapore Malay Teachers College in 1878, followed by the Malacca Malay College in 1990, Sultan Idris Training College in 1922, and the Malay Women's Training College in Malacca in 1935. In 1951 the Malayan Teachers' College was established at Kirkby, England as it was 'dictated by the fact that Malaya was then in a state of "emergency" fighting the communist insurgents' (Wong & Chang, 1975, p. 47). Currently, there are 27 ITEs with a total enrolment of 22,729 which are spread out in all 14 states of Malaysia (Malaysia, 2008c).

Prior to 1996, all teacher training colleges offered pre-service teacher training programmes at only the certificate level. In 1996, these colleges started diploma-level teaching programmes and in 2005, the teachers' colleges were upgraded to ITEMs that confer a Bachelor's degree in teaching. In short, the ITEMs conduct both pre-service and in-service training at certificate, diploma and degree levels as well as any other teacher education courses approved by the government. According to the Teacher Education Division, Ministry of Education (Malaysia, 2008c), the main purpose of ITEMs is to enhance the teaching profession by producing quality, skilled and responsible teachers and that the Ministry of Education intends to achieve a target of having 100% graduate teachers in secondary schools and 50% graduate teachers in primary schools by the year 2010 (Malaysia, 2008c). Presently there are about 800 to 1000 students in each of the 27 ITEMs (Malaysia, 2008c). The trainee teachers for all teacher education programmes are required to do a stipulated period of practice teaching in schools where they are supervised and assessed by mentor teachers and lecturers. Upon successful completion of the teacher education programme, graduates are posted to either primary or secondary schools as probationary teachers prior to confirmation as fully fledged teachers.

In addition to the in-service courses conducted by ITEMs, Institute Aminuddin Baki was established in 1979 as an educational training institute to run courses, workshops and seminars for professional development of staff in educational service, and international training programmes upon request from international organisations such as the Association of Southeast Nations (ASEAN), the Commonwealth and UNESCO.

The public universities offer diplomas, undergraduate and post-graduate degree programmes in education mainly to enable graduates to become professional teachers and gain teaching positions in government schools in Malaysia. The first School of Education (now known as Faculty of Education) was established in 1963 at the University of Malaya to train graduate teachers for secondary schools. The second teacher education programme was offered by the University Science Malaysia in 1970 followed by the National University of Malaysia in 1972. With the establishment of more public universities in Malaysia, such as University Putra Malaysia, more teacher education programmes are offered at both undergraduate and post-graduate levels.

Currently, there are 13 public universities in Malaysia that offer teacher education programmes, some of which are jointly offered with the ITEMs. Only 12 public universities offer post-graduate programmes in education at both Master's and doctoral levels (Malaysia, 2008d). Part-time and distance education programmes are also provided by the public universities, notably from University Science Malaysia and University Putra Malaysia. In 1997, the Sultan Idris Training College was upgraded to university status as Universiti Pendidikan Sultan Idris. The latter was established as a focus university of education to meet the country's objective of having 100% graduate teachers in secondary schools by 2010. In meeting the growing demands for qualified educators in the public and private sectors, the private HEIs (such as Open University of Malaysia, Tun Abdul Razak University, SEGI University College and Asia e University) provide programmes in education at different levels of study and specialisations.

As Malaysia's national school system is centralised, it is inevitable that teachers are trained to translate the national educational policies into practice. In this light, teacher education has to cope with ever-changing demands of current events and educational policies that influence the modus operandi of teacher education. For instance, when mathematics and science were taught in English, the teachers were subsequently trained under the English for Teaching Mathematics and Science (ETeMS) programme. MOE reported on 1 May 2008 that around 122,000 teachers had undergone the ETeMS programme for both primary and secondary schools throughout the country (http://www.moe.gov.my/bs/, 30 September 2009). With the decision to revert the teaching of these subjects from English to Bahasa Malaysia, it would imply that teachers who were trained under ETeMS would have to reorientate themselves to teaching the subjects in Bahasa Malaysia, and subsequently the modus operandi of the teacher education programme in Malaysia.

Prior to 2005, the ITEMs conferred teaching certificates at certificate and diploma levels and were expected to train primary school teachers, while the universities were expected to train secondary school teachers. Whilst it is in the tradition of universities to confer degrees, since 2005 the ITEMs (under MOE) also confer a Bachelor's degree in teaching. The current Vice-Chancellor of University Sains Malaysia, Dzulkfli Abdul Razak (2009), pointed that 'this notion alone is odd, since degree-awarding institutions by definition should be under MOHE, which is also the legitimate body to confer recognition to all other university degrees in Malaysia without exception'. This is yet another challenge to teacher education as it would lead to several concerns in the teacher education programmes provided by ITEMs and the universities under two different ministries, namely MOE and MOHE. Dzulkfli Abdul Razak pointed out that the student teachers at ITEMs may not be able to optimise the benefits of a university milieu that offers the breadth of knowledge and interactions with the diverse campus population. He further added that 'many of the education faculties in the local universities today are held in abeyance because of the seemingly "duplicative" move' and if 'the prevailing education faculties are not optimally used, and worse, could lead to closure when it comes to the crunch' (Dzulkfli Abdul Razak, 2009).

One of the six thrust areas in the EDMP 2006-10 is on elevating the teaching profession by making teaching a respected profession in order to mould responsible future generations. This posed a challenge to teacher education, as the teaching profession seems to lack prestige and first job preference, in terms of getting the right candidates to become teachers. The issue of 're-branding' to change the negative perception of the teaching profession and to improve the quality of teachers are some of the concerns raised by academicians, educationists and the public (Yaacob Wan Ibrahim, 2007). In meeting this challenge, the then Minister of Education, Hishammuddin Tun Hussein (2008), acknowledged that Malaysia needed to adopt a two-pronged teacher education strategy, namely recruitment and rewarding teachers, to recruit qualified teacher education candidates and to ensure that in-service teachers remain motivated to serve.

Calderhead & Shorrock (1997) stated that 'how we conceptualise the work of teachers inevitably influences how we think about their professional preparation, and ultimately shapes suggestions for the further improvement of teacher education' (p. 1). In the case of Malaysia, the direction of teacher education is reflected in the Philosophy of Teacher Education formulated in 1982. The Philosophy of Teacher Education states:

> the desire to educate and produce teachers who are noble and
> caring, knowledgeable and skilful, creative and innovative,
> resilient and competent, scientific in outlook, committed to

uphold the aspirations of the nation, proud of their heritage and dedicated to the development of the individual and the preservation of a united, progressive, and disciplined society. (SEAMEO-INNOTECH, 2003)

In summary, teacher education in Malaysia has been developed in tandem with the goals and objectives in the national educational policies and curriculum, and teachers are generally trained to translate the national educational policies into practice.

Towards Excellence in Tertiary Education

Tertiary education, especially at degree levels, has expanded very rapidly in the past three decades. Initially the expansion was confined largely to the public sector. However, by the 1990s the private sector began to play an increasingly important role and has contributed substantially to its growth. As an example, the higher education capacity in Malaysia has grown from the establishment of the nation's first university, University of Malaya in 1961 with a modest enrolment of 1010, to the 2007 estimated enrolment of 921,548 students in 20 public universities, 32 private universities and university colleges, four branch campuses of international universities, 21 polytechnics, 37 public community colleges, and 485 private colleges (Malaysia, 2008d). Table III shows the distribution of enrolment and output of HEIs.

Research findings appear to indicate that the factors associated with this expansion in Malaysia are in general similar to those of other developing countries. For instance, Lee & Healy (2006) reported that compared with members of ASEAN (see Table IV), the growth enrolment ratios for Malaysia increased significantly from 2% in 1965 to 23% in 2000. However, Malaysia's expansion was still behind Thailand (32%) and the Philippines (30%) in 2000.

An important factor is the increase in the number of school-going children. As more children complete primary and secondary education, more of them proceed to higher education. Rapid globalisation and technological changes have also spurred the need for a highly educated and flexible workforce to manage a changing economy effectively. Recent policies and plans as contained in official reports (Malaysia, 2001a, 2001b, 2006b) indicate that the government is aware of such changes and demands as well as the need to respond to them. As a consequence, public investment in higher education has increased substantially and the private sector has been encouraged to complement the government's effort in providing accessibility to tertiary education, especially in critical areas. Perceived economic, social and cultural benefits have also encouraged individuals and government to invest more in higher education. The enactment of the Private Higher Educational Institutions Act in Parliament in 1996 was the government's acknowledgement of the contribution of private HEIs in Malaysia. The Act also provided the necessary regulatory framework for the liberalisation and privatisation of HEIs on a larger scale to meet the manpower and economic needs of Malaysia (Lee, 1999; Tan, 2002).

Institution and level	Admission	Enrolment	Output
Public higher educational institutions			
Matriculation	6957	10,242	4509
Certificate	1470	1349	166
Diploma	26,255	83,833	18,321
Bachelor's degree	75,127	270,156	59,844
Post-graduate diploma	1779	2956	2065
Master's degree	16,158	36,094	8655
Doctoral degree	3644	12,243	785
Professional	450	1249	196
Others	1260	1212	81
Subtotal	133,100	419,334	94,622
Public higher educational institutions			
Certificate	47,875	60,617	18,269
Diploma	91,483	177,773	32,685
Bachelor's degree	43,261	151,591	26,590
Master's degree	2924	8540	962
Doctoral degree	303	1331	55
Subtotal	185,846	399,852	78,561
Polytechnics			
Certificate	15,019	30,861	13,723
Diploma	25,555	54,419	19,060
Subtotal	40,574	85,280	32,783
Community colleges			
Certificate	9181	16,289	5287
Diploma	468	793	279
Subtotal	9649	17,082	5566
Grand total	369,169	921,548	211,532

Table III. Admission, enrolment and output of higher educational institutions in Malaysia. Source: Malaysia (2008d).

In addition to the above factors, individual and parental preferences to a great extent influence the pattern of demand for higher education, which, in turn, influences its pattern of expansion. As far as Malaysians are concerned, research findings indicate that in general, the higher the fathers' income bracket, the higher the level of enrolment in higher education (Leong et al, 1990; Chew et al, 1995; Lee et al, 2001; Chew & Siow, 2009; Quek & Chang, 2009). Parents' educational background (Aziz et al, 1987; Chew et al, 1995; Li & Min, 2001) and academic achievement of secondary school graduates (Lee et al, 2001) are also closely associated to the demand for higher education. Other factors such as family background, ethnicity and gender (Singh, 1980; Leong et al, 1990; Lee et al, 2001; Chew & Siow, 2009), geographic location (Leong et al, 1990; Malaysia, 1996), school effects and the spirit of individualism (Lee et al, 2001) also influence the demand for higher education.

Country	1965	1975	1985	1995	2000
Philippines	19	18	38	30	30
Singapore	10	9	12	34	N/A
Indonesia	3	2	7	11	N/A
Thailand	2	4	20	20	32
Malaysia	2	3	6	11	23
Brunei	N/A	N/A	N/A	7	14
Vietnam	N/A	N/A	N/A	4	10

Table IV. Expansion of higher education in the ASEAN region as measured by gross enrolment ratios (%). Source: Lee & Healy (2006).

Currently, even though there are 595 tertiary institutions, the access to higher education is still considered insufficient to meet society's growing demands for tertiary education to meet the needs of the nation. Compared with the same cohort in some developed countries, especially the OECD's data for 1996, it is indicated that student enrolment for the 18-21 age cohort in Malaysia was low. It was 11% at the non-degree level compared with 26% in the USA and 12% in the UK, while at the degree level it was 5% in Malaysia compared with 41% in the USA and 39% in the UK. The challenge to MOHE is to further increase the accessibility of tertiary education in line with the concept of democratisation and lifelong education, particularly in the field of science and technology (Malaysia, 2003).

Another challenge is to achieve a balanced production of skilled and semi-professional workforces. According to the Education Development Plan (Malaysia, 2003), the enrolment ratio for first degree, diploma, and certificate programmes in both public and private HEIs is unbalanced and does not meet the nation's needs for a skilled and semi-professional workforce. As in 2003, the enrolment ratio of first degree to diploma and certificate is 1:4 as compared to 1:2 in developed countries (Malaysia, 2003). In meeting this demand, the MOHE needs to establish more HEIs, especially polytechnics and community colleges and to encourage the establishment of private HEIs that emphasise science and technology and other critical fields.

The attempt to increase students' participation rate has caused the lecturer to student ratio to increase from 1:15 in 1990 to 1:20 in 2000

(Malaysia, 2003). As a result, the HEIs are facing a shortage of academic and professional teaching staff with experience in various critical fields. In addition, most of the existing training schemes do not require the teaching staff to undergo industrial training or experience. Thus, the challenge to MOHE as well as the HEIs is to acquire adequate numbers of quality teaching staff with appropriate qualifications and experience, and to provide opportunities to upgrade and expand their knowledge and skills. Such initiatives include increasing training programmes (locally and abroad), providing a more competitive salary scheme, and inculcating a research and development culture among lecturers and students.

In enabling the production of human resources capable of meeting the challenges of globalisation and knowledge economy towards establishing Malaysia as a centre of educational excellence, MOHE as well as HEIs need to offer well-developed education programmes with dynamic curriculum, up-to-date infrastructure and quality teaching staff. The establishment of the Malaysia Qualifications Agency is one of MOHE's efforts to monitor and legislate the quality of education programmes at HEIs, both public and private. However, the challenge remains with HEIs to maintain self-regulatory policies and procedures to ensure quality and excellence in their educational programmes and to ensure that these meet national and international standards. In this context, another challenge for MOHE is to produce graduates who are not only equipped with knowledge and skills in their field of studies but also have value-added capabilities to raise their position in the world of work (Lee & Siow, 2009; Quek & Chang, 2009). Towards this end, MOHE and HEIs need to further advance the initiatives 'to develop students' critical, creative and innovative thinking to enable them to contribute towards the nation's progress and ready to compete in the international arena' (Malaysia, 2008c, p. 73).

As a proactive initiative to produce traits and qualities in students required to face challenges in the knowledge economy and the innovation field in the twenty-first century, the National Higher Education Strategic Plan (NHEP) was launched by the Prime Minister on 27 August 2007. It was formulated with a vision to transform higher education in the context of strengthening Malaysia's position as an international hub of higher education excellence (Malaysia, 2008c). The NHEP outlines seven strategic thrusts which form the foundation for the development of the National Higher Education until 2020, namely widening of access and increasing equity, improving the quality of teaching and learning, enhancing research and innovation, strengthening of HEIs, intensifying internationalisation, enculturation of lifelong learning, and reinforcing delivery systems of the MOHE. As far as intensifying internationalisation (Thrust 5) is concerned, the NHEP proposes to effect collaborating networks with foreign HEIs; increase international student enrolment to about 10%, especially in private HEIs; increase participation of international students in competitive courses by about 5%; send students for post-doctoral studies in renowned overseas universities; develop opportunities for student mobility with credit transfer; and establish Malaysian international scholarships.

Conclusion

Since the gaining of Independence, the national education system in Malaysia has undergone tremendous changes for development and progress that can be clustered into three distinct phases, namely from the *Razak Report* of 1956 to the Cabinet report of 1979; from the Integrated Primary School Curriculum and New Integrated Secondary Curriculum to their revision in 2000; and to a transformed version in 2008. Whilst there were changes in each phase, it could be concluded that there is a common chord in education, namely to produce a united, disciplined and trained society as espoused as early as the *Razak Report* in 1956 and reaffirmed in the National Philosophy of Education and various educational policies. In satisfying the needs of the nation and promoting its cultural, social, economic and political development, two prongs of implementation are apparent, namely national unity and a skilled workforce, whereby each of them took centre stage at different phases. During the first phase, national unity could be said to be at the forefront while a skilled workforce gained prominence during the second phase in the national educational system. However, the interchange between the prongs of taking centre stage has led to the overshadowing of the other prong. In the last phase, besides producing a skilled labour force, there is a need to create Malaysians' awareness, identity and values regarding national development and unity. Towards this end, it could be seen that these two prongs are given equal prominence in order to synergise the plurality of Malaysians in realising the attainment of 1Malaysia. Nonetheless, the balancing act of these two prongs still remains a tremendous challenge to Malaysia's educational system as education is generally regarded to be borderless.

The essence of education in Malaysia rests on the development of the whole child in all aspects, namely intellectually, emotionally, spiritually and physically, balanced and harmonious, based on a firm belief in and devotion to God. This is the National Philosophy of Education, which assumes that by developing the whole child, it would bring about the realisation of these two prongs. Thus, as discussed in this chapter, it is paramount for the development of whole child to have accessibility, equality and quality education from early years to the tertiary level. It is noted that any educational policies that are put in place would require teachers to become the principal agents of change in order to effect the educational transformations to new dimensions.

Acknowledgements

The authors wish to acknowledge the invaluable contributions of Ms Choo Min Joo and Ms Yoon Sook Jhee.

Notes

[1] The sex ratio is equal to total number of males in year t divided by total number of females in year t and multiplied by 100 (Malaysia, 2008a).

[2] The term 'Bumiputera' means 'sons of the soil' and refers to the Malays and other indigenous people of the country.

[3] This includes permanent residents, foreign workers with work permits, expatriates and foreign students.

[4] http://www.bernama.com/bernama/v5/newsgeneral.php?id=452204 (3 November 2009).

References

Abdul Razak Hussein (2009) Encyclopædia Britannica. http://www.britannica.com/ EBchecked/topic/277552/Abdul Razak (accessed 12 October 2009).

Aziz, U.A., Chew, S.B., Lee, K.H. & Sanyal, B. (Eds) (1987) *University Education and Employment in Malaysia*, Research Report No. 66. Paris: International Institute for Educational Planning.

Calderhead, J. & Shorrock, S.B. (1997) *Understanding Teacher Education. Case Studies in the Professional Development of Beginning Teachers*. London: Falmer Press.

Chew, S.B., Lee, K.H. & Quek, A.H. (Eds) (1995) *Education and Work: aspirations of Malaysian secondary school students*. Kuala Lumpur: Faculty of Education, University of Malaya.

Chew, S.B. & Siow, H.L. (2009) Expansion of Higher Education, in S. Nagaraj, S.B. Chew, K.H. Lee & R.H. Admad (Eds) *Education and Work: the world of work*, pp. 26-57. Kuala Lumpur: Faculty of Economics and Administration.

Chiam, H.K. (2008) Child Care in Malaysia: then and now, *International Journal of Child Care and Education Policy by Korea Institute of Child Care and Education*, 2(2), 31-41. http://www.kicce.re.kr/english/data/03.Malaysia(1).pdf (accessed 30 September 2009).

Curriculum Development Centre, Ministry of Education Malaysia (2007) Early Childhood Care and Education Policy Implementation Review 2007. http://www.unescobkk.org/ education/appeal/ programme-themes/ecce/ecce-resources/ (accessed 30 September 2009).

Dzulkfli Abdul Razak (2009) Teacher Training Colleges in Wrong 'Place', *New Straits Times Online*, 5 July. http://www.nst.com.my/Current_News/NST/index_html (accessed 28 September 2009).

Education Act 1996 (Act 550) and selected regulations (1996) Kuala Lumpur: Percetakan Nasional Malaysia Berhad.

Hishammuddin Tun Hussein (2008) Malaysia Adopts Two-Pronged Teacher Education Strategy to Pursue EFA, *Bernama Online*, 18 December. http://www.bernama.com.my/bernama/v5/index.php.

Hussein Onn (2009) Encyclopædia Britannica. http://www.britannica.com/EBchecked/topic/277552/Hussein-Onn (accessed 12 October 2009).

Lee, K.H., Quek, A.H. & Chew, S.B. (Eds) (2001) *Education and Work: the state of transition*. Kuala Lumpur: Faculty of Education, University of Malaya.

Lee, K.H. & Siow, H.L. (2009) Preparedness of the Future Workforce, in S. Nagaraj, S.B. Chew, K.H. Lee & R.H. Admad (Eds) *Education and Work: the world of work*, pp. 208-252. Kuala Lumpur: Faculty of Economics and Administration.

Lee, M.N.N. (1999) *Private Higher Education in Malaysia*. Penang: School of Educational Studies, Universiti Sains Malaysia.

Lee, M.N.N. & Healy, S. (2006) *Higher Education in South East Asia: an overview*. Asia Pacific Programme of Educational Innovation for Development (APEID). Bangkok: UNESCO.

Leong, Y.C., Cheong, S.Y., Chew, S.B. et al (1990) *Factors Influencing the Academic Achievement of Students in Malaysian Schools*. Kuala Lumpur: Educational Research Planning Division, Ministry of Education.

Li, W. & Min, W. (2001) *Tuition, Private Demand and Higher Education in China*. Beijing: Graduate School of Education, Peking University.

Mahathir Mohamad (Tun, The Right Honorable (Fourth) Prime Minister of Malaysia) (1991) The Way Forward – Vision 2020. http://www.wawasan2020.com/vision/ (accessed 10 January 2010).

Malaysia (1985) *Report of the Cabinet Committee to Review the Implementation of Education Policy*. Kuala Lumpur: Berita Publishing.

Malaysia (1996) *Economic Report 1996/97*. Kuala Lumpur: Percetakan Nasional Malaysia Berhad.

Malaysia (2001a) *Eighth Malaysia Plan 2001-2005*. Kuala Lumpur: Percetakan Nasional Malaysia Berhad.

Malaysia (2001b) *The Third Outline Perspective Plan, 2001-2010*. Kuala Lumpur: Percetakan Nasional Malaysia.

Malaysia (2002) *The Compulsory Education Act. Section 29A Education Act (Amendment)*. Kuala Lumpur: Ministry of Education.

Malaysia (2003) *Education Development Plan 2001-2010: generating educational excellence through collaborative planning*. Kuala Lumpur: Ministry of Education Malaysia.

Malaysia (2006a) *Ninth Malaysia Plan 2006-2010*. Kuala Lumpur: Percetakan Nasional Malaysia Berhad.

Malaysia (2006b) *Education Development Master Plan 2006-2010*. Kuala Lumpur: Ministry of Education Malaysia.

Malaysia (2008a) *Social Statistics Bulletin Malaysia*. Kuala Lumpur: Department of Statistics.

Malaysia (2008b) *Mid-term Review of the Ninth Malaysia Plan 2006-2010*. Kuala Lumpur: Percetakan Nasional Malaysia Berhad.

Malaysia (2008c) *Education in Malaysia: a journey to excellence*. Putrajaya: Educational Planning and Research Division.

Malaysia (2008d) *Perangkaan pengajaian tinggi Malaysia 2008* [Statistics on Malaysian higher education 2008]. Putrajaya: Ministry of Higher Education.

Mohd Najib bin Tun Hj Abd Razak (Dato' Seri, The Right Honorable Prime Minister of Malaysia) (2009a) 1Malaysia Speeches (September 2009). http://www.1malaysia.com.my/index.php?option=com_article_list&Itemid=59&lang=en (accessed 30 September 2009).

Mohd Najib bin Tun Hj Abdul Razak (2009b) Najib: 1Malaysia a concept for the world, *Star Online*, 7 October 2009. http://thestar.com.my/news/story.asp?file=/2009/10/7/nation/4854896&sec=nation (accessed 27 November 2009).

Muhyiddin Yassin (2009) Math and Science Back to Bahasa, Mother Tongues, *Star Online*, 8 July. http://thestar.com.my/news/story.asp?file=/2009/7/8/natin/20090708144354&sec=nation (accessed 29 September 2009).

New Straits Times (2009) All Round Skills to be Focus of New Curriculum. 19 April. http://archives.emedia.com.my/bin/main.exe?f=doc&state=pcdma9.2.1 (accessed 27 March 2010).

Quek, A.H. & Chang, L.H. (2009) Career Mobility, in S. Nagaraj, S.B. Chew, K.H. Lee & R.H. Admad (Eds) *Education and Work: the world of work*, pp. 121-166. Kuala Lumpur: Faculty of Economics and Administration.

Razak Report (Report of the Education Committee) (1956). Kuala Lumpur: Government Printing Office.

SEAMEO-INNOTECH (2003) Adult and Non-formal Education. http://www.seameo-innotech.org/.../malaysia/malaysia14.htm (accessed 30 September 2009).

Sharifah Maimunah Syed Zin (2003) Paper presented at the International Conference on Science and Mathematics Education, 'Which Way Now?', Kuala Lumpur, University of Malaya City Campus, 14-16 October.

Singh, J.S. (1980) Higher Education and Social Mobility, *Southeast Asian Journal of Social Science*, 8(1-2), 55-63.

Tan, Ai Mei (2002) *Malaysian Private Higher Education: globalisation, privatisation, transformation and marketplace*. London: Asean Academic Press.

UNESCO (2009) *Education for All (EFA) Global Monitoring Report 2009. Overcoming Inequality: why governance matters*. Oxford: Oxford University Press. http://www.unesco.org/en/efareport (accessed 30 September 2009).

Wong, F.H.K. & Chang, P.M.P. (1975) *The Changing Pattern of Teacher Education in Malaysia*. Kuala Lumpur: Heinemann Educational Books (Asia).

Wong, F.H.K. & Ee, T.H. (1971) *Education in Malaysia*. Kuala Lumpur: Heinemann Education Books (Asia).

Yaacob Wan Ibrahim (2007) Malaysian Education System at Crossroad – the way forward, paper presented at the 11th Malaysian Education Summit 2007: Malaysia Education Winning in the Global Race, Petaling Jaya, 16-17 April. http://www.isis.org.my/files/pubs/papers/YWI_Malaysian_Edu_Syst.ppt (accessed 20 September 2009).

CHAPTER 7

Education in Myanmar: opportunity for limited engagement

RICHARD MARTIN

SUMMARY Clearly it is a time to reassess the situation for education in Burma. There are small but significant opportunities for overseas institutions or philanthropic organizations to engage in distance education, particularly tourism, information technology training and foundation courses for students who have completed their high school education. Linking with the work of the British Council and possibly with small private colleges could provide other pathways for development and support. If this proves successful then possibly the Asian Development Bank and World Bank might be encouraged to re-engage and provide limited technical assistance. Developments of this kind will have to be done carefully, but it seems that the Burmese Government would not oppose such gentle approaches to reform.

Sanctions and censure imposed upon Myanmar (formerly known as Burma) with the intention of encouraging an emergent civil society and the development of democratic institutions appear to have failed, at least for the time being, but with severe consequences for the education sector in Myanmar: it should be noted that most countries still call Myanmar 'Burma' but it has been decided to use the name used by the government. There is a strong view among developed countries that current international policies will remain intact especially given the military dominating the elections of November 2010, which have also been heavily criticised as lacking fairness. However, with the release of Aung Sung Suu Kyi (also in November 2010) there are hopes for a possible change in such policies. There is the other view that any new international approach must address the issues associated with this transition, because Myanmar is one of the poorest, most ethnically diverse and conflict-prone societies in South-East Asia. Additional viewpoints suggest that forward-looking international policies should support encouragement of political liberalisation, peace building and socio-economic development; and that the status quo approach of coercive diplomacy should be replaced with a policy of improving communication with the military regime, which is suspicious and lacks any consistent thinking. Recent discussions between the USA and the Myanmar government indicate that this may be changing, albeit at a slow pace.

This chapter aims to address the needs of the education sector in Myanmar. It suggests that, in the absence of any immediate change to the current setting, there are other avenues that can be pursued in order to reduce the plight of young people wishing to gain an education, improve their skills and get meaningful work. Despite the imposition of the sanctions, it does appear that the European Commission (EC) is now considering a slightly less stringent approach and is considering additional assistance in the education and health areas. This development bodes well: education and health issues are inextricably linked.

The chapter does not attempt to provide a comprehensive analysis of the education system in Myanmar owing to the limited availability of data and problematic means to access and gather such. Rather, its focus is on areas where considerable opportunities exist to develop links and provide small but meaningful projects funded by philanthropic or private organisations in the West, in the same way as has happened in Vietnam, Cambodia and Laos over the past 20 to 30 years. If small, privately funded development assistance money is funnelled into Myanmar, then perhaps official development assistance (ODA) may again emanate from multilateral organisations such as the World Bank and the Asian Development Bank (ADB), as they review their existing policies of non-engagement. As illustrated, a number of NGOs and the EC already operate successfully in Myanmar, with the reluctant and tacit approval of the Myanmar government; however their influence is limited due to lack of funding and poor coordination. An attempt should be made to correct this shortcoming.

It is suggested that philanthropic or private organisations in the West should review the situation and, in cooperation with the small but growing private sector in Myanmar, forge partnerships in the areas of English language teaching, skills development and trades, and then also seriously consider training students in the tourism sector where there are only a few restrictions currently in place by the Myanmar government. As in Cambodia, Vietnam and Laos, education and training assistance in the tourism sector is seen as non-controversial, from the government's point of view (tourist visas are easily obtained for one month and individual Western teachers are encouraged to work in Myanmar). This is a golden opportunity for the West to influence and assist in opening up a country which has been intellectually, economically and morally in decline since the advent of the current military regime.

To achieve real improvements in education, it is also vital that the ADB and the World Bank also review their policies towards Myanmar though this is a somewhat farfetched aspiration in view of the previous US administration of George W. Bush. However, donors need to take a long-term approach to working in Myanmar, as is evidenced currently by the approach taken by the EC.

Background

Myanmar is a pariah state, shunned internationally because of its rejection of democratic institutions and its poor human rights record. International universities and vocational colleges have been reluctant to become involved in providing courses owing to restrictions placed by the Myanmar government and the lack of control they can exercise in ensuring academic standards are met. As a result, its education system at all levels remains limited and antiquated, with only a few Myanmar young people getting the opportunity to study abroad or to be exposed to modern international scholarship. However, despite the policies of the government, the recent political unrest and sanctions imposed by the international community, some opportunities do now exist for Western education institutions and NGOs to engage with Myanmar and to have a positive influence on its next generation.

Myanmar has an estimated population of over 50 million [1] of which 60% are under the age of 18 years. Yet 40 years ago, Myanmar was a country with a progressive education system.

Ethnic Myanmars make up 68% of the population [2] with the other major minority groups being the Shan, Karen and Rakhine. Chinese and Indians are predominant in commercial activities and can obtain basic technical qualifications from abroad or are employed as labourers. The middle class is small but growing and has some interest in promoting education. However, Western nations have focused on human rights issues and overseas development assistance has trickled to basic assistance provided by the United Nations Children's Fund (UNICEF) via the EC, France, Germany and the United Kingdom (UK), just to mention a few in both the health and education sectors. The World Bank and the ADB have not provided any assistance for many years. However, as the EC points out: 'Burma [Myanmar] enjoys a certain "comfort zone" with its immediate neighbors' (European Commission, 2007, p. 6). This is particularly true as Myanmar has many natural resources and China, Russia, Thailand, Singapore and India have compromised their integrity through providing arms in exchange for exploiting natural resources. The United Nations (UN) again has failed with its systems of vetoing within the Security Council thus inhibiting any real action. Indeed the UN – a good idea in its inception – has failed in any decision-making process in a number of states such as Palestine, Zimbabwe, North Korea and many other nations. It is the author's view that the UN is an organisation wasting resources on a huge bureaucracy, achieving little except providing short-term humanitarian assistance.

Information/Data

This chapter suffers from the common problem in Myanmar of the lack of up-to-date or reliable information. A number of organisations such as the ADB, some foreign governments, the BBC and various NGOs have conducted their own surveys, but much of these data are also out of date or contradict each other. A recent Save the Children in Myanmar analysis reports, for example that: 'Official literacy rate for 2006 was supposed to be 94.35per cent according to the recent "Education For All Statistics" [3] but a recent UN survey found the functional literacy rate to be only 53per cent and case studies from remote area show figures as low as 10-20per cent' (Save the Children in Myanmar, 2006, pp. 21-22), which is a large difference from the officially published statistics from UNESCO. A useful recent report is one issued recently by the EC (European Commission, 2007). This report does suggest some useful changes to international policy on Myanmar. The World Bank and the ADB have provided no assistance for a number of years; this is not a one-way blockage as the Myanmar government has resisted acceptance of assistance due to the conditions placed by these two international organisations.

This chapter relies heavily, therefore, on interview material collected by the author in 2008-09. In the absence of much else, these interviews provide the most useful basis for identifying areas of contemporary need and opportunities for constructive international engagement. The British Council has remained and operated in Myanmar for a number of years and provides an extremely valuable service in the education sector.

One of the big problems is lack of infrastructure, especially in Information Technology (IT). Access to the Internet is highly restricted and slow and even when students are able to use it they are monitored by the security forces. Students tend to use access through NGOs, embassies and especially the British Council which have their own secured networks. Online access to courses is virtually useless and the only way students are able to use curriculum electronically is through the use of CDs.

Interviews

For the information presented in this chapter, the author interviewed, in Myanmar, international agencies and embassies, Buddhist monks, local government officials, secondary teachers and students, and academics. Additionally, interviews were held in Bangkok from international agencies and embassies which had responsibilities in Myanmar and other countries in the region.

The Education System

Education has been always an important factor in Myanmar society going back many hundreds of years, but its quality has been diminished as a result of underinvestment. The education system in Myanmar can be divided into two area of access: the 'formal' area which is government funded, not including monastic education, and the 'non formal' area, which includes the private sector, monastic and non-government organisations. Presiding over both sectors is the Ministry of Education (MOE), a bureaucracy that lacks credibility and, like all Myanmar ministries, is staffed at the higher levels mainly by military personnel who have limited knowledge of their portfolios. It is, therefore, ill-equipped to spearhead much-needed education reform. Similar situations existed in countries such as Indonesia only 15 years ago, but at that time aid was still being offered by the ADB, the World Bank and NGOs.

The government, through the MOE, funds and operates almost exclusively the public education system, including establishment of the curriculum, the provision of teacher training, the provision of infrastructure, quality assurance and the general operation of the system. The system is outdated, under-funded and ineffective in meeting the meets of the society, parents and most importantly students.

Access by the Myanmar government to ODA in the area of education has been restricted to two large international aid organisations: the Japanese International Cooperation Agency (JICA) and UNICEF; these organisations are the only ones permitted to work directly with the MOE (Save the Children in Myanmar, 2006). In 2007, however, the European Commission became involved, albeit in a small, but growing way. The Myanmar government has been reluctant for many years to allow other organisations to provide assistance to the public education sector. This is a result of a policy based on the government's own paranoia. The government also generally rejects the fact that conditions are usually attached to formal aid. JICA has been operating in Myanmar for some years and while not able to initiate any new projects owing to observance of sanctions, it administers a number of education and health programmes but with great difficulty, especially in dealing with the various Myanmar ministries, particularly the MOE. The MOE has its own internal challenges and is a largely neglected and under-resourced ministry, even though the Myanmar people have traditionally valued education. Following the move of the government from Yangon (formerly Rangoon) to Naypyidaw in 2007, access to the MOE officials has become even more difficult, and JICA, UNICEF and all other international NGOs working in education, as in other sectors, now find it nearly impossible to maintain cooperation, let alone develop new programmes.

Quality Assurance and Curriculum

Issues relating to quality assurance are virtually non-existent due to the lack of training of staff and issues owing to variable standards of training of staff at school and university levels. Due to the isolation from the Western education systems, there are virtually no benchmarks to indicate whether in fact quality assurance in any tiers of education can be benchmarked.

The Myanmar's government's Education for All (EFA) or Mid-decade Assessment Report (Union of Myanmar, 2007, pp. 163-186) has a chapter on education quality which has statements which are not backed up by any empirical data; there is no comparison with other countries in the region and cannot be tested by outside sources due to restrictions within the government. It talks about child-friendly schools but no evidence is given that this is indeed a priority.

It also talks about the difficulty of improvement in teachers and teacher methodology but wages for teachers are so low that they seek other work and children are often left to fend for themselves. The EFA (p. XI) mentions that primary and secondary curricula have been revised and updated and teaching learning practices have improved but fails to explain how the Myanmar government can do this without outside assistance. There is no benchmarking with other countries in the region and thus this statement lacks credibility. UNICEF is the only organisation allowed to assist in Myanmar but does not have the expertise, skills or money to effect any meaningful change.

The MOE's level of impact is negatively affected by inadequately trained staff and by the current and relatively new Minister who lacks the necessary influence, mainly because he does not come from a military background to introduce new programmes and reforms, even micro in nature, to the education system. Furthermore, lack of effective decision making within the Ministry hampers policy development, and offers of foreign aid from foreign governments or NGOs are viewed suspiciously. Accordingly, it has been, and continues to be, difficult to engage in any real dialogue with the government.

The government [4] has committed itself officially to the UNESCO Global Education for All. It produced a publication in August 2007 (Union of Myanmar, 2007). The data in the publication are questionable and unreliable due to lack of verification. The six goals outlined are:

(1) Ensuring that significant progress is achieved so that school-age children have access to and complete a compulsory and free basic education of good quality by 2015.
(2) Improving all aspects of the quality of basic education: teachers, education personnel and curriculum.
(3) Achieving significant improvement in the levels of functional literacy and continuing education for all by 2015.
(4) Ensuring that the learning needs of the young people and adults are met through non-formal education, life skills and preventive education programmes.
(5) Expanding and improving comprehensive early childhood care and education.

(6) Strengthening education management and the Education Management Information System.

Despite the commitment by the Myanmar government, only lip-service is paid to these ideals. Until there is a significant change in government policy, international assistance will not be provided.

According to the EC:

> The strategies outlined in the national action plan remain largely unfulfilled, due to a lack of funding and a lack of trained staff to manage the education system. So far, public investments have focused on constructing more primary schools, whereas other key areas such as training, textbooks, teachers' salaries and early childhood development remain to be addressed. (European Commission, 2007, p. 4)

Linking to the EFA are six broad areas of the National Health Plan, which again lacks funding and exhibits low level of technical expertise in the health sector.

Monastic Education

The Buddhist monastic school system in Myanmar is an old and antiquated educational system with a very long history, dated back to the period of King Anawrahta in the eleventh century. The schools provided important educational needs throughout Myanmar's history and they were the only source of education for all sorts of lives ranging from royal princes to unskilled workers. The Buddhist monastic schools helped to raise Myanmar's rate of literacy considerably above those of other Far Eastern countries in the early 1900s. In 1931, 56% of males over the age of five and 16.5% of females were literate – approximately four times as high as those reported for India at the same time.[1]

At present, the monastic schools only assist in providing basic educational needs of the country especially for children from needy families and orphans – filling the significant gap within the education system. The primary school children of Myanmar attend the Buddhist monasteries to acquire literacy and numeracy skills as well as knowledge of the Buddha's teachings. Thus, the schools provide not only curriculum education but also ethics and moral foundation for the children. Their role as principle educational providers has ceased for many years but their contribution is still significant in twenty-first-century Myanmar. Supplementing the government's basic education sector, monastic schools provide the government an alternative education system. The schools also provide underprivileged children all the basic educational needs exactly as the public government elementary schools can offer by using the same curriculum.

Generally, Myanmar's monastic schools accept children from needy families who live near the school's vicinity and who are unable to attend government schools. Many of these orphans who attend monastery schools in Yangon and Mandalay are from remote areas and have been sent by senior monks from their villages and small towns. Some schools operate similarly as boarding schools and some as day schools, depending on the situation and support of the public.

The schools are required to cooperate closely with township education authorities to be officially recognised. But the operation and finance rely heavily on donations and collaboration from the public. The fees of most of the students at the schools are covered by such donations but in some cases, parents are able to make a small contribution. However, the level of educational qualifications of Buddhist monks is low and thus reflects the standard of education that they are able to provide the students.

In the 2004-05 academic years, there were nearly 1190 monastic schools, providing primary and secondary education to more than 100,000 children in Myanmar.[5] In addition to lacking resources, monastic education, mainly Buddhist in orientation, provides education to those students who cannot enter government schools due to a variety of reasons including economic, social and geographic factors. Despite there being some concerns regarding the Buddhist clergy resisting government policy, and recent arrests on such matters as development of democratic institutions in the country and linkages with Aung San Suu Kyi, monastic schools are an important contributor to the country's education system.[6]

Monastic schools have received some assistance from NGOs but this has been sporadic and tends to be focused on severely disadvantaged areas or parts of the country where border disputes have arisen. While there are some opportunities for further engagement with monastic schools, until the issues of sanctions are resolved it is not considered an area where much can be done effectively unless there is a change in government policy or an overall plan be drawn up to assist this group. Some community schools do also exist in those villages without access to a government-supported primary school and some UN agencies and international NGOs have undertaken some piecemeal work (Asian Development Bank, 2003).

Few students follow on from primary to secondary education and less to vocational education training, or to higher education from Buddhist schools. In terms of Western education standards, reaching the end of Buddhist secondary education in Myanmar equips only a few to enter what can be described as a quality higher education. For those who do graduate from secondary schooling and seek admission to tertiary education overseas, there is a gap of at least one year, even for those with sufficient language competence. Bridging, or foundation studies courses are minimal and many applicants falsify their qualifications with the assistance of local teachers.

Financing Education: the context for international assistance

Public expenditure on education is estimated to have averaged 18.1% of the state budget in November 2008 but only 1.1% of GDP at the beginning of the period (UNESCO, 2008). However, it must be remembered that these are figures given to the Myanmar government to publish and are not audited. Government expenditure goes into training the military and buying new equipment although this is denied by the authorities.

Table I below, issued by UNESCO, gives some comparisons with other countries in the region. It indicates that Myanmar has the lowest level of public expenditure on education as a percentage of GDP. Even these estimates may, however, provide an inflated sense of the extent of expenditure on education.

	Public expenditure on education as per cent of GNP	Public expenditure on education as per cent of total public expenditure
Cambodia	2.1	15.3
Indonesia	1.4	9.8
Lao PDR	2.3	11.6
Malaysia	8.5	20.0
Myanmar	1.3	18.1
Thailand	5.1	28.3
Asia-Pacific developing country average (21 countries)	4.7	16.2

Table I. Estimated public expenditure on education, 1990-2005 (per cent). Source: UNESCO (2008).

Unlike other countries in the region such as Vietnam, Cambodia and Laos, international assistance has been minimal since the early 1990s due to a combination of the government of Myanmar's unwillingness to accept assistance and the sanctions imposed by the international community. In regards to ODA: 'it was estimated to be US$121 million in 2002 which represents a per capita ODA expenditure of approximately US$2.50, the lowest in the region and far below the average for least developed countries' (Save the Children in Myanmar, 2006, **2007?** p. 15).

The Public Education Sector: issues and needs

Sectors in Education in Myanmar

Pre-school education. Less than 10% of the population attend pre-school (Asian Development Bank, 2003, p. 74). Most children who attend are from wealthier families and in the major urban areas such as Mandalay and Yangon. While within the ambit of MOE, most pre-schools are privately funded and are not considered to be a high priority. However, pre-school programmes do offer some opportunities for NGOs and private sector involvement, mainly in the urban areas. Pupils usually commence at age five. UNICEF has provided assistance in relation to the introduction of new textbooks and other teaching materials.

Primary education. There are three years of lower primary schooling with children usually commencing at age six and completing at age nine although this is dependent upon a number of factors such as high repetition rates, and low student retention and completion rates. There are then two years of upper primary. According to the draft report commissioned, but not yet published by the Asian Development Bank in 2003, 63% of children enter first grade (Asian Development Bank, 2003, p. 7). However, the US government estimates that only 40% of the population have access to basic education. Information published by UNESCO estimates that primary school enrolment was 89% in 2002 and 100% in 2005.[7] UNICEF estimates that current enrolment figures are more accurately placed at 83%.[8] Anecdotal evidence from NGOs and embassies working in Myanmar state that teachers are directed to enrol 100% of students at the beginning of each term and then after that many children do not attend school. Primary education, including pre-primary, covers the first five years of schooling and children usually commence their education at age five. Access to schooling at this level is generally patchy due to limited resources, lack of qualified teachers and issues to do with remoteness from urban areas or townships; accordingly children have variable opportunities to attend. Dropout rates are high, maybe up to 50% (Asian Development Bank, 2003, p. ix), even though the government indicates that only 6.9% of children in primary and 6.1% in lower secondary education [9] leave school before the end of fifth grade due to a number of factors, but mainly due to economic pressures from families for their children to assist them in subsistence farming or other economic enterprises (Save the Children in Myanmar, 2006, p. 20).

The language of instruction is the mainstream Myanmar language and there is strong anecdotal evidence that children from ethnic minorities suffer because of lack of language skills. International assistance in this area is not encouraged by the Myanmar government. Despite this, ethnic minority children are not discouraged to use their native tongue, however there are challenges associated with being bilingual or multilingual in an education system which lacks resources. Despite multiple inadequacies the gender balance for this level of education seems reasonable. However, NGOs cannot contribute to the primary schools under existing government policy.

Secondary education. Secondary education commences for four years at lower secondary and two years at upper secondary level Secondary education includes lower secondary level (middle school) consisting of grades 5 to 8 and upper secondary (high school) covering grades 9 and 10 (Asian

Development Bank, 2003, p. 13). Due to the high dropout rates in primary education, those entering secondary level face another huge hurdle to finish secondary school (Asian Development Bank, 2003, p. ix). Economic pressures within families for children to enter the workforce prevent many children from remaining at school. There are higher dropout rates in secondary level than there are in primary level, as a result of greater costs, both real and opportunity, associated with attending school (pp. 34-36). This is primarily because parents are concerned about the low quality of education and because they need their children to provide economic input at home or at work. Again, the primary causes of the failure of the system are: overcrowding, teaching methodology, teacher morale, and ethnic issues. As in primary education, the MOE is very reluctant to allow foreign organisations to contribute to this level. Opportunities do exist for assistance to be provided to private, monastic or community schools if international organisations are willing to be involved.

Grade 11 is assumed to be the equivalent of the English GCE O level examination, however due to a number of factors such as deficient teaching methods and the lack of adequate facilities for science subjects, those who have passed Grade 11 would not be admitted to even foundation courses in the UK, Australia, and the USA, among others. Additional study needs to be undertaken to bring students up to a level that would allow admittance to a tertiary institution overseas. The only exception is perhaps in South-East Asia countries particularly Singapore.

There are some private schools in Myanmar for parents rich enough to be able to pay for international qualifications. However, the numbers are small and students have to study up to Grade 12 with an International Baccalaureate qualification to indicate that their English is at a sufficient level to study at an overseas university teaching in English.

Against this background of what appears to be an organised system, primary and secondary schooling lack adequate facilities such as buildings and equipment and, most of all, teachers are trained to teach an already outdated curriculum. In addition, teachers' wages are miserably low and as a consequence attendance rates are also completely unsatisfactory.

Technical and vocational education. As in other countries in the region, the attraction for students to enter this area is relatively low due to a number of factors including the perception that engaging in a trade is seen to be 'low status', and historically wages in trades or non-professional occupations have been low. However, the employment opportunities for those who wish to gain a trade or vocational qualification or enter employment in the tourism sector are relatively good. Myanmar in the last few years has opened access to tourists wanting to visit the country despite the sanctions enforced by Western governments and donor organisations. Occupancy rates for hotels are increasing and the demand for skilled staff to service the tourist industry is increasing steadily especially for organised tours especially from tourists visiting from neighbouring countries (e.g. China, Taiwan, Thailand). The government plays no role in the training of tourist operators and hotel staff are provided with training by management. Despite the control exercised by the central government, tourists are able to go virtually anywhere in the country with the exception of sensitive border areas in the east and west of the country.

In the traditional trades such as plumbing, building, electrics, mechanics, among others, there are little or no formal training courses and those which are taught are of a poor standard using outdated curricula and inadequate facilities. As a consequence, ongoing maintenance of buildings, water and sanitation facilities and other infrastructure throughout the country remains a serious problem inhibiting development. There are constant electricity blackouts and as such most businesses have back-up electricity generators.

The government is less than proactive when it comes to technical and vocational training and considerable opportunities exist for foreign-quality private-based providers to contribute to improving skills in this area. The use of foreign teachers and/or the introduction of up-to-date curriculum to improve the quality of training in this sector would also provide significant benefits.

Tertiary education. The present government has deliberately neglected the higher education sector. This neglect was reflected in the temporary closure of a number of campuses in major urban areas. The government also suppresses ethnic minorities and democratic groups from action that might split the nation or cause civil disturbance (Bureau of Democracy, Human Rights and Labor, 2006, section G).

It is reported by the Myanmar authorities that there are about 30 universities, and another 35 institutions are listed as colleges operated by the Ministry of Education. Tertiary education is mostly under the control of the MOE and access is free. However, the British Council reports that there are another 92 tertiary or polytechnic (TAFE) schools which are operated by other ministries and the Public Services Selection and Training Board (British Council, 2008). Nominal salaries for tertiary teachers are, on the surface, pitifully low, with university lecturers being paid around US$15.00 per month. It should be noted, however, that most of those working in these institutions receive considerable benefits such as heavily subsidised housing, food, preferred treatment of their families by the government and other fringe benefits, which accounts for why these positions are highly prized. This situation is similar to those who currently work in the higher education or the public sector in Laos, Cambodia and Vietnam, where 'position' and 'status' within society is highly valued. However, moonlighting by academics is common and there is a proliferation of private colleges offering marginally better quality outcomes for students than public institutions, and some diversification of curriculum content.

The most well-known Myanmar tertiary institution, Yangon University, now offers courses in arts, sciences and law exclusively, with an estimated enrolment of 14,500 students (13,500 undergraduate and 1000 postgraduate).[10] Previously, subjects such as medicine, economics and education were offered, but new single-discipline universities have been established under separate ministries to teach in these areas. The Yangon campus has been split into two, one focusing on undergraduate studies and the other on postgraduate studies; this has been done to reduce the possibility of social unrest and the University was closed for periods during the 1990s. There is little concern about the quality of teaching or education outcomes, although academic staff are monitored to ensure that they do not encourage students to become politically active. As in other education levels, inadequate infrastructure, outdated teaching equipment and poorly qualified teachers are major inhibitors and are reflected in other universities and colleges. According to discussions with various foreign teachers, higher education institutions in Myanmar are increasing in numbers but decreasing in quality. Graduates who gain qualifications overseas tend not to return, thus leaving the country poorer. Access by foreigners wishing to visit and meet academics or staff is not encouraged, and meetings have to be made informally and with some reluctance from individuals. Most of the universities are single discipline and it is suggested that one of the reasons for this is that the Myanmar government can maintain more control on students and possible unrest than in multidisciplinary universities.

Currently the main market for international student qualifications is in Yangon with a number of agents representing various English-speaking countries. According to a survey conducted by the British Council 'out of 1285 IELTS candidates from April to December 2007, 37.2 per cent of them were Singapore bound, and 33.2 per cent were Australia and New Zealand bound' (British Council, 2008). It is interesting to note that the Australian government has placed a ban on all students whose rank in the army is above Colonel or equivalent level from obtaining a student visa; this may also apply to the Burmese Civil Service as well.

For students who wish to study abroad, Myanmar is mainly an undergraduate market. Over the past few years, undergraduate studying overseas in Australia has increased its share of the market and it has been reported that 'the number of enquiries for studying in Australia has doubled from those received in 2005/06' (British Council, 2008). Despite the sanction from the US government, institutions from the USA have increased their marketing activities as well using the American Centre to promote education and culture. Ironically, the USA has also built a new category 2 Embassy in Yangon (the second biggest of its kind).

In an interview in 2007 with the chargé d'affaires of the US Embassy in Yangon, it was said that despite the USA not giving any direct aid it does give aid through the United Nations. This position of not providing aid seems in direct contradiction to providing aid to non-democratic countries such as Laos, Vietnam and North Korea! It is almost similar to the US stance on Cuba, although this may change under the new Obama administration. Despite this, the US government continues to offer around seven Fulbright Scholarships to Myanmar students every year.

Below are figures (Table II) illustrating the number of visas to universities approved for Myanmar students by the UK and Australian governments for four years. Unfortunately, it has not been possible to provide figures for the USA.

Year	2005/06	2006/07	2007/08	2008/09
Australia	105	157	224	233
UK	315	295	395	80

Table II. Number of visas approved by the Australian and UK governments for Myanmar international students. Source: Australian and UK government statistics.

Teacher training. This is an area where much needs to be done but as it is under the responsibility of MOE, there is little that foreign organisations can do for the present. At both primary and secondary levels, there is a severe shortage of qualified teachers, resulting from a number of factors including lack of adequate training at teacher colleges and low wages. The system continues to rely on rote learning as the principal method of instruction. Teacher training colleges 'can only accommodate half the candidates required for enrolment expansion and attrition from the existing stock of teachers' (Asian Development Bank, 2003). Poor motivation and high absenteeism among teachers reflect a significant turnover rate which MOE solves by requiring administrative staff to take on teaching responsibilities. The problems are chronic and can only be solved by long-term systemic change.

English language training and other skills development. English language training (ELT) to assist students wishing to study higher education abroad is offered generously by the British Council, which conducts testing for ELT and professional courses. Open access to British Council offices is available in Yangon and Mandalay, and many young Myanmars seek information on overseas study. The American Centre, which is separate physically from the US Embassy in Yangon but funded by the US Department of State, has a comprehensive library and provides good access to education materials and resources for students. There is also a proliferation of lower quality English language schools teaching mainly in Yangon and Mandalay; however there are many quality control issues surrounding these institutions.

English is seen as a vehicle to a better job and a future for young people. Many opportunities exist for foreign organisations to form cooperative agreements with local providers for enhancing ELT although this is dependent upon the payment of fees for English language proficiency examinations training (IELTS AND TOEFL), however parents are either reluctant to pay these fees or do not have the money for the costs of tuition.

What can be termed as 'other skills development' covers courses relating to IT training, professional development courses such accounting, auditing, banking, among others, whether in-country or online. It does not seem to be as seriously affected by restrictive government policy in the formal sector. It is a burgeoning market but operating in a corrupt system.

There are also opportunities for overseas institutions to assist in providing pathways for students who wish to transit from the Myanmar secondary education system and then study overseas. These courses are an intermediate, work-related higher education qualification. They are designed in conjunction with employers to meet skills shortages at the higher technician and associate professional levels. They are offered by universities in partnership with higher education colleges and further education colleges. Flexible study methods make them available to people already in work, unemployed people, or those wanting to embark on a career change. On successful completion, foundation degree graduates can revisit their career options, and may choose to progress to further professional qualifications or to an honours degree.

To date only one organisation, the Yangon Institute of University Studies, a privately funded Myanmar academy, has operated such courses. It had an agreement with three universities in Western Australia which allowed graduates to enter these institutions. The Australian principal resigned due to a disagreement with the management because the standards of teaching and subsequent results from the students did not meet Australian immigration standards for IELTS testing.[11]

Conclusion

It is now time to re-assess the situation for education in Myanmar. Small but significant opportunities exist for overseas universities or philanthropic organisations to engage in distance education, tourism training, IT training and the establishment of foundation courses for students who have completed their secondary education. Linking with the work of the British Council or other reputable organisations in Myanmar could provide other pathways of support. If this proves successful, then possibly the United Nations agencies, the ADB and the World Bank might be encouraged to re-engage in providing limited technical assistance. Finally, indications from the European Commission imply that this organisation and its partner countries suggest that they are prepared, albeit in a measured and small way, to provide assistance over the next few years. These kinds of developments will need to be cautiously and carefully implemented, but it seems that the Myanmar government might not necessarily oppose such gentle approaches to reform. It is worth quoting from a recent book by Thant Myint-U, grandson of the former United Nations Secretary General:

So, what of the future? There are no easy options, no quick fixes, no grand strategies that will create democracy in [Myanmar]/Burma overnight or even over several years. If [Myanmar]/Burma was less isolated, if there was more trade, more engagement – more tourism in particular – and if this was coupled with a desire by the government for greater economic reform, a rebuilding of state institutions, and a slow opening of space for civil society, then the condition for political change would occur over a decade or two ... There is a second approach and much worse scenario that [Myanmar's]/Burma's international isolation will only deepen through an unholy alliance between those who favor sanctions and insider hardliners who advocate a retreat from the global community, that this isolation will further undermine institutions of Government, that a new generation will grow up less educated and in worse health. (Thant, 2006, p. 348)

One concludes that the first scenario is the only one pursuing; especially if the international community really cares about improving the education and health of the people of Myanmar. The present UN position is only hurting the youths in the country; certainly the present government cares little about world politics as long as it receives assistance from China, India, Singapore, Thailand and Russia. Despite this gloomy conclusion, the USA, the World Bank and the ADB might wake up and find that cooperation is better than confrontation. Otherwise, China India and Russia will make sweet pickings for the vast natural resources of Myanmar and the population will never regain its prominence as an educated, cultured and progressive nation.

Notes

[1] *CIA World Fact Book: August 2007* estimates it to be lower than this at around 47.3 million.

[2] *CIA World Fact Book: August 2007.*

[3] Based upon the Dakar Framework for Action: Myanmar. The Six Goals of Education for All (EFA), as agreed at the World Education Forum in Dakar, Senegal, are: (i) expand early childhood care and education, (ii) provide free and compulsory education of good quality by 2015, (iii) promote the acquisition of life-skills by adolescents and youth, (iv) expand adult literacy by 50% by 2015, (v) eliminate gender disparities by 2005 and achieve gender equality in education by 2015, and (vi) enhance educational quality (Union of Myanmar, Ministry of Education, October 2008).

[4] Ministry of Myanmar Education website, April 2008.

[5] *Myanmar Times*, December 2007.

[6] *Myanmar Times*, December 2007.

[7] UNESCO Institute for Statistics, 21 August 2007. It must be remembered that these figures are provided by the Burmese government and are obviously inaccurate.

[8] Meeting with UNICEF, Rangoon, 21 August 2007.

[9] Myanmar; Government's EFA Mid-assessment Review 2004-05 (Union of Myanmar, Ministry of Education, October 2008).

[10] Wikipedia, 29 October 2009.

[11] Australian Department of Immigration and Citizenship: Overseas Student Program: assessment levels. Form 1219i.

References

Asian Development Bank (2003) Myanmar: education sector review: draft report. Manila.

BBC News (2006) Country Profile: Burma.

British Council (2008) Burma Market Introduction. http://www.britishcouncil.org/eumd-information-background-burma.htm

Bureau of Democracy, Human Rights and Labor (2006) *Country Reports on Human Rights Practices: 2005 (Burma)*. Washington: US Government.

European Commission (n.d.) The EC Burma Strategy paper 2007-2013. http://www.eeas.europa.eu/myanmar/csp/07_13_en.pdf

Martin, R. (2007) The Dilemma of Higher Education in Burma, *International Education*, 47(Spring), 19-22.

Save the Children in Myanmar (2006) *Situation Analysis of Children in Myanmar.* (Unpublished)

Thant, Myint-U. (2006) *The River of Lost Footsteps.* New York: Farrar, Straus and Giroux.

UNESCO (2008) *Education at a Glance: Myanmar.* Paris: UNESCO.

Union of Myanmar (2007) *EFA. Mid-decade Assessment Report.* Yangon: Union of Myanmar.

CHAPTER 8

Philippines: education for development?[1]

LORRAINE PE SYMACO

SUMMARY Similar to other countries, especially developing ones, education in the Philippines is seen by policy makers as a way to equip its human resource with the necessary skills needed for the knowledge society. However, issues arising from 'massification', or access over quality, often undermine the relative 'returns' supposedly of such expansion in education. This chapter deals with the education system of the Philippines, some basic statistics and issues relevant to the system, specifically the higher education sector.

Introduction

Confronted by the contemporary trends in global socio-economic, cultural and political conditions, the Philippines has situated education as an essential component in its development plans. Higher education, specifically, is considered a critical factor in facing the challenges of the new millennium and government discourse encircles the need to promote the idea of the connection and significance of knowledge, attitudes and skills, supposedly imparted by higher education to the world of work and the economy in general. Higher education is seen as a 'key player in the educational and integral formation of professionally competent, service-oriented, principled and productive citizens' (Commission on Higher Education [CHED], 2001, p. 7). Its three-fold purpose of (i) teaching, (ii) research and (iii) extension services (CHED, 2001) is seen as being instrumental in the enhancement of the socio-economic development of the country. The Philippines has a large number of higher education institutions (HEIs) that cater to providing this triple function. Its higher education system is characterised mainly by private institutions, while the state university colleges (SUCs) of the public sector serve as alternative options to those wishing to obtain a tertiary-level degree at lower cost. At present, there are 1484 private higher education institutions in the Philippines and 522 public higher education institutions, of which 35% are SUCs (CHED, 2008). The weighty importance given by Filipinos to education is seen not only in the above numbers, but also in the number of schools in primary (44,691) and secondary (10,006) education (Department of Education of the Philippines [DepEd], 2010). As in other developing countries, in the Philippines education is seen as a 'solution' to rise above poverty. However, numerous issues continue to face the educational system of the country such as lack of quality and efficiency particularly in government schools at all levels; lack of teacher supply especially in the basic and secondary levels – thus resulting in multi-grade systems (where one teacher will handle and combine one, two or three class levels in one classroom) especially prominent at the basic level; access and equity issues relative to ethnic and minority religious groups, in particular Muslims; and corruption because of weak government controls and an inefficient bureaucracy.

The following sections will highlight the educational system of the Philippines, along with some of the issues facing it. Given the significant role of higher education in producing human resources to respond to the challenges of the 'knowledge society', a considerable part of this chapter focuses on the higher education sector of the country.

National Context

The Philippines, which experienced more than 300 years of colonial rule under the Spanish and Americans, manifests its diverse colonial background in its educational, religious and political institutions. The majority of its population (over 94 million, as projected for 2010) are Christian, making it one of the two Christian-majority nations in South-East Asia, along with Timor-Leste. The Philippines under Spanish rule was mostly converted to Christianity (Spanish education at that time was Church influenced), except for the crucial failure to win over (from Islam) some parts of Mindanao, the southern part of the country. It was not until the arrival of the USA at the turn of the twentieth century that Mindanao was brought under central control, although religious and cultural conflicts persisted to a large extent (Campo & Judd, 2005). The dichotomisation caused by the Muslim and non-Muslim divide in terms of educational and economic mobility, among others, will be discussed further in this chapter.

The current educational system of the country is distinctly influenced by the American system. The Philippines uses English as the medium of instruction in educational institutions, though there are some cases of the use of local dialect/s among indigenous people in certain institutions, primarily at the primary/secondary level. There is scant evidence however on the number of indigenous students exclusively learning, or schools exclusively teaching, in the local dialect, since indigenous students are usually integrated in mainstream schools.

There are three government agencies on education and training in the Philippines. The Department of Education (DepEd) caters to basic education, the Commission on Higher Education (CHED) to higher education, and the Technical Education and Skills Development Authority (TESDA) to vocational and technical education.

Basic Education Statistics

Primary education (also known as elementary level) is defined as the level that has as students those of 6-11 years; secondary level (also known as high school) has as students those of 12-15 years. Education in the Philippines consists of six years at primary level (some private schools require seven years) and four years at secondary level. The total then is one of the least number of years worldwide spent in basic education before entrance to university (average age 16 years).

Primary-level education had a total enrolment of 13.6 million for the academic year 2008-09, with net enrolment at 85.12%. Secondary level on the other hand had a total enrolment of 6.7 million for the same academic year, with net enrolment at 60.74% (DepEd, 2010). Given the number of students enrolled in the primary and secondary levels, the total teacher workforce for the former was 405,588 and for the latter 193,224 (DepEd, 2010). In the Philippines, wastage at the primary and secondary levels is also experienced similar to that in other developing countries, where children, especially girls, are forced to drop out of school to help the family (Brock & Cammish, 1997). For the primary level, the school-leaver rate was 6.02%, and at secondary level it was 7.45% for the years 2008-09 (DepEd, 2010).

The Department of Education was reorganised in 2001 in a reformation of the then Department of Education, Culture and Sports. The functional role of the institution was divided into two main structural parts: (a) the Central Office, which oversees the organisation of basic education (primary and secondary) at the national level; and (b) the Field Offices composed of regional and local agencies that ensure the implementation of the mandate of the Department (DepEd, 2010).

Higher Education as between the Public and Private Sectors

The USA introduced state education in the Philippines in the early twentieth century. This was done in order to bring about a 'thorough socio-cultural, economic and political reorientation of a society' which was at the time shaped by the long colonial rule of the Spaniards (Sanyal et al, 1981, p. 34). When the country gained independence from the USA in 1946, there was only one state university, the University of the Philippines. The system of public higher education has since expanded greatly, and now there are 522 public higher education institutions, of which 35% are state universities/colleges and local universities/colleges (CHED, 2008). The state colleges and universities are governed by a charter enacted by the legislative branch of the government, which guarantees autonomy as regards curricular and academic standards, the appointment and payment of faculty members, and the determination of the institution's priorities (Sanyal et al, 1981).

Private education, on the other hand, consists of three types as to ownership and management: (a) stock corporations, which are non-sectarian; (b) non-stock corporations, which are sectarian; and (c) foundations. At the outbreak of the Second World War in the Philippines in 1941, there were 106 HEIs (Sanyal et al, 1981). The current total is 2006, of which 1484 are private institutions (CHED, 2008). There is widespread recognition of the massive role played by private HEIs in the expansion and heightened importance of tertiary education (CHED Memorandum Order 32, 2001). The CHED is circumspect regarding the involvement of these institutions as regards quality education, research capacity and extension work, but given the number of private HEIs, the regulation of the sector is a difficult mission. The Commission, therefore, relies greatly on the principle of self-management, practically granting autonomy to HEIs that have proven to the public, the government, and even the international community their public responsibility and the quality of the education they provide. An average annual rate of growth of 3.14% was recorded in the number of private HEIs during the six-year period between 1995 and 2000 (CHED, 2004). Figure 1 provides an illustration of the Philippine higher education system (TESDA, 2006).

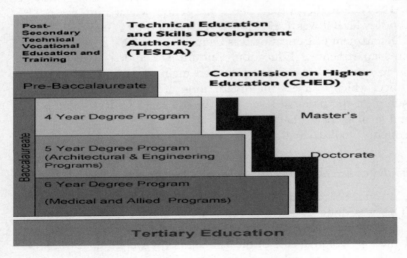

Figure 1. Higher education system in the Philippines.

The Geography of Social Exclusion in the Philippines

The Philippines is an archipelago of 7100 islands in South-East Asia. It has an estimated land mass of about 300,000 square kilometres, and three main island groups represent the country: Luzon in the north, Visayas in the centre, and Mindanao in the south. The dominant urban centre, the National Capital Region where Metro Manila is located, is in Luzon, where (as of 2007) 13% of the 88.57 million Filipinos live (Monsod et al, 2004; National Statistics Office [NSO], 2010).

Studies on social exclusion (Byrne, 1995; Warrington, 2005) draw attention to the failure of socially excluded individuals to access vital social services such as education. Despite educational policies set down with a view to creating equal access and, more often than not, a prerogative to choose the education institution that one wishes to enter, the country's geographical and topographical features could frustrate the attainment of these aims. Geography therefore plays an important role in access to education. Pacione states that:

> A fundamental deficiency of the market model of education is that it is geographically naive and therefore socially regressive. It does not and cannot address adequately the difficulties of those people and places disadvantaged by the operation of the market.
> (Pacione, 1997, p. 172)

The topographical variation of the country has posed major challenges in the provision of the necessary infrastructure (Monsod et al, 2004), leading to problems of access to proper educational facilities at all levels to people who are geographically isolated. Lack of teachers in the country, more so in remote areas, gives rise to problems in instruction quality, in particular where multi-grade systems exist. This also creates the issue of non-specialist teaching in schools.

This brings to fore the issue of the proposed expansion of basic education in the country. Criticism of the country's 'short' number of years (i.e. 10 years) in basic education has given rise to calls for an additional two years, with the rationale that the Philippines is falling behind most countries globally in terms of quantitative amount of time spent in basic education. Notwithstanding the serious impediments such an expansion would bring to the current system, proponents of this education expansion seem to forget that the country's education system presently faces insurmountable problems as aforementioned, not to mention the increase in budget this expansion would require, given the already restricted resources that the Philippines' basic education system has to deal with. The failure of the government to attune to the needs of the basic education system of the country also makes it difficult to achieve the country's Education for All (EFA) 2015 goal (Rodriguez, 2008).

Additional two years will only aggravate problems like lack of
buildings, teachers, textbooks, etc. First things first, we must
prioritise our educational problems. (School principal)
Their [government advocates of expansion] children do not study
in public schools. I suggest for them to go to the field so they will
see the real scenario. (School principal)

Given the proposed projects of the newly installed government (which started
in June 2010) such as adopting a 12-year formal education cycle among other
things, a conservative estimate of 5% of Gross Domestic Product is foreseen
to be required for education (Diokno, 2010). Considering the unstable
financial position and the weak economy of the country, resource allocation
and spending should be prioritised to already existing problems.

Issues in Philippines EFA

The goal of universal access to primary education and the Millennium
Development Goals of the United Nations-sponsored Dakar Accord have
focused on the increasing need to address the issue of access and equity in
education, especially at primary and basic levels. This has in turn led to a rise
in the number of secondary-level enrolments, and a significant increase in
enrolment rates for higher education is likely. In response to the Dakar
Accord, the Philippines in 2006 drafted a country Education for All 2015
national action plan, of which the central goal is to generate functional
literacy and to '[provide] all Filipinos with basic learning needs' (NEDA,
2006, p. 1). The Functional Literacy Education and Mass Media Survey
(FLEMMS) reports in 2008 that out of the 67 million Filipinos who are
between 10 to 64 years of age, nine million are functionally literate (National
Statistics Office, 2010). But, despite this, it is said that

Having non-readers is one of main problem in our schools.
Sometimes we get non-readers in high school because they have
bad training in elementary. (School principal)

Despite the 'no-read no-pass' policy of the Department of Education, some
schools do accept non-readers and make possible the advancement of non-
reader students from one level to the next. The overall dismal performance of
students has also elicited the creation and implementation of the 2010
Secondary Education Curriculum, which focuses on the principle of
'teaching and learning from doing and understanding' (Bureau of Secondary
Education, 2010).

But aside from the issue of non-readers, an equally pressing problem is
the existence of malnutrition in some schools. Malnutrition among students
is not restricted to remote areas; certain schools in cities face the same
predicament. Feeding programmes by the government are arranged, aside
from school initiatives, to address the problem.

This is one of the main problems in our schools. Pupils attend class without eating ... we are coordinating with the government and other stakeholders to solve this problem. (School principal)

It should be noted that the FLEMMS 2008, as discussed earlier, reports that the Autonomous Region of Muslim Mindanao (ARMM) has the lowest literacy rate in the country. This brings about issues of access and equity among Filipino Muslims as discussed in the following section.

The Madrasah System in the Philippines

Filipino Muslims are a minority in the Philippines, representing only 5% of over 76 million Filipinos, according to the 2000 national census. The International Religious Freedom Report of 2003 notes that some scholars refute the official figure given and suggest it is grossly understated, since the conflict in Mindanao Island prevented census takers from calculating and mapping the true total population of Muslims (Bureau of Democracy, Human Rights and Labour Affairs, 2003). These scholars estimate that Muslims constitute around 8 to 12% of the total population. The majority of the Muslim communities in the Philippines are found in Mindanao, the second largest island and home to the greatest diversity of ethnic groups in the country, including 13 Islamised ethno-linguistic groups. Five provinces with a Muslim majority have been identified, all in Mindanao.

The Madrasah system of privately administered Islamic schools has existed in the Philippines since Islam was introduced to the country by Muslim traders and missionaries in the late thirteenth century. Over the next 200 years, Islam became part of the cultural identity of the peoples of the Philippines. The dichotomisation of educational policy in the Philippines began when Spain colonised the country and tried to suppress Islam and introduce Christianity as the dominant religion. This aggressive stance by the Spanish was followed by a series of armed conflicts in the country, especially involving Muslims (Majul, 1999).

According to Milligan (2004), in the 1970s there were 1000 Madaris (plural form of Madrasah) operating in western Mindanao, and most of their curricula were modelled on those in the Middle East, from where they obtained financial support to supplement the tuition fees that the Madaris exacted from their students. Whether the number of Madaris continued to grow slowly or declined over the following years cannot yet be confirmed because of limited data, which is hardly surprising given that the Madrasah system had not been recognised. However, the Arabic Language and Islamic Values Education programme introduced by the government has been pilot tested and conducted in selected schools with migrant Muslims.

The first university in Mindanao was established in 1962 to provide higher education to Muslims (Stark, 2003). Nowadays, there are 68 higher education institutions in ARMM, with a total of 40,897 students enrolled. This accounts for only 1.7% of total higher education enrolment in the country in 2004 (CHED, 2008). There are no data, however, which indicate the percentage of Muslims actually enrolled in the higher education institutions found in ARMM. Despite the number of HEIs in the region, the non-recognition of the Madrasah system (primary and secondary) by the government has relegated it to the status of an unregulated community/private enterprise, and this has led to the failure of a significant number of Muslim youths to gain access to recognised HEIs. Precisely for this reason, it is unequivocally claimed that pupils in Madaris are greatly disadvantaged compared with those who undergo formal education (Arquiza, 2006). This has also in effect hampered the formation of human capital among the Filipino Muslim populace, and hindered their ability to participate in the labour market and broaden their individual capabilities and opportunities.

Higher Education in the Philippines

Higher education access is continually expanding in the Philippines, as evidenced by the massive increase in enrolment in this sector between 1994 and 2002. The substantial population in higher education in the Philippines is in fact comparable with that of many developed countries (Nebres, 2001), and enrolment for the academic year 2004-05 was estimated as 2.4 million (CHED, 2007). The increase in the perceived importance of higher education is shown by the formation of the Philippines Commission on Educational Reform in 1998. The Commission highlighted the need to: (a) optimise scarce resources and allocate them efficiently, (b) improve the quality of higher education, (c) construct a strong faculty development programme, and (d) develop an effective system of accreditation (Nebres, 2001). All these point to the efforts of the government to improve the higher education sub-sector in order to train the labour force needed to respond to the increasing demand for a higher quality workforce worldwide in the twenty-first century. Further recognition in the country of the importance of higher education led to the formation of the Commission on Higher Education in 1994, and the Medium-term Development Plan for Higher Education (CHED, 2007) also stresses the importance of higher education in achieving the country's national development plans, which are supported by the contribution of the tertiary sector in terms of manpower development, research, and other services.

Enrolment Trends

The enrolment share of the private higher education sector has been consistently greater than that of the public sector. In 1998-99, 71.2% of total enrolment was in the private sector, and only 28.8% in the public sector. The trend continued until 2004-05, though at a slower rate, with about 66% enrolled in the private sector and 34% in public institutions (CHED, 2007).

Higher education enrolment increased at an average annual rate of 4.07% in the eight academic years from 1994-95 to 2001-02, with a slight decline in the average annual rate of 0.9% in the academic years 2001-02 to 2003-04.

Since the founding of the Commission in 1994, numerous improvements have been made in higher education in the Philippines. For instance, access to higher education has improved significantly from the 1990s to the present, as evidenced by: (a) higher enrolment levels, (b) the proliferation of HEIs in the country, (c) the strengthening of student attendance, and (d) higher participation rates (Edralin, 2001; CHED, 2008). With the objective of attaining acceptable international standards, attempts have been made to improve the quality of university education. Notwithstanding the increase in access, issues of quality and equity continue to persist, the latter especially prominent, as aforementioned, among Filipino Muslims and the poorer members of society. In order to address quality and relevance issues, the formation of Centres of Excellence and Centres of Development, the encouragement of accreditation programmes, and the use of international benchmarking have been among the initiatives developed.

Mass Expansion of Higher Education in the Philippines:
state university colleges, 'diploma mills' and corruption

In the context of the massive demand for higher education, the proliferation in the Philippines of state university colleges and second-rate private institutions has contributed to the creation of 'diploma mills' in the country. Despite their claim to improve access to education for students who cannot afford the higher costs of a good number of private HEIs, most of the SUCs, along with some private institutions, are seen as providing education of average quality at best. The impression of overinvestment in higher education is corroborated by the burgeoning number of such institutions found in the country.

> My impression is we have overinvested you know in higher
> education. The Philippines is kind of an outlier; we have too many
> graduates ... we have provided too much education with very little
> growth ... it's also very cruel because you build an expectation.
> They can find a job just because they have a degree that's not
> always true. Their education is substandard. (University
> professor)

> The government does not control. In fact the government has
> been putting up universities left and right and they are all very
> poor quality. (University president)

The problems highlighted by 'diploma mills' or 'fly-by-night' schools in the Philippines have attracted a great deal of attention to its quality of education. 'Diploma mill' schools are institutions that award degrees to graduates who are seen as unworthy of such degrees and unfit to practise their professions. Mirone (1999) mentioned the negative view of physiotherapy programmes in the Philippines, brought about by certain courses that continue to produce second-rate or unqualified physiotherapists. The significance in the Philippines of acquiring a degree, generally regardless of whether it is awarded by a reputable university or not, is based on the fact that culturally a degree is considered a 'necessity' to attain success. For the Filipino, a university degree certificate is a representation of the hope to finally 'rise above poverty, especially for poorer households. The false expectations that are created by such 'diploma mill' institutions are debatable, with some arguing that it is cruel to build up false expectations, while others claim that false hope is better than no hope at all.

> Because people are going there because they need hope ... but
> better than no hope. (Business executive of a local company)

In addition to the controversies over the mediocre education provided by some SUCs, there has also been criticism of the misappropriation of funds in terms of the investment made to build and sustain such establishments, and different groups of stakeholders have called for better allocation of government funding and the primacy of quality over quantity. There are political reasons for the failure to control the rise in the number of SUCs; to oppose a politician's effort to create a state university college will elicit political 'tension'. There is also widespread corruption in budget allocation.

> If you can only see how these congressmen operate. When I was
> not yet part of the Commission, I always thought that there is
> hope for the Philippines. But when I got in, I told myself, only a
> miracle will help us. It's better to abolish the senate and congress.
> It's not the Commission that is hopeless but the politicians.
> (Government official)

The Philippines ranks 139 out of 180 countries in the 2009 Corruption Perceptions Index, only ranking higher than Myanmar, Cambodia, Timor-Leste and Laos in the South-East Asian region (Transparency International, 2009). Given this, it is not surprising that corruption in the education sector is prevalent in the Philippines. The Commission on Audit recently described the Commission on Higher Education's call centre laboratories project as anomalous, highly irregular and overpriced by 150 million Philippine Pesos (PHP) (Esplananda, 2007, 2008), and misuse of funds and charges of graft against CHED officials has also been documented (Crisostomo, 1998; Gallano, 2001). Apart from the CHED, the director of the TESDA was charged in 1998 with irregular transactions amounting to 9.2 million PHP for the printing of textbooks (Cabacungan et al, 2008), with the government eventually dismissing the case against the agency's director, who happened to be a strong ally of the country's president at that time. In addition to the corruption uncovered in government education agencies in the Philippines, many similar cases have also been revealed among higher education institutions, including bogus lists of teaching members and the setting-up of educational institutions despite lack of credit, because of important connections in the government.

> A university tried to put up a nursing school and listed names of teaching staff of another university as part of their team. It was later found out and the application for the nursing programme was rejected but no case was filed. (University president)

In view of the widespread corruption in the Philippines, the government acknowledges how such wastage can affect access to services, especially for the underprivileged, and how such a culture of corruption creates a vicious circle of low standards and underdevelopment. Initiatives to fight corruption and to enhance transparency and accountability have been set up, and the effectiveness of sanctions against graft and corruption is monitored. A memorandum of understanding, signed in 2003, created the 'lifestyle check coalition', bringing together experts and resources from government agencies, civil society groups and non-governmental organisations in order to identify and gather information about politicians suspected of unusual standards of living which might potentially be attributable to activities involving corruption (NEDA, 2006). The first anti-corruption institution in Asia was established in the Philippines in 2008, and the government insists that this is a 'marker' that the country is 'monitoring' corruption, since international standards have to be met before the setting-up of such an institution in the country (Kwok, 2008).

Responding to Market Needs?

Despite assertions by the Philippine government that the higher education sector is being made more responsive to the needs of the country, problems remain such as mismatching and the educated unemployed. In the Philippines, the lack of job opportunities makes the country vulnerable to the adoption of educational programmes which are deemed popular in the short term and which open doors to overseas employment. As an illustration of this, the increase in the number of nursing institutions may be cited. There has also been a significant decline in the number of students enrolling for medical degrees, and a parallel phenomenon has been the emergence of qualified medical doctors who shift careers and train as nurses in order to work overseas. Impelled by the significant monetary benefits earned by professional nurses abroad, the exodus of Philippine doctors is an alarming issue for the country's health system. The loss of skilled human resources and of educational investment are a cause of legitimate dismay in the Philippines, and there are also costs in terms of the investment in physical infrastructure to accommodate more nursing schools – investment that may be more economically productive for the country if the funding goes to other ventures.

> It's really a shame because to be a doctor requires so much investment, by the parents, by the people themselves, and therefore by the country. (Government official)
> Even computer schools are offering nursing courses. There's a massage parlour that has been turned into a nursing school. A massage parlour turned into a nursing school! The proliferation is caused because the government allows it to happen. (University president)

The large number of nursing students currently enrolled in tertiary institutions may also pose a problem of over-supply for the nursing profession in the future, as occurred during the 1980s with the rise in popularity of the physiotherapy programme. That development and its aftermath may be precursor of the pattern we are now seeing in nursing. The failure of industry and institutions to absorb local graduates of various specialisations is not only manifested in the burden of unemployment but also in the large-scale international migration of skilled Filipinos and the preference of others to perform tasks significantly below the educational status they have achieved. The 'push' and 'pull' theory of migration as discussed by Kline (2003) explains that the impetus of both these forces must act in tandem for labour migration to occur, the 'push' factors central in donor countries and the 'pull' factors in the receiving nations. Nursing migration, as Kingma explains (2001), results from educational, economic and social 'push' and 'pull' factors. The case of nurses leaving their home countries in search of professional advancement, where they deem a receiving country as having more and better resources and opportunities for their training, builds up educational 'pull' factors, and much higher overseas wages and much better working conditions compared with what their home country offers them make up both economic and social 'pull' and 'push' factors. In the Philippines, the adverse employment situation and the economic and political factors related to an aggressive labour export policy clearly illustrate 'push' factors in employment migration (Hawthorne, 2001). The idea of exporting its skilled people in general leads the government to view economic development through overseas employment as an avenue for growth. The remittances brought back to the country by skilled and unskilled Filipino overseas workers serve as a dynamic source of import income on which the country has become highly dependent. These remittances totalled US$14.4 billion and 1.1 million Filipino workers were employed overseas in 2007 alone (National Statistics Office, 2008).

The tendency to rely on labour export is vividly portrayed in the 'Ladderised Programme', which is envisioned to propel Philippine economic development through investment in exported manpower of the country. This is predicted to optimise incomes, hence remittances, of low and unskilled labour through the adaptable 'upgrading' transfer of skills; for instance, a household helper can train and 'qualify' to be a quasi-caregiver through minimal training, thereby ensuring better wage benefits for the worker. This is parallel to the 'Super Maid' project by the government, which envisages that household helpers can 'upgrade' their skills through further skills training. Despite the contention of the government that these programmes will save the country's economy especially during global financial uncertainties (with the assumption that layoffs will be minimal), the dependence of the government on its human resource exports (specifically the unskilled labour sector) shows the concept of further sliding its unskilled human resource trade to the level of exploitation. It is not only economically unsound in the long run but also results in long-term dislocations in the Filipino family and in Filipino society in general.

But despite the mass departure of more qualified and experienced nurses for overseas employment as aforementioned, the recruitment industry for nurses in the Philippines laments the lack of training of current nursing graduates in the country and the insufficiency of more 'qualified' nurses that companies from overseas are willing to employ (Uy, 2008). Nursing graduates who cannot penetrate the global scene are inclined to work in call centre institutions instead. Licensed nurses are now opting to find jobs in call centre companies, attracted by higher pay compared with what is offered by government-run or privately owned hospitals (Jaymalin, 2008).

The popularity of call centres in the Philippines is another phenomenon which merits attention. Call centre careers are becoming such a common option for employment for new university graduates that the Commission on Higher Education recently launched a campaign to build up call centre laboratories in the Philippines. In a country with an 8% unemployment rate and a market that fails to offer commensurate value to the competence achieved by college graduates, those graduates who resolve to settle in the country, either because of failure to gain overseas employment, or for personal reasons, are drawn to the economic possibilities offered by call centres. It is not surprising, for instance, that a university graduate in molecular biology should work in a call centre, drawn there by the higher pay and frustrated by the lack of prospects of finding employment in his/her field of specialisation. Call centre institutions are also considered by some as jobs 'for the time being', while they wait for better opportunities in the future. Although some argue that English language proficiency has declined significantly in the country, the relatively good command of English of Filipino university graduates, compared with the English of their counterparts from other countries in the region, and the low-priced labour market, attract foreign investors to set up their call hubs in the Philippines.

> We also have a problem in terms of English. English proficiency
> has declined considerably. In 1986 when Cory Aquino came to
> power, they insisted on using Filipino as a medium of instruction
> for nationalistic purposes which is stupid. I say it's stupid because
> English is the single most competitive edge we have compared to
> our neighbours. (Business executive of a multinational company)

Closing Remarks

This chapter highlighted the education system of the Philippines and some of the issues currently faced by the system. Despite the obvious setbacks that the system faces as discussed, government initiatives to put a premium on its education sector have always been a main item at the forefront of most of its development plans. However, despite this, there is apparent lack of focus and orientation to make the country's education system effective. It is manifest that the education system of the country lacks a competitive edge (in terms of government spending, among others) compared with most of its developing/developed neighbours in the region. The sincere desire of the average Filipino to attain a better life through means of attaining a university degree should be a compelling motive for the government to seek the most effective and practical ways to improve the national education system, public and private. This is but to recognise that a great good fortune has been bestowed on the government by the Filipino people's deep and persistent conviction that 'education is the key to a better future'.

Note

[1] Parts of this chapter result from the author's doctoral research, and a published article on the Madrasah in the Philippines. Details can be found in the References list.

References

Arquiza, M. (2006) Philippine Ethnic and Muslim Minorities: educating children the traditional way, *Mountain Research and Development*, 26(1), 24-27.

Brock, C. & Cammish, N. (1997) *Factors Affecting Female Participation in Education in Seven Developing Countries*, 2nd edn. London: Department for International Development.

Bureau of Democracy, Human Rights and Labour Affairs, US Department of State (DRL) (2003) The International Religious Freedom Report 2003. http://www.state.gove/g/drl/rls/irf/2003/24813.htm (accessed 15 July 2009).

Bureau of Secondary Education (2010) Policy Guidelines on the Implementation of the 2010 Secondary Education Curriculum (SEC). http://bse.portal.ph/ (accessed 30 September 2010).

Byrne, D. (1995) Deindustrialisation and Dispossession: an examination of social division in the industrial city, *Sociology*, 29(1), 95-115.

Cabacungan, G., Ortiz, M. & Sinay, D. (2008) Arroyo Dared to Prosecute TESDA Chief for Corruption, *Philippine Daily Inquirer*, 10 January.

Campo, S. & Judd, M. (2005) The Mindanao Conflict in the Philippines: roots, costs, and potential peace dividend. http://www.worldbank.org/conflict (accessed 11 October 2008).

Commission on Higher Education (CHED) (2001) *Long-term Higher Education Development Plan.* Pasig City: CHED.

Commission on Higher Education (CHED) (2004) Paper presented at the International Conference on Access to Higher Education, Manila, Philippines, 23-24 March 2004.

Commission on Higher Education (CHED) (2007) *Medium-term Development Plan for Higher Education 2005-2010.* Pasig City: CHED.

Commission on Higher Education (CHED) (2008) Recognized Higher Education Institutions. http://www.ched.gov.ph/.

Commission on Higher Education (CHED) Memorandum Order 32 (2001) Pasig: CHED.

Crisostomo, S. (1998) COA Uncovers P700-M CHED Funds Misuse, *Philippine Star*, 7 September.

Department of Education of the Philippines (2010) Basic Education Statistics. http://www.deped.gov.ph/factsandfigures/default.asp (accessed 9 September 2010).

Diokno, B. (2010) Evaluating the Philippine Primary Education System, *The International Journal of Educational and Psychological Assessment*, 5(2), 255-264.

Edralin, D. (2001) *An In-depth Study of the College/University Industry Linkages in the Philippines.* Pasig City: CHED.

Esplananda, J. (2007) CHED Project Overpriced by P150M, *Philippine Daily Inquirer*, 19 October.

Esplananda, J. (2008) COA Finds CHED Project Anomalous, *Philippine Daily Inquirer*, 12 February.

Gallano, R. (2001) CHED Exec in P1.22-M Graft Charges, *Manila Times*, 31 January.

Hawthorne, L. (2001) The Globalisation of the Nursing Workforce: barriers confronting overseas qualified nurses in Australia, *Nursing Inquiry*, 8(4), 213-229.

Jaymalin, M. (2008) Nurses Now Opting to Work in RP Call Centres as Medical Transcriptionists, *Philippine Star*, 2 September. http://www.philstar.com/index.php?Headlines&p=49&type=2&sec=24&aid=200 80901180 (accessed 2 September 2008).

Kingma, M. (2001) Nursing Migration: global treasure hunt or disaster-in-the-making, *Nursing Inquiry*, 8(4), 205-212.

Kline, D. (2003) Push and Pull Factors in International Nurse Migration, *Journal of Nursing Scholarship*, 35(2), 107-111.

Kwok, A. (2008) First Anti-corruption Centre to be Built in RP, *Inquirer.net*, 27 August. http://newsinfo.inquirer.net/breakingnews/nation/view/20080827-157083/UPDA TE-First-anti-corruption-center-to-be-built-in-RP (accessed 27 August 2008).

Majul, C. (1999) *Muslims in the Philippines.* Quezon City: University of the Philippines Press.

Milligan, J. (2004) Islamization or Secularization? Educational Reform and the Search for Peace in Southern Philippines, *Current Issues in Comparative Education*, 7(1), 30-34.

Mirone, J. (1999) Transnational Factors Influencing the Establishment of Educational Standards for Professional Licensure, *Higher Education in Europe*, 24(2), 213-218.

Monsod, S., Monsod, T. & Ducanes, G. (2004) Philippines' Progress Towards the Millennium Development Goals: geographical and political correlates of subnational outcomes, *Journal of Human Development*, 5(1), 121-149.

National Statistics Office (2008) Census Data. http://www.census.gov.ph/data/quickstat/index.html.

National Statistics Office (2010) Almost Nine out of Ten Filipinos are Functionally Literate. http://www.census.gov.ph/data/pressrelease/2010/pr10142tx.html (accessed 9 September 2010).

Nebres, B. (2001) The Philippines: current trends. http://www.bc.edu/bc_org/avp/soe/cihe/newsletter/News24/text009.htm.

National Economic Development Authority (NEDA) (2006) *Medium-term Philippine development plan.* Pasig City: NEDA.

National Statistics Office (NESO) (2010) National Census of Population. http://www.census.gov.ph/ (accessed 29 September 2010).

Pacione, M. (1997) The Geography of Educational Disadvantage in Glasgow, *Applied Geography*, 17(3), 169-192.

Rodriguez, R. (2008) Hard-pressed to Achieve the EFA Goals by 2015 in the Philippines, *Prospects*, 38(3), 393-399.

Sanyal, B.C., Perfecto, W.S. & Arcelo, A.A. (1981) *Higher Education and Labour Market in the Philippines.* New Delhi: Wiley Eastern.

Stark, J. (2003) Muslims in the Philippines, *Journal of Muslim Minority Affairs*, 23(1), 195-209.

Symaco, L.P. (2009) Higher Education and Development in the Philippines and Malaysia: an analysis of the perceptions of the main stakeholders in government, education and business. DPhil thesis, University of Oxford.

Symaco, L.P. & Baunto, A. (2010) Islamic Education in the Philippines with Reference to Issues of Access and Mobility, *The International Journal of Educational and Psychological Assessment*, 5(2), 223-236.

TESDA (Technical Education and Skills Development Authority) (2006) *The Philippine Technical Vocational Education and Technical System.* Taguig City: TESDA.

Transparency International (2009) Corruption Perceptions Index. http://www.transparency.org/policy_research/surveys_indices/cpi/2009/cpi_2009_ table (accessed 29 September 2010).

Uy, V. (2008) No Nurses Surplus Just Unqualified Graduates – recruiters, *Inquirer.net*, 1 September. http://globalnation.inquirer.net/news/news/view/20080901-158050/No-nurse-surplus-only-unqualified-graduates–recruiters (accessed 2 September 2008).

Warrington, M. (2005) Mirage in the Desert? Access to Educational Opportunities in an Area of Social Exclusion, *Antipode*, 37(4), 796-816.

CHAPTER 9

Singapore: schools for the future?

JASON TAN

SUMMARY Singapore's education system has received growing international attention and interest following its students' stellar performances in the Third International Mathematics and Science Study in 1997. Under the tight control of the People's Action Party government, which has enjoyed uninterrupted political dominance since 1959, the education system has functioned as a means of supporting national economic development and fostering social cohesion. The chapter critiques the official rhetoric surrounding these two major policy objectives and highlights various policy tensions.

Introduction

Singapore, a former British colony with a population of just under five million, has made rapid economic progress over the past four decades since attaining political independence in 1965. By the early 1980s, it had become known as one of the four Asian Tiger economic powerhouses and, alongside Brunei, enjoyed one of the highest per capita incomes in South-East Asia. More recently, it has received international attention because of its students' outstanding performances in the Third International Mathematics and Science Study in 1997, as a result of which a small but growing number of school districts in the United States have adopted modified versions of Singaporean mathematics and science textbooks. With an ethnically diverse population within a relatively small land area, Singapore has been ruled by 50 years by the same governing party. The People's Action Party (PAP) has, since coming to power in 1959, accorded education key priority in terms of serving the needs of economic development and social cohesion. To this day, education has remained the second largest item in the government's annual budget after defence.

This chapter provides a brief overview of the various levels of schooling. It then focuses on macro-policy trends and initiatives in the Singaporean education system over the past two decades. It highlights the growing marketisation of the education system, the continuing preoccupation with fostering social cohesion through the schools, and the all-encompassing Thinking Schools, Learning Nation initiative, that aims at promoting changes in teaching and learning in schools in support of national economic competitiveness within the global economy. The chapter also points out ongoing policy tensions, challenges and dilemmas. Policy rhetoric that promotes social cohesion appears at odds with a well-entrenched view of education as a tool for sorting the elite out from the rest at an early age, as well as with policies encouraging aggressive inter-school competition. At the same time, rhetoric about encouraging choice and diversity in educational provision co-exists with powerful centralising and homogenising policy surveillance mechanisms.

Levels of Schooling

Pre-primary

Pre-primary schooling in Singapore is entirely in the hands of the private sector. There are various providers such as religious bodies, for-profit organisations, and the PAP, and the institutions that provide this form of schooling are commonly referred to as kindergartens or as child-care centres. The Education Ministry registers all kindergartens while the Ministry of Community Development, Youth and Sports takes charge of licensing child-care centres. Pre-primary schooling is not compulsory, and the Education Ministry has on several occasions insisted that it intends to leave pre-primary provision in private sector hands. No official figures are available on enrolment, and on the number of children who do not enrol in pre-primary schooling. Over the past two decades, many kindergartens and child-care centres have begun to link their daily activities more closely to the perceived literacy needs of the first year of primary school, with children being taught to write in English and one other official language (Mandarin Chinese, Tamil or Malay).

Primary

In 2000, the Ministry of Education published a report advocating compulsory schooling in government and government-aided schools for six years. Parents who wish to home-school have to apply for individual exemption and prove their competence to conduct home-schooling. Their children will have to sit for the national Primary School Leaving Examination along with other children in mainstream schools. Likewise, parents who wish to enrol their children in privately run religious schools will have to apply for exemption. The first cohort of children to be affected by the relevant legislation enrolled for Primary 1 in 2003. The legislation was introduced at a time when enrolment in primary schooling was practically universal and was viewed in part as an attempt to stem further growth in enrolments in Islamic religious schools (Tan, 2002).

The six years of primary schooling are nominally free of charge and are highly subsidised by the Education Ministry. In 2006 the Education Ministry announced that the practice of streaming students at the age of nine or ten, which had been introduced in 1979, would be abandoned in favour of subject banding from 2008 onwards. Under the streaming policy, primary students had to sit for national examinations in English language, mathematics and a second language at the end of the third year of primary schooling. Their results would determine which of three streams they were to be in for the rest of their primary schooling. Students in the lowest ability stream would remain in primary school for another five years, unlike students in the other two ability streams, who would undergo another three years of primary schooling. Following the publication of an Education Ministry report in 1991, the streaming exercise was delayed by a year and all students were to complete their primary schooling in six years. The recent attempt in 2008 to blur the previously rigid streaming policy was undertaken in response to repeated complaints from the public that streaming at such an early age was premature, overly divisive and had serious consequences for students' subsequent educational advancement and life-chances.

Secondary

Students' results in the national examinations at the end of Primary 6 determine which stream – Express, Normal (Academic), and Normal (Technical) (in descending order of students' academic performance and societal prestige) – they will be streamed into for the four or five years of secondary schooling. The respective percentages for these three streams in the case of the Secondary 1 cohort in 2008 were 61.5, 25.5 and 13.0 (Ministry of Education, 2009). Not all secondary schools house all the three streams. In fact, a select few schools have only the Express stream. The majority of secondary schools run the Express, Normal (Academic), and Normal (Technical) streams. Although mobility from one stream to another is possible, upward mobility, say, from the Normal (Technical) to the Normal (Academic) stream, is in reality rather uncommon.

Express-stream students sit for the national General Certificate of Education Ordinary Level examination, which the Education Ministry runs in collaboration with the University of Cambridge Local Examinations Syndicate, at the end of four years. Success in this examination determines admission to pre-university courses, polytechnics (which offer three-year diplomas), or institutes of technical education (which offer one- to two-year technical or vocational courses). Normal (Academic)-stream students sit for the General Certificate of Education Normal Level examination at the end of four years, after which the better-performing ones may opt to sit for the Ordinary Level examination after an additional year of study. A small number of these students may be nominated by their school teachers to be examined in a few Ordinary Level subjects at the end of four years of study. Normal (Technical)-stream students are in general being prepared for post-secondary enrolment in institutes of technical education after four years of secondary schooling. In a small number of elite schools, students are spared the ordeal of facing major examinations at the end of four years, and sit instead for major examinations such as the General Certificate of Education Advanced Level examination (conducted jointly with the University of Cambridge Local Examinations Syndicate), the International Baccalaureate diploma, or Advanced Placement examinations at the end of six years of secondary schooling.

Schooling is no longer nominally free at the secondary level. Secondary schools charge much higher fees than do their primary counterparts. As in the case of primary schools, the Education Ministry exercises a heavy presence in terms of issues such as teacher qualifications and major curriculum policies.

Pre-university

Between 20 and 25% of the secondary school cohort proceed to pre-university courses. These courses last either two years in one of 17 junior colleges, or three years in a centralised institute. The vast majority of these students sit for the General Certificate of Education Advanced Level examination. Similar to the cases of primary and secondary schooling, pre-university schooling costs are highly subsidised by the government. The pre-university curriculum is a very academic one and is highly geared towards university preparation. Students in Advanced Level programmes generally study a total of six or seven subjects at different levels of depth. Table I shows the number of schools at different levels and enrolment figures in 2008.

Type of school	Number	Enrolment
Primary	174	272,097
Secondary	154	201,531
Mixed level (primary/secondary, secondary/pre-university)	14	30,981
Pre-university	14	24,323
Total	356	528,932

Table I. Number of schools in Singapore, 2008.

The Marketisation of Education since the 1980s

One of the major features of the Singaporean education system landscape since the mid-1980s has been the marketisation of education. This term refers to the use of the language of market economics, including the use of terms such as choice, competition, diversity, in education. A key manifestation of the marketisation of education has been the encouragement of greater school autonomy through the independent schools scheme and the autonomous schools scheme. Another initiative has been the active promotion of inter-school competition through the annual publication of school ranking league tables and the institution of school quality awards. Schools have also been encouraged to develop niche programmes and secondary schools and junior colleges have recently been allowed greater discretion in the admission of students through direct admission exercises in which school authorities may select students based on a few specified areas of talent. This sort of competition among schools is supposed to promote diversity and choice and to improve overall educational standards.

A major milestone in the marketisation of education was marked when the then Deputy Prime Minister Goh Chok Tong spoke in 1985 of the need to allow more autonomy within schools, and of giving the right to appoint staff, devise school curricula and choose textbooks, while conforming to national education policies such as bilingualism and common examinations. Goh asserted that prestigious schools had lost some of their individuality and special character through centralised control. He thought that principals and teachers should now be allowed greater flexibility and independence to experiment with new ideas.

Goh's sentiment was echoed the following year by the then Prime Minister Lee Kuan Yew, who felt that government domination of educational provision meant a lack of competition and diversity. At the end of 1986, 12 school principals were invited to accompany the then Minister for Education Tony Tan to study the management of 25 'acknowledged successful schools' in the UK and the USA, and to see what lessons could be learned for Singapore. The principals' report recommended greater autonomy for selected schools.

Accepting the recommendations, Tan stated that several well-established schools would be allowed to become independent schools. While remaining public institutions, they would be given autonomy and flexibility in staff deployment and salaries, finance, management and the curriculum. These schools were to serve as role models for other schools in improving the quality of education. They would also help to set the market value for good principals and teachers by recruiting staff in a competitive market. Parents, teachers and students would enjoy a wider variety of schools to choose from. By 1993, a total of eight secondary schools, all of them well established and prestigious, had become independent.

Right from the introduction of the independent schools scheme, there was intense public criticism over its elitist nature and the high fees charged by the schools. In the wake of the 1991 general elections, which saw the governing party returned to power with a reduced parliamentary majority, the government took steps to defuse public criticism of the scheme. First, it limited the number of independent schools, thus reversing its earlier announcement that it wanted to see more schools turn independent. Another step was the establishment in 1994 of a new category of schools called autonomous schools. In the first three years, 18 existing non-independent secondary schools, all of which had above-average academic results, were designated as autonomous schools. These schools receive 10% more in annual per capita government grants than non-autonomous schools. They are supposed to provide a high-quality education while charging more affordable fees than independent schools. The Education Ministry claimed that parents and students would thus have a wider range of choices.

After a decade-long hiatus during which the number of independent schools remained static, the Ministry allowed the establishment of a few brand-new independent secondary schools. In 2009, there were a total of 13 independent schools and 27 autonomous secondary schools. To date, both the independent schools scheme and autonomous schools scheme have been confined almost entirely to the secondary sector.

To date, the results of increased school autonomy have been mixed. It is clear that these schools are by no means 'private' in terms of total governing and financial autonomy from the Education Ministry. The Education Ministry continues to wield considerable control over the independent schools by such measures as providing substantial financial subsidies to independent schools and approving appointments to their governing boards. In particular, the imposition of national curricular requirements and the pressures imposed on most of these schools by their having to prepare their common national examinations and being subjected to the same quality assurance mechanisms as non-independent schools (see the next section for more details), restricts the scope for curricular innovation in most independent schools and all the autonomous schools. In addition, the range of subjects offered in these schools is largely identical (with a few notable exceptions) to that in non-independent, non-autonomous schools. As long as principals are held accountable for their students' performance in national examinations, they cannot afford to stray too far from the mainstream curriculum. Furthermore, none of the independent schools or autonomous schools is allowed to stray from key national policy initiatives.

A major feature of Singaporean education over the past decade, and one that has gone hand in hand with the granting of increased school autonomy, has been the intensification of competition among schools. Besides improving the quality of education, competition is supposed to provide parents and students with a wider range of choices and to improve accountability by forcing schools to improve their programmes. This competition has been fostered in various ways. For instance, in 1992 the various local newspapers began publishing the annual ranking league tables of secondary schools and junior colleges. The official justification for this practice was that parents and students must be provided with better information in order to make intelligent and informed choices (Goh, 1992; Parliamentary Debates Singapore, 64, 1 March 1995, Col. 27).

The introduction of explicit measures to promote competition among schools aroused a great deal of controversy and criticism. One of the major criticisms is that competition led some schools to focus narrowly on those outcomes that were relevant for public ranking. It took a number of years before the Education Ministry announced in 2004 that it would be moving away from raw numerical rankings of secondary schools in favour of broad performance bands. The public ranking of all junior colleges was halted that year. Furthermore, the Ministry broadened the range of indicators upon which schools are to be assessed, through the use of the Masterplan of Awards. The Masterplan involves the annual presentation of awards to schools for achievement in various categories such as aesthetics, sports, physical health, character development, organisational effectiveness, student all-round development, staff well-being, and teaching and learning. It is arguable that the Masterplan may result in some schools using more of the same covert strategies that they have been using thus far, this time in a wider spectrum of school processes and activities, in order to boost their schools' performance in as many of the aspects that are being assessed as possible.

The competitive stakes have now extended to student recruitment as the Education Ministry formalised the practice of Direct School Admission (DSA) for secondary schools in 2004 and for junior colleges in 2005. The scheme allowed these schools full discretion to conduct selection interviews and devise their individual selection criteria to offer admission to a limited percentage of their annual student intakes before they sat the qualifying national examinations. The DSA will certainly allow these schools and junior colleges to fuel their competitive edge further by recruiting (and competing for) students with academic, artistic or sporting abilities, as well as poaching coaches with proven track records in securing medals for their teams in competitions. It may intensify the tendency on the part of some schools to narrowly focus on co-curricular activities that are proven award winners, to concentrate obsessively on student participation in co-curricular activities more for competitive stakes than for intrinsic enjoyment, and to exclude students without a proven track record of competitive achievement from participation in high-profile co-curricular activities.

Another serious consequence of all of this intense competition is that of a growing prestige hierarchy of schools and social stratification. The trend of academic selectiveness on the part of top schools, which has been extended to other fields of endeavour with the introduction of the DSA, will inevitably lead to a further stratification of schools, with the independent schools and autonomous schools at the top and the rest below. Equally worrying is evidence that students from wealthier family backgrounds are over-represented (as are students from the majority ethnic Chinese community) in most independent schools. The government is well aware of the potential impact of social stratification on social cohesion as well as on its own political legitimacy. While maintaining that all Singapore schools are 'good schools', it claims that it is only right to nurture the more able students as the whole country will ultimately benefit (Parliamentary Debates Singapore, 59, 20 January 1992, Col. 365). What strikes the casual observer of the Singaporean education scene is how hardly any schools show any overt interest in positioning themselves within the education market as schools that cater to disaffected or low-achieving students.

Fostering Social Cohesion through National Education

Forging a sense of national identity has been a preoccupation for the Singaporean government for the past five decades. This is linked to the top political leadership's 'garrison mentality', which manifests itself in a perennial concern with issues such as the country's limited territorial and natural resources, the maintenance of the country's economic and social achievements, and the country's vulnerability as the only majority-Chinese state in the midst of a majority Malay/Muslim population in the neighbouring countries Malaysia and Indonesia. Since 1966, all students have had to participate in common daily rituals such as the recitation of the national pledge and the singing of the national anthem, in a bid to forge some sort of common national identity that transcends ethnic-based identities within the context of a multi-ethnic society classified officially as 76.8% Chinese, 13.9% Malay, 7.9% Indian and 1.4% Others (Leow, 2001a, p. 35).

At a Teachers' Day rally in September 1996, the then Prime Minister Goh Chok Tong lamented the lack of knowledge of Singapore's recent history among younger Singaporeans, as reflected in the results of a street poll conducted by a local newspaper. The Ministry of Education had also conducted a surprise quiz on Singapore's history among 2500 students in schools, polytechnics and universities. The results proved equally disappointing.

Goh claimed that the gap in knowledge was the direct result of a deliberate official policy not to teach school students about the recent political past and the events leading up to political independence. However, he felt that this ignorance was undesirable among younger people, who had not personally lived through these events. He claimed too that these events, constituting 'our shared past', ought to 'bind all our communities together, not divide us ... We should understand why they took place so that we will never let them happen again' (Goh, 1997a, p. 425). Goh highlighted the possibility that young people would not appreciate how potentially fragile inter-ethnic relations could prove to be, especially in times of economic recession. Not having lived through poverty and deprivation meant that young people might take peace and prosperity for granted.

Goh's remarks came on the heels of the increasing concern on the part of senior government officials over how to satisfy the consumerist demands and material aspirations of the growing middle class. For instance, in 1996 former Prime Minister Lee Kuan Yew commented that:

thirty years of continuous growth and increasing stability and prosperity have produced a different generation in an English-educated middle class. They are very different from their parents. The present generation below 35 has grown up used to high economic growth year after year, and take their security and success for granted. And because they believe all is well, they are less willing to make sacrifices for the benefit of the others in society. They are more concerned about their individual and family's welfare and success, not their community or society's well being. (Lee, 1996, p. 30)

Likewise, Goh had in 1995 claimed that:

[g]iving them [students] academic knowledge alone is not enough to make them understand what makes or breaks Singapore ... Japanese children are taught to cope with earthquakes, while Dutch youngsters learn about the vulnerability of their polders, or low-lying areas. In the same way, Singapore children must be taught to live with a small land area, limited territorial sea and air space, the high cost of owning a car and dependence on imported water and oil. Otherwise, years of continuous growth may lull them into believing that the good life is their divine right ... [students] must be taught survival skills and be imbued with the confidence that however formidable the challenges and competition, we have the will, skill and solutions to vanquish them. (Teach Students, 1995, p. 1)

As a result of this official alarmist rhetoric, the National Education policy initiative was launched in 1997. It aimed at developing social cohesion in students through:

– Fostering Singaporean identity, pride and self-respect;
– Teaching about Singapore's nation-building successes against
  the odds;
– Understanding Singapore's unique developmental challenges,
  constraints and vulnerabilities; and
– Instilling core values, such as meritocracy and multiracialism, as
  well as the will to prevail, in order to ensure Singapore's
  continued success. (H.L. Lee, 1997)

Lee called on every teacher and principal to pass on six key National Education messages:

– Singapore is our homeland; this is where we belong;
– We must preserve racial and religious harmony;
– We must uphold meritocracy and incorruptibility;
– No one owes Singapore a living;
– We must ourselves defend Singapore; and

– We have confidence in our future.
(Ministry of Education, 1997a)

Several major means were suggested for incorporating National Education in all schools. Firstly, every subject in the formal curriculum would be used. Certain subjects, such as social studies, civic and moral education, history and geography were mentioned as being particularly useful in this regard. Social studies at the primary level would be started earlier, at Primary 1 instead of Primary 4. It would also be introduced as a new mandatory subject for all upper secondary students in order to cover issues regarding Singapore's success and future developmental challenges. The upper secondary history syllabus would be extended from 1963, where its coverage had hitherto ended, to include the immediate post-independence years up until 1971.

Secondly, various elements of the informal curriculum were recommended. All schools were called upon to remember a few major events each year:

– Total Defence Day, to commemorate Singapore's surrender
  under British colonial rule to the Japanese in 1942;
– Racial Harmony Day, to remember the outbreak of inter-ethnic
  riots in 1964;
– International Friendship Day, to bring across the importance of
  maintaining cordial relations with neighbouring countries; and
– National Day, to commemorate political independence in 1965.
(Ministry of Education, 1997a)

In addition, students would visit key national institutions and public facilities in order to feel proud and confident about how Singapore had overcome its developmental constraints. A further means of promoting social cohesion and civic responsibility would be through a mandatory six hours of community service each year. An National Education branch was established in the Ministry of Education headquarters to spearhead this initiative.

The high degree of priority accorded National Education reflects the PAP's concern that social cohesion might suffer, should the economy falter and fail to sustain the high growth rates of the past few decades. Social stratification has assumed growing prominence on the government's policy agenda, especially in the wake of the 1991 general elections, when the PAP was returned to power with a reduced parliamentary majority. Whereas the issue of income stratification was largely taboo in public discussions up until 1991, there has been growing acknowledgement on the part of the PAP government since then of the potential impact of income disparities on social cohesion. For instance, Goh Chok Tong has acknowledged that highly educated Singaporeans are in a more advantageous position compared with unskilled workers and that there is a great likelihood of widening income inequalities and class stratification (Goh, 1996). He has drawn an explicit link between income inequalities and the need to maintain social cohesion.

However, he thinks that 'we cannot narrow the [income] gap by preventing those who can fly from flying ... Nor can we teach everyone to fly, because most simply do not have the aptitude or ability' (Goh, 1996, p. 3). In the late 1990s, Goh introduced the terms 'cosmopolitans' and 'heartlanders' to illustrate the class divide between the well-educated, privileged, globally mobile elite, on the one hand, and the working-class majority, on the other (Parliamentary Debates Singapore, 70, 1999, Col. 2284). A PAP member of parliament expressed his fervent hope that Singaporeans would not 'allow our system of education [to] create a bipolar society of cosmopolitans and heartlanders that will be destructive for nation-building' (Parliamentary Debates Singapore, 71, 1999, Col. 87). More recently, these income gaps show no sign of closing and may in fact be widening (see for instance Loh, 2007).

This tension between social inequalities and social cohesion permeates the underlying framework of National Education. Different emphases are planned for students in various levels of schooling. For instance, students in technical institutes are to

> understand that they would be helping themselves, their families
> and Singapore by working hard, continually upgrading themselves
> and helping to ensure a stable social order. They must feel that
> every citizen has a valued place in Singapore. (Ministry of
> Education, 1997a)

Polytechnic students, who are higher up the social prestige ladder, are to be convinced that 'the country's continued survival and prosperity will depend on the quality of their efforts, and that there is opportunity for all based on ability and effort'. Junior college students, about four fifths of whom are bound for university, must have the sense that 'they can shape their own future' and must appreciate 'the demands and complexities of leadership' as future national leaders (Ministry of Education, 1997b, p. 3).

One sees in these differing messages clear and unmistakeable vestiges of the stratified view of society espoused by Lee Kuan Yew more than 30 years earlier. Speaking to school principals in 1966, Lee stressed that the education system ought to produce a 'pyramidal structure' consisting of three strata: 'top leaders', 'good executives', and a 'well-disciplined and highly civic-conscious broad mass'. The 'top leaders' are the 'elite' who are needed to 'lead and give the people the inspiration and the drive to make [society] succeed'. The 'middle strata' of 'good executives' are to 'help the elite carry out [their] ideas, thinking and planning', while the 'broad mass' are to be 'imbued not only with self but also social discipline, so that they can respect their community and do not spit all over the place' (Lee, 1966, pp. 10, 12, 13). Lee also lamented the tendency among many Singaporeans to be more concerned with individual survival, rather than national survival, a theme that both he and Goh later repeated within the setting of a much more materially prosperous society. It is somewhat difficult to reconcile this stratified view of society, in which individuals are still being pigeonholed based on their academic achievement, on the one hand, with visions of a socially cohesive society, on the other. The claims of a government document *Singapore 21* that 'every Singaporean matters' and of 'equal opportunities for all' (Government of Singapore, 1999) tend to be belied by the persistent reliance on academic achievement as a primary indicator of an individual's societal worth, as well as Lee's longstanding belief in the primarily genetic basis of an individual's intelligence, creativity and leadership qualities (see for instance, Parliamentary Debates Singapore, 66, 1996, Cols 331-345; Parliamentary Debates Singapore, 70, 1999, Cols 1651-1653).

The task of holding on to citizens' sense of loyalty and commitment will come under increasingly severe strain as globalisation and its impact mean that Singaporeans are exposed via overseas travel, the Internet and news and print media to social and political alternatives outside of Singapore. Increasing wealth also means that individuals are able to send their children to be educated at foreign universities, after which work opportunities beckon. It has also been government practice for four decades now to sponsor top-performing students in the GCE Advanced Level examinations for undergraduate studies in prestigious universities such as Oxford, Cambridge, Harvard and Stanford instead of at the three local publicly funded universities. It is perhaps ironic, if somewhat unsurprising, that the well-educated elite, in other words, the very individuals who have been accorded generous support and funding in their schooling in the hope that they will take on the mantle of national leadership, are the most globally mobile, and are the best placed to take advantage of economic opportunities around the world, to the point of contemplating emigration. This policy dilemma was exemplified in the late 1990s when parliamentarians debated the merits of publicly naming and shaming individuals who had been sponsored for their undergraduate and/or postgraduate studies in elite foreign universities, only to repay the government the cost of their studies upon completion of their studies instead of returning to Singapore to work for the government (Parliamentary Debates Singapore, 68, 1998, Cols 855-996). A few years later there were echoes of the 'cosmopolitans–heartlanders' issue in the wake of Goh Chok Tong's National Day rally speech about two categories of individuals, the 'stayers' (Singaporeans who were 'rooted to Singapore') and the 'quitters' ('fair weather Singaporeans who would run away whenever the country runs into stormy weather') (Parliamentary Debates Singapore, 75, 2002, Cols 1110-1201).

Another worrying trend is the persistence of ethnic disparities in educational attainment. Ethnic Chinese are heavily over-represented in local public universities and polytechnics, forming 92.4% and 84.0% of the respective total enrolments in 2000, as compared with their 76.8% representation in the overall population. Ethnic Malays (2.7% and 10.0%, respectively) and Indians (4.3% and 5.2%, respectively) are correspondingly under-represented (Leow, 2001b, pp. 34-36). Despite ethnic Malay and ethnic Indian students having made tremendous quantitative improvements in educational attainment over the past four decades, their public examination results continue to lag behind those of their Chinese counterparts. Disproportionately large percentages of Malay and Indian students are streamed into the slower-paced bands or streams at both primary and secondary levels. This gap also translates into ethnic minority under-representation (and working class under-representation) in some of the most prestigious primary and secondary schools and a corresponding over-representation in some of the least prestigious schools (see for instance, Davie, 2002). To date, the Singaporean government has steadfastly rejected the idea of instituting special ethnic-based admission quotas, preferring instead to insist on academic merit as the primary admission criterion for advancement through the various levels of the highly competitive schooling system. Instead, it has preferred financial assistance measures such as the waiver of secondary school fees for ethnic Malays, and subsidising the operating costs of various ethnically based organisations that are attempting to improve educational achievement through tuition classes, scholarships and family education programmes.

There is evidence that five decades of common socialisation in a national school system have still not managed to eradicate racial prejudice among school students (Lee et al, 2004). A Malay member of parliament told Parliament in 2002 that he had heard that once schools had an over-representation of ethnic Malay students, non-Malay students, especially ethnic Chinese students, shied away from choosing such schools (Parliamentary Debates Singapore, 74, 2002, Col. 1893). The existence of Special Assistance Plan primary and secondary schools, which are almost entirely ethnic Chinese in enrolment, as part of the Education Ministry's intention to promote Chinese language and culture, has been the subject of periodic discussion because of their perceived ethnic exclusivity (see for instance, Parliamentary Debates Singapore, 55, 1990, Col. 371; Parliamentary Debates Singapore, 64, 1995, Col. 486; Parliamentary Debates Singapore, 70, 1999, Col. 1027; Parliamentary Debates Singapore, 76, 2003, Col. 1635). Moreover, the practice of streaming students into various tracks at the primary and secondary levels within the context of a highly competitive, high-stakes education system has, since its inception in 1979, contributed to prejudice on the part of students in faster-paced streams, and teachers as well, towards students in slower-paced streams (Kang, 2004). The marketisation of education may further accentuate the segregation of students along ethnic and class lines across schools as more and more schools scramble in a very utilitarian fashion to, on the one hand, recruit students who are 'assets', in other words, students who can best contribute to measurable indicators of school performance, and minimise the recruitment of students who are perceived to be 'liabilities', on the other hand.

In the past few years, there have been belated policy reforms as part of a tacit official admission of the divisive impact of education policies that aim deliberately to identify and set apart the academic elite at an early age. For instance, there have been moves to blur some of the boundaries across different academic streams at the primary and secondary levels; to encourage greater interaction between primary students enrolled in the Gifted Education Programme and their other schoolmates and to provide some semblance of upward mobility from lower-prestige academic streams to higher-prestige academic streams. The Ministry of Education has also tried to encourage the teaching of conversational Chinese and conversational Malay in a bid to stimulate students' cross-ethnic mixing.

Further compounding the situation in recent years has been a renewed heightening of awareness of religious differences, especially between Muslims and non-Muslims. For instance, in early 2002 another domestic controversy broke out over the Education Ministry's insistence that female Muslim students not be allowed to don Islamic head veils in state-run schools. These ethnic-based controversies have been complicated in recent years by the influx of individuals who are often highly educated professionals and others on temporary work permits who work in lower-prestige jobs, from such countries as the People's Republic of China and India. These non-citizens comprised about a third of the entire population in 2009. These individuals have had at times to cope with resentment among some Singaporeans over perceived competition for jobs, a phenomenon that has been acknowledged by Goh (Loh, 2007). National Education will have to grapple with the task of socialising the children of the new immigrants, as well as how it ought to play out in the case of students whose parents may have no intention of seeking Singaporean citizenship, but who have chosen nevertheless to enrol their children in Singaporean schools. Even in the schools arena, there is worry among some parents, teachers and local students about the added competitive element that talented foreign students are perceived to represent (Quek, 2005; Singh, 2005). It is rather ironic that such large numbers of highly educated foreigners are being attracted to work and live in Singapore while thousands of its own highly educated individuals are choosing to relocate elsewhere.

Towards Thinking Schools

Another policy initiative that has generated a tidal wave of reforms in the past decade has been Thinking Schools, Learning Nation (TSLN), which was launched in 1997. Driven explicitly by official concern about Singapore's economic competitiveness within the global economy, TSLN included a reduction in curricular content from primary to pre-university levels to allow more time to be devoted to thinking skills and processes, and the revision of assessment modes. A whole list of desired outcomes, such as creative, critical, analytical and flexible thinking, the exercising of initiative, communication skills, problem solving, cooperative team work, and research skills, were announced. Goh Chok Tong claimed that TSLN had to instil a passion for learning among students instead of having them study merely for the purpose of obtaining good examination grades (Goh, 1997b). TSLN has since become a major policy umbrella encompassing multiple policy prongs such as Innovation and Enterprise, the Information Technology Masterplan, Ability-driven Education (where every child's potential is supposed to be developed to its fullest), 'Teach Less, Learn More', the review of primary, secondary and pre-university curricula, as well as the revision of university undergraduate admission criteria.

Just after the announcement of the TSLN initiative, the Education Ministry published the report of an external review it had earlier commissioned to study the school system (Ministry of Education, 1997c). Team members noted that teachers' adeptness at drilling students in answering examination questions had extended to those questions involving 'higher-order thinking skills'. The report also noted with disapproval the pernicious effects of the public ranking of schools. Although project work was praised for its potential to develop creativity, teamwork, communication skills, and independent learning, the report lamented the fact that students often viewed projects as chores instead of as a means to develop their learning. In addition, teachers lacked adequate knowledge and time to guide students in their research. These comments came on the heels of comments in the local press that rising Ordinary Level and Advanced Level examination pass rates merely reflected the high prevalence of examination preparation techniques (Nirmala & Mathi, 1996), as well as laments by parliamentarians over the apparent lack of creativity and thinking skills among students and members of the workforce (Parliamentary Debates Singapore, 53, 1989, Cols 550-551; Parliamentary Debates Singapore, 55, 1990, Cols 310-311). Furthermore, they create a sense of déjà vu as one contemplates Goh Keng Swee's claim in 1967 that schools were over-emphasising examination preparation and engaging in 'parrot-like teaching' (Goh, 1995, p. 128).

What was perhaps ironic about these criticisms of the school system in the mid-1990s was that they coincided with what appeared to be Singaporean students' stellar performance in the Third International Mathematics and Science Study. This accomplishment was hailed by the Education Ministry as providing 'confidence in our school system, curriculum and teaching methods' (J. Lee, 1997, p. 3). It was pointed out that the study was 'not made up of typical examination questions that our pupils are familiar with. [The test items] assessed them on creative problem-solving skills and their ability to respond to open-ended questions' (Chiang, 1999, p. 70).

On the surface, TSLN appears to be an inclusive concept that benefits all students. Over the past decade Education Ministry rhetoric would have it that TSLN has been a steady and consistent success in all schools. Within the context of an education system where students' life-chances are highly dependent on their examination success, how likely is it that the teaching of critical and creative thinking skills as embodied in TSLN will take root and flourish? It appears the ever-tightening grip of disciplinary mechanisms such as intense inter-school competition and the Masterplan of Awards may serve as inhibitory brakes on the flourishing of creativity and critical thinking skills in schools. The gradual emergence in more schools of alternative forms of teaching and assessment aimed at promoting critical and creative thinking may not prove enough to persuade principals, teachers, students and parents that these are not yet more additional hoops to be cleared through more of the same strategies, such as repeated coaching and practice of previous years' examination questions, that have proved successful in enhancing examination scores. In other words, many teachers and students may be co-opting new policy initiatives, well intentioned though they might be in theory, into well-entrenched modes of teaching and learning. A decade on, there is little evidence that TSLN has made a dent in the prevalence or profitability of private tutoring and the sale in public retail outlets of numerous workbooks and school examination papers, or to the widespread practice of providing students facing high-stakes examinations with endless hours of drilling, often to the marginalisation of peripheral subjects such as art, music and physical education.

Conclusion

By many measures, the Singaporean education system has achieved quantitative success, achieving almost universal attendance for 10 years of schooling while enjoying funding levels that are probably unmatched in the rest of South-East Asia. Pass rates in national examinations have been steadily rising since the mid-1980s and the proportion of each age cohort proceeding to post-secondary schooling has increased dramatically too over the past two decades. It has been officially acknowledged that much of this success may have been accounted for through intensive drilling and coaching practices by classroom teachers. What has not been officially acknowledged is the possible role played by the widespread phenomenon of private tutoring.

One of the major challenges lying ahead is to change well-entrenched drilling and coaching practices in schools in favour of pedagogical approaches that favour creative and critical thinking instead. Despite more than a decade of the Thinking Schools, Learning Nation initiative, there is evidence that crucial gate-keeping national examinations continue to exert an inhibiting and conservative influence on principals, teachers, parents and students, official talk of creativity and innovation notwithstanding. It is likely that in a large number of schools, perfunctory acknowledgement is given to officially touted teaching and learning methods, while the real business of examination preparation carries on unabated.

Another challenge is how to manage the balance between diversity and uniformity. In spite of official attempts in recent years to promote greater flexibility of academic options and a wider array of school provision, other features of the education landscape push towards uniformity. One of these powerful surveillance mechanisms is the annual publication of performance league tables and the awarding of medals for different areas of school achievement. These measures serve as a powerful, if somewhat indirect, means of ensuring that almost all schools remain 'on track'. So crucial are the schools in terms of economic development and social cohesion that the Education Ministry is likely to be unwilling to allow totally unfettered diversity.

Yet another perennial problem is the management of disparities in educational attainment along social class and ethnic lines. There is widespread evidence that minority ethnic groups such as Malays and Indians are under-represented in higher education institutions, despite official attempts to provide financial assistance to various community organisations that are attempting to improve these students' educational attainment. There are no official figures on how many students enter primary school each year not having first attained basic literacy in a school system that begins on the assumption that each child has already attended a pre-school. Although the 1990s saw the initiation of compensatory programmes such as the Learning Support Programme in primary schools to assist such children, there is still evidence that students from less well-off homes and ethnic minorities are under-represented in the most prestigious schools. These disparities fly in the face of official attempts such as National Education to foster social cohesion. Similarly, well-entrenched elitist policies and other practices such as streaming may be said to be divisive and to segregate students rather than bring them together.

The Singaporean education system has attained a certain amount of regional and international renown, to the extent that there are regular visits and exchange programmes by foreigners keen to emulate its success or to attend courses in Singaporean educational institutions. This success is trumpeted even as officialdom attempts a bold remaking of fundamental ways of teaching and learning. What bears watching is whether the next phase of educational success, involving the fostering of social cohesion amid growing income disparities and centrifugal forces, and the gearing of the school system towards the needs of the global economy, will flourish in a schooling system well accustomed to an inordinate focus on success in high-stakes examinations as a sorting mechanism for determining students' subsequent life-chances.

References

Chiang, C.F. (1999) Education: new directions, in G.L. Ooi & R.S. Rajan (Eds) *Singapore: the year in review*. Singapore: Times Academic Press.

Davie, S. (2002) Malay Enclaves in School a Concern, *The Straits Times*, 23 February, p. 4.

Goh, C.T. (1992) *National Day Rally Speech 1992*. Singapore: Ministry of Information and the Arts.

Goh, C.T. (1996) Narrowing the Income Gap, *Speeches*, 20(3), 1-4.

Goh, C.T. (1997a) Prepare Our Children for the New Century: teach them well, in J. Tan, S. Gopinathan & W.K. Ho (Eds) *Education in Singapore: a book of readings*. Singapore: Prentice Hall.

Goh, C.T. (1997b) Shaping Our Future: 'thinking schools' and a 'learning' nation'. http:/stars.nhb.gov.sg/stars/public/viewHTML.jsp?pdfno=1997060209.

Goh, K.S. (1995) *The Economics of Modernization*. Singapore: Federal Publications.

Government of Singapore (1999) *Singapore 21: together, we make the difference*. Singapore: Singapore 21 Committee.

Kang, T. (2004) Schools and Post-secondary Aspirations Among Female Chinese, Malay and Indian Normal Stream Students, in A.E. Lai (Ed.) *Beyond Rituals and Riots: ethnic pluralism and social cohesion in Singapore*. Singapore: Eastern Universities Press.

Lee, C., Cherian, M., Rahil, I., Ng, M., Sim, J. & Chee, M.F. (2004) Children's Experiences of Multiracial Relationships in Informal Primary School Settings, in A.E. Lai (Ed.) *Beyond Rituals and Riots: ethnic pluralism and social cohesion in Singapore*. Singapore: Eastern Universities Press.

Lee, H.L. (1997) The Launch of National Education. http://www1.moe.edu.sg/ne/KeySpeeches/MAY17-97.html.

Lee, J. (1997) Singapore Students Top Maths and Science Practical Test, *The Straits Times*, 20 September, p. 3.

Lee, K.Y. (1966) *New Bearings in our Education System*. Singapore: Ministry of Culture.

Lee, K.Y. (1996) Will Singapore Survive Lee Kuan Yew? *Speeches*, 20(3), 23-33.

Leow, B.G. (2001a) *Census of Population 2000 Statistical Release 1: demographic characteristics*. Singapore: Department of Statistics.

Leow, B.G. (2001b) *Census of Population 2000 Statistical Release 2: education, language and religion*. Singapore: Department of Statistics.

Loh, C.K. (2007) Cracks in Society are Showing, *Today*, 17-18 November, pp. 1, 3.

Ministry of Education (1997a) About NE. http://www1.moe.edu.sg/ne/AboutNE/SixMSGs.html.

Ministry of Education (1997b) *Launch of National Education*. Ministry of Education press release 017/97. Singapore: MOE.

Ministry of Education (1997c) *Learning, Creating and Communicating: a curriculum review*. Singapore: MOE.

Ministry of Education (2009) *Education Statistics Digest 2009*. Singapore: MOE.

Nirmala, M. & Mathi, B. (1996) Do More A's Mean Brighter Students ... or just students who are more exam-smart? *The Straits Times*, 31 March, p. 2.

Quek, T. (2005) China Whiz Kids: S'pore feels the heat, *The Straits Times*, 13 February, pp. 3-4.

Singh, S. (2005) But Montfort Principal Says: we are improving local standards, *The New Paper*, 15 February, pp. 2-3.

Tan, J. (2002) *Why Have Compulsory Education in Singapore?* Occasional Paper No. 4. Hong Kong: Comparative Education Policy Research Unit, City University of Hong Kong.

Teach Students to Live with S'pore's Constraints: PM (1995) *The Straits Times*, 5 March, p. 1.

CHAPTER 10

Timor-Leste: building a post-conflict education system

BOB BOUGHTON

SUMMARY Timor-Leste, South-East Asia's newest nation, achieved its independence in 2002, after five hundred years of colonial occupation, and a brief period of direct United Nations rule. Its population of only one million people remains among the poorest in the region, though this is set to change in coming years as a result of revenue flowing into the state budget from its newly-won offshore oil reserves. The first independence government, which was led by FRETILIN, the party which had launched the liberation struggle in 1974, was committed to a rapid expansion of education and health services, and significant progress has been made, particularly in primary schooling and adult literacy. A major political crisis in 2006-07 revealed the ongoing differences between elements of the old Resistance, the Catholic Church and the international donors, and, while stability has returned to the country, the legacies of colonialism and war are expected to have a major impact on the emerging education system in the foreseeable future.

After centuries of colonial occupation, Timor-Leste achieved its independence in May 2002, becoming the first new nation of the twenty-first century. This tiny country, whose population is less than one million, occupies the eastern half of a small island in the Indonesian archipelago, approximately 450 kilometres from Australia's northern coastline. One hundred kilometres wide, and less than 500 long, the country is divided along its southwest-northeast axis by a high and rugged mountain range. Isolated settlement patterns and successive waves of immigration and colonisation have produced a richly diverse ethnic mix of Melanesian, Malay-Polynesian, Chinese, Indian, Portuguese and African heritage (Gunn, 1999, pp. 12-14). For over 400 years, Portugal was the ruling authority. Then, in the final decades of the twentieth century Timor-Leste suffered a new and even more destructive invasion, from its nearest and largest neighbour, Indonesia. For 24 years, between 1975 and 1999, the country experienced a protracted, devastating conflict, costing the lives of nearly a third of the local population (CAVR, 2006).

Colonialism bequeathed to Timor-Leste an underdeveloped economy with minimal infrastructure and no functioning democratic institutions. Today, almost 50% of the adult population remain illiterate, with the figure rising much higher away from the capital, Dili, and the few large towns in the country's 13 administrative districts. Fifty-four per cent of the population are aged 19 or younger, and 16% are under five (Democratic Republic of Timor-Leste. National Directorate of Statistics [DRTL.NDS], 2006). Over 70% of the population survive from subsistence agriculture and fishing in the rural areas, many in small hamlets isolated by terrain and lack of infrastructure. Asia's poorest country, its strategic location and rich energy resources attract the attention, not all of it welcome, of its powerful closest neighbours, Indonesia and Australia, and from the major global powers. These circumstances combine to make quality critical education essential to the new nation's ability to articulate and pursue its own interests, and thereby secure the sovereignty and independence for which its people paid so high a price.

A decade has passed since the UN-supervised ballot of August 1999, in which 78.5% of the population voted, in the face of widespread violent intimidation, to reject the offer of so-called autonomy within the Indonesian Republic. Since that time, Timor-Leste has slowly been building its first independent and democratic education system. The three key actors in this process, the Resistance, the Catholic Church and the international community, approach the problems of educational development with ideas and practices formed from the very different experiences and roles they played during the colonial past, and the complex, contradictory relationships they developed internally and with each over that time. The shape of the system they are building, therefore, is highly contested, like the country's history itself, which comprises five distinct but overlapping periods of educational development:

1. Portuguese colonial rule 1516-1974;
2. Decolonisation 1974-75;
3. Indonesian military occupation and the Resistance 1975-99;
4. UN administration 1999-2002;
5. Independence 2002-11.

This chapter provides a brief account of the different stages in the development of the colonial education systems of Portugal and Indonesia, and of the counter-hegemonic anti-colonial education ideas and practices which arose out of, and in opposition to, those systems. It then analyses educational developments since 1999, highlighting how these were shaped by the relationships and contradictions of the colonial period. The chapter concludes with a discussion of the current state of Timor-Leste's education system, and some of the major issues and challenges it faces.

Education and Portuguese Colonialism

The Portuguese arrived in Timor in the sixteenth century, but a civilian administration was not established until the mid-1700s. Full control over the territory was only achieved at the end of the pacification campaigns 1894-1906 (Hill, 2002, p. 6). From the very beginning, the Catholic Church played a major role in the colonisation process. Between 1512 and 1701, it was the effective governing power, with its own military garrisons under the direct command of Dominican and Jesuit missionaries. The civil authority took over in 1702, but the Portuguese state made no effort to educate the local population until the mid-nineteenth century when it opened a few schools for children of local chieftains (*liurais*). The Church, meanwhile, established its first primary school in 1904, and by 1909 was running 17 schools across the territory (Carey, 1999, p. 78). In 1940, the fascist Salazar regime in Portugal signed a Concordat with the Vatican, delegating responsibility for all education in the Portuguese colonies to the Church (Hill, 2002, p. 18). A Missionary Statute forbade the speaking of languages other than Portuguese within the schools (Hill, 2002, p. 35). Following a failed anti-colonial rebellion in 1959, the state began expanding its educational provision, but the Church retained control of most rural schools, and state-provided education beyond basic primary schooling was restricted to the so-called *assimilados*, people of mixed heritage who had adopted the Portuguese language and lifestyle. In the early 1970s, the vast majority of Timorese were still illiterate, while most children and young people had access to only the most rudimentary education, all of it in Portuguese. A small handful of *assimilados*, however, had completed their secondary schooling, and worked in the colonial administration. Within this group, in particular among young students from a Jesuit-run seminary in the hills above the colonial capital Dili, the first stirrings of modern Timorese nationalism took hold in the late 1960s and early 1970s. A limited number of scholarships were also awarded at this time, and a small but significant group of Timorese students were studying in Portugal by 1974 (Carey, 1999, p. 78; Hill, 2002, pp. 52-54).

Three decades on, the effects of Portuguese colonial rule continue to impact on the current educational environment. Firstly, and most importantly, Portuguese rule was marked by extreme educational neglect of the vast majority of the Timorese people, the rural-dwelling population, who never acquired literacy or a literate culture, and were largely excluded from meaningful political participation in their country's governance. This legacy remains in the high illiteracy among older adults and the absence of a strong culture of education in many rural areas. Secondly, Portuguese colonialism gave the Catholic Church enormous influence over what little education did occur, and the Church's authority in relation to educational matters remains strong today, despite the clear separation of Church and state in the new Constitution. Thirdly, the intellectual and cultural formation of educated Timor-Leste nationals was intimately bound up with the Portuguese language and Lusophone culture and history, an influence which the leadership of the anti-colonial Resistance shared with their counterparts in other Portuguese colonies, and which continued throughout the period of Indonesian rule. Moreover, a large body of colonial scholarship on Timor and its people developed during 500 years of Portuguese rule, creating an extensive natural and social science archive written in Portuguese, as well as a nascent literature. This archive is an integral part of the new nation's intellectual heritage, on which the education system must now draw to construct a new post-independence knowledge of its natural, social and cultural history (Gunn, 1999).

Education for Decolonisation

In April 1974, Portuguese army officers in Lisbon overthrew the dictatorship in what became known as the 'Carnation Revolution', initiating a decolonisation process in all the overseas territories. In Dili, young nationalist intellectuals formed FRETILIN (Revolutionary Front for the Independence of East Timor) [1], a political party committed to independence. They were joined by Timorese university students returning home from Lisbon, where they had been exposed to the revolutionary ideas of the national liberation movements in Mozambique, Angola and Guinea Bissau (Cabral, 2002). Adopting their African counterparts' mass 'popular education' approach to decolonisation, the Lisbon group returned with a literacy manual based on the method of radical Brazilian educator, Paulo Freire. In early 1975, FRETILIN led a group of young supporters, mainly high school students, into the districts, mobilising communities to establish literacy classes, health posts and agricultural cooperatives. One participant, who later became a Vice-Minister of Finance in the independence government, recalled:

> The education we delivered was accompanied by socialisation.
> People had to understand the objective situation that stopped
> people having human dignity ... . The objective was literacy
> through conscientisation, to raise awareness of people to struggle
> against colonialism. (Aicha Basurewan, cited in Durnan, 2005,
> p. 96)

As FRETILIN's support grew rapidly in the countryside, conservative *assimilados*, supported by the Catholic Church hierarchy and manipulated by Indonesian intelligence, launched a pre-emptive 'anti-communist' coup, seizing power in Dili. In response, FRETILIN called for an armed people's insurrection. When Timorese troops in the Portuguese army deserted to join them, FRETILIN was able to establish its own liberation army, called

FALINTIL.[2] The remnants of the Portuguese administration withdrew to an island offshore, while FRETILIN put down the coup, and prepared for the anticipated invasion from Indonesia. With tacit support from the USA and Australia, and under the cover of Timorese partisans recruited from the anti-FRETILIN forces, the illegal invasion began in October 1975 with commando raids across the border (Jolliffe, 2009). This escalated to a full-scale invasion in December of that year. Two weeks prior to the invasion, FRETILIN announced a unilateral declaration of independence, forming the first government of the Democratic Republic of Timor-Leste (Jolliffe, 1978, 2009).

As the invading Indonesian army took over Dili and the major towns, 80% of the population retreated into the mountains, where they lived in 'liberated zones' governed by FRETILIN's revolutionary administration. This was modelled on the concept of a 'people's war' which the African nationalist leader Amilcar Cabral had adopted in Guinea Bissau (Cabral, 2002, p. 151). In each zone under FRETILIN's control, the political leadership shared power with military commanders, governing through a system of Commissions. The Education Commission was under the control of FRETILIN's women's organisation, OPMT [3], whose founder, Rosa 'Muki' Bonaparte, one of the Lisbon group, was executed by the Indonesians on the first day of the invasion. The OPMT slogan was 'Fight, Learn, Produce'. The rudimentary education system included literacy classes for adults and children, some basic revolutionary theory, and the history of the Timorese struggle for independence (Alves et al, n.d., p. 18). This experiment in revolutionary education, despite its brevity, is a key part of the heritage of many of today's leaders, including several members of the first independence government, a significant number of officials and teachers in the Ministry of Education, and a younger generation of leaders who experienced this system directly as children, or else learned of it through the youth and student organisations which formed during the next wave of resistance in the 1980s and 1990s (Cabral & Martin-Jones, 2008; Da Silva, 2004; Durnan, 2005; CAVR, 2006, ch. 3).

At the end of 1978, the Indonesian army succeeded in overcoming the first phase of military resistance in the liberated zones. Over the next 20 years, a new form of resistance was built, via a clandestine network under the direct authority of the FALINTIL commanders, some of whom remained behind in small guerrilla groups to continue the armed struggle. The internal struggle was supported by a diplomatic front led by FRETILIN exiles and their families, some of whom had been sent out for this purpose prior to the invasion. In each of these 'fronts', the armed front, the clandestine front, and the diplomatic front, the Resistance continued to educate its members and their children, countering the Indonesian-ising education system introduced by the invaders. The different experiences in these three fronts helped to form the educational thinking of the movement, but it also led over time to complex differences within the Resistance as a whole. These differences continue today in educational debates on many issues, including the type and purpose of post-independence education, the balance between traditional Indigenous knowledges and scientific modernism, the appropriate languages of instruction, the most relevant international models, and the role of the Catholic Church.[4]

Indonesian Colonial Education

The Indonesian occupation force adopted an educational strategy to complement its military one, seeking to win support for the integration of Portuguese Timor (Portugal remained the internationally recognised administering power until 1999) into the Republic of Indonesia. A provincial administration was established, with a Timorese governor, and an education department controlled from Jakarta. While the Catholic Church maintained an uneasy truce with the new civil power, continuing to operate its own schools, Indonesian-controlled educational provision was slowly extended into the countryside. In theory, this meant six years of primary education, three years of junior secondary education, and three years of senior secondary academic or vocational education; with post-school provision of two years of polytechnic education, or three to four years of university education (World Bank, 2004, p. 4). Primary schools were staffed by Timorese teachers, but almost all secondary teachers and the higher levels of educational administration were reserved for 'transmigrasi', settlers from other parts of Indonesia. By 1999, according to the World Bank, some gains had been made:

> Between 1976 and 1998, enrollment in primary education
> increased from 13,500 to 165,000 students. By the mid-1990s,
> primary education was available in most villages. Over the same
> period, junior secondary enrollment grew from 315 to 32,000
> students, and senior secondary education enrollment grew from
> 64 to 14,600 students (World Bank, 2004, p. 4)

Nevertheless, Timor-Leste lagged well behind the Indonesian enrolment average, and was 'far from meeting the national requirement of 9 years of compulsory basic education for children between the ages of 7 and 15' (World Bank, 2007). For young people aged 16-18 in 1999, less than half had reached Grade 9, and less than a quarter of those were from the poorest 25% of the population. The Bank attributed this to 'the low level of public expenditure on education during the Indonesian administration ... [which] resulted in poor quality and high repetition and low retention rates'. The other problem the Bank identified was that, while Indonesian primary education was free, 'households had to pay for books, school supplies, uniforms, transport and lunches and secondary schools charged annual and monthly fees' (World Bank, 2007). Given the subsequent role of the World Bank and key international donors in Timor-Leste's post-independence education system, it is important to note that, throughout this period, the Indonesian government, including its education system, continued to receive significant support from the donor community.

In its history of the occupation, Timor-Leste's Commission for Truth and Reconciliation agreed with the World Bank, arguing that 'the large investment in education increased the physical availability of facilities, but did not produce a corresponding improvement in its quality'. It pointed to a literacy rate which, after 20 years, was 'still only 40% ... lower than that in any country in the Asia Pacific region' (CAVR, 2006, ch. 7, p. 9, para. 119). However, the CAVR's [5] explanation was that the Indonesian school curriculum was designed to support the military pacification of the country, and undermine the independence movement:

> The use of schools for propaganda and indoctrination severely interfered with the education of an entire generation of East Timorese youth. Education was used in this way as part of an integrated security approach whose overriding objective was to ensure that pro-independence sentiment did not take root in a new generation ... teaching children the skills that would enhance their prospects and enable them to fulfil their human potential was secondary. (CAVR, 2006, ch. 7, p. 9, para. 148)

Consequently, many families sent their children to Catholic schools, where they were less likely to be the subject of surveillance by school-based spies and informants; while many other children and young people simply refused to take part (Pinto, 2001; Rei, 2008). The contradictory role of the education system in the independence struggle was re-emphasised when a new generation of Timorese high school and university students began forming their own resistance organisations in the mid-1980s. In 1991, this new wave of student activists forced the situation of their country back onto the world stage, when Indonesian troops fired on a peaceful demonstration at the Santa Cruz cemetery in Dili, killing 273 unarmed demonstrators (Jardine, 1995).

These events remind us that the Indonesian educational legacy went far beyond its lack of progress in reducing illiteracy or extending primary and secondary education; or the failure to train teachers and administrators to staff the system. For nearly 24 years, Timor-Leste was subjugated by a brutal and arbitrary military rule. This systematic institutionalised repression, including its educational aspects, helped produce and educate a new generation of independence activists, but it also did enormous damage, not only to individuals caught up in it, but to every aspect of the social fabric. According to the CAVR:

> An estimated 102,800-183,000 civilians died ... about 18,600 of these were direct killings or disappearances mainly committed by the Indonesian security forces and the rest, at least 84,200 but possibly much higher, were due to hunger and illness. (CAVR, 2006, p. 5)

Given a population of approximately 600,000 in 1975, at least one expert has concluded this was an attempted genocide (Robinson, 2003).

A feature of this period was the growing influence of the Catholic Church. Its socially conservative hierarchy had been outspoken critics of FRETILIN in 1974-75, but by the early 1980s the Timorese clergy had moved to a more nationalist position, defending their congregations against the human rights abuses of the new regime. While it did not formally affiliate to the independence movement until 1998, the Catholic Church gradually became the only legally sanctioned institution within the country able to speak out against the excesses of the military occupation, and to defend key aspects of the country's national identity, especially its language and culture. The decision by the Church to use Tetum in its liturgy and its schools helped maintain it as a national language. The Catholic secondary college in Dili also taught the Portuguese curriculum until the Indonesian authorities shut it down in 1992 (Oxfam GB, 2003, p. 68). The Church's international connections helped many young Timorese university students obtain overseas scholarships to Indonesia and beyond. Catholic foundations also helped to finance the first Timorese university, which opened in Dili in 1986 (CAVR, 2006, p. 448). The Church's position was nevertheless complicated by the increasing presence of Indonesian clergy, and the complex relationships between the Vatican and its Indonesian bishops and congregation (Carey, 1999). Individual nuns, priests and Catholic laity played crucial roles in the Resistance, and Bishop Belo became internationally recognised for his courage in speaking out against Indonesian atrocities; but at the same time, the Church played a role in, and benefited from, the Indonesian presence. It maintained its large land-holdings, for example, and the regime's requirement that all Timorese affiliate to a religion boosted Church membership and authority to a level even greater than in Portuguese times. Finally, despite the role in supporting the Resistance, the Church never abandoned its social conservatism, including its opposition to socialism and to women's reproductive rights.

The Indonesian occupation ended as it had begun, with extreme violence. As the Resistance grew in strength during the 1990s, and as the Suharto regime in Indonesia entered into its final days, the occupation force and its local militia increased the level of repression, in an effort to maintain its failing grasp on power. In May 1998, Suharto was forced to step down by the Indonesian pro-democracy movement, some of whose student leaders had strong links with the clandestine Timorese student organisations which operated in Indonesian universities (Pinto, 2001; Rei, 2008). In the lead-up to the August 1999 ballot on autonomy, Timorese students once again left their high schools and the university, to travel to the countryside in a courageous popular education campaign to win support for the independence option, and to provide local manpower for the UN mission supervising the voting (Da Silva, 2004). The vote precipitated a last wave of violence, organised by the Indonesian military as they withdrew:

Before a UN-sanctioned military force arrived to restore order in late September, hundreds of people had been killed and an estimated 400,000 people – more than half the population – had been forced to flee their homes ... Seventy percent of all buildings had been deliberately burned or rendered uninhabitable. (Robinson, 2003, pp. 1, 44)

Public infrastructure came in for special attention, and 90% of the schools were damaged, 80% destroyed completely. Moreover, almost all the 'transmigrasi' teachers brought in to help the process of 'Indonesianisation' departed, 'precipitating the collapse of the [Indonesian] education system' (World Bank, 2003, p. 2).

Educational Reconstruction under the United Nations

Following the withdrawal of the Indonesians, the United Nations became the occupying power for the next two and a half years, backed up by a multilateral peacekeeping force of 10,000 troops led by Australia. The World Bank played a major role, through its management of an international trust fund for reconstruction, to which donor countries contributed. Within the UN system, the United Nations Children's Fund (UNICEF) was the main agency involved with school education, while the United Nations Development Programme (UNDP) recruited a workforce of international advisers. The initial priority was to rehabilitate and re-open the schools, and recruit a workforce to replace the Indonesian teachers and administrators. Local leadership of the process was provided by an interim body whose members were drawn from the National Council for the Timorese Resistance (CNRT), the umbrella body which had united the different elements of the Resistance in the last years of the occupation (United Nations Security Council, 2002a, 2002b; World Bank, 2004).

During the emergency phase, many young students from the Resistance travelled to the districts to re-open schools and run literacy classes. This 'grass-roots' locally led movement for educational reconstruction was treated as marginal to the international effort, and operated with far less resources (Durnan, 2005). Moreover, its ideology, which harked back to the 'popular education' initiatives of the early independence movements' leaders like Vicente Sahe and Rosa Muki Bonaparte, did not sit comfortably with the human capital approach driving World Bank educational planning (Boughton, 2009). It also challenged the Church-influenced leaders within CNRT, including Father Filomeno Jacob, the Jesuit priest who was education minister in the transitional administration. These conservative influences helped establish the character of the reconstructed Ministry of Education.

By the end of the UN period, 700 primary schools and 100 junior secondary schools were functioning, and school enrolments had grown to 240,000, 25% greater than in the last year of Indonesian rule. Six thousand

Timorese teachers staffed the new system, many with minimal qualifications. One hundred and fifty Portuguese teachers were also teaching in the schools, and providing Portuguese language classes to their Timorese counterparts (United Nations Security Council, 2002b, p. 9). Given the lack of teacher training, the continued dependence on Indonesian curriculum and resources, and the complexity of delivering these in the official languages of Portuguese and Tetum, the quality of the education was seriously problematic. However, around 5000 students had enrolled or re-enrolled in courses at the national university, which had re-opened in November 2000, many of them in teacher education.

The most significant development for education was the new Independence Constitution, adopted on 22 March 2002 by an elected Constituent Assembly. The Preamble declared it to be 'the culmination of the historical resistance of the Timorese People which intensified following the invasion of the 7th of December 1975', and acknowledged the contributions made by all three fronts, as well as the specific contribution of the Church. The progressive character of the Constitution, and its heritage in the experience of the Resistance, are also clear from its objectives. These include a commitment to a socially just society, including equality between men and women, and its international solidarity provisions, which commit the new nation to supporting national liberation in other parts of the world. In respect of education, Article 59 makes an unequivocal commitment to free public education:

> The State shall recognise and guarantee that every citizen has the
> right to education and culture, and must promote the
> establishment of a public system of universal and compulsory
> basic education that is free of charge in accordance with its ability
> and in conformity with the law.[6]

Article 13, another key clause for the education system, makes Tetum and Portuguese the country's official languages, while requiring the state to 'value and develop Tetum and the other national languages'. Timor's complex language ecology (Hajek, 2000) is further recognised in Article 159, under which 'Indonesian and English shall be working languages within civil service side by side with official languages as long as deemed necessary'. The Lusophone heritage is specifically valorised in Article 8.3, requiring the new nation to 'maintain privileged ties with the countries whose official language is Portuguese'.

Education since Independence

On 20 May 2002, the UN flag was lowered, and the new flag of independent Timor-Leste was raised, finally re-establishing the sovereignty first asserted by FRETILIN in November 1975. In the August 2001 Constituent Assembly elections, 57% of the population voted for FRETILIN.

FRETILIN's Secretary-General, Mari Alkatiri, one of three surviving founders from 1975, became the prime minister. In separate elections, the presidency was won overwhelmingly by Kay Rala Xanana Gusmao, the charismatic Resistance commander-in-chief captured by the Indonesians in 1992. Alkatiri chose a non-FRETILIN member, Armindo Maia, as his first education minister, part of his strategy to include in his Council of Ministers non-aligned people with expertise in their field. Maia had been rector of the university in the last years of the occupation, and enjoyed good relationships with the Church.

In Timor-Leste, ministers are not parliamentarians, but work within their own ministry offices as the most senior administrator, assisted by senior civil servants and advisers. Maia's senior foreign advisers, many of whom were appointed under UNTAET [7], included nationals from Portugal, Brazil, Cape Verde, the United States and Australia. Some were employed through UN agencies, usually UNICEF or UNDP, while some were World Bank employees or consultants. With advisers reporting to the minister, to the international agency employing them, and often to their own national embassy, lines of accountability were extremely confused. Differences in the political and personal histories of the national Timorese officials compounded this complexity. The first Director General of Education, who had been educated in Portuguese times, had joined the pro-Portuguese party during the 1974-75 decolonisation period and been jailed by FRETILIN during the 1975 civil war. By contrast, some of his directors were FRETILIN militants, some of whom were FALINTIL fighters during the occupation; while others were Indonesian educated, and had previously been active in different parts of the clandestine movement. There were significant differences between the ex-activists, depending on which part of the movement they had worked in, and these differences were expressed in affiliations to different post-independence political parties, including FRETILIN, ASDT and PD.[8] Other officials were exiled returnees, educated in Portugal, Australia or any one of a dozen other countries. These complex political, educational and personal histories necessitated a high degree of negotiation over almost every aspect of the Ministry's functioning, and provided ample opportunity for internationals with competing agendas to mobilise support among different Timorese factions. This occurred most often over the issue of language of instruction, but extended into almost every aspect of the emerging system, from its policy and legislative context to its school-term timetabling to its preferred method of assessment. In the first three years of the new administration, the education sector was therefore characterised by a highly factionalised and conflicted process, as different international agencies and different bilateral donors joined forces with different Timorese political groupings to argue over the shape which the new education system should take. The various fault lines came to the surface in two national education conferences in 2003, and dominated debates over the next few years (Oxfam GB, 2003).

From 2002 until 2006, the educational debates continued against a background of ongoing political tension, as the new government sought to establish an institutional framework and implement its program. In this period, the government had to manage rising expectations and frustrations, especially among disaffected veterans and elements of the security forces. Meanwhile, it was maintaining a tough stance in negotiations with Australia over the ownership of the seabed oil and gas resources between the two countries, which was vital for financing its radical social program without recourse to international loans. Core to FRETILIN's program was its commitment to free education and health care, a position running counter to the orthodox neoliberal view of the World Bank and International Monetary Fund. Even before independence, the Bank's views had exercised significant influence on the first National Development Plan, resulting in a document which was an odd mix of FRETILIN social objectives and neoliberal economic orthodoxy. However, there had been little doubt in the minds of the majority of the population about what it was they had fought for, with education being nominated by 70% of the population as the first development priority in nationwide consultations on the National Development Plan (East Timor Planning Commission, 2002).

Political Crises 2005-07

Tensions between the government and its political opponents were exacerbated by the re-emergence of conflict between FRETILIN and the Church in 2005, when the government moved to enforce the Constitutional guarantee of religious freedom by abolishing the Indonesian practice whereby religious instruction was a compulsory and examinable subject in secondary schools. A Church-sponsored demonstration mobilised several thousand people from the districts who were trucked into Dili and took over the streets around the parliament for several weeks. While a compromise solution was reached, the Church's action helped set in train a series of further challenges to the government's legitimacy, culminating in an attempted coup d'état in April 2006, involving significant desertions from the army and the Dili police command to the anti-government forces. Once again, an international peacekeeping force had to restore security, as the crisis shattered the fragile truce whereby the various elements of the old united Resistance front had agreed to keep their differences within the framework of constitutional democracy. This left FRETILIN, the country's largest political party, on one side, with the president, backed by the Church and key elements of the international community, on the other.

The crisis had major educational consequences. In Dili especially and in a small number of districts, communal and gang violence erupted on a scale not seen since 1999, sponsored by different political factions seeking to obtain advantage from the situation. One hundred and fifty thousand people were forced to leave their homes, and take refuge in hastily erected IDP [9] camps. Thousands of children stopped attending schools, and many teachers and FRETILIN-aligned ministry officials lost their homes. The Ministry of Education's warehouse containing the new curriculum and resource materials was burned. The Cuban education mission, which had arrived only a month earlier to begin work on the national adult literacy campaign, was also targeted, as evidence of FRETILIN's communist sympathies. In June 2006, Alkatiri, in an effort to avoid further bloodshed, agreed to an ultimatum from President Gusmao, and resigned as prime minister. His place was taken by Gusmao's ally, José Ramos Horta, but while FRETILIN's power was significantly reduced, it continued to control most ministries, including education. FRETILIN's Rosaria Corte-Real, who had been vice-minister, replaced Amindo Maia, who resigned at the height of the crisis. Backed by her vice-minister Ilda da Conceição, also a woman and a former FALINTIL fighter and OPMT leader, Corte-Real used the next 12 months to oversight completion of a strategic plan for free universal primary education, initiate a pilot program providing daily meals to children in the poorest schools, finalise the UNICEF-sponsored bilingual primary school curriculum and launch the Cuban-backed national adult literacy campaign.

The political instability continued until the presidential and parliamentary elections during the first half of 2007. These ended with a new president, José Ramos Horta, and a new prime minister, Xanana Gusmao, who headed a coalition government of several anti-FRETILIN parties, known as Aliança de Maioria Parlamentar (AMP). FRETILIN's parliamentary representation was reduced to 21, and while it remains the country's largest political party, it is now the opposition.

The Situation Today

The minister for education in the new AMP government is Dr João Câncio, previously director of the country's largest and most successful private tertiary education provider, the Dili Institute of Technology. Dr Câncio, who has a PhD in management from an Australian university, has instituted a major administrative decentralisation program, creating five new administrative education regions. This decentralisation is supported by a World Bank and donor-funded program to improve the capacity of the Ministry's senior managers and regional directors to provide education policy leadership. A strong advocate of the role of the private sector, the minister is also moving to create a new policy and regulatory framework, with a focus on achieving the Millennium Development Goals, and on separating executive and policy functions from delivery. The Church has received a significant increase in government funding support. The new minister has changed the school year to a calendar year, abandoning the previous practice based on the Portuguese school year. In 2009, the final three months of the year were devoted to intensive teacher training, part of a move to raise the quality of teaching by tying wage levels to the newly adopted teacher competency standards.

A new Basic Law for Education passed in 2008 guarantees all children under 17 years of age access to nine years of free basic education. The strategic plan for universal primary education developed by the previous government continues to be the chief policy instrument in achieving this goal. However, while significant progress was made between 1999, when the estimated net enrolment ratio was between 60-70%, until 2004, when it reached 78%, it has since fallen back below the 1999 level, to 63% in 2007. The 2006-07 political crisis was one factor, but these figures also reflect the peculiar post-war demography of Timor-Leste, where 40% of the population are under 15 years of age, with the youngest cohorts forming the largest groupings (DRTL.NDS, 2006, p. 71). Substantial funding is earmarked in the current budget for new school buildings, to help solve the growing access problem. The low participation rates are the combined effect of the high fertility rate (7.8 average births per woman over her lifetime) which is producing rapidly growing cohorts of primary school-age children, insufficient schools and teachers, and the high prevalence of illiteracy and poverty in rural communities in particular, which results in an unwillingness among parents to send children to school on a regular basis. These factors are clearly interrelated, since high fertility is associated with early pregnancies among young women, which would be reduced if there was more opportunity, access and encouragement for them to stay on at school. Likewise, the high rates of adult illiteracy are associated with poor health, low nutrition, and lack of capacity to improve agricultural productivity, which together help to maintain families in poverty and reduce their capacity to release children from income-generating or food-producing labour.

The situation in the secondary system is much less clear, in part because the government shares responsibility for secondary education with the Catholic Church, which does not have the same level of accountability and reporting. In 2005-06, the World Bank reported there were 200 secondary schools, of which 135 were junior secondary and only 65 were senior secondary. The net enrolment ratio of the latter was 33%. In the senior secondary system, 585 teachers were teaching 264,333 students, giving a student–teacher ratio of 45:1 (World Bank, 2007, p. 18). The new government is placing more emphasis on vocational skills in junior secondary schools. It has transferred control of the agricultural colleges from the Ministry of Agriculture to the Ministry of Education, which is also working with the private sector to build other technical schools or polytechnics, based on models from Australia. A recently established National Commission for UNESCO has announced a focus on improving science and technology education.

The tertiary and higher education sector continues to receive the least attention in term of policy development, funding and donor support. After the 1999 violence, thousands of students who had been studying in Indonesia returned with their studies incomplete. Some are only now managing to complete their studies through the national university, UNTL, or one of the 19 other tertiary institutions currently operating. In 2007, one experienced Timor scholar commented:

> It is regrettable that UNDP only belatedly looked to assist the rationalisation of the higher education sector in East Timor in a dismaying situation where private universities have proliferated, where facilities are primitive, where standards are low, where teachers are under-credentialled or not trained, where text books are lacking and in a situation where a host of other factors – not excluding language choice – contrive to choke the rational allocation of educational resources, not to mention the production of knowledge ... few other new nations have sought or have been obliged to rebuild their university systems using almost exclusively local human resources. (Gunn, 2007, p. 110)

The new Basic Education Law provides for the regulation and auditing of higher education providers. In July 2008, an initial assessment led by a World Bank consultant approved 7 of the 14 providers who applied, including UNTL. In November 2009, the Ministry of Education announced the establishment of a National Commission for Academic Assessment and Accreditation, to begin work in 2010. Meanwhile, the range of courses available in the country and the quality of instruction have forced many students to travel overseas on scholarships in order to gain professional qualifications. One of the most significant international contributions has come from Cuba, which, under an arrangement negotiated with the previous government, is training 648 Timorese medical and allied health students in Cuba on full scholarships, of whom the first 18 returned in 2009, while a further 148 are being trained through a new medical program established by the Cubans at UNTL (Leach, 2008-09). President Horta has also been actively seeking more scholarships from countries in the Association of Southeast Asian Nations region, including Malaysia and the Philippines; and from Australia.

The new government continues to give strong support to the Cuban-led national adult literacy campaign, initiated in 2005. Since classes began in June 2007, more than 95,000 adults have completed its 13-week course, which is delivered by local village monitors using audiovisual materials, supervised by 35 Cuban technical advisers. By opening the way to a more literate culture especially in rural areas, this campaign will, if maintained and followed up with ongoing post-literacy and basic adult education activities, reduce the number of children and young people dropping out of school, as families and communities become more engaged with the value of education and its contribution to development and independence (Boughton, 2008, 2010). Currently, less than 60% of children who enrol in Grade 2 actually reach Grade 5. This low retention rate, coupled with the low level of enrolments to begin with, produced an estimate prior to the crisis of 8000 young people leaving school each year without acquiring basic literacy (Democratic Republic of Timor-Leste, Ministry of Education & Secretariat of State for Solidarity and Labour (DRTL, ME & SSSL), 2005). The new government has decided, with strong support from UNICEF and the World Bank, to focus its non-formal education strategy on young people aged 16-24, a position supported by many analyses of the 2006-07 crisis, which laid much of the blame for the violence on young unemployed youth.

There is also a growing technical and vocational education and training (TVET) sector. This is the responsibility of the Secretary of State for Employment and Training (SSET), whose principal source of advice is the International Labour Organization. The SSET has adopted a TVET model based on a national qualifications framework and competency-based training standards, both of which will be developed via a National Labour Force Institute with significant input from private sector employers. Responsibility for provision will be largely left to non-government and private providers. This model has implications for other parts of the education and training system, and the Education Ministry will be involved in the development of teacher training and literacy standards, as well as the pathways between the TVET sector and the formal education sector (Boughton, 2009).

Conclusion

For most of the second half of the last century, newly independent countries and the social movements which fought to create them debated what sort of education systems they would build under the general concept of 'decolonisation'. Indeed, when FRETILIN formed in 1974, 'decolonisation' was central to their discourse and those of the new government in Portugal. Decolonising education is a very special kind of education, since it must help a previously dominated people learn to be free. This makes education more than human capital building; rather, it is a central aspect of the right of self-determination, the right of a people, as the UN Covenants put it, 'to freely determine their economic, political and cultural development' (United Nations, 1966). Clearly, the capacity of 'a people' to create the institutions whereby such rights can be freely exercised is, at the same time, seriously undermined by the educational legacies of past colonial systems which aimed to extinguish those same rights.

It would be hard to overstate the complexity of the educational challenges which faced the Timorese leadership in September 1999. This chapter has emphasised the way the legacy of conflict and violence which is endemic to colonialism continues to disrupt the process of nation building long after the fighting ceases. Education is one of the principal ways in which the legacy of conflict can be overcome, and a renewed national identity created. But this can only occur to the extent that the international community supports the decolonisation process, rather than treating education primarily as a support for economic development; or worse, as the means to reinstate colonial dependence in a new form. It also requires the international community to see beyond the apparent 'deficits' in the educational legacy the colonial powers leave, to the internal and often underground educational traditions borne out of the struggle for independence. As the editors of a special issue of the *International Journal of Lifelong Education* on 'Women, War and Learning' wrote:

> survivors of conflict have their own good knowledge of their lives and experience ... [and] their survival has more often than not been based upon their agency and intelligence and their ability to adapt, improvise, and innovate. The goals of lifelong education cannot be achieved unless the survival and resistance learning acquired in war is the basis for [future] learning. (Mojab & Dobson, 2008, pp. 120, 122)

The problem of constructing a new national identity and culture in Timor-Leste, while at the same time building an economic base appropriate to that identity and culture and supporting its growth and development, is the most fundamental challenge of the post-conflict education system. While the Resistance generated an understanding of national identity in opposition to the identity of the occupier, this identity was never uncontested, even when the national struggle enjoyed overwhelming support. Moreover, national unity in a Resistance movement is held together in part by the actions of the occupier, and in part by the highly disciplined command structure required in armed and clandestine struggle. When both of these are removed, and the 'national resistance' has to transform, not just its own supporters, but the whole country into 'the nation', a new set of problems emerges. To build a transformative education system capable of supporting a people's move from colonial subjection and resistance to an independent, freely determined future, is a mammoth task. This chapter demonstrates that a decade is a very short time, when put against the much longer period during which powers much greater and stronger than Timor-Leste have conspired to prevent this happening.

Notes

[1] In Portuguese, Frente Revolucionária do Timor-Leste Independente.

[2] Forças Armadas de Liberatação National de Timor-Leste (Armed Forces for the National Liberation of East Timor).

[3] Organizaçao Popular da Mulher Timor (Popular Organisation of Timorese Women).

[4] The diversity of views on these questions can be seen in the proceedings of the Civil Society Education Conference and the National Education Congress, both held in 2003.

[5] The acronym is from the Portuguese: Comissão de Acolhimento, Verdade e Reconciliação de Timor-Leste (Timor-Leste Commission for Reception, Truth and Reconciliation).

[6] An official English translation of the Constitution, which has no page numbers, was downloaded from the website of the Government of Timor-Leste, at http://www.gov.east-timor.org/constitution/constitution.htm. The originals are in the two official languages, Portuguese and Tetum.

[7] United Nations Transitional Administration in East Timor.

[8] ASDT (Social Democratic Association) and PD (Democratic Party) were smaller parties formed by independence supporters, many of whom had originally been part of FRETILIN.

[9] Internally Displaced People.

References

Alves, M.D.F., Abrantes, L.S. & Reis, F. (n.d., *c*.2003) *Written with Blood*, trans. N. Sarmento & L. Alves. Dili: Office for Promotion of Equality, Prime Minister's Office, Democratic Republic of Timor-Leste.

Boughton, B. (2008) East Timor's National Literacy Campaign and the Struggle for a Post-conflict Democracy, paper presented at the Australasian Asian Studies Association Conference, Melbourne, 1-3 July. http://www.arts.monash.edu.au/mai/asaa/bobboughton.pdf.

Boughton, B. (2009) Challenging Donor Agendas in Adult & Workplace Education in Timor-Leste, in L. Cooper & S. Walters (Eds) *Learning/Work. Critical Perspectives on Lifelong Learning and Work*. Cape Town: HSRC Press.

Boughton, B. (2010) Back to the Future? Timor-Leste, Cuba and the Return of the Mass Literacy Campaign, *Literacy and Numeracy Studies*, 18(2), 23-40.

Cabral, E. (2002) FRETILIN and the Struggle for Independence in East Timor 1974-2002: an examination of the constraints and opportunities of a non-state nationalist movement in the late twentieth century. Unpublished PhD thesis, Lancaster University, UK.

Cabral, E. & Martin-Jones, M. (2008) Writing the Resistance: literacy in East Timor 1975-1999, *International Journal of Bilingual Education and Bilingualism*, 11(2), 149-169.

Carey, P. (1999) The Catholic Church, Religious Revival, and the Nationalist Movement in East Timor, 1975-98, *Indonesia and the Malay World*, 27(78), 77-95.

CAVR (2006) Introducing ... Chega! The Report of the Commission for Reception, Truth and Reconciliation in Timor-Leste (CAVR). http://www.cavr-timorleste.org/chegaFiles/introducingChegaEng.pdf (accessed 5 September 2009).

Da Silva, A.B. (2004) Potential of Education for Conflict Transformation and Identity Reconstruction in the Cultural Context of Uato-Lari and Uato-Carbau. Paper presented at the Catholic Teachers Training Center, Baucau, September 2004.

Democratic Republic of Timor-Leste, Ministry of Education & Secretariat of State for Solidarity and Labour (DRTL, ME & SSSL) (2005) *Education and Training. Priorities and Proposed Sector Investment Program.* Dili: DRTL.

Democratic Republic of Timor-Leste. National Directorate of Statistics (2006) *Census of Population & Housing 2004. National Priority Tables.* Dili: NDS.

Durnan, D. (2005) Popular Education and Peacebuilding in Timor Leste. Unpublished Master of Professional Studies (Honours) dissertation, University of New England, Armidale.

East Timor Planning Commission (2002) *East Timor National Development Plan.* Dili: Republic of East Timor.

Gunn, G.C. (1999) *Timor Loro Sae. 500 Years.* Macau: Livros do Oriente.

Gunn, G.C. (2007) The State of East Timor Studies after 1999, *Journal of Contemporary Asia,* 37(1), 95-114.

Hajek, J. (2000) Language Planning and the Sociolinguistic Environment in East Timor: colonial practice and changing language ecologies, *Current Issues in Language Planning,* 1(3), 400-414.

Hill, H. (2002) *Stirrings of Nationalism in East Timor: Fretilin 1974-1978: the origins, ideologies and strategies of a nationalist movement.* Otford, Sydney: Otford Press.

Jardine, M. (1995) *East Timor: genocide in paradise.* Tucson: Odonian Press.

Jolliffe, J. (1978) *East Timor. Nationalism and Colonialism.* St Lucia: University of Queensland Press.

Jolliffe, J. (2009) *Balibo.* Carlton North: Scribe.

Leach, M. (2008-09) The Neglected State-builder: Cuban medical programs in the Pacific, *Arena Magazine,* no. 98, pp. 8-9.

Mojab, S. & Dobson, S. (2008) Women, War, and Learning, *International Journal of Lifelong Education,* 27(2), 119-127.

Oxfam GB (2003) National Conference on Education, Dili, Timor-Leste, April.

Pinto, C. (2001) The Student Movement and the Independence Movement in East Timor: an interview, in R. Tanter, M. Selden & S.R. Shalom (Eds) *Bitter Flowers, Sweet Flowers: East Timor, Indonesia and the world community,* pp. 31-42. Sydney: Pluto Press.

Rei, N. (2008) *Resistance: a childhood fighting for East Timor.* Brisbane: UQP.

Robinson, G. (2003) East Timor 1999. Crimes against Humanity. A Report Commissioned by the United Nations Office of the High Commissioner for Human Rights July 2003. Published as an annex to the Report of the Commission for Truth and Reconciliation (CAVR).

United Nations (1966) International Covenant on Civil and Political Rights. Adopted by General Assembly resolution 2200A (XXI) of 16 December 1966. http://www2.ohchr.org/english/law/ccpr.htm (accessed 19 May 2011).

United Nations Security Council (2002a) *Report of the Secretary-General on the United Nations Transitional Administration in East Timor (UNTAET) 17 January 2002.* New York: UNSC.

United Nations Security Council (2002b) *Report of the Secretary-General on the United Nations Transitional Administration in East Timor (UNTAET) 17 April 2002.* New York: UNSC.

World Bank (2003) Timor-Leste Education. The Way Forward. A summary report from the World Bank, 1 December. Originally prepared for the National Education Congress, November 2003.

World Bank (2004) *Timor-Leste Education since Independence from Reconstruction to Sustainable Improvement* (Report No. 29784-TP). Washington: World Bank Human Development Sector East Asia and Pacific Region.

World Bank (2007) *Social and Economic Development Brief.* (Prepared by the World Bank Group and the Asian Development Bank, in consultation with Development Partners). http://www.adb.org/Documents/Books/ESDB-Timor-Leste/ESDB-Timor-Leste.pdf

CHAPTER 11

Thailand:
educational equality and quality

NATTHAPOJ VINCENT TRAKULPHADETKRAI

SUMMARY This chapter primarily examines the issues of educational equality and quality in Thailand. It provides a brief overview of the national context as well as the education system, with particular focus on early childhood education, basic education, higher education and teacher education. Thailand's progress on achieving the six Education for All goals is later analysed, along with factors which could promote and hinder such progress.

National Context

Thailand is a constitutional monarchy headed by King Bhumibol Adulyadej. Thailand, with a population of just over 66,480,000 people, is a predominantly Buddhist country with 94.6% of the Thai population who are Buddhist. Around 4.6% of the entire population is Muslim who live mainly in its southern provinces, while a small Christian population (approximately 0.7%) live mostly in Bangkok and the northern provinces. Generally speaking, Thailand is a relatively homogeneous and peaceful country. However, recent violence in the three southernmost Muslim provinces, namely Yala, Pattani and Narathiwat, as well as an on-going political unrest in the capital city, seem to suggest otherwise. A discussion of how these events may have an impact on education is provided later in this chapter.

Unlike other countries in the region, Thailand has never been colonised by foreign powers. This legacy manifests in various ways from the use of Thai as the official language to how Thai society has its own unique socio-cultural values which, as it will also be discussed in this chapter, are believed to have an impact on teaching and learning.

Thailand has a GDP of about $272.8 billion, making its GDP per capita standing at $8013 (International Institute for Management Development [IMD], 2009). In its annual *World Competitive Yearbook*

(WCY), which measures a country's competitiveness, in terms of growth and economic performance as well as *soft factors* of competitiveness, such as environment, quality of life, technology and education, the IMD (2009) ranked Thailand 26th out of 57 economies as covered by the WCY. Other countries in the region include Singapore (3rd), Malaysia (18th), Indonesia (42nd) and the Philippines (43rd).

According to the United Nations Development Programme's (2007a) *Human Development Report*, which measures a country's level of development using three basic dimensions of life expectancy, education and standard of living, Thailand was ranked 78th in the Human Development Index, behind Singapore (25th), Brunei (30th) and Malaysia (63rd). These three countries are categorised as having high human development. Other countries in the region including the Philippines (90th), Vietnam (105th), Indonesia (107th), Lao PDR (130th), Cambodia (131st), Myanmar (132nd) and Timor-Leste (150th), are categorised, along with Thailand, as having medium human development.

Educational Context

Administrative and Organisational Structures

The Ministry of Education (established in 1892 and formerly existing since 1887 as the Department of Education) is responsible for overseeing education in Thailand. The Ministry comprises five main Offices: the Office of the Permanent Secretary for Education is the main organisation responsible for 'providing the Education Minister with information to initiate and implement policies which aid and manage a budget plan and include the evaluation of the Ministry of Education's operation performance'. It also acts as 'a coordinating unit for administration and cooperation among ministries and government offices' (Ministry of Education [MoE], 2008b, p. 7). The Office of the Education Council (OEC) is 'the main policy development organisation for planning and setting national education standards. OEC is also responsible for education research and assessment' (MoE, 2008b, p. 7). The Office of the Basic Education Commission (OBEC) coordinates 'the continuity of activities to achieve government policy for social development and also implements the policies of the Ministry of Education. OBEC assesses the results of activities implemented by all Educational Service Areas, which then leads to improvements in policy-based tasks' (MoE, 2008b, p. 7). The Office of the Higher Education Commission (OHEC), once the Ministry of University Affairs, is responsible for education at both undergraduate and graduate levels. The OHEC has 'the authority to strategise, manage and promote higher education with respect to the academic freedom and excellence of degree-granting institutions' (MoE, 2008b, p. 8). The Office of the Vocational Education Commission is responsible for 'vocational and professional life long learning. The provision of technical and vocational education and training is offered through the formal school system, in both the basic and vocational education streams, as well as through non-formal education opportunities' (MoE, 2008b, p. 8). Unlike in the past, efforts have been made recently to ensure that overlapping of responsibilities among these different bodies is avoided.

Early Childhood Education and Basic Education

The Thai education system comprises 12-year free basic education: six years of *Prathom* (or primary education, P1 to P6), three years of *Mattayom Ton* (or lower secondary education, M1 to M3), and three years of *Mattayom Plai* (or upper secondary education, M4 to M6). Mattayom Plai is divided into academic and vocational streams. Students who choose the academic stream usually intend to enter a university. Vocational schools offer programmes that prepare students for employment or further studies. Compulsory education lasts nine years, covering Prathom and Mattayom Ton. In addition to the 12-year free basic education, the government decided, in 2009, to extend the free education scheme to also include three years of early childhood education (for age groups 3 to 5). More details of this scheme will be discussed later in this chapter.

The current Thai education system stems from the reforms set by the 1999 National Education Act, which implemented new organisational structures, promoted the decentralisation of administration and called for innovative learner-centred teaching practices. Considerable changes in the structure of management and administration have taken place since 2002 in order to reduce replication of roles and responsibilities within the Ministry of Education bodies. Emphasis is, however, on the decentralisation of administrative responsibilities to local level with the consolidation of education planning at the central level. As a result, 175 Education Service Areas (ESAs) were established in 2003, which subsequently increased to 185 in 2008. The main areas of responsibilities which have been transferred from the Ministry to Education to ESAs range from academic, budget and human resources to general affairs (OEC, 2006). The management of educational decentralisation in Thailand has not always been as smooth running as it was hoped to be. It is widely acknowledged that many managerial-level officers at ESAs still find their roles and responsibilities relatively ambiguous. Further, since educational decentralisation is a recent phenomenon in the country, the majority of those involved in the running of ESAs (i.e. civil servants) are said to still espouse the traditional mentality of 'receiving' orders from the central government. Similarly, the government is still used to 'giving' orders to ESAs, and fails to decentralise its educational management effectively (OEC, 2006).

The latest curriculum reform in Thailand was launched in 2008, providing a core curriculum for each of the eight core subjects: Thai language, mathematics, science, social studies, religion and culture, health and physical education, arts, careers and technology, and foreign languages

(MoE, 2008a). For each subject and for each grade level (P1–M6), programmes of study set out what pupils should be taught, and attainment targets set out the expected standards of pupils' performance. According to the Ministry of Education (2008b, p. 3): 'Flexibility is built into the curriculum in order to integrate local wisdom and culture, so that it is consistent with set learning standards in each of the core subject groups. The promotion of thinking skills, self-learning strategies and moral development is at the heart of teaching and learning in the Thai National Curriculum.' Later in this chapter, the author, based on his earlier work, argues how attempts to reform teaching and learning in Thailand may be hindered by some of the Thai socio-cultural factors.

Higher Education

Until recently, on graduating from high school, students needed to pass the CUAS (Central University Admission System), which contains 50% of O-NET (Ordinary National Educational Test) and A-NET (Advanced National Education Test) results and the other half of the Grade Point Average of the last three years of secondary education. The new Aptitude Test, introduced in March 2009 and supervised by the National Institute of Educational Testing Service (NIETS), replaced the A-NET. The new test comprises the *compulsory* General Aptitude Test, which covers reading, writing, analytical thinking, problem solving and English communication, and the *voluntary* Professional Aptitude Test, which offers a choice of seven subjects. Both types of Aptitude Test can be taken up to a maximum of three times, with the best scores counted (NIETS, 2009).

Most Bachelor degree courses are of four-years' full-time study, with the exception of some academic disciplines such as medicine, dentistry, and veterinary medicine (six years). Master's degrees last from one to two years, and are conferred on course credits with either a thesis or a final exam. Students, on completion of a Master's degree, may apply for an admission exam to a doctoral degree lasting from two to five years, conferred on coursework, research and the successful submission of a dissertation (Fry, 2002).

Of the 165 higher education institutions in Thailand, 65 are public universities and 13 are *autonomous* public universities (Commission on Higher Education, 2009). In recent years, more public universities have become autonomous, in order to increase the efficiency of their academic, personnel and financial administration. This trend, according to Bovornsiri (1998), is part of the higher education loan's contract agreement with the Asian Development Bank, which requires taking state universities out of the Thai civil service system.

Teacher Education

Teacher training is offered either in universities by the Ministry of University Affairs or in teacher training colleges, many of which have now become *Rajaphat* (the King's scholars) Universities, and which are administered by the Ministry of Education's Department of Teacher Education. Programmes include courses in teaching methodology, school administration, optional specialisation, supervised practical teaching experience, and general education subjects.

Completion of upper secondary education (Mathayom 6) is required for access to basic teacher training programmes. Primary and lower secondary school teachers are required to complete a two-year programme leading to the Higher Certificate of (or Diploma in) Education. To teach at the upper secondary school level, the minimum requirement is a four-year Bachelor of Education degree, provided either at a teacher's training college or in a university faculty of education. Prospective teachers with a Bachelor's degree in other subjects must take an additional one-year full-time course to complete a Bachelor of Education degree (Office of Commercial Services, 2002).

Many Thai state school teachers are attracted to the profession only because of guaranteed employment, a pension and the high social respect for the profession. However, there is little financial incentive to teach in a state school. Teachers' salaries are exceptionally low when compared with other professions. Many newly qualified teachers, instead, choose employment in the better rewarded private sector, resulting in a shortage of teachers and the overcrowding of classes in some public schools (Pillay, 2002).

Education and the Tenth National Economic
and Social Development Plan (2007-11)

The Tenth National Economic and Social Development Plan is a five-year strategic plan (2007-11), based on 'a collective vision of Thai society as a "Green and Happy Society", where Thai people are endowed with morality-based knowledge and resilience against the adverse impacts of globalisation' (MoE, 2008b, p. 9). The main objective of the National Development Plan is to increase capacity for the improvement of the Thai people's quality of life. According to the Office of the National Economic and Social Development Board (2009), the Tenth Plan sets, among others, four education-related targets:

1. Increase the average period of education received to 10 years.
2. Improve test scores (higher than 55%) in core subjects, at all levels.
3. Raise the percentage of the mid-level workforce to 60% of the national labour force.
4. Increase the ratio of research personnel to population by 10:10,000.

The government aims to achieve these targets by, for example, investing in raising the quality of the entire educational system, to address the training and development of teachers, curricula, instructional media and information technology, in the hope of improving test scores to higher than 55% in core subjects at all levels. It also aims to ensure that every Thai citizen has access to no fewer than 12 years of basic education, free of charge, as well as to increase access to further education through student loan schemes, and provide supplementary scholarships for both domestic and overseas education. The government hopes that these strategies will ultimately help ensure that the average period of education that each Thai citizen receives will increase to 10 years, and help boost the production of knowledgeable and capable graduates, increasing the numbers of the mid-level workforce. Further, the government aims to develop the standard of higher education institutions to 'guarantee a high level of academic and professional services, to achieve excellence in research and innovation, and produce and develop a workforce that corresponds to structural changes within the manufacturing and services sector; accelerate the development of high quality workforce with clear career paths to enhance the country's competitiveness in various sectors' (MoE, 2008b, p. 9). Further, by putting more focus on improving access to and quality of higher education, the government hopes to meet one of its targets of increasing the ratio of research personnel to population by 10:10,000. Evidently, education has thus a crucial role to play in helping Thailand to develop both socially and economically. The government acknowledges this and has made investment in education an integral part of its policy.

Equality and Quality

Equality of Education

Equality of education is here taken to refer to *access* to education, ranging from early childhood, primary education and secondary education to higher education. Gross Enrolment Ratio (GER) and Net Enrolment Ratio (NER) are adopted, wherever possible, as the main indicators of access to education.

Based on the 2005 and 2006 data as gathered by Office of the Basic Education Commission (2007), a regional and national overview of Thailand's equality of education are discussed here.

Access to early childhood education (ages 3-5). In 2005, there were 2,410,120 Thai children whose ages fell within the national pre-school age range, from three to five years old. Some 1,776,786 children were enrolled in pre-school programmes across the country, but only 1,296,868 were actually between the ages of three and five. The rest were either slightly younger than three or slightly older than five years old. From these statistics, it is possible to calculate the GER or 'the total enrolment in a specific level of education, regardless of age' (UNESCO, 2008, p. 409) in pre-school education by dividing the total pre-school population (i.e. 1,776,786 children) by the total pre-school-age population (i.e. 2,410,120 children) and multiply it by 100 to convert it to a percentage. Accordingly, the 2005 GER in pre-school education was 73.72%. Based on the given statistics, it is also possible to work out the NER, an 'enrolment of the official age group for a given level of education, expressed as a percentage of the population in that age group' (UNESCO, 2008, p. 411). This can be done by dividing the total pre-school-age population currently enrolled in the pre-school programme (i.e. 1,296,868 children) by the entire pre-school-age population (i.e. 2,410,120 children) and multiply it by 100 to convert it to a percentage. Subsequently, the 2005 NER in pre-school education was as low as 53.81%. If we are to adopt the NER as an indicator to measure the level of equality in Thailand's pre-school level, then Thailand still certainly has a long way to go to ensure that the remaining 46.19% of Thai children whose age fell within the national pre-school age range do enrol in the pre-school programme. This trend was also representative regionally, with one exception of Bangkok and its vicinity (see Table I). The region which was far behind other regions in terms of providing equal access to children at the pre-school level was the north-eastern part of Thailand, where a high number of provinces within the region had either a *low* or *very low* Human Achievement Index (United Nations Development Programme, 2007b).

	GER	Rank	NER	Rank
Bangkok and its vicinity	75.92	3	70.29	1
Central	79.28	2	54.62	3
East	80.66	1	57.98	2
North	72.92	5	54.47	4
Northeast	69.48	6	46.13	6
South	75.34	4	52.78	5
Three southernmost provinces (Pattani, Yala and Narathiwat)	72.18		51.25	
Total	73.72		53.81	

Table I. Thailand's 2005 GER and NER data at pre-primary level.

Access to primary education (ages 6-11). In 2006, there were some 5,609,712 Thai children whose ages fell within the national primary education age range, from 6 to 11 years old. Some 5,693,040 children attended primary schools across the country, but only 4,973,682 of them were of the official primary education age group. The rest were either slightly younger than six or slightly older than 11 years old. Based on these statistics, Thailand's 2006 GER and NER in primary education were 101.49% and 88.66% respectively (see Table II).

	GER	Rank	NER	Rank
Bangkok and its vicinity	106.92	2	90.43	4
Central	105.95	3	91.04	3
East	111.89	1	96.93	1
North	102.00	5	88.76	5
Northeast	94.47	6	82.40	6
South	104.39	4	96.18	2
Three southernmost provinces (Pattani, Yala and Narathiwat)	104.19		91.02	
Total	101.49		88.66	

Table II. Thailand's 2005 GER and NER data at primary level.

Access to secondary education (ages 12-17). In 2006, there were some 5,663,529 Thai children whose ages fell within the national secondary education age range, from 12 to 17 years old. Some 4,650,554 children attended secondary schools across the country, but only 4,334,143 of them were of the official secondary education age group. The rest were either slightly younger than 12 or slightly older than 17 years old. Based on these statistics, Thailand's 2006 GER and NER in secondary education were 82.11% and 76.53% respectively (see Table III).

	GER	Rank	NER	Rank
Bangkok and its vicinity	93.21	1	74.10	6
Central	83.60	3	79.58	2
East	89.40	2	84.37	1
North	81.09	4	75.30	5
Northeast	77.70	6	75.59	4
South	78.53	5	76.94	3
Three southernmost provinces (Pattani, Yala and Narathiwat)	64.38		73.35	
Total	82.11		76.53	

Table III. Thailand's 2005 GER and NER data at secondary level.

The GER at the secondary education level perhaps distinguishes the three southernmost provinces from other regions of the country most dramatically. While Pattani, Yala and Narathiwat enjoyed a GER of 104.19% at the primary education level, the rate reduced significantly to merely 64.38% at the secondary education level, compared with the average national rate of

82.11%. Perhaps this could be explained by the fact that almost 80% of the population in this southernmost region are Muslim (OEC, 2005), and that once children have completed their primary education, their parents usually send them to privately run religious schools, called *pondok*, which, according to Medrano (2007), is 'very simple in structure; generally, it is attached to a mosque. The name, pondok, refers to the huts that the boys stay in while pursuing their studies. A pondok school is deeply personal and intimate, and is traditionally built around its teacher, the local *imam*, or its founder (who could be both). The language of instruction at many pondoks is Malay' (p. 57) as '[t]he teaching of Malay [is an] important feature of the cultural heritage of Islamic education in southern Thailand' (p. 58). Muslims do also live in other parts of the country, such as the central region. However, due to the small number of Muslims in that region, *pondok* schools are not as readily available as they are in the three southernmost provinces in Thailand, and Muslim children are thus, out of necessity, enrolled in state-run Buddhist schools instead. Children of other faiths, such as Christianity, do not appear to face the same issue as their Muslim counterparts. Perhaps Thai Christians may find it easier to assimilate in Thai Buddhist culture, while Thai Muslims – due to their ethnic, linguistic and religious uniqueness – find it harder to do so. Accordingly, the surprisingly low GER at the secondary education level for children in Pattani, Yala and Narathiwat might be explained by socio-cultural factors as opposed to lack of schools or funding.

The government acknowledges that if Muslim children only receive religious education in their secondary schooling and are refused opportunities to acquire necessary skills such as linguistic, arithmetic, and critical and analytical thinking skills that they can learn from other subjects, such as Thai, English, French, mathematics and science, the likelihood of them growing up unemployed or unable to cope with living in the era of globalisation is quite high. Worse, they may be, as it will be discussed subsequently, brainwashed to become terrorists. The government has pushed for the *pondoks* to become private Islamic schools. In some areas, this school is referred to as a *madrasa(h)*. According to Medrano (2007), private Islamic schools 'may offer non-Koranic subjects, such as science and math, as well as the teaching of foreign languages (Arabic and English)', and that '[t]hese schools are usually registered with the government' (p. 57). Further, the government also intends to develop an Islamic curriculum which could be integrated and taught in Thai Buddhist schools (OEC, 2005).

Access to higher education. According to MoE (2008b), over 2.2 million students are currently enrolled in the higher education sector and participation rates of university- age students have increased significantly over the last few years from an average of 26% to the current average of 40%. In recent years, there has been a significant increase in higher education opportunities with 78 public universities and 89 private higher education institutions.

Quality of Education

The notion of educational quality is multi-dimensional, and can be measured using different indicators. In this chapter, the concept of educational quality is taken to refer to how well students perform academically and it will be measured using their test scores.

Based on the data gathered from Thailand's National Institute of Educational Testing Service (2008a, 2008b), a brief overview is given of how well Grade 12 Thai students performed regionally and nationally in O-NET exams.

One damning and alarming fact, as deduced from Table IV, is how poor the educational quality in Thai state schools really is. In Thai, the highest annual average national score since 2005 was merely 50.70%. In mathematics, the highest was only 36.57% in 2008, followed by 34.88% in science in 2006. The worst performed subject nationally was English. Even with the highest average score, this came to only 32.37% in 2006. The average national scores of all four subjects from 2005 to 2008 are all under 50%. From 2007 to 2008, a *slight* improvement in educational performance can be seen in English (0.13% increase) and mathematics (4.08% increase), while the performance continued to deteriorate in science (0.72% decrease) and Thai (2.97% decrease). Since the data adopted here are derived entirely from Grade 12 ONET scores, they can hardly be used to represent educational performance across educational levels. Nevertheless, it is hoped that this will serve as an indicator of how well Thailand has performed educationally at a national level.

	2005	2006	2007	2008	Mean (2005-08)
Thai	48.62	50.33	50.70	47.73	49.35
Science	34.01	34.88	34.62	33.90	34.35
Mathematics	28.46	29.56	32.49	36.57	31.77
English	29.81	32.37	30.93	31.06	31.04

Table IV. Average national O-NET exams score from 2005 to 2008.

Drawing from the 2008 statistics, the regional differences in Thai educational performance (at Grade 12) are distinct (see Table V). Bangkok appeared to be leading all other regions in all four subjects. In fact, Bangkok performed better than the national average. In science, Bangkok's average O-NET score was 5.62% higher than the national mean, followed by 8.49% higher in Thai, 8.62% higher in English and 10.26% higher in mathematics. In contrast, the three southernmost provinces (Pattani, Yala and Narathiwat), where violence has been escalating over the past few years, performed well below other regions and hence the national average. In English, the region's average score was 3.62% lower than the national mean, followed by 4.68% lower in science, 7.43% lower in mathematics, and 10.51% lower in Thai.

	Thai	Science	Mathematics	English
Thailand	47.73	33.90	36.57	31.06
Bangkok	56.22	39.52	46.83	39.68
Bangkok vicinity	50.86	35.54	35.18	32.56
Central region	45.86	32.97	35.05	29.04
Eastern region	47.92	34.35	37.86	30.51
Western region	48.71	34.28	37.14	30.12
Northeastern region	41.86	31.22	31.55	27.83
Northern region	45.68	33.33	34.98	29.31
Southern region	44.70	30.02	33.98	29.39
Three southernmost provinces (Pattani, Yala and Narathiwat)	37.22	29.22	29.14	27.44

Table V. Thailand's regional disparities in academic achievement in 2008.

Even within the same region, disparity in educational attainment may also exist between public and private institutions. Private schools in Thailand, as monitored by the Office of the Private Education Commission, are either run for profit or are fee-paying, but not-for-profit, schools which are often run by charitable organisations. According to the Office of the Education Council (2007b), the private sector has saved the government about 10.43% of the total education budget or approximately THB 22,508 million in 2002. Due to this contribution, private schools are partially funded by the government. From 2000 to 2008, it appears that more students in Thailand have access to private education at all education levels, increasing from 15% of those who had access to private education in 2000 to 17% in 2004 and an estimated 25% in 2008 (OEC, 2007b) (see Table VI).

	2000	2004	2008 (Estimated)
Early childhood education	75:25	72:28	65:35
Primary education	86:14	84:16	77:23
Lower secondary education	94:6	89:11	83:17
Upper secondary education	87:13	80:20	72:28
Higher education	78:22	80:20	75:25
Total	85:15	83:17	75:25

Table VI. Public/private student ratio in Thailand.

Drawing from the data compiled by the Office of the Education Council (2007b), the educational attainment in private education is generally higher than the attainment in the public sector in all four compulsory subjects across the three educational levels (Prathom 6, Mathayom 3 and Mathayom 6) (see Table VII). Two exceptions are Mathayom 6 Thai and science where the national average performed better than the private sector in 2004. While the private sector's educational attainment has been consistently getting worse, the same trend is reflected in the national average too. The notion that private institutions are performing better academically is not the case at the higher education level. All seven Thai universities that were included in the 2008 Times Higher Education–Quacquarelli Symonds (THES–QS) World University Rankings were all public institutions. This ranking is further discussed below.

	2002		2003		2004	
	National average	Private sector	National average	Private sector	National average	Private sector
Prathom 6 *(Grade 6)*						
Thai	20.25	22.78	18.10	21.99	17.69	19.41
Maths	19.95	23.40	16.68	20.51	17.51	20.50
English	18.96	22.92	16.46	20.59	14.94	17.91
Science	-	-	16.97	20.27	16.64	18.79
Mathayom 3 *(Grade 9)*						
Thai	18.66	20.00	21.59	22.80	15.32	15.95
Maths	15.63	18.22	14.00	15.51	13.95	15.07
English	18.13	23.21	15.17	18.32	12.91	15.47
Science	-	-	15.23	16.58	14.88	16.24
Mathayom 6 *(Grade 12)*						
Thai	-	-	22.25	23.33	24.63	23.27
Maths	-	-	13.60	15.51	14.03	14.22
English	-	-	19.57	24.40	16.23	18.74
Science	-	-	24.41	26.41	22.17	21.76

Table VII. Comparisons of educational attainment between that of national average and that of private sector (2002-04).

Three other indicators of Thailand's educational performance can be found in the Trends in International Mathematics and Science Study (TIMSS) and the Programme for International Student Assessment (PISA) scores as well as the World University Rankings.

TIMSS is an international assessment of the mathematics and science knowledge of fourth- and eighth-grade students around the world. The assessment was developed by the International Association for the Evaluation of Educational Achievement (IEA), and is taken every four years with the most previous one conducted in 2007. Only four South-East Asian countries are part of the PISA assessments: Thailand, Singapore, Malaysia and Indonesia. The trends of these countries' performances were similar in both assessments in that Singapore led the other three countries by far, with Indonesia last in the cohort. According to IEA (2008a), out of 49 participating countries across the world, Singapore was right at the top of the science (eighth-grade level) assessment ranking, with the score of 567. Both Thailand and Malaysia scored 471, while Indonesia scored 427. In the mathematics (eighth-grade level) assessment, Singapore came third (593), only narrowly beaten by Chinese Taipei (598) and South Korea (597). Thailand (441) was beaten by Malaysia (474), while Indonesia scored 397 (IEA, 2008b).

PISA, on the other hand, is an international assessment of 15-year-old school children's scholastic performance in mathematics, science and reading. PISA is coordinated by the Organisation for Economic Co-operation and Development (OECD), and is taken every three years with the most previous one conducted in 2006. Only two South-East Asian countries are part of PISA assessments: Thailand and Indonesia. According to the OECD (2007), Thailand scored 413 in science, while Indonesia and the OECD countries averagely scored 393 and 499 respectively. Whilst Thailand's and Indonesia's scores were not that far apart, they were certainly far behind the OECD countries' average score. The same trend can be seen in the mathematics and reading assessments. Thailand scored 417 and 417 in mathematics and reading assessments respectively, while Indonesia scored 391 and 393, and the OECD countries averagely scored 498 and 492, respectively.

As it has been previously pointed out, both TIMSS and PISA assessments examine the educational achievement of primary- and secondary-school-aged students. In order to look at the educational performance of Thailand's higher education institutions against those of others in the same region, the 2008 World University Ranking data are analysed. Based on the THES–QS's (2008) World University Rankings 2008, data on how well universities in Thailand and those in the South-East Asian region performed are gathered and shown in Table VIII. While Singapore was the only country in the region that made it to the world's top 100 universities tier with National University of Singapore (30th) and Nanyang Technological University (77th), Thailand's Chulalongkorn

University (166th) was the only university from the region that made it to the 101st-200th tier with two other Thai universities ranked 251st and 400th respectively. Only three other South-East Asian countries made it onto the list. Malaysia had two and three universities ranked in the 201st-300th and 301st-400th tiers respectively. Only one and two Indonesian universities were ranked in the 201st-300th and 301st-400th tiers respectively, while only two universities in the Philippines made it onto the list in the 201st-300th tier.

	Top 100	101-200	201-300	301-400	401-500	500+	Total number of universities in this ranking
Thailand	-	1	1	1	2	2	7
Brunei	-	-	-	-	-	-	-
Cambodia	-	-	-	-	-	-	-
Indonesia	-	-	1	2	-	4	7
Lao PDR	-	-	-	-	-	-	-
Malaysia	-	-	2	3	-	-	5
Myanmar	-	-	-	-	-	-	-
Philippines	-	-	2	-	2	-	4
Singapore	2	-	-	-	-	-	2
Timor-Leste	-	-	-	-	-	-	-
Vietnam	-	-	-	-	-	-	-
Japan	4	5	4	9	6	7	35
China	5	5	2	1	4	1	18
South Korea	2	1	2	2	3	6	16
India	-	2	2	1	3	3	11

*Data are gathered from THES–QS World University Rankings 2008.
**These scores are the mean scores of all ranked universities up to the 400th-ranked university. This is due to the fact that further down the rankings, fewer data are available to evaluate each university and the statistical appropriateness of discerning one university from the next begins to decay. Responses for institutions in our survey drop off exponentially from the top of the table; by the time it gets past 400 the results become highly sensitive to error. As a result, precise positions beyond 400 are not published.

Table VIII. Higher education performance of Thailand, as compared with the 10 other South-East Asian countries, as well as Japan, China, South Korea and India.

Beyond the 400th university cut-off point, Thailand had, in fact, four other universities that made it to the overall ranking; so did Indonesia and the Philippines (with only two other universities). However, as fewer data were available further down the rankings to evaluate each university, 'the statistical appropriateness of discerning one university from the next begins to decay. Responses for institutions in the survey drop off exponentially from the top of the table, by the time it gets past 400, the results become highly sensitive to error' (THES–QS, 2008, p. 5). Precise positions beyond the 400th-ranked university were thus not published.

Thailand and Education for All (EFA)

Only six years before the 2015 target date, Thailand already appears to be on track to achieve most of the Education for All (EFA) targets.

At the World Conference on Education for All back in 1990, a global movement was launched in Jomtien, Thailand to 'universalise primary education and massively reduce illiteracy by the end of the decade' (UNESCO, 1990). Ten years later, these goals were, however, far from being achieved. The international community met again in Dakar, Senegal to reaffirm their commitment to achieving Education for All by the year 2015 as well as identifying six key measurable education goals aimed to meet the learning needs of all children, youth and adults. As it will become apparent, two of these goals also echo two of the eight Millennium Development Goals (MDGs): MDG 2 on universal primary education and MDG 3 on gender equality in education by 2015.

Drawing from the *2009 EFA Global Monitoring Report* (UNESCO, 2008), eight educational statistics are discussed below to measure Thailand's progress on the six EFA goals, in comparison with those of the 10 other South-East Asian nations.

EFA 1: Expand early childhood care and education is concerned with the well-being of pre-primary-aged children and their access to education. While there are various indicators adopted to measure these two aspects of EFA 1, given the space limitation, only that of the latter will be discussed here. Using the 2006 statistics as reported in the *2009 EFA Global Monitoring Report* (UNESCO, 2008), the Gross Enrolment Ratio in pre-primary education in Thailand is as high as 92%, second only to Malaysia who scored 125%. (A score above 100% is likely explained by a situation where the actual number of pre-primary education students exceeds the number of children whose age falls within the national pre-primary education age range.) Brunei, the Philippines and Indonesia ranked third, fourth and fifth with scores of 51%, 45% and 37% respectively. Both Cambodia and Lao PDR come sixth with 11%, while Timor-Leste (7th) and Myanmar (8th) scored 10% and 6% respectively. (The pre-primary education GER data for both Singapore and Vietnam are missing from this year's report.)

EFA 2: Provide free and compulsory primary education for all is primarily concerned with children's access to primary education. One aspect of EFA 2 discussed here is the Net Enrolment Ratio in primary education. While Malaysia (1st), Myanmar (1st) and Indonesia (2nd) scored 100%, 100% and 96% respectively, both Thailand and Brunei ranked third with 94% access to primary education. The Philippines (4th), Cambodia (5th) and Lao PDR (6th) provided respectively 91%, 90% and 84% access to primary education, while only 68% of Timor-Leste's (7th) primary-age children gained access to education. (The primary education NER data for both Singapore and Vietnam are also missing from this year's report.)

EFA 3: Promote learning and life skills for young people and adults is concerned with learning needs of all youth and adults. The discussion of Thailand's performance on EFA 3 is based on the Youth Literacy Rate (ages 15-24). Using data collected from 2000 to 2006, Thailand (and Indonesia) ranked third, achieving a 98% rate of youth literacy. Brunei (1st), Singapore (1st) and Indonesia (2nd) achieved 100%, 100% and 99% respectively, while Myanmar (4th), the Philippines (5th) and Vietnam (5th) scored 95%, 94% and 94% respectively. Cambodia (6th) and Lao PDR (7th) scored 85% and 82%. (Timor-Leste's Youth Literacy Rate (15-24) data are missing from this year's report.)

EFA 4: Increase adult literacy by 50%. The Adult Literacy Rate (15 and over) data, gathered from 2000 to 2006, are used here to discuss Thailand's current performance in EFA 4. Thailand (and Singapore) ranked second, achieving 94%, after only Brunei (1st) with 95%. The Philippines (3rd), Malaysia (4th), Indonesia (5th), Myanmar and Vietnam (both 6th) achieved respectively 93%, 92%, 91% and 90% adult literacy rates, while Cambodia (7th) and Lao PDR (8th) achieved 76% and 72% respectively. (The Adult Literacy Rate (15 and over) data for Timor-Leste are missing from this year's report.)

EFA 5: Achieve gender parity by 2005, gender equality by 2015. While the former is concerned with achieving equal participation of girls and boys in primary and secondary education, the latter is associated with ensuring that educational equality exists between boys and girls. The Gender Parity Index (GPI), 'a ratio of female to male values (or male to female, in certain cases) of a given indicator' (UNESCO, 2008, p. 409), for the GER at primary and secondary levels is adopted here to measure Thailand's progress in eradicating gender disparity in primary and secondary education. At the primary education level, Thailand, as well Malaysia and Myanmar, all achieved gender parity. The GPI for both Brunei and the Philippines is 0.99, while that of Indonesia, Cambodia, Timor-Leste and Lao PDR is 0.96, 0.93, 0.92 and 0.89 respectively. (The GPI data for GER in primary education for both Singapore and Vietnam are missing from this year's report.) At the secondary education level, with the exceptions of Cambodia and Lao PDR, all other countries in the region (including Thailand) achieved gender parity with the number of girls exceeding that of boys in the enrolment in some cases. (The GPI data for GER in secondary education for both Singapore and Vietnam are missing from this year's report.)

EFA 6: Improve the quality of education. While it is fully acknowledged that there is more to educational equality than quantifiable and measurable outputs, for the purpose of quick comparison, the two following statistics are used: Pupil/Teacher Ratio in Primary Education and Total Expenditure on Education (as a percentage of Total Government Expenditure). At the end of the 2006 school year, around 50% of the whole region (Brunei, Malaysia, Thailand, Indonesia, Vietnam, and Singapore) all reported to achieve the rate of fewer than 25 pupils per teacher nationally (25 pupils/1 teacher ratio being the world average). The Pupil/Teacher Ratio for the other countries in the same region, however, appears to be more than 30, with Cambodia ranked bottom providing on average one teacher for every 50 pupils. While the data on Total Expenditure on Education are missing from half of the countries in the region, those of the remaining countries are reported here. Thailand, as well as Malaysia, ranked first in the region for spending the highest percentage (i.e. 25%) of total government expenditure on education. Indonesia (2nd), the Philippines (3rd) and Lao PDR (4th) spent 18%, 15% and 14% respectively.

Promising Avenues and Blind Alleys

Since 2003, the Thai government has expressed its intention to transition from being an aid recipient to being an aid donor, and thus to stop receiving any more financial aid from other governments (Department of Foreign Affairs and Trade, 2009; United Nations Thailand, 2009). This, however, did not seem to adversely affect the educational provision in the country. On the contrary, efforts have been made by the government to ensure that Thai children have equal access to education. In 2009, the government announced its plan to ensure that Thai children receive 15 years of free public education via its 15 Year Free Education Scheme with a budget of approximately THB 11 million in the 2009-10 academic year. The annual subsidy amounts to THB 1700 per student at pre-school level, THB 1900 at primary school level, THB 3500 at lower secondary school level and THB 3800 at upper secondary school level (OBEC, 2009). This money is not to be spent directly on pupils, but to be spent by their schools on improving the school facilities and covering day-to-day expenditures. At this point, it may appear as though bigger schools with a large amount of students would secure much more funding from the government than smaller schools. In reality, further additional funding has been put in place to ensure that smaller state schools, with small budgets, do get additional funding wherever necessary. In addition to this, each Thai student will also be entitled to a fixed annual financial assistance to spend on textbooks, school uniforms, learning materials and learning enhancement activities. Many poor families in the past have struggled to cover such expenses. With this guarantee of financial assistance from the government, more children from poorer households will now have access to education that they would otherwise have not been able to afford. Further, initiatives such as the royal-sponsored distance learning TV channels, established since 1996, provide educational benefits and equal opportunities to Thai students nationwide especially in the remote and far-reaching areas of the country where the lack of (quality) teachers is still evident.

As it has been previously mentioned, the reform of basic education has recently been implemented which places a great deal of emphasis on child-centred learning and learning through a discovery approach. Drawing from Hofstede (1994), Trakulphadetkrai (2007), nevertheless, argued that unless some of the deep-rooted Thai socio-cultural values are *relaxed*, the chance of implementing any meaningful education reform in Thailand is minimal. Three cultural dimensions are particularly relevant, namely *Power Distance*, *Individualism*, and *Uncertainty Avoidance*.

According to Hofstede (2009), Thai society scored 64 on the Power Distance Index (PDI), compared with merely 35 and 40 for British and US societies respectively (see Table IX). Generally, in a large power distance situation, teachers are treated with absolute respect. 'Students in class speak up only when invited to; teachers are never publicly contradicted or criticised' (Hofstede, 1994, p. 34). The educational process is, thus, very much teacher centred, with little input from students. Hofstede (2009) also examined the culture of five other South-East Asian nations, which all happened to have a higher PDI score than Thailand: Vietnam (70), Singapore (74), Indonesia (78), the Philippines (94) and Malaysia (104).

	Power Distance Index (PDI)	Individualism Index (IDV)	Uncertainty Avoidance Index (UAI)
Thailand	64	20	64
Indonesia	78	14	48
Malaysia	104	26	36
Philippines	94	32	44
Singapore	74	20	8
Vietnam	70	20	30
UK	35	89	35
USA	40	91	46

Table IX. Hofstede's (2009) Power Distance Index (PDI), Individualism Index (IDV) and Uncertainty Avoidance Index (UAI) scores.

In the Individualism Index (IDV), Thai society scored merely 20, while British and US societies scored as high as 89 and 91 respectively. This index is associated with how much members of society are willing to act or think differently from other members of the same society. Hofstede (1994, p. 62) suggested that students in a low IDV-scored society, like Thailand, who conceive of themselves as part of a group, believe that 'it is illogical to speak up without being sanctioned by the group to do so', highlighting how Thai children might not be willing to express their own unique views and ideas in classrooms. Holmes & Tangtongtavy (2000) assert that 'a [Thai] person with a good idea may hold back on an initiative so as not to appear that he's trying to grab the spotlight' (p. 84). Even if an idea is given, only a few people would dare to comment on or criticise it. Holmes & Tangtongtavy comment that 'criticism is generally [interpreted] in a much more personal way than is the case in the West, it is not seen as a purely professional manner' (p. 99). Further, to give a wrong answer, either by a teacher or student, would entail a *loss of face*, a situation that in Thai culture must always be avoided. Thai society's score of 20 resonates well with those of the other South-East Asian five nations: Indonesia (14), Singapore (20), Vietnam (20), Malaysia (26) and the Philippines (32).

In the Uncertainty Avoidance Index (UAI), Thai society scored 64, while British and US societies scored 35 and 46 respectively. Generally, students from strong uncertainty-avoidance countries appear to have a low level of tolerance for uncertainty, and tend to associate difference with danger. They appear to prefer situations where there is only one correct answer which they can find, and expect their teachers to be the experts who have all the answers. On the other hand, members of societies with low UAI appear to have a high level of tolerance for uncertainty, and tend to associate difference with curiosity and new knowledge. They appear to prefer open-ended situations, and dislike the thought of having only one correct answer. Thailand's score of 64 is the highest among Hofstede's (2009) six examined South-East Asian nations: Singapore (8), Vietnam (30), Malaysia (36), the Philippines (44) and Indonesia (48). What is worth mentioning is that Singapore has a score which is much lower than Western societies, and UAI is the only index that distinguishes Singapore from other South-East Asian countries most dramatically.

Successful education reform requires leadership and consistency in policies. Thailand, however, has experienced a high level of political instability over the past few years. Less than three years after Thaksin Shinawatra was deposed in the 2006 military coup, four prime ministers have taken his office: Surayud Chulanont (October 2006-January 2008), Samak Sundaravej (January 2008-September 2008), Somchai Wongsawat (September 2008-December 2008) and Abhisit Vejjajiva (December 2008-present). Education ministers are no exception to this constant political change. In 2008 alone, Thailand witnessed as many as four education ministers, representing two political parties and a military junta-appointed government. Inevitably, the consequence is a lack of leadership and of coherent education policies.

Further, the Muslim extremist separatist movement in the three southernmost provinces of Thailand (Pattani, Yala and Narathiwat) was also believed to be behind the arson attacks on some 57 (Buddhist) schools. Along with these incidents, some 49 teachers and 20 students were either seriously injured or brutally killed in separate attacks, and around 6000 young children became orphans as the result of the violence (OEC, 2005). As a result, schooling in the region has consistently been interrupted, either in the form of permanent or temporary school closures. Teachers (and sometimes students and their families) migrate to other more peaceful regions in the country. Fewer teachers from other parts of the country are willing to work in the three southernmost provinces for fear of their safety, which together ultimately creates a shortage of qualified teachers in the region. If this problem continues to manifest, efforts in education reform in this part of the country will be seriously hindered. Evidence of this can be seen in the O-NET scores of the region which have consistently been the lowest in the country.

Efforts to improve the quality of and increased access to education have also been hindered by factors such as natural disasters. One of the most disastrous events was the 2004 Indian Ocean tsunami, which not only wiped out a large number of schools in the south of Thailand (Krabi, Phang Nga, Phuket, Ranong, Satun and Trang), but also took away more than 8000 lives, including those of Thai teachers and pupils in the affected area. As it has been previously mentioned, the Thai government has, since 2003, declined to receive any financial assistance from other governments. Efforts, however, have been made by the government, NGOs and the private sector, via donations, to build new schools and infrastructures in the affected region. According to the government, each Thai orphan would receive THB 25,000, while those who were affected by the tsunami but whose parents are still alive would receive THB 15,000 (Ministry of Education, 2006). Equally important, post-traumatic mental and financial support must also be made available to those affected, including around 1500 orphaned children. The sense of normality, especially among young children, must be quickly resumed, or else this could affect their school attendance and hence their long-term academic performance.

Conclusions

Overall, equality of or access to education in Thailand appears to be satisfactory although more could be done to ensure that more pre-school children enrol in pre-school programmes, as the NER for early childhood education is merely 53.81%. Bangkok and its vicinity appear to have the highest NER, while the northeast seems to have the lowest. The NER for primary education is 88.66% with the east having the highest rate and the northwest, once more, having the lowest. The NER for secondary education is 76.53%, with the east having the highest rate, and the three southernmost provinces (Yala, Pattani and Narathiwat) having the lowest NER in the country. If the poverty in the northeast and violence in the three southernmost provinces are allowed to continue, this could negatively affect the overall national participation rate.

Drawing from statistics discussed previously, educational quality in Thailand is alarmingly low. Given the fact that Thailand has spent more than most of the countries in the region, i.e. between approximately 20% to 25% of its total government expenditure on education and yet the national and regional average scores of nearly all subjects across all levels are below 50%, this shows how money has not been spent effectively to improve the quality of teaching and learning. Political unrest in Thailand, which often results in constant change of governments, leadership and policies, means lack of continuity and real effort to reform the education system. Further, it is imperative for teachers and pupils to be made aware of how certain deep-rooted Thai socio-cultural values may be counter-productive to effective teaching and learning. The government cannot be allowed to be complacent by just knowing that it has injected a lot of money into education. More meaningful efforts must be made to ensure that the country meets the Education for All goals by 2015.

References

Bovornsiri, V. (1998) Country Report: Thailand. In *Recent Reform and Perspectives in Higher Education: report of the seminar including a range of countries from Asia-Pacific and Europe*. Bangkok: National Institute for Educational Research.

Commission on Higher Education (2009) Higher Education in Thailand. http://inter.mua.go.th/main/index.php (accessed 15 September 2009).

Department of Foreign Affairs and Trade (2009) Thailand Country Brief. http://www.dfat.gov.au/geo/thailand/thailand_brief.html (accessed 15 November 2009).

Fry, G.W. (2002) Synthesis Report: from crisis to opportunity, the challenges of educational reform in Thailand. Prepared for the Office of the National Education Commission and the Asian Development Bank (TA 3585-THA).

Hofstede, G. (1994) *Cultures and Organizations: software of the mind*. London: HarperCollins.

Hofstede, G. (2009) Cultural Dimension. http://www.geert-hofstede (accessed 10 September 2009).

Holmes, H. & Tangtongtavy, S. (2000) *Working with the Thais: a guide to managing in Thailand*. Bangkok: White Lotus.

IEA (International Association for the Evaluation of Educational Achievement) (2008a) *TIMSS (2007) International Science Report*. Amsterdam: IEA.

IEA (2008b) *TIMSS (2007) International Mathematics Report*. Amsterdam: IEA.

International Institute for Management Development (IMD) (2009) *IMD World Competitiveness Yearbook 2009*. Lausanne: IMD.

Medrano, A.D. (2007) Islamic Education in Southern Thailand, *Explorations*, 7(2), 57-60.

Ministry of Education (MoE) (2006) Report on Assistance to Schools and Students who were Affected by the Tsunami. http://www.inspect10.moe.go.th (accessed 15 November 2009).

Ministry of Education (MoE) (2008a) *Rhark-sood Gaen-grarng Garn Suk-sa Khan Puen-tharn 2008* [Basic education core curriculum 2008]. Bangkok: MoE.

Ministry of Education (MoE) (2008b) *Towards a Learning Society in Thailand*. Bangkok: MoE.

National Institute of Educational Testing Service (NIETS) (2008a) *Prieb-tieb Kar-stithi Puern Tharn Pon-garn Tod-sorb O-NET Mathayom 6 (2005-2008)* [Statistical comparisons of O-NET Grade 12 test results (2005-2008)]. Bangkok: NIETS.

National Institute of Educational Testing Service (NIETS) (2008b) *Kar-stithi Prieb-tieb Pon-garn Tod-sorb Tarng-garn Suk-sa Ra-dub Chart Puern-tharn (O-NET) Mathayom 6 (2008)* [Statistical comparisons of Ordinary National Educational Tests (O-NET) in Grade 12 (2008)]. Bangkok: NIETS.

National Institute of Educational Testing Service (NIETS) (2009) GAT and PAT. http://www.niets.or.th (accessed 15 September 2009).

Office of Commercial Services (2002) *Teacher Development for Quality Learning: the Thailand education reform project*. Brisbane: Queensland University of Technology.

Office of the Basic Education Commission (OBEC) (2007) *Rai Ngarn Garn Pra Mern O-Ghart La Koon-Na-Parb Garn Suk-sa Khorng Kon Thai* [Report on evaluation of Thai people's educational opportunity and quality]. Bangkok: OBEC.

Office of the Basic Education Commission (OBEC) (2009) *Naew Tarng Garn Dum Nern Ngarn Tarm Na-yo-baai Rean Free 15 Pee Yharng Mee Koon Na Parb* [Guidelines for implementing the 15 years free education with quality policy]. Bangkok: OBEC.

Office of the Education Council (OEC) (2005) *Pan Yoot-tha-sart Pa-thi-Roop Garn-suk-saa Sarm Jung-wad Chai-dan Pak-tai Peur Sarng San-thi-sook 2005-2008* [Roadmap for educational reform in the three southernmost provinces for peace 2005-2008]. Bangkok: Office of the National Education Commission.

Office of the Education Council (OEC) (2006) *Rai-ngarn Garn Wi-jai Pra-mern-pol Garn Gra-jaai Um-naj Garn Bor-ri-harn Lae Garn Jad-garn Suk-sa Hai Khet Peun-tee Garn Suk-sar Cha-bub Sa-roob* [Evaluation report on educational decentralisation to Educational Service Areas – summary version]. Bangkok: OEC.

Office of the Education Council (OEC) (2007b) *Paen Yoot-tha-sart Song-serm Garn Mee Suan-ruam Khorng Ek-ga-chon Naai Garn Wad Garn-suk-sa Khan-puen-tharn* [Roadmap for encouraging involvement from the private sector in the provision of basic education]. Bangkok: OEC.

Office of the National Economic and Social Development Board (2009) Summary of the Tenth National Economic and Social Development Plan (2007-2011). http://www.nesdb.go.th/Default.aspx?tabid=139 (accessed 15 November 2009).

Organisation for Economic Co-operation and Development (2007) *PISA 2006 Science Competencies for Tomorrow's World*. Paris: OECD.

Pillay, H. (2002) Teacher Development for Quality Learning: the Thailand education reform project. Consulting report prepared for the Office of the National Education Commission and the Asian Development Bank, March.

Times Higher Education–Quacquarelli Symonds (2008) *World University Rankings 2008*. London: THES–QS.

Trakulphadetkrai, N. (2007) A Study of Thai Culture as Affecting the Learning of Thai Pupils in Different Primary School Contexts. Dissertation submitted to the University of Oxford for the degree of MSc in comparative and international education.

UNESCO (1990) The World Conference on Education for All 1990. http://www.unesco.org/education/efa/ed_for_all/background/world_conference_jo mtien.shtml (accessed 15 September 2009).

UNESCO (2008) *2009 EFA Global Monitoring Report*. Paris: UNESCO.

United Nations Development Programme (2007a) *Human Development Report 2007/2008*. New York: UNDP.

United Nations Development Programme (2007b) *Thailand Human Development Report 2007*. Bangkok: UNDP.

United Nations Thailand (2009) Thailand Country Brief. http://www.un.or.th/thai/thailand/development.html (accessed 15 November 2009).

CHAPTER 12

Vietnam as an Outlier: tradition and change in education

PHAM LAN HUONG & GERALD W. FRY

SUMMARY The focus of this chapter is the evolution of Vietnamese education from past to present. Though Vietnam is a developing country, the authors argue that in terms of educational success and potential, it is an exceptional 'outlier', primarily related to its unique history, which involved struggles against both outside invaders and natural disasters, and its rich Confucian traditions which highly value education, literacy, learning, and teachers. The current Vietnamese educational system is a legacy and amalgam of many external international influences, namely Chinese, French, Russian, American, and more recently global forces. Vietnam has overcome many wars and a lack of natural resources to improve economically and educationally. After the introduction of market mechanisms in 1986, education has flourished particularly in terms of dramatic growth in education at all levels, including an increasing role of the private sector, particularly at the higher education level. Many note Vietnam's economic potential as a rising phoenix, a nation on the move, or ascending dragon. To realize this dynamic future, Vietnam has adapted both its economic and educational systems to be more responsive to the powerful forces of globalization and the new ASEAN economic community (AEC) becoming a reality in 2015. The future of Vietnam as a dynamic Asia-Pacific knowledge economy depends heavily on its current commitments to foster both human resource development and innovation. Vietnamese education has impressive potential and promise.

Whether the Vietnamese mountains and rivers will attain glory and whether the Vietnamese land will gloriously stand on an equal footing with the powers in the five continents, this depends to a great extent on your studies. (Special letter written to Vietnamese pupils by President Ho Chi Minh on 3 September 1945, the day after the declaration of the independent Democratic Republic of Vietnam, cited in Phạm, 1998, p. 13.)

To cross a river, you should build a bridge; to have your children well-versed in letters, you should love the teacher. (Vietnamese proverb, cited in Phạm, 1998, p. viii)

Introduction: Vietnamese exceptionalism?

Though Vietnam does share many common characteristics with other developing nations, it is in no way a typical case. In fact, in many respects it is what Gladwell (2009) has called 'an outlier'. Reflecting its being a 'special case', Vietnam has been referred to as a country rising (Ratliff, 2008), an ascending dragon (Kamm, 1996), a rising phoenix, and a country on the move (Mai, 2008). A concrete example is the success of Vietnamese students in international mathematics competitions. In the August 2009 International Math Olympiad in Germany, a Vietnamese student of Nung ethnicity won the gold metal beating 565 competitors from 140 nations (VietNamNet/VNS, 2009). In the 2007 International Math Olympiad Vietnam finished tied for third out of 93 competing nations. Thus, Vietnam is exceptional in many ways.

To understand contemporary Vietnam, it is critical to understand five important and persisting themes of Vietnamese history. The first theme is the Vietnamese struggle against outside invaders such as the Chinese, Mongols, French, Japanese, and Americans. In eventually defeating these outside invaders, the Vietnamese demonstrated ingenuity, creativity, and persistence. A second theme relates to threats from natural disasters such as flooding and typhoons. For example, a complex system of dykes protects the city of Hanoi from flooding by the Red River. A third theme and particularly relevant to education are Chinese Confucian cultural and intellectual influences. A fourth theme is the importance of the traditional Vietnamese village, which is at the heart of Vietnamese culture (Phan et al, 1993). A fifth and final theme is *nam tiến* (march to the South). Given Vietnam's large population relative to cultivable land area, historically Vietnam expanded steadily to the south at the expense of other cultural groups such as the Chams and Khmers, for example.

Perhaps what is most special about Vietnam is the nature of diverse but powerful external influences on its culture, society, and educational system. The major external influences that have shaped Vietnamese education and human resource development are Chinese, French, Russian, American, and now global forces. Anthony Reid (1988-93), in his insightful writing about Southeast Asian history, notes that Southeast Asian societies are highly adept at adapting and modifying external forces of change to fit their own unique cultural and historical settings. Thus, Vietnam's current educational system is both a unique and creative amalgam of indigenous, Chinese, French, Russian, American, and global influences.

Historical Background: Vietnam as distinct from China

Until recently some international scholars held the view that Vietnam did not have its own educational tradition in ancient times but rather depended entirely on China for its education (Dương, 2005). However, research on ancient Southeast Asian culture has led to the discovery of relics of documents, handwriting, ceramics, and bronze work that show a rather advanced indigenous culture. Ancient documents from China mention Vietnamese poetry and a Vietnamese calendar which differ from similar Chinese documents from the same period. In the early stages of its development, going back 4000 years ago, Vietnam consisted of the Đông Sơn civilization. If there had not been some form of traditional education, Vietnam could not have built such a civilization.

The Đông Sơn society was formed from two groups of people. One Austronesian group (of the same origin as Indonesians) came from the south, and the other, the Mongoloid, moved down from the North (Phạm, 1996). The first Vietnamese state was called Văn Lang. Education from this ancient period can be divided into two basic genres: education in the family or in the community, and education focusing on beliefs and religion (Dương, 2005).

In education in the family and community, 'senior persons' passed on their knowledge and experiences to young people. Parents and grandparents taught children. Relatives taught each other about the responsibility of everyone in the family and the way to live in nature. Young people received technical training from older relatives to learn how to make handicrafts. The tradition of 'respect for old people' existed in Vietnam going back to ancient times. Women had an important role in society. Women were also trained and occupied a social position equal to that of the men in the community. Only when Chinese culture later dominated Vietnam did the role of women become diminished.

In general, education by the community was combined with that in the family, which focused on education for knowledge, morality, and technical competence. The Vietnamese belief system is an integral part of Vietnamese culture. Its character was influenced by the agricultural culture (see Phạn et al, 1993). The Vietnamese worshiped nature and emphasized harmony between negative and positive forces.

The values and educational ideas in ancient Vietnam were handed down from generation to generation through many important legends which remain a part of Vietnamese education today.

Historical Background: the feudal period and its two phases

First Phase: domination by the Chinese
Imperial Regime (111 BC to 938 AD)

In 111 BC, King Han Vu of China attacked King Triệu of Vietnam (Nam Việt) and prevailed. King Han Vu renamed Nam Việt 'Giao Chỉ' and divided it into nine administrative districts. This was the beginning of the time when Vietnam was dominated by a Chinese imperial regime, and this domination lasted over 1000 years. To rule over the Vietnamese people, the Han mandarins tried to assimilate Vietnam as a part of Han (China) by force and cultural influence. Han writing, culture, and religions (Buddhism, Taoism, and Confucianism) were brought to Vietnam.

One of the first strategies for assimilation of the Vietnamese people was the opening of schools. Most of the credit for bringing Chinese studies to Vietnam belongs to Sĩ Nhiếp (137-226 BC). In 187 BC, Sĩ Nhiếp was appointed as the Governor of Giao Chỉ. He opened schools and was venerated as *nam bang học tổ* (the educational king of the South). His statue still stands in Tam A today. The aim of these schools was to serve the purposes of the organs of the Han court and did not provide any certificate for completion of study. Together with public schools, Buddhism played an important role in the development of Vietnam in this early period. At the start of the third century, Luy Lou became the first Buddhist center in Vietnam. At this time classrooms were built in all pagodas and temples. The monks of various Buddhist factions opened schools or classes to teach content such as prayers, religious dogma, and moral education. It can be said that the monks were the first teachers of Vietnamese formal education. The pagodas and temples played a central cultural, spiritual, and educational role in the Vietnamese community.

Second Phase: Vietnam as an independent nation

After over 1000 years of Chinese domination, Vietnam achieved independence in 938, and at that point began to build an independent educational system following the Chinese model. Education only began to develop officially during the reign of the Nhà Lý dynasty when it established the Quốc Tử Giám School in 1076, which was the first university in Southeast Asia (Sagemueller, 2001). Between the eleventh and the thirteenth centuries, the educational content in all schools included ideas and ideals such as Buddhist, Taoist, and Confucian doctrines, called the 'three religions united'. In the seventeenth century Taoism was abandoned, Buddhism lost influence, and Confucianism became the ruling ideology and philosophy for all schools.

The Vietnamese Confucian system emphasized three primary relationships (king–subject, father–children, husband–wife), and five virtues: *nhân* (kindness toward others), *nghĩa* (understanding one's duty), *lễ* (knowing how to relate to those under and above you in the social hierarchy), *trí* (knowledge), and *tín* (trustworthiness). Central to this system were two words: *trung* and *hiếu* (be faithful to the king and have respect for one's parents). Aside from learning morality and the responsibilities of a citizen, students also studied some literature and history but not the sciences or technology. The pedagogy was memorization. Those who passed the classical examinations were highly celebrated as they were 'brought home in glory and with thanks'. This policy was certainly about 'mobilizing talent', but on the other hand it also gave birth to the value of obtaining degrees for the sake of social respectability and status without regard to the quality of education, a pattern that persists in Vietnam today (Pham, 2006).

Vietnamese Education in the French Colonial Period

Prior to the seventeenth century, Vietnam's writing system was comprised of Chinese characters. In the thirteenth century, a Vietnamese style of Chinese characters (*Chữ Nôm*) was introduced, but the elite mandarinate continued to privilege traditional Chinese writing and characters. The complexity of either system of characters contributed to the persistence of elitist education and limited the possibilities of widespread functional literacy. Then, in the seventeenth century, with the assistance of Alexandre de Rhodes, a French missionary and scholar, the Vietnamese developed a relatively simple Romanized Vietnamese script for writing tonal Vietnamese known as *quốc ngữ* (Phạm, 1998, p. ix) used in this chapter. This innovation was to have profound and unanticipated consequences on the evolution of education in Vietnam. This new writing system made the Vietnamese language far more accessible to ordinary Vietnamese, with great implications for raising mass consciousness to foster both political and social change. The *quốc ngữ* simplified writing system was adopted in Cochinchina (the southern part of colonial Vietnam) in 1878.

A major motivation for France's interest in colonizing Vietnam was its naïve dream that the Mekong River, which flows from China into the Mekong Delta and into the South China Sea (Vietnamese refer to it as the Eastern Sea), could be navigable and become a major economic gateway to China (Garnier, 1994; Osborne, 2000). Also, Vietnam had rich natural resources such as rubber, timber, tin, coal, and rice. Though the real reason for colonization was economic, the French justified their invasion of Vietnam based on the assassination and alleged mistreatment of French missionaries by the Imperial Vietnam government. Once present and in complete control of Vietnam in the late eighteenth century, they also stressed their *mission civilisatrice* (civilizing mission) to lift up the 'backward and primitive' Vietnamese to appreciate the high culture and intellect of French civilization.

The goal of the French was to replace the Chinese-influenced feudal Confucian system with an elitist modern educational system that privileged the French language. The curricula developed had little relevance to Vietnam and mirrored those in France. Both primary and secondary education were almost identical to those of the *métropole* (Thompson, 1968, pp. 287-288). The system was designed to serve the children of local French colonizers and to train a highly limited number of Vietnamese to become functionaries in their colonial system (interpreters and petty administrators, for example). By 1918 the simplified *quốc ngữ* Romanized writing system had been adopted throughout Vietnam and replaced the traditional Confucian system. Ironically and as an example of unintended consequences, the Romanized writing system contributed importantly to increased political consciousness and rebellion against the French colonial rulers (Trương, 1967; Marr, 1971, 1981; Woodside, 2000).

The Current Vietnamese Educational System and Situation

As a background to understanding contemporary education in Vietnam, two tables of basic statistical indicators are presented. The first provides basic development indicators. The second provides key educational indicators. Table I indicates that Vietnam is a rapidly developing economy which has succeeded in reducing both fertility and poverty. For a developing country its level of income inequality is relatively low as indicated by the .34 Gini coefficient. Table II indicates the overall success of the Vietnamese educational system in quantitative terms but does not address directly serious and persisting *quality issues*, which are discussed below in detail.

In such quantitative terms, the Vietnamese educational system has expanded dramatically in recent years (Nga, 2004, pp. 426-427). For the 2007-08 academic year Vietnam had about 23 million students. That number represents an increase of 2.86% from the 2000-01 academic year. The number of vocational students increased by a factor of 2.14. The number of intermediate vocational students increased by a factor of 2.41. The number of undergraduate students increased by a factor of 1.75 and the number of university students per 10,000 people increased by a factor of 1.6. The number of graduate students increased by a factor of 2.5. The percentage of trained laborers (out of all laborers, trained or untrained) increased from 20% in 2000 to 31.5% in 2007 (Nguyễn, 2007).

The network of educational providers has expanded throughout the country. Every village has preschools and primary schools. Every district has middle and high schools. Vocational schools, junior colleges, and universities have been built in every province or city. Such schools have even been built in some of the less developed and remote areas such as the Central Highlands, the northwest, and the Mekong Delta. Many mountain districts and provinces also have boarding schools for students from diverse ethnic nationalities.

Statistical indicators	Socialist Republic of Vietnam	Sources
Population	86,967,524 (2009)	USAID, 2009
Population growth rate (%)	0.98 (2009)	USAID, 2009
Percentage of population that is majority (Kinh, %)	85.73 (2003)	Dept of State, 2009
Number of ethnic groups	54	Dept of State, 2009
Fertility rate (births per woman)	1.8 (2009)	USAID, 2009
Life expectancy at birth (years)	71.6 (2009)	USAID, 2009
Population < age 15 (%)	24.9 (2009)	USAID, 2009
GDP ($US)	$84.98 billion (2008)	Dept of State, 2009
GDP, PPP (current international $)	$240,093 million (2008)	World Bank, 2009c
GDP real growth rate (%)	6.23 (2008)	Dept of State, 2009
Exports to US ($US)	$12.9 billion (2008)	Dept of State, 2009
Imports from US ($US)	$2.8 billion (2008)	Dept of State, 2009
Gini coefficient	37.8 (2007)	UNDP, 2009
Human development index	0.725 (2007)	UNDP, 2009
Internet users (per 100 population)	20.45 (2007)	UN Stat Div, 2009b
Population below poverty line (%)	14.8 (2007)	USAID, 2009

Table I. Basic statistical indicators for the Socialist Republic of Vietnam

The whole country has over 9000 community education centers, about 700 regular educational centers, 1300 computer study centers, and some distance education centers. Furthermore, many international institutions are now operating in Vietnam. This reflects the emergence of a knowledge and learning society in Vietnam.

In 2008, 42 out of 63 provinces in Vietnam reached the standard of compulsory primary and middle school education. The percentage of the population over 15 that is literate is 94%. The average number of years of schooling among the population over 15 is now 9.6 (Ministry of Education and Training [MoET], 2008).

The policy on social equity in education has been implemented. In general education, 53% of students are allowed to pay reduced tuition fees. Poor students can borrow money from national banks to help pay tuition fees.

Statistical Indicators	Socialist Republic of Vietnam	Sources
Gender parity index		
Primary	0.94 (2001)	UN Stat Div, 2009b
Secondary	0.92 (2001)	UN Stat Div, 2009b
Tertiary	0.74 (2001)	UN Stat Div, 2009b
Adult literacy rate (%)	90.3 (2007)	UNDP, 2009
Net enrollment rate (%)		
Primary	93.4 (2001)	World Bank, 2009b
Secondary	61.9 (2001)	World Bank, 2009b
Tertiary	13.0 (2008)	Nguyen Thi Le Huong, 2008
Ratio of pupils to teachers		
Primary	20.4 (2007)	World Bank, 2009a
Secondary	21.8 (2007)	World Bank, 2009a
Public expenditure on education (% of GDP)	5.0 (2005)	MoET
Public expenditure on education (% of total government spending)	>20% (2008)	MoET
Percentage of educational expenditures covered by the state	80% (2005)	Vu Quang Viet
School life expectancy (years)	10 (2001)	UN Stat Div, 2009a
Males	11 (2001)	UN Stat Div, 2009a
Females	10 (2001)	UN Stat Div, 2009a
Percentage of repeaters (%)		
Primary	3.3 (2000)	World Bank, 2009a
Secondary	1.7 (2000)	World Bank, 2009a

Table II. Key Educational indicators for the Socialist Republic of Vietnam.

Educational Management and Policies

Vietnamese educational management is highly centralized. The Ministry of Education and Training is the government agency which manages all educational activities in Vietnam. Under the MoET are the educational departments of the provinces and educational offices of districts. Undergraduate institutions are managed by MoET for academic activities, but some institutions are also managed by other ministries, provinces, or cities for other kinds of activities. Resolution 14 calling for higher education reform, approved on 2 November 2005, provides more autonomy for college and universities (Hayden & Lâm, 2007).

Legal Status

Vietnam's 2005 Education Law stipulates the rights and responsibilities of every institution, organization or person related to education in the country. The 2005 Education Law supersedes the Education Law of 1998 and provides a variety of additional regulations that were not addressed by the earlier law. With these changes, the Vietnamese government hopes to underscore its commitment to quality and equitable education for its populace.

Policy of Social Mobilization for Education

After the policy of *Đổi mới* (renovation, change in economic structure emphasizing the use of market mechanisms and private incentives) was introduced in 1986, Vietnam began a process of changing its educational system and structure to be in accord with the new economic policy. Eventually, this resulted in a policy of social mobilization for education to enable the realization of social and economic potential contributions to education. The passage of Resolution Number 05/2005/NQ-CP (number designating policy decisions by the Vietnamese government), which called for such mobilization in support of health care and education, clearly mandated major changes in education. That resolution mobilized the high potential of Vietnamese society, expanded the size and diversified models and styles of schools and programs, increased facilities, and contributed to the growing social demand for education at all levels. It also created more jobs for educators.

Private institutions have been rapidly developing. In the 2007-08 academic year, there were 6000 preschools, 95 primary schools, 33 middle schools, 651 high schools, 308 vocational institutions, 72 intermediate professional schools, and 64 undergraduate institutions which are considered private institutions. Also, the number of private school students is increasing. The percentage of students in private schools was 11.8% in 2000 but increased to 15.6% in 2008. Among those students, students in general education schools made up 9%, students in intermediate professional schools represented 18.2%, students in vocational schools constituted 31.2%, and undergraduate students were 11.8% (MoET, 2008).

The policy of social mobilization has aided in the expansion of the capacity of Vietnamese education. However, the religious community has still not been mobilized to an extent which matches its potential to contribute to education.

Issues Related to Ethnic Diversity

Vietnam has considerable ethnic diversity. There are a total of 54 diverse ethnic nationalities (Đỗ, 1998; Nguyễn, 1998; Phạm, 2008) representing approximately 13% of the nation's population. Regarding diverse ethnic nationalities, the network of institutions in the mountains and islands that belong to ethnic nationalities is completely supported by the state. Some ethnic nationality students (from 30 major ethnic groups) can study in their mother tongue at the primary level. There were 278 schools targeted at ethnic groups with 86,000 students in the 2007-08 academic year. Graduates of such schools have the same rights as those graduating from mainstream schools. In certain remote mountainous areas, there are special boarding schools for children of ethnic nationalities.

While the Vietnamese Communist Party has an impressively long history of including these ethnic nationalities in all aspects of governance (starting in the 1930s), in the new market economy gaps have emerged between the Kinh (ethnic Vietnamese majority) and ethnic nationalities (Asian Development Bank, 2002; McElwee, 2008). For example, those from such ethnic communities were three times less likely to have a university education that someone from a Kinh background and those of a Kinh background were nearly twice as likely to have completed some secondary education (Van de Walle & Gunewardena, 2001, p. 185). The average educational attainment level (years of schooling) of the Kinh-Hoa head of household was 7.36 while that of an individual from an ethnic community was only 5.53 (Baulch et al, 2004). These data, however, are from surveys in the 1990s. Data from 1999 indicate that the net enrollment rate for lower secondary education for the majority Kinh was 64.8% while for the Khmer-Vietnamese it was 22.5%, for the Tay 51.0%, for the Nung 39.2%, but only 4.5% for the highland Hmong and 11.8% for the Dao (Baulch et al, 2004, p. 282). Baulch et al (2004) also emphasize the disparities among the ethnic groups. The Tay, Nung, Muong, and Khmer do far better than the Hmong and those indigenous to the Central Highlands. A number of policy interventions have been introduced since 1993 to assist these disadvantaged groups. The most important of these is called the Hunger Eradication and Poverty Reduction Program, which provides additional resources to the poorest communes of the country. However, the effectiveness of this program is limited by its insufficient targeting and spreading resources too thinly (Baulch et al, 2004, p. 286).

Special Education

Vietnam has 1.1 million disabled children. Among them, only 269,000 can go to general education schools and special schools, and 5000 children receive financial assistance for school supplies and equipment (Nguyễn, 2007). Given financial constraints on the state system therefore, only some of these children receive special services. Priority goes to those with the greatest disabilities.

Educational Management Staff

There are 10,400 educational administrators working for the MoET, provincial offices, and district offices, and 80,000 administrators work at schools from the preschool to the university level. Administrators make up 10% of the personnel of schools nationwide. However, 60% have not yet been trained in educational management (Nguyễn, 2007).

Educational Finance

In recent years, the budget for education has been increasing (see Table III). Average expenditures for education have increased by an impressive 28% per year. Over 20% of the national budget was allocated for educational expenditures in 2008. Aside from the national budget, there is individual and international support for projects as well as major soft loans from the World Bank and the Asian Development Bank (ADB). NGOs such as Save the Children and CARE are also active in Vietnam (Fry & Phạm, 2007), but major external finance for education is from international organizations such as the World Bank and ADB. In addition, tuition fees and other contributions of the people make up 20-30% of education funding. With respect to tuition fees, there are none for primary school students. For secondary school students, fees are 35,000 VND (US$2.10) per month for students in the city, 25,000 VND (US$1.50) per month for students in rural areas and 15,000 VND (US$1.00) per month for those in remote distant areas (Nguyễn, 2007).

	2000	2001	2002	2003	2004	2005
Total educational expenditures (million VND)	23,219	25,882	34,088	37,552	54,223	68,968
Percentage of expenditures for education/GDP	3.2	3.2	4.7	3.7	4.6	5.0

Table III. Expenditures for education in Vietnam 2000-2005.
Source: Vũ Quang Việt, calculated based on the data of MoET, 2005).

Tuition fees in undergraduate public institutions are extremely low. They are 1.8 million VND (US$112.50) per academic year for university students, 1.5 million VND (US$94) for students of junior colleges, and 1 million VND (US$63) for vocational students. With those low tuition fees, most institutions have poor facilities. The salaries of lecturers are low, contributing to job dissatisfaction and moonlighting. Because of that, it is difficult to raise the quality of institutions. The state has estimated it will increase tuition fees in the coming years to 400,000 VND per month/student, almost three times the current rate. The state also has a plan to provide scholarships for gifted poor students, and other poor students can borrow money from banks (MoET, 2009).

During the academic year 2007-08, the government covered tuition fees for 750,000 students, and in 2009 the number is expected to grow to 900,000. The MoET plans to divide university and college fees into two groups – domestic training institutions, and institutions running in conjunction with international partners. Fees will not be exempted, as before, but students studying to become teachers will be entitled to special loans. If, after graduation, the student teaches for a minimum five-year period in a state-run school, the fees will be waived.

Teachers in Demographic Perspective

Currently Vietnam has a teaching staff of over 1,000,000 teachers and lecturers. In recent years, the number of Vietnamese teaching staff has been increasing rapidly. Between the 2001-02 and 2005-06 academic years, teaching staff at all levels increased by a total of 15%. The great majority (77%) are teaching at the primary and secondary school level, and 15.9% are teaching at the preschool level, reflective of Vietnam's awareness of the critical importance of preschool education. Furthermore, 4.8% are teaching at the postsecondary level (MoET, 2008). However, there is an imbalance with respect to teaching staff in a number of areas. For example, only 2.2% of the total teaching staff are teaching at the vocational/technical school level (MoET, 2008). Given the rapidly changing structure of the Vietnamese economy with increasing industrialization, this is a major concern (Nga, 2004, p. 464).

There is also a lack of balance between the various regions of Vietnam. In urban areas there are enough teachers, generally speaking. But in remote rural regions far from the city there is a serious lack of teachers, especially in the northwest, the Central Highlands, and the Mekong Delta. Regarding disciplines, there are adequate numbers of mathematics and literature teachers, but in the areas of music, art, and physical education, there are shortages.

The role of private education varies dramatically by level. For example, for preschools, two thirds of teachers work for a private school. However, only slightly over 10% of university teachers work for a private institution (Phạm, 2009).

Regarding gender, the percentage of women among teaching staff is quite high, especially in preschools and primary schools. Currently, women make up 95% of preschool teachers, 78% of primary school teachers, 55.6% of secondary school teachers, 43.5% of vocational and middle technical school teachers, 48.5% of junior college teachers (those teaching at postsecondary institutions which offer only up to two years of education and do not offer a Bachelor's degree), and 39.6% of university teachers. This ratio of women to total lecturers has been increasing more rapidly at the higher education level in more recent years.

The shortage of teaching staff in Vietnam will become a serious problem in the near future. The number of lecturers has been increasing but not at a fast enough pace to keep up with the recent explosion in the number of students enrolled in schools and universities.

Quality of Teachers

In general, teachers have a sense of determination to overcome difficulties and to adapt to new requirements for the renovation and improvement of the education sector. Among them, many teachers were awarded important honors such as 'Labor Hero', 'National Teachers', and 'Excellent Teachers'. The MoET has conducted numerous programs to further develop teachers' skills. Further, Decision Number 09/2005/QD-TTg, dated 11 January 2005, of the minister for the project 'Building and Increasing the Quality of Teaching Staff and Educational Managers in the Period, 2005-2010' has specified concrete plans for the development of Vietnamese teachers and teaching. The Ministry has published standards for teachers and schools, both regarding numbers and quality. There are three basic standards related to morals, knowledge of teaching, and skills in teaching. However, the number of teachers meeting the standard is limited.

Among preschool teachers, still 21.59% have not met the standard. Many teachers have been trained over a short period of time and their teaching level is quite low. In mountainous areas and remote places, teachers are often not yet trained in modern progressive pedagogy.

At primary schools there are still many teachers who were provided with little training, and they are not able to teach using the new textbooks required by the MoET. Currently, approximately 10% of primary school teachers exceed the standard for teachers, and 8% of teachers have not met the standard. For lower secondary schools, 3.81% of teachers do not meet the standard for teachers, and they have not yet acquired a junior college degree. The number of teachers with a Bachelor's degree from the University of Pedagogy is only 20%. In upper secondary schools, 3.81% of teachers do not meet the minimum standard. They are generally physical education, foreign language, and computer teachers who do not have a university degree. Only a few teachers have Master's degrees (3%).

The hiring of university-level teachers is made by the president or rector. Hiring of primary and secondary school teachers is done by provincial education departments. Though the policy is to reduce the number of under-qualified teachers, they may be hired out of necessity when schools lack teachers. For such hiring, it is not necessary to seek an exception from the MoET.

At vocational schools there are over 8000 teachers, 70% of whom have a community college degree or higher, with 68.7% meeting the standard. In middle technical schools, the total number of teachers is 14,230. Among them, 10,677 teachers have a junior college degree, and 5.7% have a higher degree. However, 14.7% of teachers still do not meet the standard. In general in Vietnamese society study in the vocational/technical stream is much less prestigious. This contributes to the difficulty of recruiting top students and teachers to this important sector, growing in importance because of Vietnam's rapid industrialization.

In higher education, there were 38,217 lecturers in the academic year 2007-08. Among them are 303 full professors, making up only 0.79%, 1805 associate professors (4.72%), 5643 with a doctoral degree (14.77%), 8064 with a Master's degree (14.77%), and 15,045 lecturers with only a university or junior college degree. In general, the number of lecturers has been increasing (approximately 3000 per academic year during the most recent five years).

According to Vietnam Net Bridge September 15, 2008), 198 new universities and junior colleges were established in the period 1998-2008. The number of non-state universities and colleges increased fourfold (from 16 to 64), while the number of lecturers and students increased only twofold. The numbers of permanent lecturers at universities is actually much lower than reported numbers. Vạn Xuân Technology College reported that it had 20 faculty with doctorates and 105 with Master's degrees, but the actual payroll only showed one faculty member with a doctorate and only six with Master's degrees. Phú Xuân University enrolls students for finance and banking, but it has only one lecturer in this field – with only a Bachelor's degree.

Lecturers are seriously lacking in newly upgraded universities. Phú Yên and Phạm Văn Đồng Universities, for example, only have two lecturers with doctorates. Also, the ratio of professors to total lecturers has been decreasing in recent years. In Vietnam, of the total number of people who have attained the title 'professor' or 'associate professor', only 30% actually teach. The rest are in management or work in some other profession. The result is that universities lack teachers who are trained at a high level. Most of the 30% still teaching are in their 50s or older because of a lack of funding for advanced study, beginning in the early 1980s. Also given extremely low salaries, many faculty teach at multiple institutions to supplement their income. For example, at public universities, 10-15% of those teaching are part-time instructors. Currently, some universities are inviting professors from abroad (including overseas Vietnamese) to teach, and many of them are members of cooperation projects between Vietnam and international institutions. The number of teacher training colleges has been increasing continually. Every year, pedagogical universities, colleges, and middle technical schools train 18,000 teachers for lower secondary schools and high schools and 13,000 teachers for primary schools and preschools.

To diversify the curricula available for all schools and their responsiveness to the rapidly changing labor market, many faculties have been added to the training system at universities such as music, art, gymnastics, foreign languages, informatics, and technology. Informal forms of training have been developed such as in-service courses, special sessions, and distance education. However, according to the statistical information available, the number of teachers is increasing but not quickly enough to meet the needs of society. Most provinces lack teachers. The Mekong Delta lacks 30,000 teachers. Even Ho Chi Minh City is lacking 1600 teachers for this academic year (2008-09). The educational department of the city has to move quickly to select new teachers for schools to meet the demand. However, at all levels there are not enough teachers to meet the standard. This lack of teachers has been a problem for many years. The reason is the number of students has been increasing every year. On the other hand, the use of teachers is not always rational and salaries are too low. For example, urban teachers may be assigned to mountainous regions without adequate preparation, or the extensive experience of certain teachers may not be fully utilized. Thus, some teachers have defected to obtain higher salaries in the private sector. For the past several years, the state has issued appropriate policies to encourage teachers by providing them with more benefits, opportunities to develop themselves as teachers, and praise for excellent teachers or medals for exemplary educational performance. Teachers receive a slightly higher monthly salary, and students of pedagogical universities do not have to pay tuition fees. The conflict between the rapid expansion of the educational system and the lack of teachers is a problem that remains difficult to solve.

Renovation of Educational Programs, Textbooks, and Curriculum

In the first years of the twenty-first century, Vietnam laid down a policy for the renovation of the program of general education (Instructions 14/2001/CT-TTG of Minister by Decision 40/2000/QH10 of Parliament). This renovation was necessary because of the demand for manpower for socioeconomic development and because of the need for Vietnam to integrate with international education. According to the new program promulgated in May 2006, new textbooks are being written for classes from primary to high school. These texts are better than the previous ones, more current, and more global in scope. However, those books still need to be improved and the teachers need to be trained before teaching with them. This has been difficult.

In the universities, standardization, modernization, diversification, linking theory with practice, and the demand for manpower are all needs requiring a new curriculum. At the end of 2005, in accordance with Decision 14/2005/NQ-CP of the government calling for the renovation of Vietnamese higher education, the MoET promulgated 90 framework programs for branches of higher education. Based on those programs, the universities and colleges can build programs for themselves. The curricula are being rewritten by different professors in universities. They are trained in different countries. Current programs and curricula are weighted excessively toward theory or follow international models with inadequate adaptations to the Vietnamese context. They are still not adequately responsive to the practical needs of society.

Teaching Methods

In general, teachers have tried to improve their teaching skills. A large part of the teaching staff have taken retraining courses to improve their teaching. They all are expected to master two key working tools: English and information technology skills. Many teachers have actively improved their teaching skills and the content of their curricula. They have applied new teaching methods that can develop and stimulate learners' creativity resulting in students being able to learn more effectively on their own. Some lecturers in the universities have re-tailored their curricula as well as improved training methods in accordance with the development of the new economy as well as new science and technology. Many teachers' training seminars have been held to improve teaching methods and curricula. However, such training has not been uniformly provided across diverse regions and schools.

Educational methods in many places are still highly traditional. The most popular method of teaching is still rote learning with the teacher talking and the students taking notes. In recent years, the MoET as well as many schools and universities have expressed concern about this problem, but their capability to remedy it is limited. The reason is that the level of teachers is not sufficient to grasp new methods, and textbooks and/or curricula are not yet adequate, still containing many errors, and are not fully progressive. Facilities and infrastructure are also lacking. For example, as of September 2008, some 17,342 schools or 62% of 27,595 schools nationwide have no connection to the Internet (Quách, 2009). So it is difficult to implement new pedagogies. Also, the style of administration does not encourage new methods and there is no system for checking and evaluating teacher effectiveness. There is also no means of evaluation of schools to determine which are doing well and which are not. To address this issue, in 2003 the MoET established the Department for Testing and Education Quality Accreditation. This department is developing standards for quality and will contract either local or international bodies to assess schools or universities. Thus far, 20 universities have been assessed, though no results have yet been announced publically. Educational evaluation in Vietnam is at an early stage of development.

Also, many students have not changed their idea of educational methods. Thus, they may not like the new, more innovative pedagogies. Further, they do not have the opportunity to research documents (because of a lack of books in the library or lack of access to the Internet) on their own and engage adequately in practice. So, among the factors listed above, the lack of facilities and poor infrastructure are important weaknesses at all major levels of education. Also at the higher education level, there is a serious problem with individuals investing in obtaining bogus degrees from for-profit postsecondary institutions. Unfortunately, there appears to be little awareness or concern about this issue.

Examinations and Assessment

Vietnamese students used to take many examinations at every level from the primary to the undergraduate level. It was a complicated and expensive system. Starting in 2010, students have only one examination to graduate from high school. The university also uses the results of this examination to decide on admission to their institutions. It is important to note that the university entrance examination is merit based and free from corruption and nepotism (Vallely & Wilkinson, 2008, p. 4). Thus, the students who are admitted are indeed the most talented.

For the university level, the state has established a standard to assess and rank universities. However, only 20 universities have been assessed thus far; other universities will be assessed in the coming years. Interestingly Trần (2009) conducted an assessment of how Vietnamese universities are carrying out the 'third mission' of higher education to reach out and to serve the larger society via provision of research, technology transfer linkages, and other kinds of linkages.

Educational Disparities

Even though Vietnam was highly successful in the 1990s after the introduction of the *Đổi mới* policy in achieving impressive economic growth, reducing poverty, and dramatically expanding formal education, both income and educational inequality not only persisted but increased (Liu, 2001; Glewwe et al, 2002). Also Van de Walle & Gunewardena (2001) find significant ethnic disparities with respect to educational attainment.

The overall Gini coefficient of inequality of education for Vietnam at the national level is .25 (Rew, 2009), indicating that educational disparities are less than economic ones. This is relatively low, indicating a reasonably equal distribution with respect to educational attainment. However, an examination of disaggregated data by province reveals significantly greater disparities both among and within provinces (Holsinger et al, 2004). The Gini, for example, for Lai Châu province is a high .53. In contrast, the Gini for Thái Bình province is a low .18. Interestingly, the majority Kinh ethnic group represents only 17% of the population in Lai Châu, while it represents 99.9% of the population in Thái Bình. Of 61 Vietnamese provinces, 22 have a higher Gini than the national average (Rew, 2009). The coefficient of variation (V) is an excellent measure of inequality (Fry & Martin, 1991, pp. 291-292). Based on the level of educational attainment in each of

Vietnam's 61 provinces, the V is a relatively low .14. A V was also computed for the disparities in the Ginis for all 61 provinces. That was a higher .27, but still relatively low.

The Crisis in Higher Education

Given Vietnam's relative success in providing educational access for most of its population to attain primary and secondary education, the major contemporary issue relates to problems of quality across the educational system, as noted above, and what has been termed a crisis in higher education (Harvard Vietnam Program, 2008; Vallely & Wilkinson, 2008). While there has been a huge increase in numbers of students going on to postsecondary education (both public and private), there has only been a modest growth in faculty numbers. Vietnam now has 369 universities and colleges (Nguyễn, 2008).

A major report commissioned by the prime minister of Vietnam, Nguyễn Tấn Dũng, prepared by the Kennedy School of Government at Harvard, presents a candid and harsh critique of Vietnam's higher education system. The system is described as substandard and employers (both domestic and international) express dissatisfaction with the relevant skills of recent graduates (Harvard Vietnam Program, 2008, p. 23). Only 10% of university faculty hold doctorates. Not surprisingly, given their qualifications and the need to moonlight because of low salaries, research productivity is low. Researchers at one of Thailand's leading research universities such as Chulalongkorn or Mahidol produce more than the faculty at all of Vietnam's universities combined (Phạm, 2009). In 2007, for example, researchers at Vietnam's three leading research institutions produced a total of only 96 articles in peer-reviewed journals, while researchers at a single Thai university, Mahidol, produced 950 articles and researchers at Seoul National University produced 5060 articles (Vallely & Wilkinson, 2008, p. 2).

Some basic statistics also show serious problems in higher education. As of 2000, only 2% of Vietnam's population were comprised of university-educated workers. This compares unfavorably with India's 8% and China's 5%. In 2005, Vietnam's higher education enrollment ratio was only 10-16% compared to Thailand's rate of 43%. South Korea's ratio is now over 80%.

The Kennedy School Report cites influential Vietnamese commentators such as General Võ Nguyên Giáp and Vietnam's brilliant mathematician Professor Hòang Tụy (2007) who are critical of the state's management of education and argue that the state has not orchestrated critically needed higher education reforms despite Decision 14 (approved on 2 November 2005), which called for a 'comprehensive reform' of higher education.

The Role of Education in Vietnam's Future:
an ascending dragon

Interestingly, Vietnam shares some important commonalities with both South Korea and Japan, which augur well for its future and its being an increasingly important economic player in the dynamic Asia-Pacific region. All three nations historically share a common strong Confucian heritage, which gives high status and recognition to education and teachers, with a reverence for learning. Also, for centuries and millennia they have been wet rice cooperative cultures (that is, where it is necessary to work in groups to grow rice in flooded fields, often facing harsh or difficult conditions) contributing to a collectivist rather than an individualistic orientation. Thus, Vietnam has valuable social cohesiveness as a society and culture. All three nations recovered from and had to transcend horrific and costly tragedies of war in the past century. Vietnam actually suffered from three major wars. All three are mountainous countries with limited arable land for cultivation. This provides natural incentives for using space in creative and efficient ways. Finally, South Korea and Vietnam both share a bitter colonial heritage which they struggled against with courage and determination. With the exception of wet rice cooperative culture in Southeast Asia generally and Confucian culture in Singapore, these striking commonalities with South Korea and Japan make Vietnam an outlier among both Southeast Asian countries and many other developing nations often rich in natural resources. Vietnam's high secondary enrollment rates for a low-income country also reflect its outlier status (Bender, 2009). The remarkable academic achievements mentioned at the beginning of the chapter further demonstrate Vietnam's exceptionalism.

To realize its great development potential, it is essential that Vietnam enhance its human resource development through quality improvements at all levels of education and training. A positive development is the government's decision to invest US$24 billion in the education sector from 2008-10 (*Viêt Nam News*, 2008). Vietnam actually spends an impressive amount (in terms of percent of national budget) on education. The problem is that it is not getting adequate 'bang for its dong'. The nation must dramatically improve its use of education funding to improve the quality of education at all levels, but particularly higher education. It is imperative to improve the incentives to attract increasing numbers of the best students to go into teaching at all levels.

Thomas Rohlen, an anthropologist who studies Japan, states that this nation is distinctive in its 'devotion to the idea that self-cultivation through the disciplined pursuit of knowledge is the path to human perfection' (McConnell, 2000, p. 139). The same mindset exists among many Vietnamese with their high motivation to learn and to study, reflected in the quotation by Ho Chi Minh at the beginning of this chapter. Vietnam is indeed an ascending dragon (Kamm, 1996). Its commitment to higher education reform and realization of genuine quality improvements are crucial to it becoming an integral part of what has been termed an 'Asian Renaissance', a region of dynamism and creativity (Gill et al, 2007) and what Mahbubani (2008) calls the 'new Asian Hemisphere'.

Acknowledgment

We appreciate the research assistance of Lisa Vu.

References

Asian Development Bank (2002) *Indigenous Peoples/Ethnic Minorities and Poverty Reduction, Viet Nam.* Manila, Philippines: Environment and Social Safeguard Division, Regional and Sustainable Development Department, Asian Development Bank.

Baulch, B., Truong T.K.C., Haughton, D. & Haughton, J. (2004) Ethnic Minority Development in Vietnam: a socioeconomic perspective, in P. Glewwe, N. Agrawal & D. Dollar (Eds) *Economic Growth, Poverty, and Household Welfare in Vietnam*, pp. 273-310. Washington, DC: The World Bank. Regional and Sector Studies 29086.

Bender, M. (2009) Why are Some Low-income Countries Better at Providing Secondary Education, *Comparative Education Review*, 54(4), 513-534.

Đỗ, P. (1998) *Vietnam – image of the community of 54 ethnic groups.* Hanoi: The Ethnic Cultures Publishing House.

Dương, T.T. (2005) *Suy nghĩ về GD truyền thống và hiện đại* [The thinking of traditional and modern education]. Ho Chi Minh City: NXB Trẻ [Tre Press].

Fry, G. & Martin, G. (1991) *The International Development Dictionary*. Oxford: ABC-Clio.

Fry, G. & Phạm, L.H. (2007) Children's Issues in Vietnam, in P. Jyotsa (Ed.) *The Greenwood Encyclopedia of Children's Issues Worldwide*, pp. 535-558. Volume I: Asia and Oceania. Westport, CT: Greenwood Press.

Garnier, F. (1994) *The French in Indo-China*. Bangkok: White Lotus (translated from the French and originally published in 1884).

Gill, I.S., Kharas, H.J. & Bhattasali, D. (2007) *An East Asian Renaissance: ideas for economic growth*. Washington, DC: World Bank.

Gladwell, M. (2009) *Outliers: the story of success.* London: Penguin.

Glewwe, P., Gragnolati, M. & Zaman, H. (2002) Who Gained from Vietnam's Boom in the 1990s? *Economic Development and Cultural Change*, 50(4), 773-792.

Harvard Vietnam Program (2008) *Choosing Success: the lessons of East and Southeast Asia and Vietnam's future, a policy framework for Vietnam's socioeconomic future, 2011-2020.* Cambridge, MA: John F. Kennedy School of Government, Harvard University.

Hayden, M. & Lâm, Q.T. (2007) Institutional Autonomy for Higher Education in Vietnam, *Higher Education Research & Development*, 26(1), 73-85.

Hoàng, T. (2007) Năm mới nói chuyện cũ [New year, old story], *Tia Sáng*, 2 February. http://www.tiasang.com.vn.

Holsinger, D.B., Collins, J.M., Rew, W.J., Luo, J., Lindsay, A.J. & Jimenez, L. (2004) *The Education Gini Coefficient: an underutilized tool for educational policy analysis – the case of Vietnam.* Provo, UT: David M. Kennedy Center for International Studies, Brigham Young University.

Kamm, H. (1996) *Dragon Ascending: Vietnam and the Vietnamese.* New York: Arcade Publishing.

Liu, A.Y.C. (2001) Markets, Inequality, and Poverty in Vietnam, *Asian Economic Journal*, 15(2), 217-231.

Mahbubani, K. (2008) *The New Asian Hemisphere: the irresistible shift of global power to the east.* New York: Public Affairs.

Mai, L.Q. (2008) *Vietnam on the Move*, 5th edn. Hanoi: Thế Giới Publishers.

Marr, D.G. (1971) *Vietnamese Anticolonialism: 1885-1925.* Berkeley: University of California Press.

Marr, D.G. (1981) *Vietnamese Tradition on Trial, 1920-1945.* Berkeley: University of California Press.

McConnell, D.L. (2000) *Importing Diversity: inside Japan's JET program.* Berkeley: University of California Press.

McElwee, P.D. (2008) Ethnic Minorities in Vietnam: are globalization, regionalism, and nationalism hurting or helping them? in L. Prasit, D. McCaskill & B. Kwanchewan (Eds) *Challenging the Limits: indigenous peoples of the Mekong region*, pp. 55-76. Chiang Mai: Mekong Press.

MoET (Ministry of Education and Training) (2008) *Dự thảo chiến lược giáo dục Viet Nam trong thời kỳ 2009-2020* [The strategy of Vietnamese education in the period 2009-2020]. Hanoi: MoET.

MoET (2009) *Dự thảo đổi mới cơ chế tài chính giáo dục 2009-2014* [Renovation of educational financial mechanism in the period 2009-2014]. Hanoi: MoET.

Nga, N.N. (2004) Trends in the Education Sector, in P. Glewwe, N. Agrawal & D. Dollar (Eds) *Economic Growth, Poverty, and Household Welfare in Vietnam*, pp. 425-465. Washington, DC: The World Bank. Regional and Sector Studies 29086.

Nguyễn, H.C. (2007) *Giáo dục Việt Nam trong những năm đầu của thế kỷ XXI* [Vietnamese education at the beginning of the XXI century]. Hanoi: Nhà xuất bản Giáo Dục [Education Press].

Nguyễn, T.L.H. (2008) Vietnam Higher Education: reform for the nation's development, presentation at Macau SAR, China, 26 September.

Nguyễn, V.H. (1998) *Vietnam Museum of Ethnology.* Ho Chi Minh City: Tran Phu Printing Company.

Osborne, M.E. (2000) *The Mekong: turbulent past, uncertain future.* New York: Atlantic Monthly Press.

Phạm, D.D. (1996) *Văn hóa học đại cương và cơ sở văn hóa Việt Nam* [Overview of Vietnamese culture and the essence of Vietnamese culture]. Hanoi: NXB Khoa học xã hội [Social Science Press].

Pham, L.H. (2006) *Giáo dục Quốc tế- một vài tư liệu và so sánh* [International education – comparative perspectives), Ho Chi Minh City: Ho Chi Minh National University Press.

Phạm, D.T. (2008) *54 Ethnic Groups in Vietnam*. Hanoi: VNA Publishing House.

Phạm, L.H. (2009) The Internationalization of Vietnamese Higher Education, paper presented at the 3rd Comparative Education Conference, Ho Chi Minh City University, 16 October.

Phạm, M.H. (1998) *Vietnam's Education: the current position and future prospects*. Hanoi: Thế Giới Publishers.

Phạn, H.L. (1993) *The Traditional Village in Vietnam*. Hanoi: Thế Giới Publishers.

Quách, T.N. (2009) *Ứng dụng công nghệ thông tin trong ngành giáo dục hướng đến một nền giáo dục điện tu* [The application of information in Vietnamese education]. Hanoi: MoET.

Ratliff, W. (2008) *Vietnam Rising: culture and change in Asia's tiger club*. Oakland: The Independent Institute.

Reid, A. (1988-93) *Southeast Asia in the Age of Commerce, 1450-1680*. New Haven: Yale University Press.

Rew, W.J. (2009) Provincial, Ethnic, and Gender Disparities in Education: a descriptive study of Vietnam, in D.B. Holsinger & W.J. Jacob (Eds) *Inequality in Education: comparative and international perspectives*, pp. 307-323. Hong Kong: Comparative Education Research Centre.

Sagemueller, E. (2001) *Văn Miếu: the temple of literature*. Hanoi: Map Publishing House.

Thompson, V. (1968) *French Indo-China*. New York: Octagon Books (originally published in 1937 by Macmillan).

Trần, N.C. (2009) Reaching out to Society: Vietnamese universities in transition, *Science and Public Policy*, 36(2), 91-95.

Trương, B.L. (1967) *Patterns of Vietnamese Response to Foreign Intervention: 1858-1900*. New Haven, CT: Asia Studies, Yale University. Monograph Series No. 11.

United Nations Development Programme (2009) Human Development Report 2009. http://hdrstats.undp.org/indicators/.

United Nations Statistics Division (2009a) Indicators on Education. http://unstats.un.org/unsd/demographic/products/socind/education.htm.

United Nations Statistics Division (2009b) Millennium Development Goals Indicators. http://mdgs.un.org/unsd/mdg/Data.aspx.

United States Agency for International Development (2009) Country Health Statistical Report. http://pdf.usaid.gov/pdf_docs/PNADO791.pdf.

United States Department of State (2009) Background Note: Vietnam. http://www.state.gov/r/pa/ei/bgn/4130.htm#econ.

Vallely, T.J. & Wilkinson, B. (2008) *Vietnamese Higher Education: crisis and response*. Cambridge, MA: ASH Institute, Harvard Kennedy School.

Van de Walle, D. & Gunawardena, D. (2001) Sources of Ethnic Inequality in Vietnam, *Journal of Development Economics*, 65, 177-207.

Viêt Nam News (2008) Education Sector Gets $24 Billion. 16 September. http://vietnamnews.vnagency.com.vn/showarticle.php?num=02EDU160908.

VietNamNet/VNS (2009) Numbers Wizard the Pride of Bac Giang. http://www.lookatvietnam.com/2009/09/numbers-wizard-the-pride-of-bac-giang.html.

Vũ, Q.V. (2007) Sự cần thiết của học phí đại học [The necessity of higher tuition fees for universities], *Lao Động*, no. 217, 19 September.

Woodside, A. (2000) An Enlightenment for Outcasts: some Vietnamese stories, in J.N. Wasserstrom, L. Hunt & M.B. Young (Eds) *Human Rights and Revolutions*, pp. 113-126. Lanham, MD: Rowman & Littlefield Publishers.

World Bank (2009a) Education Trends and Comparisons: Vietnam. http://go.worldbank.org/JVXVANWYY0.

World Bank (2009b) Gender Disaggregated Data: Vietnam. http://go.worldbank.org/JVXVANWYY0.

World Bank (2009c) World Development Indicators Database. http://siteresources.worldbank.org/DATASTATISTICS/Resources/GDP_PPP.pdf.

CHAPTER 13

Aspects of Gender and Education in South-East Asia

COLIN BROCK & PEI-TSENG JENNY HSIEH

SUMMARY The gender factor in access to, and progress within, education is nearly always to the disadvantage of girls and women. In general in South-East Asia the situation is better than the global average. Most of the countries are 'middle income' in global terms, but Cambodia, Laos, Timor-Leste and Vietnam have profiles more like those of South Asian and Sub-Saharan African countries. Overall access and progress for females is generally in advance of males at primary and secondary level. However, at post-secondary level most females are in traditional female-oriented career training programmes even though the incidence of female engineers in some countries is impressive. Where problems exist in access and discrimination, they tend to be associated with issues of ethnicity, language, religion and geography. The massive incidence of archipelago situations in Indonesia and the Philippines is a constraining factor. Females tend to be disadvantaged in situations of migrant workers and also in terms of working while of school age in some countries. Overall, however, the relatively positive picture engenders the cultural capacity building that is necessary for sustainable development, especially in the predominantly rural communities.

Introduction

One of the foremost scholars on the connections between gender and education, Lalage Bown, encapsulated the issue in characteristically direct fashion: 'women are development' and 'without women, no development' (1985). She was illuminating the consequence of the gender gap mainly in terms of Sub-Saharan Africa, but these sentiments apply equally to South-East Asia, and for that matter anywhere in the world. It speaks for more than mere gender parity, a Millennium Development Goal already comprehensively missed. Rather she recognises the added value of female

245

education through its contribution to the survival and enhancement of the prime unit of socio-economic development: the family. The international community may set goals, and governments – including in South-East Asia – may pass regulations in law, but it is at the level of the individual family that decisions are made and actions taken. This applies, albeit differentially, whether it be a poor subsistence farming community or an affluent professionally populated suburb of a city. It applies to the distinctive region with which we are concerned here from basic subsistence communities in Kalimantan, Indonesia, to the nomadic 'water gypsies' of the Philippines, to the entrepreneurs of Singapore.

In this chapter we begin with some of the key general principles relating to gender, education and development in global terms, then to the profile of South-East Asia in this regard before identifying particular examples in some of the countries in the region.

Gender, Education and Development: a global synopsis

In the compilation of their annotated bibliography on gender, development and education for the United Kingdom Department for International Development, Brock & Cammish (1997a) found that in the broad range of social science literature, education rarely figured in the discourse. It was mainly confined to the literature of the field of 'educational studies' where issues relating to learning and teaching, such as access to literacy acquisition for adult women and basic schooling for girls, were seen to be key. As more organised interest in the phenomenon of development progressed after the Second World War, through the establishment of the United Nations and its component parts, as well as other multilateral and bilateral agencies such as the development banks and government ministries, the visibility of the gender factor struggled to emerge. It was boosted by Western feminism in the 1960s and 1970s, itself the beneficiary of outstanding pioneers for women's rights from the eighteenth century onwards.

The first and lengthy phase of gender and education work related to so-called 'developing countries' consisted mainly of numerous researches generating, recording and replicating data concerning female disadvantage in education. It related both to the widespread lack of enrolment and participation of girls in formal schooling, and to equally widespread illiteracy among adult women. The perspective was mainly an economic one (King & Hall, 1993). The next phase was concerned more with access to schooling and the factors affecting the participation of girls (Brock & Cammish, 1997b) and was followed by more theoretical considerations beyond access (Heward & Bunwaree, 1999). Such studies in effect related to some of the key considerations of anthropological work in the 1980s (LeVine & White, 1986; Todd, 1987) such as gender relations at the heart of the family and in the world of work. Issues discussed then such as power relations and educational disparity between parents, and the age-sex hierarchies in societies remain as powerful factors in South-East Asia as elsewhere. Cultural factors are dominant in restraining development, which needs stronger female participation in order to progress. This means change, which needs social space in which to emerge. Such space was termed the cultural capacity for change by Brock & Cammish (1997c) and defined as 'the extent to which and the rate at which a society is capable of absorbing cultural change' (p. 118).

Gail Kelly (1990), taking into account the beginnings of improvement in girls' enrolment in school, distinguished between a number of factors: access to formal education; equality of process in education; quality of cognitive outcomes; and the political outcomes of women's education. She concluded with a question and answer:

Why has the expansion of women's schooling failed to eradicate persistent inequalities in the public spheres of work and politics?

The answer to such a question is complex. First, equality of access to education is only part of the issue. Rarely have the issues of equality of educational processes been addressed. (p. 139)

She was writing in the year of the enormously influential 'World Conference on Education for All' held in South-East Asia at Jomtien in Thailand. Even then the South-East Asian region had mostly moved ahead of the global average in terms of reaching towards a gender balance in enrolment in school but, as with all other regions of the world, was experiencing the problems of inequality in the worlds of work and politics identified by Kelly.

At Jomtien in 1990, temporal aspirations were voiced for the attaining of global gender parity in education that were far too optimistic, as evidenced at the follow-up meeting a decade later at the World Education Forum in Dakar, Senegal in 2000. This meeting gave rise to the 'Dakar Framework for Action', which in turn generated the Education for All (EFA) Millennium Development Goals (MDGs) and then the EFA Global Monitoring Reports (GMRs). The EFA GMR of 2003-04 went out under the title *Gender and Education for All: the leap to equality.*

Asia, Asia/Pacific/South-East Asia: issues of scale and disparity

According to Boden & Green (1994):

Mazumdar (1989) characterises the current education system in Asia as a compromise between indigenous knowledge systems, western imposed scientific-rational education values and control systems, and movements arising out of reactions to imperialism, which include liberal democratic, secular and socialist as well as religious, cultural revivalist and fundamental movements.

Projections of appropriate gender roles are, she argues, 'central to this compromise' (p. 4).

Although this statement was made in the context of Asia as a whole, all of its content is applicable to Asia/Pacific, and within that South-East Asia. The issue of scale is always important in comparative and international educational discussion, and the issue of gender and education is significant at all scales of observation and discussion. Real impacts of scale are too subtle to be accommodated by datasets subdivided by political units only, but that is where we must begin.

The Dakar Forum was itself informed by a series of regional preparatory forums, including the Regional Framework for Action in Asia and the Pacific held at Bangkok, Thailand in January 2000. Given that the regional inputs were based on the UNESCO world regions, one of which is 'Asia/Pacific', these meetings did not generate data specifically on South-East Asia. Consequently the aggregate regional figures tend to be dominated by larger developing countries, especially China and India, and a few highly developed nations such as Australia and Japan. Nonetheless, some of the so-called 'Gains' and 'Challenges' for the region identified in the Regional Framework for Action for Asia and the Pacific were clearly relevant to gender and education in South-East Asia. Among such 'Gains' were: increased primary school enrolment; increased functional adult literacy; increase in international assistance and advocacy for basic education; more partnerships in education between the private sector and civil society. Among the 'Challenges' identified in 2000 with relevance to gender and education in South-East Asia were: growing disparities within countries, especially between urban and rural communities; a lack of emphasis on non-formal modes of education at the basic level and in the workplace; a lack of attention to the retention of students in school as opposed to enrolment; the need to recast curricula to address the actual risks and challenges facing young people; a need to increase the visibility of disadvantaged groups; disruption of education by armed conflict; disparities between large countries and small island states.

This last issue is somewhat curious in that the two most populous countries in the Association of Southeast Asian Nations (ASEAN), Indonesia and the Philippines, are each composed of thousands of islands. They also have a relatively good profile in gender and education terms. Furthermore, the two small states of the regional association, Brunei and Singapore, also have positive profiles in this regard, but we have to dig down to the intra-national, local scale, to identify and comprehend the realities.

Sub-regional Disparities with Reference to Gender and Education

Sadiman (2004) highlighted both disparities *in*, and challenges *to* education in South-East Asia, pointing out that: a) of a total regional area of nearly five million square kilometres, 25% is water; b) of a regional population of some

550 million, nearly half are in one country, Indonesia; and c) national populations range from 250 million there to less than 400,000 in Brunei.

Within every one of the 10 ASEAN nations and Timor-Leste, with the exception of Singapore, the dichotomy between urban and rural contexts is stark, especially in the poorer countries. According to the World Bank, GDP ranged in 2009 from US$677 in Cambodia to US$6975 in Malaysia among the poor and middle-income countries. Most are ethnically diverse, with numerous local social languages. This raises questions about the nature of literacy, the levels of which, as will be mentioned below, are above the global average for both genders. Where there is such ethnic diversity, women and girls tend to experience double disadvantage. This is also the case in archipelago situations, of which there are many in this region. Parents are naturally concerned about their children, especially girls, going off-island to school. This may well be necessary in order to attend secondary school. The same may also apply to mountainous areas with scattered clusters of rural populations, where such small concentrations are known to geographers as 'land islands'.

Poor communities do not necessarily have to be geographically remote to experience exclusion and related female disadvantage in education. The South-East Asia region contains some of the major concentrations of the urban poor, especially in the Philippines. Sadiman (2004) estimates that over the region as a whole about 30% of the population are in real poverty, ranging from over 40% in Lao PDR and the Philippines to less than 10% in Malaysia. In such situations, parents often do not see schooling for their children as relevant to the immediate challenge of daily survival. The opportunity costs are just too high. Brock & Cammish (1997b) found that in the predominantly rural populations of the disadvantaged majority, the prime factor operating against parents sending their children to school and/or keeping them there was poverty. The second most influential factor was the fact that the majority of societies are patriarchal in kinship and therefore power. This is also the case in South-East Asia.

These and other disparities need to be borne in mind when considering the aggregate composite figures in official large-scale datasets such as those that will be discussed below with regard to gender, schooling and post-compulsory education in this region. Enrolment data are not the only indicators, but the easiest to collect on an annual or other periodical basis. Data on attendance and wastage are more telling in terms of the realities, including gender disparity in favour of males. This tends to increase with secondary schooling as evident in the rural areas of Vietnam, Indonesia and the Philippines despite the aggregate figures for all three being among the best in Asia for female enrolment. These favourable profiles overall are due to the strong policies adopted in these countries to encourage the enrolment of girls in school. Such policies are enacted by central governments in response to international initiatives like the MDGs, but their implementation may often depend on sub-national political units.

These units may have different status and power across the 10 nations of the ASEAN region. Their responses to educational needs, including those of girls where they are not being met, may vary considerably from country to country and within countries.

Lack of knowledge of the roles and responsibilities of sub-national units with regard to education is another factor that obscures the educational realities on the ground, such as the differential performance of internal political units with regard to supporting the education of both boys and girls.

With the above caveats in mind we can now proceed to discuss the data and selected literature regarding gender and education in South-East Asia by sector, beginning with the overall picture of literacy, and then moving to primary and secondary schooling and aspects of post-school education.

Gender and Sectors of Education in South-East Asia

A prime outcome of all sectors of education is to maximise the acquisition of literacy. So before examining the primary, secondary and post-secondary sectors with regard to gender it is worthwhile to ascertain what the data exhibit with regard to this fundamental outcome of the learning process.

Literacy

The EFA GMRs are useful recent sources of information that are relatively credible, though one must always treat with caution datasets compiled from returns from governments. The GMR for 2003-04 provided figures for adult and youth literacy, the former being with regard to all over the age of 15, while the latter was limited to those in the age range 15 to 24. The most recent figures included there are for the year 2000. Prior to that, Boden & Green (1994) referring to the previous two decades had indicated that:

The data show that in almost all countries, female illiteracy is higher than male – often two times as high or more. These gender differentials persist in spite of the fact that female illiteracy has been falling, in some cases faster than male illiteracy since 1970. (p. 20)

They recognise Cambodia as one of the worst cases in Asia in the 1970s and 1980s, with 1990 figures indicating the adult literacy rate as being only 48% for females, as opposed to 77% for males. Well-known special circumstances applied to Cambodia at that time, but Lao PDR was even lower at that time: 43% and 70% respectively. Boden & Green (1994) commented on Malaysia having problems of female literacy in respect of ethnicity, relating mainly to Muslim Malays. This did not appear to apply to Indonesia, the most populous Muslim country in the world, but Malaysia was, and is, much more multicultural in its demographic structure.

When youth literacy is considered, the percentage of literate females in Lao PDR in 1990 was 61%, in Cambodia 81% and in Malaysia 94%. Much of this improvement can be ascribed to post-colonial initiatives of newly independent governments.

According to the 2003-04 GMR the East Asia/Pacific region exhibited literacy figures above the world average in 2000. Whereas the global average of adult literates that year was recorded as 82.2% for males and 74.2% for females, the figures for East Asia/Pacific were given as 92.5% and 80.6% respectively. By contrast youth literacy (15-24) was more gender balanced and from 2000 onwards saw significant female gains. This reflected increased take-up of school by girls. By 2007 the East Asia/Pacific region showed both genders on 98% youth literacy, the global figures being 96% for males and 91% for females.

Within the South-East Asia component of the region there is significant disparity, but with females everywhere narrowing the gap. In nearly half the ASEAN countries by 2007 there was parity, but in Malaysia and Myanmar the youth literacy of females was slightly in advance of that of males. Female disadvantage was, however, still in evidence marginally in Vietnam but more clearly in Lao PDR and Cambodia. These are the least industrialised and urbanised of the South-East Asian nations and have experienced more social and economic disruption than others. The same applies to Timor-Leste, outside ASEAN but still in the geographical region, where a long and violent conflict for independence from Indonesia came to an end in 2002. Immediate and significant efforts at educational redevelopment were then made (Nicolai, 2004), but it has few statistics as yet in the EFA GMRs.

Primary/Basic Education

This is arguably the most important sector as without it there is little chance of access to subsequent sectors. The Jomtien Conference of 1990 was a key turning point in that it led swiftly to a redirection of funding towards the primary sector with, in most cases, a reduction of support for other sectors, especially higher education. This was based on the findings of the World Bank and other economists that the aggregate development of all individuals making up a community in terms of attaining functional literacy and numeracy was the most likely way of achieving national socio-economic development. There was consequently increased investment in primary/basic education by multilateral and bilateral development agencies as well as by the governments of less developed countries. Such investment, for its potential effects to be maximised, needs to be paralleled by significant and coordinated development in adult education, especially female literacy enhancement. Unfortunately, such 'joined up' planning and implementation rarely occurs.

Also somewhat lacking, and not surprisingly so, is access to pre-primary schooling in South-East Asia, with according to the GMR of 2003-04 only Thailand showing over 50% of the pre-school age group enrolled. Brunei,

Malaysia, the Philippines and Vietnam were placed between 30 and 50%, while Cambodia, Indonesia, Lao PDR and Myanmar were recorded as below 30%. Such data are difficult to interpret when the official age of entering primary school varies from country to country, as well as the duration of primary schooling itself. Even then, enrolment figures whether gross or net are less indicative of the take-up of a system than those relating to retention and survival adding up to the so-called 'school life-expectancy'. Table I comprises data abstracted from the GMRs of 2003-04 and 2010, the figures available to them being for the years 2000 and 2007.

State	Repeaters (all grades)			Survival rate to grade 5			School life expectancy		
	T	M	F	T	M	F	T	M	F
Brunei	-	-	-	92	92	92	-	-	-
	(2)	(3)	(1)	(98)	(97)	(99)	(14)	(14)	(14)
Cambodia	1	-	-	98	-	-	7	8	7
	(12)	(13)	(10)	(54)	(53)	(56)	(10)	(10)	(9)
Indonesia	6	6	6	95	91	100	-	-	-
	(3)	(4)	(3)	(95)	(1)	(-)	(12)	(12)	(12)
Laos	20	21	18	53	53	54	8	9	7
	(17)	(18)	(16)	(61)	(62)	(61)	(9)	(10)	(8)
Malaysia	-	-	-	-	-	-	12	12	12
	(-)	(-)	(-)	(89)	(99)	(90)	(13)	(12)	(13)
Myanmar	1	-	-	55	55	55	7	7	7
	(1)	(1)	(1)	(73)	(-)	(-)	(-)	(-)	(-)
Philippines	2	2	1	-	-	-	11	-	-
	(2)	(3)	(2)	(73)	(69)	(78)	(12)	(11)	(12)
Singapore	-	-	-	-	-	-	12	12	12
	(.3)	(.4)	(.3)	(-)	(-)	(-)	(-)	(-)	(-)
Thailand	4	4	4	94	92	96	11	11	11
	(9)	(12)	(6)	(-)	(-)	(-)	(14)	(13)	(14)
Timor Leste	-	-	-	-	-	-	-	-	-
	(14)	(15)	(14)	(-)	(-)	(-)	(-)	(-)	(-)
Vietnam	3	-	-	86	-	-	10	11	10
	(1)	(3)	(3)	(92)	(-)	(-)	(10)	(-)	(-)

Table I. Key indicators of primary schooling from the GMRs: percentage of repeaters (all grades) (%), survival rate to Grade 5 (%), school life expectancy (years): 2000 and 2007. T = Total, M = Males, F = Female. Source: abstracted from GMR 2003-04, UNESCO and GMR 2010, UNESCO.

These figures illustrate the gender parity or female superiority in all ASEAN countries at the primary level. Girls seem to progress through the grades a little better in that there are fewer repeaters in most countries. Only Lao PDR and Cambodia show some female disadvantage, while Malaysia seems to be anomalous in that while a lower percentage of girls than boys survive to Grade 5, girls show a slightly longer school life expectancy. However, 2010 figures from the World Bank of the number of years of primary schooling experienced by females over the age of 15 in all ASEAN countries other than Singapore still show them lagging marginally behind the figure for both genders together over the age of 15, except in Brunei where there is parity. This indicates how cautious one must be when attempting to draw any conclusions from international datasets dealing in information on a macro/national scale.

Secondary and Post-secondary Education

The data for female transition from primary to secondary education are impressive, and this is borne out by GMR figures on the secondary sector itself for the South-East Asian nations. The proportions of repeaters for both genders are small, but girls repeat to a lesser degree than boys in almost all countries in the region.

However, the secondary sector is more diversified than the primary, and also across the region. There is a technical/vocational line available at some stage in most countries, as well as what the GMRs refer to as a 'post-secondary non-tertiary sector'.

This may be seen as roughly parallel to further education in England or community college in the USA. As students proceed through secondary and post-secondary education in South-East Asia a picture of divergence begins to emerge as between the genders. According to Jayaweera (1987) both the impressive take-up by females and the increasing divergence and disparity between genders are quite longstanding.

With regard to gross enrolment rates at secondary level in the 1970s Jayaweera comments that:

> Within the vocational education system, however, many women students are seen to be enrolled in courses leading to culturally demarcated 'feminine' areas of employment. (p. 461)

But with reference to Asia as a whole Jayaweera identifies just the Philippines, along with China and India, where there were 'specific measures to introduce curriculum materials that may promote gender equality' (p. 465).

Figures are given by Jayaweera (1987) for what is termed 'third level' for 1975 and 1980, with the percentage of females enrolled at this level in the following countries: Burma (now Myanmar) 39/49; Indonesia 28/28; Lao PDR 26/31; Malaysia 29/39; the Philippines 55/53; Singapore 40/39; Thailand 40/43 and Vietnam 24/26 (p. 459). In each case the first number is for 1975 and the second number for 1980.

The data from the GMRs of 2003-04 and 2010 giving the percentage of females enrolled at tertiary level in 2000 and 2007 respectively provide a different picture: Brunei 20/20; Cambodia 2/4; Indonesia 13/17; Lao PDR 3/10; Malaysia 27/33; Myanmar 15 (2000 only); the Philippines 32 (2007 only); Thailand 37/58 and Vietnam 8 (2000 only). Be that as it may, perhaps a more significant issue is that of gender disparity by field of study. This is illustrated in Table II with reference to those South-East Asian nations that submitted data to the 2010 GMR.

States	Fields of study								
	1	2	3	4	5	6	7	8	9
Brunei	52/69	9/57	13/62	8/57	7/36	-/-	7/73	-/-	4/73
Cambodia	20/69	1/57	52/62	11/57	4/36	3/-	6/73	-/-	4/73
Indonesia	15/50	1/50	50/50	8/50	16/49	5/50	4/50	-/-	1/39
Laos	22/49	20/50	40/41	3/34	6/12	5/24	2/58	2/26	-/-
Malaysia	9/55	9/58	27/63	19/55	23/37	3/79	6/61	3/64	-/-
Myanmar	2/73	48/57	28/56	22/60	-/-	-/-	-/-	-/-	-/-
Philippines	-/-	-/-	-/-	-/-	-/-	-/-	-/-	-/-	-/-
Singapore	3/70	9/66	34/58	17/46	31/28	-/-	5/71	1/51	-/-
Thailand	-/-	-/-	-/-	-/-	-/-	-/-	-/-	-/-	-/-
Vietnam	26/60	4/70	34/59	-/-	24/23	7/40	3/46	-/-	-/-

Fields of study: 1. Education; 2. Humanities/arts; 3. Social sciences/business/law; 4. Sciences; 5. Engineering/management/distribution; 6. Agriculture; 7. Health/welfare; 8. Services; 9. Unspecified.

Table II. Tertiary education in ASEAN countries by field of study in percentages of the total/percentage female in each field, 2007. Source *EFA Global Monitoring Report 2010* (UNESCO, 2011).

According to the returns to the 2010 GMR, the percentage of tertiary-level students who were female in 2007 were: Brunei 65%, Cambodia 35%, Indonesia 50%, Lao PDR 42%, Malaysia 54%, Myanmar 58%, the Philippines 54%, Singapore 49%, Thailand 54% and Vietnam 49%. Turning to the data on fields of study in Table II, the very high percentage of female Brunei students in education, presumably mostly teacher training, is clearly related to the high overall proportion of female tertiary students in that country. With its high GDP mostly derived from petroleum income, Brunei is able to invest heavily in the education of its people. With several universities in a country with a population of only about 350,000, higher education is also seen as a source of international income as well. The 2007 figures show that females make up 55% of foreign students in Brunei. So female Brunei graduates clearly have opportunities here as they do in the health and welfare fields. Indeed the only area where female students are in a minority across the region is that of engineering, management and distribution. It is interesting to see this also in Singapore, which is way ahead of the other ASEAN nations in the proportion of its total graduates being in these fields. Nonetheless with the global average of the percentage of the world's engineering, management and distribution students being 21, at least six South-East Asian nations exceed this figure: Brunei (36), Cambodia (36), Indonesia (49), Malaysia (37), Singapore (28) and Vietnam (23). It is quite likely that the Philippines and Thailand might also have done so, but they did not provide figures (for 2007) on this item to the GMR of 2010.

While the figures for gender opportunity and balance at tertiary level in the South-East Asian region are impressive and generally above the global average, it must be remembered that only a minority of the age group are enrolled in higher education. The 2007 figures published in the 2010 GMR indicate that the following percentages of the females in the tertiary age group did *not* take their education beyond secondary level: Brunei (80%), Cambodia (96%), Indonesia (83%), Lao PDR (90%), Malaysia (67%), Myanmar (85% in 2000), the Philippines (68%), Thailand (47%) and Vietnam (92% in 2000). For the majority of females who do not go beyond the secondary level factors enhancing some kind of disproportional disadvantage need to be identified, such as being in an indigenous or multicultural situation; being in a conflict or refugee situation; experiencing the burdens of child labour instead of or alongside going to school; and the issue of female teachers. These will now be discussed.

Selected Factors Adversely Affecting Female Participation

The factors mentioned above can also be disadvantageous to males as well as females, and where necessary this will be mentioned, but as indicated earlier women and girls tend to be doubly disadvantaged whenever there are constraints on participation in any form of education.

Multicultural and Indigenous Situations

Clearly being an indigenous minority is a specific and special situation, but most of the national populations of ASEAN countries are distinctly multicultural. Among the poor rural communities that make up the majority of the populations of the larger states in the area there are many cultures, some of them very localised and indigenous. This is accentuated where there are archipelago situations, which, as mentioned above, are disadvantageous to women and girls in any case. There is another form of multicultural demography derived from the colonial legacies apparent in the region: the British in Malaysia, Myanmar and Singapore, the Dutch in Indonesia and the Spanish and Americans in the Philippines. In Malaysia especially, the differential educational opportunities and experiences of the three main cultural components, the indigenous Malays and the imported Chinese and Indians, have been significant but have applied to both genders. However, there may be cultural factors within each of these main communities that have affected gender balance and parity.

In their article on gender policy and practice with regard to the education of indigenous adults, Rao & Robinson-Pant (2006) identify three main issues of concern: language policy – clearly related to literacy; the relationship between indigenous and Western learning; and learning for empowerment. Their discussion is not geographically focussed, but they exemplify the gender dimension of these key concerns with a number of references to the Karen people, who are an important minority within several countries of South-East Asia, notably Myanmar, Thailand and Malaysia. With regard to language policy Rao & Robinson-Pant challenge the orthodoxy, favoured by UNESCO, of putting the indigenous social language of home and local community first, especially with regard to adult females in minority communities. As an example they state:

> When the Karen Women's Organisation was faced with setting up
> literacy programmes for refugees on the Thai-Burmese border
> they identified three major languages spoken amongst their
> participants: Po Karen, S'Kaw Karen and Burmese. They began
> the literacy course in S'Kaw Karen as this was the first language of
> a majority of participants and was the language spoken in camp
> meetings and public places. However, they recognised that follow-
> up courses should also take place in Burmese, in response to the
> women participants' request to learn what had been perceived as
> the language of power (when they were in Burma). (p. 214)

They go on to explain that this was because these adult women, as is often the case in poor rural communities, had been excluded from opportunities to learn basic literacy in their normal traditional environments.

However, due partly to the globalisation of English and its use by aid agencies and charities both inside and outside refugee camps, the issue of the relationship between indigenous and Western learning had also to be addressed.

It is not just a matter of linguistics, but also one of the culture of education. With reference to Aikman (1999, p. 28) they illustrate this by pointing out that:

> within indigenous systems it can be difficult to separate teaching,
> learning and evaluation, which are closely woven strands and in
> which failure is unknown. The modern education system has
> therefore not just led to a loss of indigenous languages, but also to
> the 'failure' of indigenous students within such education systems.
> (p. 216)

Modern, i.e. 'Western' education systems, the structures and overall curricular priorities of which operate in all national systems, including those in South-East Asia, include the assumption of participatory methods. With respect to the Karen Women's Organisation mentioned above, they preferred to operate through traditional rote learning even though it did not involve the debating facility that would assist adult women in the power relationship within the family. This impedes the generation of cultural capacity for change that is central to advancing the education of women and girls in traditional communities.

Situations of Conflict

The Karen nation as it is known is one of several that existed prior to the British colonisation of Myanmar and Malaysia in the borderland between the dominant Burmese, Malay and Thai cultures. The British drew the international borders through the traditional territories of the Karen, Kareni and other smaller indigenous peoples.

Subsequent conflict between the politically and militarily dominant Burmese culture has led to the exodus of Karen and others, mainly into Thailand but also into Malaysia, both as refugees and as economic migrants. As the existence of the aforementioned Karen Women's Organisation would indicate, adult females tend to be in the majority and especially in the refugee camps to be the main source of teachers. The economic migrants, being illegal, remain dependent on whatever informal education they can manage, not being permitted to enrol in the mainstream schools. Those who register as refugees gain the support of the UN High Commissioner for Refugees (UNHCR) under the auspices of which numerous NGOs and other charities assist with providing formal education in the camps. They grapple with the tension between Western and indigenous approaches to learning as described above (Steadman et al, 2008). Conflict and related forced migration tends to create refugee communities that are gender imbalanced due to the disproportionate involvement of males, young and older, in the actual violent conflict itself. Due to prior schooling and literacy disadvantage of women and girls in their traditional patriarchal societies, females are again doubly disadvantaged in refugee communities. In Malaysia this is compounded by a failure to accede to the international protocols on responsibilities to refugees where the work of UNHCR and other humanitarian agencies is barely tolerated (Letchamanan, 2010).

Conflict and displacement arising from the actions of the Burmese-dominated government of Myanmar is not the only example in the region. In his UNESCO report *Education under Attack*, O'Malley (2010) also details examples from Indonesia, the Philippines and Thailand. In Indonesia he reported on attacks on Christian students and their campus in Jakarta in 2008 which left 600 female students living in a tented camp, and that earlier in 2005 in eastern Indonesia many schools had been destroyed by elite paramilitaries with the associated rape and beheading of girls (pp. 197-198). In the Philippines, there has been a longstanding and violent conflict between central government forces and paramilitaries in some parts of the southern province of Mindanao. O'Malley mentions this, but also numerous other cases of violent conflict with religious motivations on the part of both Christians and Muslims in other locations (pp. 219-221). In Thailand the prime examples come from the southern border area with Malaysia. He details an example:

> Gunmen disguised as government soldiers on motorbikes overtook
> a truck carrying a group of teachers and forced it to stop at a fake

roadblock set up by other gunmen in their group. Two Buddhist
Thai teachers were singled out and killed: Atcharapon Tehpsor, a
teacher at Ban Dusung School, who was eight months pregnant,
and Warunee Navaka, a teacher at Barn Ri Nge School. (p. 231)

Apparently 119 teachers had been killed by the beginning of August 2009 in
the Southern Federation region, along with years of destruction of schools by
arson.

Although both genders suffer from violent conflicts such as these,
sometimes leading to forced migration, it is girls and women who are at
greatest risk and disproportionately suffer disruption to their education or
teaching careers. Whether or not the massive and prolonged conflict in
Cambodia in the 1970s has any legacy for education in that country that is
gender related is difficult to determine.

The Influence of Work: migrant workers

According to an official report by Pitsuwan (2008) on the findings of a task
force of the United Nations Development Fund for Women (UNIFEM) and
the South-East Asian Regional Co-operation Office of ASEAN, there was
concern at the increasing incidence of female migrant workers at all levels of
employment. The report states that:

There is a trend of growing feminization of labour in ASEAN,
with an increasing predominance of women in contractual,
temporary, lowest paid and sometimes hazardous jobs. (pp. 2-3)

Consequently the countries of ASEAN are seeking to harmonise their labour
laws so that collective bargaining, freedom of association and facilities for
coming together can be provided. In order to achieve these objectives much
more information will have to be generated and shared. Officials in all
ASEAN member states need to be trained to recognise disadvantage and
abuse and be able to educate female migrant workers about their rights. In
particular, the report emphasises, there is a need to eliminate debt bondage, a
modern form of slavery, and strengthen the women's control over their
earnings. Letchamanan (2010) found significant numbers of migrant workers
in Sabah, Eastern Malaysia with problems for the education of their children
similar to those of refugees. This also resonates with the incidence of large
numbers of female workers from South-East Asia, especially the Philippines,
in low-paid employment in the United Kingdom, where there are also
significant numbers in the health and welfare sectors with existing training.
The concern of ASEAN governments to safeguard the well-being of female
migrant workers would seem to indicate that there are significant numbers of
girls either not achieving in school or holding qualifications beyond the
capacity of the labour market to absorb them.

The Influence of Work: child labour and gender

An illustration of the illusion created by school enrolment data, as opposed those on attendance and wastage, is the incidence, especially in the poorer sections of South-East Asian societies, of child labour. However, although there are places where child labour on the scale of the slum settlements around large Indian cities like Mumbai exists – notably Manila in the Philippines – a significant proportion of child labour in the larger ASEAN states is in home-based work. Mehrotra & Biggeri (2002) carried out a study for the United Nations Children's Fund under the title *The Subterranean Child Labour Force: subcontracted home based manufacturing in Asia*. Although the research carried a continent-wide connotation, three of the five case study countries were in South-East Asia: Indonesia, the Philippines and Thailand. The other two were India and Pakistan. The decision to include the majority of cases from this region was presumably significant. Apparently home-based manufacturing, including child labour, is a feature in the region but the majority of children involved also go to school. Unlike in South Asia it brings the majority of such children and their families above the poverty line and promotes entrepreneurial expertise. The family is the economic unit. This is similar to the case in most indigenous and travelling communities, where parents see the value of contact with formal schooling but in combination with their prime means of survival (Brock, 2011, pp. 60-67). The survey comments on dropout during upper primary and lower secondary schooling being a feature of a proportion of home-based work households, and also on the feminisation of home-based work in the South-East Asian region. They claim that in Indonesia 40% of older – presumably secondary age – girls were working as opposed to 20% of boys, more of whom combine work and school. It is claimed that the number of hours worked by such older children in Indonesia in a six-day week is 31.3 for those who do not attend school and 18.3 for those who do. Table III comprises data abstracted from the survey for Indonesia and the Philippines.

While these data derive from a 'snapshot' of a relatively small number of families in the countries concerned, it is of value in indicating that there is much greater disparity lurking beneath aggregate national-level data and that there is certainly some disadvantage to girls. With reference to what they term 'Gender and Time-use of Children' Mehrotra & Biggeri (2002) are of the view that in Indonesia, girls of school age are more likely to be working than boys at a ratio of 2:1. This, they claim, is partly due to parental insistence on the development of skills for marriage, and on top of this they are more likely to be required to undertake domestic tasks than are boys. In their summary analysis the authors comment with regard to Indonesia as follows:

> As in India and Pakistan, the education level/literacy of the
> mother increases the probability that the child will only study

rather than work; having an educated mother increases the probability by 5 per cent. (p. 51)

Family size is also an issue in that the more dependents there are in the home, the more likely that home-based work will be carried on. They conclude that 'the political economy of financing such a fund is critical to its creation in the first place' (p. 59). Here they are referring to the ability of a family to pay school fees in order to strengthen the capacity for survival both from the immediate income generation from home-based work and from the possibility that some of the children, whether boys or girls, may proceed to more lucrative employment as a result of educational success. So while the burden may fall more heavily on females to some degree, this is more akin to the situation in more developed nations rather than in the major concentrations of global poverty in South Asia and Sub-Saharan Africa.

	Age 7-12				Age 13-15			
	Work only	School only	Work + school	No work or school	Work only	School only	Work + school	No work or school
Indonesia								
Total	0.5	79.4	13.4	6.7	23.6	38.6	22.0	15.7
Male	0.0	82.2	11.9	5.9	28.1	45.6	10.5	15.8
Female	1.1	76.3	15.1	7.5	20.0	32.9	31.4	15.7
Philippines								
Total	1.2	65.7	25.9	7.2	12.1	36.3	47.3	4.4
Male	1.2	65.9	23.2	9.8	12.2	32.7	49.0	6.1
Female	1.2	65.5	28.6	4.8	11.9	40.5	45.2	2.4

Note: The above percentages are derived from data gathered from 300 home-based work households in Indonesia and 173 home-based work households in the Philippines.

Table III. Work and study status of children in Indonesia and the Philippines by age and gender in percentages – home-based work households only. Source: Mehrotra & Biggeri (2002, p. 25).

Empowerment

As Heward & Bunwaree (1999) highlighted over a decade ago female access to schooling and other forms of education is important, but empowerment of adult women is fundamental to chances of access. Bown (1991) showed how the acquisition of literacy by adult women was not just a functional facility but a massive confidence and identity booster on the path to maternal authority, that is to say the level of education of a mother in relation to that of the father.

With reference to South and South-East Asia, Chaudhuri (2010) reported on a comparative study of women's empowerment. It is a complex study involving regression analysis on six indicators: economic participation, educational attainment, wage work, fertility, the female to male ratio to living children in the family, and what respondents regarded as the ideal number of daughters as to sons in the family.

Four countries in South Asia were included: Bangladesh, India, Nepal and Pakistan, while the four South-East Asian countries were Cambodia, Indonesia, the Philippines and Vietnam. Overall for both sets of countries four key findings emerged: a) that social and religious norms hindered female empowerment; b) that feminist movements and government policies were real drivers towards empowerment; c) that advances in empowerment had been achieved despite meagre access to resources – Vietnam showed the greatest advance despite being almost the poorest; d) that empowerment can be a consequence of political turmoil – regarding which with reference to Cambodia, Chaudhuri (2010) states:

> For example, high female economic partition rate and high ratio of living women to men in Cambodia are due to major civil wars and political killings that reduced the male population. This is not the result of economic development, and is certainly not the result of any changes in women's position in society. (p. 4)

Within the overall study Chaudhuri conducted a six-country survey, four being the South-East Asian states. Cambodia emerged with the lowest levels of empowerment of all six, due to the shortest average number of years in education of females (3.2), a high incidence of non-wage labour, a decline in fertility due to war and genocide, and very strict social codes dominated by patriarchal factors. Vietnam, by contrast, despite a low GDP showed clear female empowerment due to high levels of access to wage employment, a 'two child' policy, an education span of seven to eight years and strong commitment to adult female literacy. Indonesia, with half the population of the region and high economic participation by women, showed higher levels of development but lower female empowerment. This was again put down to patriarchal and cultural pressures in a predominantly Islamic population. Finally the Philippines:

> Women of the Philippines enjoy higher autonomy than the rest of the developing world, especially in household decision-making. Estudillo et al (2001) note that women of the Philippines enjoyed equal rights in the pre-Spanish period (pre 1521). Although the Spanish clergy preached male dominance, nonetheless even during this period, the treatment of Filipino women was much more egalitarian than in other countries. Filipino women have owned land and inherited property for centuries. Husbands often hand over their income to their wives and financial and other decisions are jointly made by husband and wife. (p. 26)

The education span in the Philippines is the longest of all the countries in the study at 10+ years; there has also been free compulsory secondary education since 1986, plus a relatively low fertility rate and a strong feminist movement over the past few decades. Chaudhuri (2010) concludes that, in this region at least, women's empowerment is exhibited in resources, agency and outcomes. All have a cumulative effect which can be achieved even in very poor circumstances as the case of Vietnam illustrates.

As has been mentioned with regard to Cambodia, situations of conflict may afford female opportunity but not necessarily empowerment. In situations of violent oppression of indigenous communities empowerment may be viewed in very different terms, as described by Rao & Robinson Pant (2006) with respect to examples from Burma/Myanmar and Malaysia:

> In Burma, for example, the Karen community (a minority ethnic group) were forbidden to speak or teach in their own language, Po Karen, and were forced to give their children Burmese names. In Malaysia, belonging to the Orang Asli Community has been associated with stigma and low esteem ... In these very differing situations, empowerment has been associated with enhancing self-esteem, strengthening collective identity and promoting indigenous culture and language as well as the opportunities to set up alternative educational structures. (p. 217)

In such situations of conflict, oppression and prejudice suffered by males and females alike it is nonetheless the maternal authority of women that is key to survival.

Conclusion

A number of issues emerge from this brief and somewhat selective discussion of gender and education in South-East Asia. In broad terms, as indicated by the GMRs of 2003-04 and 2010, the region exhibits a profile that is above the world average for female enrolment and survival through the sectors of formal education from primary school to the tertiary level. This is because the majority of ASEAN states are middle-income countries. It is also clear that some states, especially Indonesia and the Philippines, by far the largest in population, have made clear efforts to confront the challenge of female disadvantage in education. The challenge exists because the majority of societies in the region are patriarchal and there are still significant numbers in poverty in poor urban and rural areas alike. The persistence of both poverty and socio-cultural constraints, including perverse male interpretations of some theological issues to their own advantage, are key factors constraining female opportunity in many parts of the world. The degree of maternal authority is key in this region, as everywhere. In South-East Asia the relatively positive educational profile of women and girls that has been improving over half a century of post-colonial independence is enabling this key factor to help to create the cultural capacity that is fundamental to sustainable development. It would also appear that ASEAN takes the matter of female disadvantage where it exists seriously, and at least in policy terms is attempting to support the infrastructure necessary to challenge it.

References

Aikman, S. (1999) *Intercultural Education and Literacy*. Amsterdam/Philadelphia: John Benjamin's Publishing Company.

Boden, S. & Green, C. (1994) Gender and Education in Asia and the Pacific. Report for the Australian International Development Assistance Bureau, Canberra.

Bown, L. (1991) *Preparing the Future: women, literacy and development*. Chard: ActionAid.

Bown, L. (1985) Without Women No Development: the role of nonformal education for women in African development, in K. Lillis (Ed.) *School and Community in Less Developed Areas*. London: Croom Helm.

Brock, C. (2011) *Education as a Global Concern*. London: Continuum Books.

Brock, C. & Cammish, N.K. (1997a) *Gender, Education and Development: an annotated bibliography*. London: Department for International Development.

Brock, C. & Cammish, N.K. (1997b) *Factors Affecting Female Participation in Seven Developing Countries*. London: Department for International Development.

Brock, C. & Cammish, N.K. (1997c) Cultural Capacity-building and Closing the Gender Gap, in K. Watson, C. Modgil & S. Modgil (Eds) *Quality in Education* (Vol. 4 of Educational Dilemmas, Debate and Diversity), pp. 118-126. London: Cassell.

Chaudhuri, S. (2010) Women's Empowerment in Asia and South-East Asia: a comparative analysis. MPRA Paper 19686. http://mpra.ub.uni-muenchen.de/19686/1/MPRA_paper_19686.pdf

Heward, C. & Bunwaree, S. (Eds) (1999) *Gender, Education and Development: beyond access to empowerment*. London: Zed Books.

Jayaweera, S. (1987) Gender and Access to Education in Asia, *International Review of Education*, 33(4), 455-466.

Kelly, G.P. (1990) Education and Equality: comparative perspectives on the expansion of education and women in the post-war period, *International Journal of Educational Development*, 10(2/3), 131-141.

King, E. & Hall, M.A. (1993) *Women's Education in Developing Countries: barriers, benefits and policies (a World Bank book)*. Baltimore and London: Johns Hopkins University Press.

Letchamanan, H. (2010) Needs and Responses: a study of education for refugee and migrant children in Malaysia. MSc dissertation, University of Oxford.

LeVine, R.A. & White, M.I. (1986) *Human Conditions: the cultural basis of educational development (Harvard Project on human potential)*. New York: Routledge and Kegan Paul.

Mazumdar, V. (1989) *Gender Issues and Educational Development: an overview from Asia*. Centre for Women's Development Studies, Occasional Paper No. 15. Delhi: CWDS.

Mehrotra, S. & Biggeri, M. (2002) *The Subterranean Child Labour Force: subcontracted home based manufacturing in Asia*. Florence: UNICEF Innocenti Research Centre.

Nicolai, S. (2004) *Learning Independence: education in emergency and transition in Timor Leste since 1990*. Paris: International Institute for Educational Planning.

O'Malley, B. (2010) *Education under Attack*. Paris: UNESCO.

Pitsuwan, H.E.S. (2008) *Report on Task Force of UNIFEM and S.E. Asian Regional Co-operation in Human Development (SEARCH)*. Report drafted by Sinapan Samydorai, Jean D'Cunha and Michael Miner. Bangkok: Association of Southeast Asian Nations.

Rao, N. & Robinson-Pant, A. (2006) Adult Education and Indigenous People: addressing gender in policy and practice, *International Journal of Educational Development*, 26, 209-223.

Sadiman, A.S. (2004) Challenges in Education in Southeast Asia, paper presented to the International Seminar on 'Towards Cross-Border Co-operation Between South and South-East Asia: the importance of India's North-East playing budge and buffer role', Kaziranga, India, 16-19 November.

Steadman, J. with Brock, C. McCorriston, M.K. & Oh, S.A. (2008) *An Assessment of Teacher Training for ZOA Refugee Care: N.W. Thailand*. ZOA Refugee Care.

Todd, E. (1987) *The Causes of Progress: culture, authority and change*. Oxford: Basil Blackwell.

UNESCO (2011) *The Hidden Crisis: armed conflict and education. EFA Global Monitoring Report 2010*. Paris: UNESCO.

World Bank (2010) World Data Bank, Education Statistics. http://databank.worldbank.org/ddp/home.do (accessed 12 November 2010).

CHAPTER 14

Higher Education in South-East Asia: achievement and aspiration

ANTHONY WELCH

SUMMARY The multifaceted jewel of South-East Asia presents a challenge to researchers attempting to do justice to its diversity. This chapter addresses the achievements of higher education in five key ASEAN member states: Indonesia, Malaysia, the Philippines, Thailand and Vietnam – as well as their ambitions for the future. Key elements of change include privatisation, measures of innovation, and internationalisation, including regionalisation. It is argued that while all five states share the ambition to extend both the quantity and quality of higher education, there are significant constraints that limit the prospects of these ambitions being achieved in the shorter term; in some states more than others.

Any survey of higher education within South-East Asia must, of necessity, be selective. Doing justice to a region of such extraordinary diversity – linguistic, cultural, religious, economic and political – is a daunting task for any analyst, but one of importance, as the region is of growing importance in world terms, and encompasses higher education systems that range from relatively peripheral to highly developed. The current volume is thus to be particularly welcomed, and the following analysis of regional higher education will hopefully add to understanding the dynamic state of higher education within the region. Arguing that higher educational developments within the region are best understood as a heady mix of ambition and constraint, the chapter sketches some of the diversity among selected systems in the Association of Southeast Asian Nations (ASEAN), and then illustrates this range, by focusing on key areas of dynamism such as privatisation, knowledge and innovation measures, and internationalisation (including regionalisation).

The current analysis embraces much of this diversity, principally focusing on the five ASEAN member states of Indonesia, Malaysia, the

Philippines, Thailand, and Vietnam, although some reference will be made to the wealthy and highly developed Singapore system. The analysis deliberately exempts Australia and New Zealand, which while part of the region geographically, and increasingly integrated into the Asia Pacific in terms of trade and cultural relations, are not ASEAN member states.

A Diverse Context

The 10 member states that together make up the Association of Southeast Asian Nations collectively house some 575 million people. In economic terms, average annual GDP growth rate for 2007 was 6.5%, but this does little justice to the range, which was always huge, and which the differential effects of the subsequent Global Financial Crisis (GFC) of 2008-09, that hurt some regional states much more than others, further varied. Levels of economic development still range widely: from the highly developed economy of Singapore, with a GDP per capita in excess of US$35,000 in 2007, to that of the Lao People's Democratic Republic, with a GDP per capita of just US$731 (ASEAN, 2009). ASEAN trade totalled US$1.4 billion, and aggregate foreign direct investment (FDI) amounted to US$52.4 billion of which the lion's share flowed to Singapore (ASEAN, 2009). While all five countries could be classed as developing, three are classed as low income. The level of Malaysia's GDP per capita now places it into a middle-income category, with Thailand not that far behind.

Economic statistics, however, express only one dimension of regional diversity – South-East Asia embraces one of the world's richest arrays of histories and cultures. Many hundreds of languages are spoken across the region, and a number of religious and ethical traditions exist, several of which have been influential in the regional history of higher learning. The region contains, for example, the most populous Muslim country in the world (Indonesia, with a population of 230 million), strong currents of Buddhism (Thailand), Christianity, Hinduism (Bali and eastern tip of Java), and numerous local religious traditions. Even within one state, the extent of diversity is extraordinary. The Indonesian archipelago alone, for example, comprises around 14,000 islands, and perhaps 600 languages or dialects, with substantial differences in wealth and higher education participation between different regions, and between rural and urban settings.

While this diversity makes analysis challenging and generalisations perilous, there are some countervailing elements held in common. A longstanding respect for learning is common to the region, including in many cases a longstanding history of higher learning. It might be a surprise to some to learn, for example, that Hanoi's Temple of Literature (*Van Mieu*), an early site of Confucian higher learning, was founded by Emperor Ly almost a thousand years ago, pre-dating the universities of Oxford, Cambridge and Paris (A. Welch, 2010a). Indonesia's famed Borobudur temple, established around 800 AD, contains many carved panels that illustrate Buddhist sutras of an educational nature, of which the most notable, the Avatamsaka Sutra, is devoted to the story of Sudhana's tireless wandering in search of the Highest Perfect Wisdom.

This long-standing respect for learning provides one plank for a platform of strong support for higher education that, notwithstanding significant differences of wealth and infrastructure, is common throughout the region. A further plank is more related to the ubiquitous goal of achieving a knowledge society, and the associated conviction that, for social and economic development to be achieved, the quality and quantity of higher education must be increased. For families, such faith in higher learning underpins a willingness to make often considerable sacrifices to make higher education available to their sons, and increasingly daughters. At a national level, nations from across the region, both rich and poor, see their future as inextricably tied to the vitality of their knowledge and innovation systems. Higher education, from this point of view, is the key production site for the highly skilled personnel who, in a more post-Fordist world, are believed to be the foundation of the emerging, twenty-first-century knowledge economies. This is all the more the case since the growth of a more neo-liberal, economically rational age over the past two or three decades, in which knowledge, like other commodities, is increasingly valued in instrumental, economic terms (Pusey, 1991).

As detailed below, however, such aspirations are not always matched by achievements. Indeed, while relatively ubiquitous in the region, such aspirations raise some difficult consequential issues. With the notable exception of Singapore, whose relative wealth and highly developed infrastructure make it something of an outlier in the context of South-East Asian higher education, no other higher education system in ASEAN has a single university listed within the well-known and carefully calibrated Shanghai Jiaotong index of the world's 500 leading research universities (Shanghai Jiaotong, 2008). Singapore's National University is ranked not far outside the top 100, while Nanyang Technological University falls slightly outside the top 300. Thus, while each of the governments of South-East Asia sees universities as institutions of national and international prestige (and, of course, as important repositories of national culture), but also crucially, as springboards to economic development, in concert with key industries such as information technology (IT), engineering and science, their ranking, at least on this measure, shows that, to some extent, ambition is not entirely matched by achievement. At the same time, of course, each country has cherished icons of higher education among its ranks: Vietnam National University, the University of the Philippines, the University of Indonesia, Chulalongkorn University and the University of Malaysia are all examples. Even if, however, universities are seen as drivers of economic growth, such rankings bring into question the extent to which they enable developing nations to leapfrog steps in the conventional path to developed country status.

To a fair extent, such differences of academic attainment are matched by broader national development indicators, as seen in Table I.

Country	HDI 1990	HDI 2002	HDI rank 2002	Life expectancy at birth 2002
Indonesia	0.623	0.692	111	78.0
Malaysia	0.720	0.793	59	73.0
Philippines	0.719	0.753	83	69.8
Thailand	0.707	0.768	76	69.1
Vietnam	0.610	0.691	112	69.0

Country	Education index 2002	GDP per capita (PPP$) 2002	Public expenditure on ed. (% of GDP) 1990	Public expenditure on ed. (% of GDP) 2002
Indonesia	0.80	3230	1.0	1.3
Malaysia	0.83	9120	5.2	7.9
Philippines	0.89	4170	2.9	3.2
Thailand	0.86	7010	3.5	5.0
Vietnam	0.82	2300	-	-

Note: PPP: purchasing power parity.

Table I. Human Development Indicator (HDIs), South-East Asia Five, 1990-2002. Source: UNDP (2005, p. 20).

Table I reveals that, while all five countries are ranked from mid to low on Human Development Index indicators, there are marked differences. The two poorest, Indonesia and Vietnam, stand well below the other three. A caveat is warranted with respect to the Malaysian case, however. The high rate of public expenditure on education as a proportion of GDP is in practice reserved to a significant degree for ethnic Malays (*Bumiputras*, often translated as 'sons of the soil'), who effectively gain preference in most areas of Malaysian society. This means that ethnic Chinese citizens, and the ethnic Indian minority in Malaysia, have often had to resort to private sector higher educational institutions (HEIs) domestically, or been forced to study overseas. While ethnic quotas in higher education were formally abandoned in 2003, they are often still claimed to persist in practice, including in areas such as scholarships and promotions. To a fair extent, the same explanation lies behind the Malaysian data in Table II, which expresses the current levels of public expenditure on tertiary education of the South-East Asia Five.

Table II reveals that most countries rank rather lowly relative to developed country averages, the significant exception being Malaysia, whose devotion of 35% of its public education budget on the tertiary sector compares favourably with developed country data. Here again, however, in practice, spending is largely restricted to ethnic Malays, giving a somewhat distorted impression of overall effort. Levels of poverty that range from 9% in Vietnam to a high 16.6% in Indonesia, and substantial Gini coefficients that range from 34.3 in Indonesia to 46.1 in Philippines, also impact on higher education participation, especially among the poor, and rural dwellers (United Nations Development Programme [UNDP], 2007; A.R. Welch, 2009). As detailed below, privatisation, including privatisation of public sector HEIs, is also having an impact on participation rates and equity, in a region often characterised by a weak record of service delivery to the poor, and with the exception of Singapore, and to a lesser extent Malaysia, significant problems with corruption (Transparency International, 2006; A. Welch, 2007b, 2010b; Amirrachman et al, 2008). The recent spiralling prices of staples such as rice and fuel, together with the GFC, have both reduced the discretionary income of poor families, thereby putting higher education further out of reach, and also significantly reduced amounts available from state budgets for education. Lastly, the demographic challenge is also huge, with rising aspirations for higher education fuelled by a very young population profile – the proportion of the total population aged under 15 ranges from 26.7% in Thailand to 37.5% in the Philippines (UNDP, 2002).

Country	Percentage of public education budget expended on tertiary sector
Indonesia	19
Malaysia	35
Philippines	14
Thailand	20
Vietnam	-

Table II. Current public expenditure on tertiary education, by country.
Source: UNDP (2007, pp. 266-267).

Privatisation: extent, forms and implications

Added to the above, substantial changes have occurred over the past decade or more to the relative size of public and private sectors in higher education in several of the systems treated above. To this, must be added a further and related trend towards privatisation of public sector HEIs. To some extent the expansion of the private sector in several of the higher education systems of South-East Asia arose from the mismatch between spiralling demand, intensified by the young demographic profile indicated above, and on the other hand, the inability, and perhaps a degree of unwillingness, on the part of the state, to expand the public sector to cater to this endlessly increasing demand. The GFC of 2008-09 only added further pressure to already tight budgets for higher education in the region. Tables III and IV show how much the balance between the public and private sectors has changed since the mid-late 1990s, across the region.

Country	Public	Private
Indonesia	44	59
Malaysia	100	0
Philippines	25	75
Thailand	60	40
Vietnam	100	0

Table III. Proportion of students in public and private institutions of higher education, South-East Asia Five countries, 1997-98. Source: Gonzales (1999).

What is clear from the above is the extent of variation, with at least two systems revealing no private higher education at all. In both Vietnam and Malaysia, until recently, private universities were not legal, although in the latter case colleges did cater to non-ethnic Malays. The most notable exception was the Philippines, which has long had a large, if poorly regulated, private higher education sector, although both Indonesia and Thailand also had significant private components.

Table IV, while focused more on institutions than student enrolments, illustrates the extent of change over the decade from the mid-1990s.

Country	Public			Private			Total
	Degree	Non-degree	Subtotal	Degree	Non-degree	Subtotal	
Indonesia	-	-	81	-	-	2431	2512
Malaysia	18	40	58	22	519	541	599
Philippines	424	1352	1776	1363	2045	3408	5184
Thailand	66	-	66	54	401	455	521
Vietnam	201	-	201	29	-	29	230

Table IV. Numbers and types of HEIs, South-East Asia, 2007.
Source: Asian Development Bank (2008).

Striking changes are evident in Malaysia where, by 2007, 22 private universities were listed, as well as 519 non-degree-granting colleges. In Vietnam, too, its strikingly ambitious plans to expand higher education now include targets that envisage an astonishing 40% of all enrolments being private ('non-public') by 2020 (Thiep & Hayden, 2006; A. Welch, 2010a). Already, private sector enrolments are calculated to be approximately 12% of total student numbers.

But much more is involved than simply a swiftly changing balance between public and private sectors. Public sector HEIs in the region are also effectively being privatised, an artefact of pressure to expand enrolments, at a time when funding from the state has plateaued, or in several cases, reduced, at least in per student terms. The pressure to diversify income sources and shore up institutional budgets has pushed public HEIs to adopt strategies that increasingly blur the boundaries between public and private.

Such strategies have largely been two-fold. The first has been to increase fees for high-demand courses, such as for example engineering or IT. A move adopted by a number of nationally recognised public HEIs in Malaysia, Indonesia and Thailand, this has led to fees at some of these institutions outstripping those in equivalent private HEIs (A. Welch, 2007a). The implications for equity are significant – poorer students who were always excluded from high-quality private sector HEIs by virtue of the high fees that they charged, are in many cases now also excluded from major public sector HEIs, on the same grounds. Effectively, their only recourse, often, is to seek entry to low-quality, low-fee private HEIs.

A second strategy used by public sector HEIs in several regional systems has been to develop parallel courses that operate in the evenings or weekends, for substantial fees. Such courses, variously termed 'extension' or 'executive' programmes, are taught by the same academics who offer similar courses within the public sector HEI, thereby adding substantially to their workload, and sometimes substantially adding to their incomes. Such parallel courses are generally considered to be of significantly lower quality than their original, are often effectively open entry, and in many cases do not confer eligibility for public sector employment – nonetheless they bring in significant additional income to hard-pressed public sector HEIs, who can ill afford to pass up such opportunities. An unfortunate by-product of this trend, however, is that the academics involved are even less available to regular students in their original institution, and have even less time to devote to research. The overall result may well be not merely to offer weak alternative programmes, but also to weaken academic standards and achievements within the originating public sector HEIs that offer such programmes. Moonlighting by public sector academics, another common feature of regional higher education, also detracts from overall teaching and research quality at affected HEIs, while the poaching of such public sector staff to teach at private sector institutions does little to strengthen the system overall.

South-East Asian Higher Education and the Global Knowledge System

The constraints indicated above must however be set against the universal regional ambition to extend both quantity and quality of higher education systems. Given this context, and the significant challenges posed that range from demographic to financial, how far are lofty regional aspirations matched by achievements on the knowledge and innovation front? How does the region measure up, in an increasingly competitive context, where institutions and nations compete for the best staff and students, and for leading research rankings, on a global level?

The data below provide something of a test for the operation of what has been termed an international knowledge system, a concept first proposed by Altbach some 15 years ago (Altbach, 1998, 2002). Deploying notions originally derived from World Systems Theory that are predicated on analysing fundamental inequalities in a capitalist world system, Altbach assigned national higher education systems to categories of core, semi-periphery, or periphery. The core was reserved largely for North American systems, and the major research institutions within those systems (together with, perhaps, equivalent major research institutions in the United Kingdom [UK], Europe, Japan and Australia), while South-East Asia was unambiguously assigned to the periphery. A review conducted by the World Bank a decade ago, in which Altbach played a role, gave some support to this position. It pointed to, for example, the global North having something like 10 times the proportion of research and development (R&D) personnel (scientists and technicians) per capita as compared with the global South (3.8% compared with 0.4%), and that the North spent about four times the proportion of GDP on R&D – 2.0% compared with 0.5% (World Bank, 2000). The same survey revealed that the North registered some 97% of all patents registered in the USA and Europe, and, together with the newly industrialising countries of East Asia, accounted for 84% of all scientific articles published (World Bank, 2000, p. 69).

Since then, however, some elements of the worldwide higher education network have changed, notably the development of a more globalised knowledge system overall, and the emergence of a much denser and more ubiquitous network of information and communications technology (ICT), that is increasingly used to foster research, including in settings that would traditionally have been characterised as peripheral (A. Welch & Zhang, 2005; A.R. Welch & Zhang, 2008). The combined effect of these developments has seen the global knowledge system assume a more multi-polar quality.

But if, as was indicated above, no university in the five South-East Asian countries listed above is currently ranked within the leading 500 research universities of the world, does this mean that no progress has been made in their knowledge and innovation systems? A more recent World Bank survey charted indices of innovation among South-East Asian systems, and compared these with developed country averages (Table V). Clearly, differences were still substantial: developed countries had more than 17 times the number of researchers per million of population than the average found across South-East Asia. In none of the South-East Asia Five was the difference less than twelve-fold. On other indices, however, significant changes were evident – the data on quality of research institutions, and university–industry collaboration, rated Malaysia little below the developed world average on the former, and somewhat higher on the latter.

	Average years of schooling	Researchers per million	Quality of scientific research institutions	University–industry research collaboration
SE Asia	6.6	210	4.1	3.6
Indonesia	4.7	207	3.9	3.4
Malaysia	7.9	299	5.0	4.7
Philippines	7.6	48	3.3	2.7
Thailand	6.1	287	4.0	3.6
Developed country average	9.5	3616	5.1	4.4

Table V. National innovation indices, by country, region and level of development. Source: World Bank (2006).

On other indices, intra-regional differences were clearly evident, albeit much less strong than those between regions. Data from Table VI show strong and persisting differences between Malaysia and other South-East Asian systems, particularly on measures of R&D as a percent of GDP. On that same measure, however, even Malaysia devoted less than one third of the developed country average to R&D.

Countries	R & D spending 2002		R & D as percentage of GDP*	
	US$ billions (PPP)	Percentage of world	1992	2002
SE Asia	3.3	0.4	0.1	0.2
Indonesia	0.3	0.0	0.1	0.1
Malaysia	1.5	0.2	0.4	0.7
Philippines	0.4	0.0	0.2	0.1
Thailand	1.1	0.1	0.2	0.2
Developed world average	645.8	77.8	2.3	2.3

Note: *Regional data are sum of R&D divided by sum of PPP GDP.

Table VI. R&D expenditure levels, and as percentage of GDP, 2002. Source: World Bank (2006).

Data on patents (Table VII) awarded reveal similar disparities, both within and between regions, but a stronger pattern of overall growth within South-East Asia, compared with the developed world average.

	Number of patents		Patents per 100,000 people		
	1990-94	2000-04	1990-94	2000-04	Per cent change
SE Asia	31	140	0.01	0.04	15.3
Indonesia	6	15	0.00	0.01	8.8
Malaysia	13	64	0.07	0.28	15.3
Philippines	6	18	0.01	0.02	10.4
Thailand	6	43	0.01	0.07	20.9
Developed world average	104,170	168,017	12.88	19.58	4.3

Table VII. Patents granted, US Patents Office, by region, country and level of development (World Bank, 2006).

A further commonly used measure of knowledge productivity is that of papers and citations. Here, however, it is important to acknowledge a strong linguistic bias. Conventional measures, based on indices such as Science Citation Index, Social Science Citation Index and Engineering Index, are biased towards English language journals. Acknowledging this additional burden for the South-East Asia Five, relative to English language systems, the measures of knowledge production in Tables VIII and IX are nonetheless illustrative both of significant differences among the South-East Asia Five and of differential patterns of growth over the past decade or two.

Country	Number of papers 1981	Number of papers 1995	Number of citations 1981–85	Number of citations 1993-97
Indonesia	89	310	694	3364
Malaysia	229	587	1332	3450
Philippines	243	294	1379	2893
Thailand	373	648	2419	8398
Vietnam	49	192	203	1657

Table VIII. Papers and citations, by country, 1980s and 1990s.
Source: World Bank (2000).

Brief comparison with developed country data, taken from the same database, are also pertinent: Australian publications for 1995 totalled 18,088, and for Japan 58,910. Citation counts for each country 1993-97 were 301, 320 and 930, 981 respectively.

Measures of papers and citations for the last decade show significant growth, and further underline substantial differences among the South-East Asia Five.

Country	Number of papers 1998-2008	Number of citations 1998-2008	Citations per paper 1998-2008
Indonesia	5410	36,804	6.80
Malaysia	14,782	60,856	4.12
Philippines	4997	37,246	7.45
Thailand	23,272	141,913	6.07
Vietnam	5207	31,959	6.14

Table IX. Papers and citations, by country, 1998-2008.
Source: Thompson Science Watch (2009).

While it might be expected that the two wealthiest systems, Thailand and Malaysia, were responsible for over 70% of the total papers produced, and almost two thirds of total citations, other results were more surprising. Malaysia's rate of citations per paper is surprisingly weak, for example, relative to the other four systems. Taken together, the two preceding tables show that each of the South-East Asia Five countries expanded their innovation indices significantly. Of the five, however, Vietnam's progress seems most striking, off an admittedly low base, while Thailand's development is also impressive.

Once again, it is important to put such progress in perspective. Over the same period, Japan produced 806,008 papers and 7,397,444 citations (a citation count of 9.18), and Australia 271,311 papers and 2,870,552 citations (a citation count of 10.58). While the gap remains substantial, the trend shows a significant narrowing of the performance differential between the South-East Asia Five, and the equivalent totals for both Australia and Japan, over the last decade or more, in terms of total papers produced. While still significant, the gap has narrowed by something like one third, in each case.

A final measure of knowledge production allows an assessment of the respective contribution of the higher education sector to total R&D performance (Table X).

	Business	Government	Higher education
SE Asia	51.3	22.1	15.7
Indonesia	14.3	81.1	4.6
Malaysia	65.3	20.3	14.4
Philippines	58.6	21.7	17.0
Thailand	43.9	22.5	31.0
Developed average	62.9	13.3	27.0

Table X. R&D performance by sector, SE Asia and developed country average. Source: World Bank (2006).

With the striking exception of Thailand, Table X reveals that the proportion that the higher education sector contributes towards total R&D performance in South-East Asia is little more than half the average of developed nations, and for Indonesia is, at 4.6%, a mere one sixth.

Globalisation, Internationalisation and Regionalisation

A further dynamic element of South-East Asian higher education is its progressive internationalisation, which now includes a growing regional component. While each of South-East Asia's systems sees their universities as contributing to national culture and its preservation and enlargement, at the same time they are no longer immune to forces of globalisation, including the increasing ubiquity of ICTs and new media, and the growing strength of English, as a medium of higher education internationalisation (Crystal, 1997; Wilson et al, 1998). The rise of China is also having an impact on its South-East Asian neighbours, including in higher education (A. Welch, 2011). Brain drain continues to be an issue of concern, despite growing recognition that brain circulation may be a more complete explanation, and that highly skilled diaspora can contribute from abroad (A. Welch, 2010a). Branch campuses have been established within the region, with overseas institutions being sometimes deliberately sought out. At the same time, at least one or two systems are vigorously expanding into Eduhubs, enrolling significant numbers of international students, from both within and without the region.

The dominance of English plays a significant role in several of these trends. It is notable, for example, that the two regional systems most active and successful in boosting their credentials as Eduhubs (Singapore and Malaysia) both trade on the fact that teaching programmes are offered in English, while the branch campuses that have been established in the region, in places such as Vietnam, Singapore and Malaysia, have largely been established by US, UK or Australian universities, or where not, such as the French business school INSEAD's presence in Singapore, at least offer programmes in English.

As indicated, however, the dramatic and ongoing rise of China means that more programmes and international partnerships are between that country and its South-East Asian neighbours, at times utilising the Chinese language as a medium. With the Chinese diaspora in South-East Asia being estimated at around 20 million, and the rise of Confucius Institutes throughout the region, this is no surprise. In addition, Malaysia's majority-Muslim status allows it to recruit among fellow Muslim countries, an opportunity it is exploiting vigorously. On a recent a visit to the Middle East, for example, the Minister of Education confirmed the connection between seeking out talented Muslim students, selected by their governments, and Malaysia's international reputation:

> Governments will only sponsor the best students and we need
> good students to help improve the rankings of our universities.

Whatever we do, we can't run away from achieving excellence.
(Bernama, 2009)

Malaysia is exploiting both these connections. The fact that approximately one quarter of Malaysians are of Chinese ethnicity has helped underpin significant growth in China–Malaysia partnerships in higher education, to the point that approximately one third of Malaysia's impressive total of some 60,000 international enrolments in its HEIs – largely in its private sector – now originate from China. Its majority-Muslim status, together with linguistic affinity, lie behind the fact that Indonesia is its largest source of international enrolments, while Bangladesh is its third largest source country.

The past decade or so has also seen several branch campuses established in Malaysia, a result of a significant, and deliberate, opening of the Malaysian system. Several UK and Australian universities moved to found branch campuses in Malaysia, the most notable of which include Monash, and Curtin University of Technology from Australia, and Nottingham from the UK. Indian institutions, like the Manipal Medical University, 'have also set up private colleges in Malaysia, through joint ventures with local partners' (Lee, 2003, p. 18). These branch campuses served two purposes for Malaysia. The first was represented by their capacity to respond to growing demand for skilled personnel, most particularly in areas such as engineering, technology, and the emerging sciences such as IT. Secondly, 'the presence of off-shore campuses will provide the impetus to both public and private local higher education institutions to improve their quality and standard of education' (Zakaria, 2000, p. 129).

The Australian Monash University (Malaysia), in Bandar Sunway, was the first such example. Opening in early 1998, it represented a partnership with the local Sunway Group Malaysia (Banks & McBurnie, 1999). Although the campus offers undergraduate programmes in engineering, arts, science, IT, nursing, and business, comparatively few are enrolled in arts subjects. An incorporated company, Monash University Sunway Campus Malaysia Sdn Bhd (MUSCM), was established to operate the University, with Monash University and Sunway as shareholders. The agreement was for a term of 12 years, including a review by both parties after eight years, to assess whether or not to continue the operations after the 12th year. The operating agreement specified that Sunway would provide infrastructure facilities under a lease arrangement, while Monash University was responsible for providing the academic staff. An early issue arose from the fact that local academic staff pay and conditions differed significantly from Monash's Australian staff who were teaching in Malaysia from time to time (Coleman, 2001). All students undertaking courses at the Malaysian campus are enrolled as Monash students and awarded a Monash degree or diploma.

The campus has continued to develop. 2005 saw the first 50 enrolments in medicine, with students taking the first two years at Monash in Melbourne, and the remainder of the programme in Malaysia. By 2007, all training for the five-year Bachelor of Medicine, Bachelor of Surgery (MBBS) was to revert to Malaysia. Containing the same structure as the course taught in Australia, with the same admission requirements and the same assessment content and standards, upon completion, students are awarded the same degree as graduates from Monash Australia. A feature of the plan was to make resources available for medical research relevant to Malaysia. Research in the medical school deployed existing strengths in the School of Arts and Sciences, in biotechnology and medical bioscience, while also leveraging Monash University in Australia's strengths in related fields such as stem cell technology, in-vitro fertilisation, assisted breeding and cloning.

The capacity of Monash to leverage its presence in Malaysia to attract investment by local firms was a further successful component of the local campus. For example, National Instruments ASEAN planned to team up with Monash University Malaysia to set up a pilot remote-access electrical engineering laboratory that will enable students to conduct experiments over the Internet. As well, some scholarships were made available for students with a record of excellence. The prospect of Monash students at one campus taking a semester or two at a campus in another country was seen as an additional advantage, while the prospects of studying in another language (Behasa Melayu) were also seen as attractive.

Singapore's small size, with a total population of only 4.6 million, and total higher education enrolments of 105,424, comprising 43,663 from universities, 58,880 from polytechnics and 2881 from teacher education in 2005, have in no way blunted its ambition to develop into an educational hub (Tan, 2008). Its Global Schoolhouse, which set out to make Singapore the 'Boston of the East', has had signal successes and some failures. It has had substantial success in attracting students from the region, with estimates that in 2004, trans-national enrolments totalled over 80,000 students, or 36% of all enrolments (Gribble & McBurnie, 2007). In 2008, all three of its universities, Nanyang Technology University, National University of Singapore and Singapore University of Management, reported that 20% of their enrolments were international.

Efforts to attract major international universities to establish branch campuses have met with considerable success, with France's INSEAD, the University of Chicago, the Georgia Institute of Technology, New York University, the University of Nevada at Las Vegas, the Technische Universiteit Eindhoven, and the Shanghai Jiaotong University all having a presence in Singapore. At the same time, however, not all such attempts have been a success – a bio-medical research facility of the US-based Johns Hopkins University, established in 1998, closed in 2006, while the first fully owned and operated foreign campus, opened by the University of New South Wales (Australia) with great fanfare, closed only months later, due to weak enrolments. The UK's Warwick University abandoned plans to establish a campus, 'amid staff concerns about possible limitations on academic freedom in Singapore' (Tan, 2008, p. 12). While government regulations preclude a breakdown of international enrolments by country, Singapore's established presence in service sector trade within the region, plus the fact that almost three quarters of Singapore's population are of Chinese descent, significant numbers of whom speak Hokkien, Teochew, or Cantonese, provide firm planks for plans to forge closer and denser relations with China, including attracting its students to Singapore's universities. While Singapore attracts significant numbers of students from India, Vietnam, Indonesia and Malaysia (Organisation for Economic Co-operation and Development, 2003), China is certainly a major current priority for its universities: 'A main recruitment target ... of these students is the PRC. Singapore government scholarships [are] being awarded at the undergraduate level to students from this country' (Tan, 2008, p. 15). Singapore and China concluded a specific Memorandum of Understanding on 29 May 2002, signed by the respective ministries of education, that has aided bi-lateral partnerships.

At the institutional level, initiatives by the National University of Singapore include two China colleges (one in Beijing, another in Shanghai), and an International MBA programme in partnership with Peking University. Nanyang Technology University's Nanyang Business School has established a partnership with Shanghai Jiaotong University (one of China's leading universities), who together offer an Executive MBA programme. Singapore Institute of Management (SUM) offers, *inter alia*, a one or two semester exchange programme with three Chinese universities: Nankai University, (Zhongshan) Sun Yat Sen University, and Xiamen University.

Conclusion

A heady mix of ambition and constraint, higher education in South-East Asia displays considerable dynamism. At the same time, the very different levels of development that characterise the member states of ASEAN mean that individual states face very different circumstances and scenarios, in the development of their higher education systems. Singapore's wealth, highly developed infrastructure and multi-ethnic workforce (many highly skilled) mean it is able to attract specialist research teams to work in its well-supported universities, something unable to be matched by, for example, Lao PDR, Cambodia, Indonesia, or Vietnam. Malaysia and Thailand represent perhaps points somewhere between these two poles.

Globalisation has had considerable effects on regional higher education. The rise of English is perhaps the first of these. As a medium of instruction, and as a measure of research output, it both poses a challenge to the strength and vitality of local cultures and languages, while also providing an opportunity for the most developed systems to deploy it as a vehicle for educational hubs that can attract students from within and without the region.

A second globalisation effect is more economic than cultural. The desire by all regional systems to expand access to higher education, in the face of rising aspirations and a young demographic profile, has not been matched by an equivalent rise in funds by the state. This has seen the rise of privatisation, and greater competition, both within and between systems. One result has been the spread of private HEIs as a notable feature of several higher education systems, as well as significant privatisation of public sector HEIs. The combined effect is troubling, in terms of access for the poor, with fees for high-demand courses in public HEIs now sometimes outstripping those at equivalent private institutions.

The differentiated nature of regional higher education also lies behind the complex pattern of internationalisation, clearly one of the most dynamic elements within the different systems. While Singapore, and to a lesser extent Malaysia, have each developed ambitious schemes for Eduhubs that are proving attractive within the region, and to an extent beyond, Indonesia, Vietnam and the Philippines are far more dependent upon attracting foreign branch campuses, where possible. Of the three, Vietnam has been the most successful in doing so. Such branch campuses, if established on a basis of mutual advantage, can assist in raising the quality of local provision, supplying much-needed highly skilled personnel, and addressing local issues in areas such as health, agriculture and transport. Relative to the costs of acquiring a degree overseas, the somewhat lower fees for programmes at such campuses are attractive, as also the lower levels of disruption to family life and work patterns. Regionalism, notably with China, but also with Australia, also offers significant potential for development.

The future of regional higher education will continue to be differentiated, with many systems still likely to remain peripheral within the global higher knowledge network, at least for the foreseeable future. Nonetheless, the increasingly multi-polar quality of global knowledge centres offers opportunities for regional higher education that its substantial aspirations and achievements will work hard to further develop.

References

Altbach, P.G. (1998) Gigantic Peripheries: India and China in the world knowledge system, in P.G. Altbach (Ed.) *Comparative Higher Education. Knowledge, the University and Development*, pp. 133-146. Greenwich CT: Ablex.

Altbach, P.G. (2002) Centres and Peripheries in the Academic Profession: the special challenges of developing countries, in P.G. Altbach (Ed.) *The Decline of the Guru: the academic profession in middle and lower income countries*. New York: Palgrave Publishers.

Amirrachman, A., Syafi'i, S. & Welch, A. (2008) Decentralising Indonesian Education: the promise and the price, in J. Zajda (Ed.) *Centralisation and Decentralisation in Education*. Amsterdam: Springer.

Asian Development Bank (2008) *Education and Skills: strategies for accelerated development in Asia and the Pacific*. Manila: ADB.

Association of Southeast Asian Nations (2009) Basic ASEAN Indicators. http://www.aseansec.org/19226.htm (accessed 20 January 2009).

Banks, M. & McBurnie, G. (1999) Embarking on an Educational Journey – the establishment of the first foreign full university campus in Malaysia under the 1996 Education Acts: a Malaysian-Australian case study, *Higher Education in Europe*, XXIV(2), 265-272.

Bernama (2009) Malaysia to Boost Muslim Progress through Education. http://www.msdwdc.org/v2/index.php?option=com_content&view=article&id=97 :-malaysia-to-boost-muslim-progress-through-education&catid=47:education&Itemid=50 (accessed 18 January 2009).

Coleman, D. (2001) The Core and the Periphery: organisational, educational and transformative trends in the internationalisation of higher education. University of New South Wales.

Crystal, D. (1997) *English as a Global Language*. Cambridge: Cambridge University Press.

Gonzales, A. (1999) Private Higher Education in the Philippines: private domination in a developing country, in P.G. Altbach (Ed.) *Private Prometheus: private higher education and development in the 21st century*, pp. 101-112. London: Greenwood Press.

Gribble, C. & McBurnie, G. (2007) Problems within Singapore's Global Schoolhouse, *International Higher Education*, 48, 3-4.

Lee, M. (2003) International Linkages in Malaysian Private Higher Education, *International Higher Education*, 30, 17-19.

Organisation for Economic Co-operation and Development (2003) *Education Policy Analysis 2003*. Paris: OECD.

Pusey, M. (1991) *Economic Rationalism in Canberra: a nation-building state changes its mind*. Cambridge: Cambridge University Press.

Shanghai Jiaotong (2008) Academic Ranking of World Universities. http://www.arwu.org:80/ARWU2008.

Tan, J. (2008) Facing Global and Local Challenges: the new dynamics for higher education. Asia-Pacific Sub-Regional Preparatory Conference for the 2009 UNESCO World Conference on Higher Education, Macao, China.

Thiep, L.Q. & Hayden, M. (2006) A 2020 Vision for Higher Education in Viet Nam, *International Higher Education*, 44, Summer, 11-12.

Thompson Science Watch (2009) Science Watch, Country Profiles. http://sciencewatch.com/dr/cou/.

Transparency International (2006) 2006 Corruption Perceptions Index. http://www.transparency.org/policy_research/surveys_indices/cpi/2006.

UNDP (United Nations Development Programme) (2002) *Human Development Report 2002: deepening democracy in a fragmented world*. New York: UNDP.

UNDP (2005) *Human Development Report for South-East Asia*. New York: UNDP.

UNDP (2007) *Human Development Indicators 2007/2008*. New York: UNDP.

Welch, A. (2007a) Blurred Vision? Public and Private Higher Education in Indonesia, *Higher Education*, 54, 665-687.

Welch, A. (2007b) Ho Chi Minh Meets the Market: public and private higher education in Viet Nam, *International Education Journal*, 8(3), 35-56.

Welch, A. (2010a) Internationalisation of Vietnamese Higher Education: retrospect and prospect, in G.H. Harman, M. Hayden & V. Pham (Eds) *Reforming Higher Education in Vietnam. Challenges and Priorities*, pp. 197-214. Amsterdam: Springer.

Welch, A. (2010b) Measuring Up? The Competitive Position of South-East Asian Higher Education, in S.S. Kaur, M. Sirat & W. Tierney (Eds) *Quality Assurance and University Rankings in Higher Education in the Asia Pacific*. Penang: University Sains Malaysia Press.

Welch, A. (2011) The Dragon, the Tiger Cubs and Higher Education. Competitive and Cooperative China-ASEAN Relations in the GATS Era, in D. Jarvis & A. Welch (Eds) *ASEAN Industries and the Challenge from China*. London: Palgrave Macmillan.

Welch, A. & Zhang, Z. (2005) Zhongguo de zhishi liusan – haiwai zhongguo zhishi fenzijian de jiaoliu wangluo [Communication networks of the Chinese intellectual diaspora], *Comparative Education Review [Beijing]*, 26(12), 31-37.

Welch, A.R. (2009) Financing Access and Equity in SE Asian Higher Education: state capacity, privatisation, and transparency, in J. Knight (Ed.) *Financing Higher Education: access and equity*. Rotterdam: Sense Publishers.

Welch, A.R. & Zhang, Z. (2008) Communication Networks among the Chinese Knowledge Diaspora: a new invisible college? In R. Boden, R. Deem, D. Epstein & F. Rizvi (Eds) *Geographies of Knowledge, Geometries of Power: higher education in the 21st century. World Yearbook of Education 2008*. London: Routledge.

Wilson, M.A., Qayyam, A. & Boshier, R. (1998) World Wide America: manufacturing web information, *Distance Education*, 19(1), 109-141.

World Bank (2000) *Higher Education in Developing Countries: peril and promise*. Washington, DC: World Bank.

World Bank (2006) *An East Asian Renaissance. Ideas for Economic Growth*. Washington, DC: World Bank.

Zakaria, H.A.b. (2000) Educational Development and Reformation in the Malaysian Education System: challenges in the new millennium, *Journal of Southeast Asian Education*, 1(1), 113-133.

CHAPTER 15

Education and Language Policies in South-East Asian Countries

KEITH WATSON

SUMMARY After discussing the importance of language for the individual, community and society the chapter then looks at how societies, especially those in South-East Asia, have become multi-ethnic and linguistically plural over a long period of time. It also plays down the relatively brief impact of colonialism on different countries of the region. Having explained the ethnic and linguistic complexity of the region, country by country, the chapter then explores the language and ethnic policies available to governments before looking at how the different countries in the region have used both these and educational policies to further their aims. It argues that while several countries have begun to recognise the linguistic rights of their ethnic minorities, the realities of creating a national identity, economic necessity and political power will always mean that the dominant group, and those groups who have access to either a national or international language, will continue to maintain their privileges at the expense of the smaller ethnic groups. In the long term this could have catastrophic results for those minorities.

The Importance of Language

The importance of language in societies cannot be underestimated yet, surprisingly, this issue had largely been ignored by most of the international aid agencies, excepting UNESCO, until relatively recently (Watson, 1994). The Delors Report (1996) was one of the first major reports on education that clearly acknowledged the crucial importance of language, not only in everyday life, but also in the classroom and it recommended that governments should give more attention to the language issues in their countries, not least because so many are now becoming multilingual as a result of immigration. This, in turn, is largely because of globalisation and the desire for a better quality of life in a country other than the one in which people were born.

As Philip Coombs wrote in his analysis of *The World Crisis in Education: a view from the Eighties*, nearly a quarter of a century ago:

> The issue of what language or languages to adopt as the medium of instruction at successive levels of education is one of the most pedagogically difficult and potentially explosive issues faced by schools in a great many countries ... Paradoxically, however, the choice of language of instruction is also one of the least appreciated of all the major educational problems that come before international forums. (Coombs, 1985, p. 256)

The issue of which language to choose has become even more pressing in countries that are already multiethnic and multilingual, such as exist in South-East Asia, and as a recent book on Africa clearly demonstrates (Brock-Utne & Skattum, 2009), because of the global pressures to adopt English as one of the languages used in many countries, since this is now recognised as the *lingua franca* of global communication as well as trade, and invariably of UN and other aid agencies (Crystal, 1997, 2003; Phillipson & Skutnabb-Kangas, 1999), it inevitably means that there will be winners and losers (Watson, 1993, 1994, 2007). This is certainly true in Asia (Tsui & Tollefson, 2007).

Writing about education in South-East Asia nearly 40 years ago, Wong (1973, p. 114) observed that:

> Language is an essential means of communication and when the language is also the mother tongue, it is one of the most important formation influences in moulding the intellect as well as the character of the child. Indeed it is a powerful instrument by which not only individuals may express their personality, but groups may also identify their collective consciousness.

At the individual level it is language that not only distinguishes humans from other species but it is a key part of what makes a person a person. Language helps us express our deepest emotions and feelings, personal thoughts and relationships with others. At the group, or community, level a specific language can provide not only a sense of identity and belonging, but it can also offer a sense of cohesion and mutual support. Amongst many ethnic groups it is both language and a common culture that bind them together, while at the same time separating them from other linguistic groups. In a region as diffuse as South-East Asia, with many small ethnic and tribal groups, this is particularly important in helping groups to maintain their identity. This is why so many ethnic groups cling to their language, as for example in Myanmar, Indonesia, Thailand and Vietnam, for fear that their culture and history might be submerged into an amorphous national one. This is especially important as these groups are also threatened by the forces of economic modernisation (e.g. roads and airports as well as schools) and by global demands for particular products (e.g. timber or palm oils) that mean their traditional habitats are being constantly eroded.

Thirty years ago Sutherland (1979) argued that language maintenance was vitally important for ethnic and linguistic minorities in multiethnic and multilingual societies if there was to be any semblance of social cohesion and harmony. More recently, as societies have become more linguistically and ethnically diverse as a result of globalisation (Castles & Miller, 1993) the issue of language rights has become more prominent (Watson, 2007). This is partly because the issue of human rights has taken centre stage in many countries and regions (Skutnabb-Kangas, 2001); partly because of fears that whole language groups are in danger of dying out (*Time Magazine*, 1997); partly because the UN and its agencies have begun to acknowledge that many smaller linguistic and ethnic groups are endangered by the remorseless global pressures for uniformity, especially in terms of educational outcomes. As a result, during the last decade or so, there have been numerous conventions that have sought to raise the profile of linguistic rights, for example the World Convention on Human Rights (1993), the International Year for the World's Indigenous Peoples (1993), the 1996 International Declaration of Language Rights, the European Convention on Human Rights and so on. As mentioned earlier, even the Delors Report (1996) recognised the need to preserve languages.

These views are all very well but over-riding political considerations have often made governments pursue a language policy of self-interest that will help them position their country favourably within the global economy. The result is a further marginalisation of ethnic and linguistic minorities. Most governments in South-East Asia, for example, have pursued language policies that will enhance their global economic competitiveness, with the result that English is playing an increasingly important role, whether or not it is widely spoken by the majority of the population (see, for example, Hsieh, 2009). Since the late 1990s Cambodia and Vietnam, for example, have been gradually replacing French with English as one of their key languages because the Association of Southeast Asian Nations (ASEAN) has been using English to conduct its affairs and to publish its reports. English has been widely used in Brunei, Malaysia, Singapore, the Philippines and Thailand for many years. It is gaining in importance in Cambodia, Laos and Vietnam as well because it is the most widely accepted language used in global markets and trading as well as by the UN agencies working in those countries (Tsui & Tollefson, 2007). The point is that which language policy to pursue is tied up with political power and economic interests. As Tsui (2007, p. 122) has observed:

> Language often plays a central role in the construction of national identity. It also may be the primary foundation upon which national ideology is constructed (Joseph, 2004) ... The establishment of national and official languages is an indispensable part of nation building.

Inevitably in multilingual societies such as those of South-East Asia, where language divisions coincide with ethnic cleavages, the dominant ethnic group will ensure that the language chosen as the national one will enhance their own political dominance. Thus, as will be shown, the Malays in Malaysia pursued a policy of making Bahasa Malaysia the national language as a means of dominating the Chinese and Indians in the country by placing additional language and educational hurdles in the way of non-indigenous people. Whereas the Chinese had been, and still are, economically powerful their chances of seizing political power were, and are, limited. The same goes for the education and language policies of Brunei, Thailand, the Philippines, Indonesia and Vietnam.

The difficulty facing governments in multiethnic and multilingual societies is how to achieve national cohesiveness, or a sense of national identity as opposed to group or community identity, without, at the same time, destroying the different existing cultural and ethnic identities that make up the whole. To put it another way:

> The challenge facing all school systems is how schools can help
> minorities to gain access to a social and economic system that is
> dominated by the values of the majority, while, at the same time,
> retaining their separate ethnic group cultures and identities.
> (Clothey, 2005, p. 389)

Thus there would appear to be two conflicting and contradictory trends in the contemporary world, not least in South-East Asia. At one level there is the desire to preserve traditional minority cultures in the face of ever-growing supranational pressures that are leading to their marginalisation. Proponents of this view argue on grounds of post-modernism and human rights. At another level are pressures to move towards a more uniform world culture with a common world language and universal urban, multinational lifestyles. Proponents of this view argue that the forces of globalisation will inevitably bring this about. In the middle of these trends and pressures are ordinary people. This chapter is about how both education and language policies impact on their lives in one region of the world, South-East Asia.

Ethnic and Linguistic Diversity and the Nation-State

While scholars such as Churchill (1996) argue that the problems associated with linguistic and ethnic diversity can be blamed on the creation of nation-states in Europe, and the transfer of this concept/model throughout the world as a result of colonialism, this is only part of the story. Countries have become multiethnic and multilingual for many reasons. This is especially true in the countries of South-East Asia.

The first, and oldest, reason is *trade*. For centuries traders have penetrated the countries of South-East Asia, initially coming from Persia and the Arab countries of the Middle East, then from India and Ceylon (Sri

Lanka) and from China. Lastly came traders from Europe. Most did not settle, or if they did it was only for a few years at a time. They did, however, bring with them religious ideas, that would later be translated into different forms of worship and styles of religious buildings. The result is such that any casual visitor to the region quickly realises that Hindu and Buddhist temples, Islamic mosques and Christian churches sit side by side and that there is a complexity of beliefs and cultures vying with each other in all countries of the region. It was traders from India, the Arab world, China, and later Europe that shaped and influenced developments in Brunei Darussalam. It was trade that led to the Chinese settling in the Philippines, Indonesia and especially Singapore, though that was not until Sir Stamford Raffles had claimed it for the British in 1819.

Following on from trade is *migration*. This is as old as history, especially in the hill tribe areas of South-East Asia where different ethnic groups have migrated from southern China and the Himalayan region over centuries and where, even now, there is no clear recognition of international borders as groups move from one place to another in search of new pastures, or, as in the case of the Myanmar/Thai border, particular ethnic groups such as the Karen, Mon and Karenni flee from government and military persecution. The Thais originated in Yunnan in southern China and migrated south into Thailand, Laos and Cambodia, taking their language with them. Indian influence, particularly Buddhist and Hindu, can be found in Myanmar, Cambodia and Laos as a result of monks travelling from country to country with their message of peace and harmony. Migration of a different kind occurred when Han Chinese began migrating to different countries of the region with the result that nearly all the countries of South-East Asia have sizeable Chinese minorities (Hall, 1981; Osborne, 1987). Indeed most of the mainland countries have been strongly influenced by the Chinese, especially Laos and Cambodia. The Chinese, and to some extent the Indians, who were brought over by the British as indentured labourers to work in the rubber plantations and estates of the Straits Settlements, now integrated into Malaysia, have always sought to retain their ethnic and linguistic identity rather than to assimilate or integrate into the mainstream of society. On the other hand they have been prepared to (or forced to) learn the national language for economic purposes (Santhiram, 1999). Even though the Malayan form of Islam has, until recently, been fairly moderate and non-threatening, assimilation with other groups has not been possible because of dietary habits, cultural traditions and religious beliefs.

It was through migration over centuries that the Chinese moved into Laos, the Philippines and Thailand. They were so economically dominant at the beginning of the twentieth century in Bangkok especially that they were labelled 'the Jews of the East' by the then Thai king, Vajiravud, and, as a result, they suffered considerable discrimination (Watson, 1976a). In both Thailand and Malaysia they have also found that education and language policies have been used to discriminate against them (Watson, 1976b, 1983,

1984, 1993). In all parts of South-East Asia, however, there are sizeable Chinese minorities with their own 'Chinatown' areas and the policies of different governments towards them have varied considerably, but usually not particularly favourably. As the *World Directory of Minorities* notes:

> Despite living in the region for more than a hundred years, ethnic
> Chinese are still regarded with fear and suspicion by most
> Southeast Asian governments, partly because of their
> entrepreneurial success. (Minority Rights Group, 1997, p. 593)

One of the reasons why Indians and Chinese, especially, were accepted in different societies is that they were prepared to do jobs that the indigenous Malays, Filipinos, Vietnamese, or Thais would not do. This was all very well when economic times were good but when competition for jobs increased in times of difficulty there was, and has been, growing resentment between different ethnic groups.

Then there is the *expansion* of one dominant group over a particular landmass. This is what happened in China, where the Han Chinese spread outwards from the Yellow River basin overrunning ethnic groups who happened to be in their path. The result is that there are at least 55 ethnic minority groups within China's borders, accounting for about 6% of the total population (Grimes, 2000). Since the early imperial days the country has been held together by one written language, Mandarin, although there are numerous dialects such as Hakka, Hokkien, Hunanese, and Cantonese which are often mutually incomprehensible when spoken.

Perhaps the most controversial reason for why countries have become multiethnic and multilingual is because of *colonialism*. While the colonial legacy has been most felt in Africa and Latin America it was never so dominant in South-East Asia. Nevertheless it did have a profound impact on the region, not least because it led to the creation of clear national boundaries in mainland South-East Asia, and Spanish, and later American, control of the Philippines led to the creation of a country out of a disparate island archipelago. Cambodia and Laos, for example, owe their existence to the involvement of the French. Vietnam's borders, however, were not necessarily shaped by the French but by geography (Osborne, 1987, pp. 67-68). Thailand's borders resulted from the astuteness of the Thai kings in playing off the British and French colonial authorities (Wyatt, 1984). Even so, some countries, most notably Vietnam and Thailand, retained their basic geographic shape despite, and because of, European involvement.

The entry of Europeans into the region began when Portugal captured Malacca on the Malay Peninsula in 1511. Their influence was soon surpassed by the Anglo-Dutch acrimonious rivalry for control of the spice trade in the East Indies, which later became known as Indonesia from the seventeenth century onwards (Milton, 1999). Only by the late nineteenth century was Dutch supremacy assured, but even then they did not dominate or control the whole of Indonesia, contrary to what has so often been suggested (Osborne, 1987, p. 63). The indigenous peoples of Indonesia continued to play an important role in the life of their own country, particularly in Sumatra and Ambon. French missionaries first arrived in Cambodia, Laos and Vietnam, having failed to convert the Chinese emperor to Christianity, beginning in the eighteenth century. They began to settle and trade in earnest from the nineteenth century onwards. The British involvement in Myanmar, Malaya, Singapore and Brunei also began during the nineteenth century, initially for trading purposes rather than with any sense of colonial control. Indeed much of their involvement was in the form of a protectorate. In the Philippines the nearly three centuries of Spanish rule exerted a strong influence on the country: first through a land-tenure system based on Spanish feudalism; second through the spread of Roman Catholicism and education. Spanish rule came to an end after their defeat in Cuba at the hands of the Americans in 1901, after which Spain ceded the Philippines to the USA. After Catholicism it is the American cultural influence that is probably strongest today, despite the USA claiming not to be a colonial power. The same is true in Thailand, which claims never to have been colonised, though there was considerable British influence on the development of the Thai education system in the late nineteenth and early twentieth centuries (Watson, 1980).

The most recent reason why countries, especially those in the developing world, have become more ethnically and linguistically diverse is because of *globalisation.* This has meant that many trans-national corporations (TNCs) and multi-lateral agencies (MLAs) have set up head offices or regional offices in cities such as Bangkok, Jakarta, Manila, Singapore and Kuala Lumpur with the result that many *farang* (foreigners) from around the globe have moved into these cities. Their numbers might be few in comparison to the overall populations but their impact has been profound since their influence has been considerable (see, e.g., Clayton, 2007) and they have brought with them English, French, Japanese and other languages.

It can be seen, therefore, that South-East Asia has been shaped by many forces, most noticeably migration, trade, territorial expansion and colonialism. Yet, although the colonial legacy can be seen through the creation of nation-states, in bricks and mortar and in a certain degree of infrastructure, in the education and legal systems that were left behind, and in the introduction of European languages, it is not as great as in other parts of the world. This is partly because of the long history of civilisation that was influenced by Confucianism. Hinduism, Buddhism and Islam all required a degree of literacy, especially amongst those who were kings and priests, which meant that there were ruling groups who were already literate. Gradually, this led to key languages that were widely understood. The Tai language, for example, is not only the principal language of Thailand and is related to Chinese – it is spoken in southern China – but it is also spoken widely by the Shans of Myanmar, the lowlanders of Laos, and in the northern parts of Cambodia, Vietnam and northern Malaysia. Variations of Malay, e.g. Bahasa Malaysia, Bahasa Maleyu, Bahasa Indonesia, are spoken in Malaysia, Brunei, Sabah and Sarawak, Indonesia and Timor. Moreover, despite the claims made by the French, Vietnamese was not only never replaced by French during the colonial period but has always been widely spoken throughout the country. Linguistic unity helped create social and cultural unity. For these reasons the wars of independence that took place at the end of the Second World War were able to generate so much support so quickly and to prove that the colonial legacy was relatively superficial (Jeffrey, 1981).

As Osborne (1987, p. 63) has said:

> In some aspects of history the European role was vital in determining developments of far-reaching importance. The establishment of international boundaries in the Southeast Asian region was one such case. But in other aspects of life the part played by the European was much less important than it was once thought to have been. French officials in Vietnam, for instance, were often depicted in histories of that country, written before the Second World War and by their countrymen, as presiding over the implantation of French culture among the Vietnamese population. The error of such a view was most clearly revealed in the extent to which Vietnamese revolutionaries were able to strengthen their capacities to challenge the French through the promotion of literacy in the Vietnamese language. *French language and culture, all French claims to the contrary, never supplanted indigenous values and the indigenous language.* (My italics)

The same applies to Laos and Cambodia. However, Kelly (2000) takes a slightly different stance, arguing that in viewing their colonial empire as an extension of metropolitan France, the French authorities tried to enforce French dominance far more ruthlessly than any other colonial power.

Finally, it needs to be acknowledged that there is a new, and perhaps more invasive reason for multiethnic and linguistically diverse societies – *globalisation*. Economic globalisation is transforming cities like Bangkok, Ho Chi Minh City, Jakarta, Kuala Lumpur and Manila into international centres with the regional headquarters of TNCs and UN agencies being located there. Not only has this brought many non-indigenous nationalities as residents, each with his/her own culture and language, but with a need to use a common *lingua franca*. This is increasingly English. The result is that the local residents have had to adapt to the outsiders' language, either through education or, as in the case of Singapore, for those well past the formal education stage, through the use of 'Singlish', a form of pidgin (Chew, 2007) or, as in the case of Brunei, 'Brulish' (Saxena, 2007).

The Ethnic and Linguistic Complexity of South-East Asia

As has been shown above, the present structure of South-East Asia has come about not through any one cause but through multiple causes. Let us therefore set out the linguistic and ethnic complexity of the region that has resulted before looking at the possible language policy options that are available, and looking at some of the actual polices pursued in different countries of the region.

South-East Asia must be amongst the world's most complex ethnic regions. Each country not only has a myriad of ethnic groups, often many very small ones, but each also has many languages. Table I sets out the main groups and languages.

Country	Main ethnic groups	Major languages
Burma (Myanmar)	135 ethnic groups Burman, Chin, Karen, Kachin, Karenni, Mon, Shan, Arakanese, Nagas	111 languages Burmese (official)
Brunei	12 ethnic groups Malay, Chinese, Dusun, Iban, Kedayan, Murut	16 languages Bahasa Maleyu (official), Chinese, English
Cambodia	5 ethnic groups Khmer, Cham (Khmer Islam), Khmer Leou (hill tribes), Chinese, Vietnamese	17 languages Khmer (official), Chinese, Vietnamese, Malayo-Polynesian
Indonesia	360 ethnic groups Javanese, Sundanese, Chinese, Dayaks, Acehnese, Balinese, Minangkabau, West Irians, South Moluccans, Bataks, Ambonese, Buganese	256 languages Bahasa Indonesia (official), English, Javanese, local languages
Laos	71 ethnic groups Lao Lum (lowlanders, Lao Theung (middle Lao, made up of 36 clans), Hmong, Tai, Chinese, Vietnamese	92 languages Lao (official language), Tai, Mon-Khmer
Malaysia (Peninsular)	22 ethnic groups Malays, Chinese, Tamils, Sikhs and other Indians, Orang Asli (19 tribal groups)	38 languages Bahasa Malaysia (official), English, Chinese, Tamil
Malaysia (Sabah)	44 ethnic groups Kadazan-Dusun, Chinese,	54 languages Bahasa Maleyu, English,

	Bajau, Murut, Malay	Chinese
Malaysia (Sarawak)	28 ethnic groups Dayak-Iban, Chinese, Malay, Bidayuh	45 languages Bahasa Maleyu (official), English, Chinese
Philippines	? 120 ethnic groups* Filipino/Malays, Muslims (Moros), Chinese, indigenous peoples	168 languages Tagalog (national language), English, Bicolano, Cebuano, Hiligaynon, Ilocano, Visayan, Pangasinan, Waray-Waray, Chinese
Singapore	4 main ethnic groups Chinese, Malays, Tamils, others (including Europeans)	26 languages Malay, Chinese, English, Tamil (all official languages)
Timor-Leste	4 main ethnic groups Timorese, Indonesians, Chinese, Malays	5 languages Tetum, Timorese, Portuguese, Indonesian, Chinese
Thailand	? 30 ethnic groups Thais, Chinese, Malays, Khmers, Mons, Highlanders	76 languages Thai (official), English, Chinese, Malay, minority languages (hill tribes)
Vietnam	54 ethnic groups Vietnamese, Chinese, Khmer, Cham, Highlanders (hill tribes)	86 languages Vietnamese, Chinese, Khmer, Tai, Hmong

*Ethnic data is not collected in the Philippines census.

Table I. Main ethnic groups and languages in South-East Asia. Sources: various, but good use made of Minority Rights Group (1997) *World Directory of Minorities* and of Grimes (2000) *Ethnologue: languages of the world.*

It can be seen from Table I that there are at least 875 ethnic minority groups in the region and 975 known languages. It stands to reason that the language policies chosen by different governments must have left, and have left, many of the smaller and more vulnerable groups, usually hill tribe people/highlanders, marginalised from mainstream economic and cultural development. Some governments have been content to leave these groups alone, provided that they have not posed a threat to the central government, but others have endeavoured to force their assimilation into mainstream society. Even so, according to the Summer Institute of Linguistics, most have preserved their distinct languages and cultural identity, rather than become absorbed in the development of the twenty-first century (Grimes, 2000). The very complexity of the South-East Asian region, however, has meant that governments have been left with dilemmas as to which language policy they should adopt. It is to these choices that we next turn.

Language and Ethnic Policy Options Available

What language policy is chosen in a multiethnic and multilingual society depends on a number of factors. One ethnic group might be dominant and seek to ensure that dominance by insisting that its language should be the national language. This is the situation in Myanmar, Brunei, Malaysia, Thailand and Vietnam. On the other hand there are occasions where a government tries to accommodate all language groups within society while recognising that one or more languages should be used for administrative purposes. Such is the situation in Singapore, the Philippines, Indonesia and, further afield, in India where the expectation is that all primary school children will be able to speak at least three, even four, languages. Then there are attempts to accommodate all groups within a society where all languages are granted equal status, though this is only possible in countries where the language groups are few in number and are roughly equal, such as in Switzerland or Canada. More common is where one language is used as a national language while allowing disparate groups to keep their languages at local or community levels as is the situation in the Philippines, Thailand and Cambodia in South-East Asia, in Russia and in many African countries. Another option, and one that is becoming increasingly common, is where a government decides for economic or politically strategic reasons to adopt an international language either as the main language or as a joint language such as is the situation in Singapore, Pakistan and Bangladesh to name but a few countries. Then there are decisions surrounding monolingualism, bilingualism or even trilingualism. Should there be some form of enforced assimilation into a main ethnic or linguistic group, or at the least integration of different groups, or should some form of cultural and linguistic pluralism be encouraged? None of the policy options is easy and they are always associated with political power, or the loss of it, and economic considerations.

The bottom line is how far the mother tongue or home language of different groups is tolerated or even encouraged through the school system, and how far it is marginalised to community use only. This is particularly important when it comes to education because if a group's mother tongue is ridiculed or ignored in schools and is largely left to the domestic scene it can have dire consequences for both emotional and cognitive development, as was shown in a study of Indian children in rural areas of Malaysia (Santhiram, 1999) and as is happening with the Chams of Cambodia

(Clayton, 2007). It is also happening in countries such as Myanmar, Indonesia and the Philippines where it is impossible to provide schooling in the mother tongue for so many different ethnic and linguistic groups.

One of the best pieces of international research into language provision, especially bilingual provision, was conducted in over 100 countries in the 1970s by Fishman (1976). He classified four policy categories. *Transitional bilingualism* is where the mother tongue is used for the first part of schooling with a gradual changeover to the main official or national language. This pattern is widely used in many Third World countries where there are so many small linguistic groups and where most of these are predominantly oral because there is no written script and where a national language has to be used for administration, the law and official communication. The second category, *monoliterate bilingualism*, is where oral/aural skills in both the mother tongue and the medium of instruction in schools are both developed but where literacy skills are only developed in the main medium of instruction, usually a state or national language. *Partial biliterate bilingualism* is the third of Fishman's categories. Here both oral and literacy skills are developed in both the mother tongue and the national/official language but where the mother tongue is confined to those subjects that have less economic value, such as art, moral education or religious studies, even literature and history. The final category is *full biliterate bilingualism* where equality of esteem is given to two or more languages in the classroom as well as outside. Children learn different subjects through different language media as happens in the European and International Schools and as is the pattern in countries such as Belgium, Switzerland and Singapore.

Education and Language Policies

Turning to the region that is the focus of this chapter, South-East Asia, it will be shown that very diverse education and language policies have been pursued. Most countries have sought to generate a sense of national unity through the school system. Apart from the textbooks used (e.g. David & Govindasamy, 2007), symbolism such as a flag-raising ceremony, a pledge of allegiance or the use of a unifying language such as has been successfully used in the USA are widely used. Thus Thailand and the Philippines use a daily flag-raising ceremony. In Singapore, one of whose key educational objectives is 'to inculcate attitudes of social discipline and responsibility, racial harmony and loyalty to the Republic', all pupils pledge allegiance to the 'nation as a united people regardless of race, language or religion'. This has been accepted because this island-state operates a meritocratic system and does not discriminate against any one ethnic group. Thai pupils pledge allegiance to the monarchy and their country on a daily basis, singing the national anthem by way of reinforcement. Interestingly, in the political disputes of the past few years both sides have claimed loyalty to the king. Filipino children are expected to identify with the Philippines as a nation despite the fact that that country consists of so many islands and peoples, not all of whom (especially the Muslims in Mindanao, Sulu and Palawan) are happy with their situation. In Malaysia 'all aspects of the government's policy are geared towards the achievement of national unity. All projects, including education, are meaningless if the people are not united,' according to Tungku Abdul Rahman, Malaysia's first prime minister, following the publication of the Razak Report (1956). As will be shown, not all polices have led to national unity, but at least the country can boast of the *Rukenegara* (the fundamental principles of the nation). This aims to foster the ideal Malaysian, regardless of racial origin, who believes in God, is loyal to king and country, upholds the Constitution, abides by the rule of law and professes upright behaviour and morality. Indonesia has something similar, the *Pancasila*, and since 1928 its slogan has been 'one country, one nation, one language'. Brunei's ideology is *Melayu Islam Beraja* (MIB), which literally means support for the Malay Islamic Monarchy. It invokes Islamic values in support of the Sultanate's absolute monarchy, though this has strong historical links to a Hindu variation of monarchy (Saxena, 2007) and entwines Malay ethnic identity, Malay culture, and Bahasa Meleyu (the official/national language). Hutchinson (1994) has described this as a 'one nation-one culture-one language' principle of many modern nation-states, Brunei's educational policy is essentially bilingual. With Brunei's importance as an oil-producing country and its long tradition as an international port English is seen as an essential part of the country's education and language policy. Nevertheless the MIB ideology is central to the Brunei school curriculum and religious studies has recently been integrated into mainstream education (Saxena, 2007).

Indonesia's education and language policy has been one of *transitional bilingualism*, with the first three years of schooling being delivered in the mother tongue, where possible, before transferring to the national language, Bahasa Indonesia. With over 300 ethnic groups and 256 different languages inhabiting over 6000 islands out of 13,677, many of whose settlements are isolated from neighbouring ones either by water or by dense jungle, this would seem to be a sensible approach to creating a sense of national unity through language. The approach is reinforced through the use of common textbooks that ensure that what is taught is remarkably similar throughout the nation. The Thai authorities, until recently, have insisted on the use of the central Thai dialect for all schooling, even among the hill-tribe peoples of the north and north-east of the country and the Malay-speaking Muslims in the south. With 80% of the population being Thai this could hardly be called *linguistic hegemony* but that is how it has seemed to the minority groups. There is now a belated recognition that linguistic rights should be acknowledged but this is not even *monoliterate bilingualism*. Myanmar has pursued a similar language policy but with the added injustice that the government has persistently harassed, murdered or displaced its ethnic minority groups. 'Many minority groups such as the Karen have as many as

20% of their population either displaced within Myanmar or taking refuge in neighbouring Thailand' (Minority Rights Group, 1997, p. 554). Both approaches show a form of positive discrimination in favour of one particular group.

Since independence from both Britain, and later the Malaysian Federation in 1965, Singapore opted for a policy of *full biliterate bilingualism*, recognising four languages as mediums of instruction in separate schools – English, Malay, Chinese and Tamil. However, although nearly 80% of the population of Singapore are Chinese (of different dialects) and the government opted for Bahasa Malaysia as the national language for reasons of regional cooperation, the majority of parents opted for English-medium schooling. The reasons given were that English was most likely to lead to employment in science and technology-related fields. The result was that with 90% of enrolments in English-medium schools Malay- and Tamil-medium schools were forced to close through lack of demand. It is fair to say that Singapore is becoming an English-speaking state. In 2004 almost 50% of primary school entrants came from English-speaking homes (*Straits Times*, 2004). However this does not mean that the government has not been concerned about the situation. It has frequently tried to encourage the use of different languages, especially Mandarin Chinese, through the 'Speak Mandarin Campaign', and although dialects are widely used in everyday living, they are declining. According to Chew (2007, p. 78) 'the switch to Mandarin has actually heralded the death of the mother culture of the majority of Singaporeans'.

Moreover, as Chew has also noted: 'It has always been a conscious choice on the part of the Singapore government not to indulge in the linguistic nationalism of many postcolonial countries' (p. 76). The result has been of positive benefit to the country. Indeed Singapore's pre-eminent position as an entrepot port has given it an edge over neighbouring countries, and with globalisation, the widespread use of English is seen as providing great opportunities as well as enormous benefits, providing good reasons for foreign investment. Inevitably English has given the country a leading advantage 'in education, academic achievement, international trade and business' (p. 76). However, because many Singaporeans speak 'Singlish', a mixture of Chinese, English and words from other languages, the government has been at pains to encourage the 'Speak Good English Movement'. This is largely the British variety of English, as opposed to the American version, but there is a sense that the better the English spoken the greater the benefit to the country. There have been heated debates over the merits of this policy and attempts to minimise the use of 'Singlish', which, for many commentators, is seen as the glue that gives the people a sense of national identity (Chng, 2003). There are others who want to encourage the use of Mandarin and other Chinese dialects for the same reasons. To the younger Singaporeans, however, these might be arcane debates since large numbers have embraced Western culture, language and lifestyles and they are as equally at home with these as with local customs and lifestyles. Many also avail themselves of opportunities to study abroad. It would seem that Singapore's pragmatic approach to language is proving advantageous in the face of globalisation.

Malaysia, in contrast, has pursued a rather different approach. The government's policies have been a mixture of *transitional bilingualism* and *positive discrimination* in favour of the Malay majority. Because of the association of English with colonialism, and the fact that it was the urban Chinese, Indians and Malays who benefited most from English-medium education, the Malay elite has always sought to encourage a strong sense of national identity by promoting Bahasa Malaysia as the joint national language. It was also seen as a means of developing the rural Malays (*bumiputras*). However, the race riots of 1969, and the subsequent Constitutional Amendment Act of 1970, led to a hardening of attitudes. Not only was Bahasa Malaysia made the official language but all English-medium schools, first at primary level and then at secondary level, were to switch to Malay medium. By 1982 English-medium schools switched to Malay medium and by 1983 the examination system had followed suit, though non-Malays were expected to gain a distinction pass rather than a simple pass. Tamil and Chinese primary schools were still allowed to teach content subjects in the language medium of their choice. There was considerable resentment at these policies by the minority ethnic communities (Watson, 1983, 1984; Omar, 1993).

Needless to say concerns were, and have continued to be, expressed about the impact these policies would have on standards of English. English is a compulsory second language in all Malay-medium national schools and Chinese and Tamil can be taught if the parents of 15 or more children request this. In Kuala Lumpur and other urban areas many children use English as their first language at home (David, 2001) but in the rural areas English is still seen as a foreign language (David & Govindasamy, 2007). There was a gradual recognition that standards of English had declined and that many students at university level struggled with subjects, such as science and medicine, that are taught in English. This led to a review of the place of English in the country, given Malaysia's need to remain competitive in a global market. The proponents of the status quo argued on the grounds of national identity; the proponents of English medium did so on economic grounds. After a long, and heated, debate about the role of English the decision was taken to reintroduce English-medium education in science, mathematics and technology.

Even so the ethnic and urban–rural divides remain, largely along linguistic and ethnic lines. According to Yong (2003) between 80% and 90% of Chinese attend Chinese primary schools and 50% of Indians study at Tamil schools, while almost all Malays, excepting about 60,000 who attend Chinese schools, attend Malay national schools. Although the government has introduced a series of textbooks in English designed to create a sense of identity with Malaysia, and that recognise all ethnic groups as equal, those living in the urban areas have a clear advantage because of their wider exposure to English (David & Govindasamy, 2007).

Globalisation has led to a rethink about the place of English within the education system and society as a whole. It has also led to a re-examination of the place of Bahasa Malaysia. National identity remains strong though there is little doubt that the *bumiputras* are still at the bottom of the heap economically. The recent decision to reverse the English language policy in 2012 so that science and mathematics are again taught in Malay is seen by many as madness. While it might benefit the *bumiputras* it will do little to help Malaysia achieve its goal of becoming an advanced nation by 2020. Malaysia likes to think of itself as on a par with Singapore but, until it is prepared to relax its obsession with Malay nationalism and the key role played by Bahasa Malaysia in this, these will always be distractions from some of the more important economic and political considerations needed for dealings with globalisation.

Brunei Darussalam, another predominantly Malay country, also has a long history as a trading centre and has sought to meld together different ethnic, linguistic and religious groups into a coherent entity. It has endeavoured to create a national ideology as well as a national/official language. The ideology, *Maleyu Islam Beraja*, has been referred to earlier. The education system is used to reinforce this, much the same as in Malaysia. As Saxena (2007, p. 151) says, 'non-Malay linguistic groups are subject to the homogenization forces of Malayanization/Bruneization'. *Positive discrimination* is widely used to favour the Malays. An O level credit pass in Malay is necessary for top positions in the civil service and upward social mobility is only possible if the non-Malays buy into the MIB. Any would-be citizen is expected to take, and pass, a language test in Bahasa Malayu. As a result many of the Chinese residents, who might be economically successful and who play a positive role in society, find themselves stateless, lacking any political identity and as second-class citizens (p. 154). Nevertheless they, and other ethnic groups, are increasingly using English as well as their mother tongues. English as a joint official language is stressed because of its importance in trade and access to technological and scientific knowledge. Thus from grade 4 it is used as the medium of instruction for mathematics, science and geography and since 1985 its use has been growing in most areas of society (Saxena & Sercombe, 2002). As with the growth of 'Singlish' in Singapore, Brunei has seen the growth of 'Brulish', a local patois, but unlike Singapore there has been no real campaign to suppress this. As globalisation spreads, and as Brunei, with its oil and natural gas, becomes more engaged with the wider world the linguistic mix will continue to grow.

Of all the countries of South-East Asia that have been most transformed, politically and economically, Cambodia must be the most prominent example. Following the nightmare years of the Pol Pot regime and the ruthless communist governments between the 1950s and 1990s it has now been/is being transformed into a capitalist market economy and a liberal democracy. It is still a relatively poor country. As a result aid agencies, UN delegations and TNCs have moved in, Not only has this led to the re-establishment of Khmer as the official language but it has also generated a debate as to which international language, French or English, should be the best language for the country. In many ways it should be English. Most of the TNCs and the MLAs use English as their working language, as does ASEAN, of which Cambodia is a member. But the French, as the former colonial power, still wish to have some influence, and they have poured money into higher education as a means of ingratiating themselves. If French is a language of higher education it naturally follows that it will have to be used at school level. On the other hand because of the importance of China and Taiwan as trading partners, Chinese could also lay claim to being included.

Clayton (2006, 2007) has explored some of the ethnic and linguistic complexities facing Cambodia. He has concluded that while English might be gaining the upper hand its widespread use can also lead to the marginalisation of groups without access to English as well as lead to a certain resistance if there is a threat to the national identity of the country. The Cambodian government recognises the rights of its minorities to be educated in their own languages and has developed a policy of multiculturalism and bilingualism, although its rhetoric is far ahead of the reality. According to Thomas (2002) it is hoped that by 2015 all ethnic groups will receive an education in their mother tongue. Some of the highlanders are being encouraged to develop their own languages, largely as a result of pressure from international NGOs, but while the Chinese and Vietnamese have gained new freedoms their schooling is largely dependent on either private or communal support. Because of trading links with Singapore and China many employees of companies are expected to know Chinese (Clayton, 2007, p. 100). The Muslim Cham community's education is mainly confined to Koranic schools using classical Arabic. Whether they will become more integrated into mainstream society only time will tell but the experience of other countries where Muslims form a minority is not encouraging. Moreover the government's determination to restore Khmer identity and language, and to encourage both English and French, means that those ethnic groups in the rural areas and the poor urban groups with limited access to those languages are being disadvantaged. The current language policy, whether intentional or not, is designed to serve the economic and political interests of the privileged few and growing contact with the wider world is bound to increase the demand for more English.

Until recently the two communist South-East Asian countries, Laos and Vietnam, pursued very similar policies, the assimilation of the ethnic minorities into mainstream lowland culture and the non-recognition of minority languages except in local situations. While the future of Laos' indigenous peoples 'appears bleak' (Minority Rights Group, 1997, p. 627) there has been some movement in Vietnam towards recognition of indigenous peoples' culture and customs, but not language rights. Vietnam is faced with the question of how to develop national identity and greater interaction with the wider world while at the same time preserving ethnic minority cultures. Thus, while the government pays lip-service to the idea of developing minority cultural identity, and presumably local languages, Vietnamese is the national language and all school textbooks are written in Vietnamese. A World Bank report (Baulch et al, 2004) highlights the tensions between cultural assimilation/Vietnamisation and the professed policy of ethnic minority recognition. As in Thailand the majority population, the Kinh, or lowland, Vietnamese, comprise about 86% of the total population. Ethnic minority groups make up the remaining 14%. There is a sense, therefore, that these groups should move towards the majority. Many of them have done so but in the highland areas knowledge of Vietnamese is limited or non-existent and most of the ethnic groups are economically poor, have a low life expectancy and suffer from poor health (World Bank, 1999). It is the lowland, Kinh, Vietnamese who largely fill the teaching, local government, police and other crucial jobs, not the ethnic minorities. While the government recognises the rights of minorities to keep their cultures, customs, and even languages the latter are essentially oral since there is no policy of bilingualism and only Vietnamese is taught throughout the education system. Courses have been established in ethnic minority cultures at Hanoi University of Culture but these are more tokenistic than anything else since, while they recognise local cultures, dress, customs and traditional dances, etc., courses are taught through the medium of Vietnamese and there is virtually no recognition given to indigenous languages.

With Vietnam's colonial history and the involvement of the USA in the long-running Vietnamese War, there are still elements of French language and culture. However, as Vietnam's economy is opened up and the country is increasingly engaged with economic globalisation English will become more important and used for commercial purposes. Also, despite the pressures placed on the Chinese community, whose numbers declined dramatically during the late 1970s and 1980s as they fled abroad, there is some resurgence within the small community that remains. Whether their usefulness in future trade with China becomes recognised is a matter of conjecture.

One other country that needs a brief mention is Timor-Leste, once East Timor, that was one of the last outposts of the Portuguese Empire. The Portuguese finally ceded independence in 1975 after a brief struggle for independence on the part of the Timorese. The country soon became involved in a long-running dispute for real independence after Indonesia invaded it in December 1975. The UN intervened in 1999 and administered the territory until it finally gained its independence in 2002. Since then the language issue has been whether to promote Tetum, Portuguese or English, which is widely spoken. While both Tetum and Portuguese are widely used in the school system Portuguese predominates at the higher education level. How long this situation will prevail remains to be seen.

Conclusions

This chapter has sought to discuss the importance of language for individuals, communities and for nation-states. It has looked at how the countries of South-East Asia became culturally and linguistically plural. It has also discussed the dilemmas faced by governments when balancing the linguistic rights of certain groups with the need to develop a sense of national coherence, while at the same time needing to respond to the challenges posed by economic and cultural globalisation.

As has been shown language and ethnic policies vary considerably, depending on how the political elites perceive their own position. Without exception the use of English has been growing throughout the countries of South-East Asia, helped by the Internet and Western culture, largely because of its position as the most widely used international language. The next generation will use it even more. However there are downsides to this development. Not only is there a danger that many indigenous languages will disappear, with all that that implies, but the realities are that those with access to English, and any national language, will be privileged. Those without such access, mainly minority ethnic groups, will remain disadvantaged. It would therefore appear as if the laudable goals of ethnic and linguistic rights are being sacrificed on the altar of economic globalisation. While South-East Asia is not alone in this the effects on many small ethnic groups could prove catastrophic in the long run.

References

Baulch, B., Truong, T.K.C., Haughton, D. & Haughton, J. (2004) Ethnic Minority Development in Vietnam: a socioeconomic perspective, in P. Glewwe, N. Agrawal & D. Dollar (Eds) *Economic Growth, Poverty, and Household Welfare in Vietnam.* Washington, DC: World Bank.

Brock-Utne, B. & Skattum, I. (Eds) (2009) *Languages and Education in Africa: a comparative and transdisciplinary analysis.* Oxford: Symposium Books.

Castles, S. & Miller, M.J. (1993) *The Age of Migration.* Basingstoke: Macmillan.

Chew, P.G.-L. (2007) Remaking Singapore: language, culture and identity in a globalized world, in A.B.M. Tsui & J.W. Tollefson (Eds) *Language Policy, Culture, and Identity in Asian Contexts.* New York: Lawrence Erlbaum Associates.

Chng, H.H. (2003) You See Me No Up? Is Singlish a Problem? *Language Problems and Language Planning,* 27(1), 45-60.

Churchill, S. (1996) The Decline of the Nation-state and the Education of National Minorities, *International Review of Education,* 42(4), 265-290.

Clayton, T. (2006) *Language Choice in a Nation under Transition: English language spread in Cambodia.* Berlin: Springer Verlag.

Clayton, T. (2007) Tradition, Culture and Language in Cambodia, in A.B.M. Tsui & J.W. Tollefson (Eds) *Language Policy, Culture, and Identity in Asian Contexts*. New York: Lawrence Erlbaum Associates.

Clothey, R. (2005) China's Polices for Minority Nationalities in Higher Education: negotiating national values and ethnic identities, *Comparative Education Review*, 49(3), 389-409.

Coombs, P. (1985) *The World Crisis in Education: a view from the Eighties*. Oxford: Oxford University Press.

Crystal, D. (1997) *English as a Global Language*. Cambridge: Cambridge University Press.

Crystal, D. (2003) *English as a Global Language*. London: Longmans.

David, M.K. (2001) *The Sindhis of Malaysia – a sociological study*. London: Association of Southeast Asian Nations.

David, M.K. & Govindasamy, S. (2007) National Identity and Globalization in Malaysia, in A.B.M. Tsui & J.W. Tollefson (Eds) *Language Policy, Culture, and Identity in Asian Contexts*. New York: Lawrence Erlbaum Associates.

Delors, R. (1996) *Learning: the treasure within*. Report to UNESCO of the International Commission on Education for the Twenty-first Century. Paris: UNESCO.

Fishman, J.A. (1976) *Bilingual Education: an international sociolinguistic perspective*. Rowley, MA: Newbury House.

Grimes, B.E. (2000) *Ethnologue: languages of the world*. Dallas: Summer Institute of Linguistics (CD-ROM).

Hall, D.G.E. (1981) *A History of South-East Asia*, 4th edn. Basingstoke: Macmillan.

Hsieh, P.-T. (2009) The Impact of Globalisation on Foreign language Policy in Taiwan: curriculum design and implementation. Unpublished DPhil thesis, University of Oxford.

Hutchinson, J. (1994) *Modern Nationalism*. London: Fontana.

Jeffrey, R. (1981) *Asia: the winning of independence*. London: Macmillan.

Kelly, G.P. (2000) Colonial Schools in Vietnam: policy and practice, in P.G. Altbach & G.P. Kelly (Eds) *Education and Colonialism*. New York: Longman.

Milton, G. (1999) *Nathaniel's Nutmeg. How One Man's Courage Changed the Course of History*. London: Sceptre.

Minority Rights Group (1997) *World Directory of Minorities*. London: Minority Rights Group International.

Omar, A. (1993) *Language and Society in Malaysia*. Kuala Lumpur: Dewan Bahasa Dan Puskaka.

Osborne, M. (1987) *Southeast Asia: an illustrated introductory history*. London: Allen & Unwin.

Phillipson, R. & Skutnabb-Kangas, T. (1999) Englishization: one dimension of globalization, in D. Graddad & U.H. Meinhof (Eds) *English in a Changing World*, pp. 19-36. Oxford: Catchline.

Razak Report (1956) Report of the Education Committee, 1956. Kuala Lumpur: Government of Malaya.

Santhiram, R. (1999) *Education of Minorities: the case of Indians in Malaysia.* Petaling jaya: Child Information and Learning Centre.

Saxena, M. (2007) Multilingual and Multicultural Identities in Brunei Darussalam, in A.B.M. Tsui & J.W. Tollefson (Eds) *Language Policy, Culture, and Identity in Asian Contexts.* New York: Lawrence Erlbaum Associates.

Saxena, M. & Sercombe, P. (2002) Patterns and Variations in Language Attitudes and Language Choices among Bruneians, in W.C. So, G.M. Jones & H.B. Beardsmore (Eds) *Education and Society in Plurilingual Contexts.* Brussels: VUB Press.

Skutnabb-Kangas, T. (2001) The Globalisation of (Educational) Language Rights, *International Review of Education*, 47(3-4), 201-219.

Straits Times (2004) 27 November, p. H5.

Sutherland, M.B. (1979) Perspectives on Education of Cultural Minorities, in A.E. Alcock, B.K. Taylor & J.M. Wekon (Eds) *The Future of Cultural Minorities.* London: Macmillan.

Thomas, A. (2002) Bilingual Community-based Education in the Cambodian Highlands. A Successful Approach for Enabling Access to Education by Indigenous Peoples, *Journal of Southeast Asian Education*, 3(1), 26-58.

Time Magazine (1997) Speaking in Tongues, 7 July, pp. 52-58.

Tsui, A.B.M. (2007) Language Policy and the Social Construction of Identity: the case of Hong Kong, in A.B.M. Tsui & J.W. Tollefson (Eds) *Language Policy, Culture, and Identity in Asian Contexts.* New York: Lawrence Erlbaum Associates.

Tsui, A.B.M. & Tollefson, J.W. (Eds) (2007) *Language Policy, Culture, and Identity in Asian Contexts.* New York: Lawrence Erlbaum Associates.

Watson, K. (1976a) A Conflict of Nationalism: the Chinese and education in Thailand, *Paedagogica Historica*, 16(2), 429-451.

Watson, K. (1976b) The Education of Racial Minorities in South East Asia with Special Reference to the Chinese, *Compare*, 6(2), 14-21.

Watson, K. (1980) *Educational Development in Thailand.* Hong Kong: Heinemann Asia.

Watson, K. (1983) Cultural Pluralism, Nation-building and Educational Polices in Peninsular Malaysia, in C. Kennedy (Ed.) *Language Planning and Language Education*, pp. 132-150. London: George Allen & Unwin.

Watson, K. (1984) Cultural Pluralism, Education and National Identity in the ASEAN Countries of South East Asia, in T. Corner (Ed.) *Education in Multicultural Societies*, pp. 216-235. London: Croom Helm.

Watson, K. (1993) Language, Education and Political Power: some reflections on North–South relationships, *Language and Education*, 6(2,3) and (4), 99-121.

Watson, K. (1994) Caught Between Scylla and Charybdis: linguistic and educational dilemmas facing policy-makers in pluralist states, *International Journal of Educational Development*, 14(3), 321-337.

Watson, K. (2007) Language, Education and Ethnicity: whose rights will prevail in an age of globalisation? *International Journal of Educational Development*, 27(2), 252-265.

Wong, F.H.K. (1973) *Comparative Studies in South East Asian Education*. Hong Kong: Heinemann Asia.

World Bank (1999) *Vietnam Development Report 2000: attacking poverty*. Joint Report of the Government-Donor-NGO Working Group. Hanoi: World Bank.

Wyatt, D.K. (1984) *Thailand: a short history*. New Haven, CT: Yale University Press.

Yong, T.K. (2003) Daunting Task to Check Polarisation in National Schools, *New Sunday Times*, 23 February.

CHAPTER 16

Quality Assurance in South-East Asian Higher Education

SOMWUNG PITIYANUWAT

SUMMARY In the South-East Asia (SEA) region, every country except Myanmar and Timor-Leste has an agency responsible for quality assurance (QA) in higher education. There are three predominant modes of QA agencies: centralized government, quasi-governmental and non-governmental agencies. Programme and institutional audit or accreditation can be seen in many countries in the SEA region. Few countries have developed a national qualifications framework (NQF). In terms of QA, common practices are accreditation, self-assessment, quality audit, site visits and reports. Concerning QA networks, the three popular international and regional networks in the SEA region are the International Network for Quality Assurance Agencies in Higher Education (INQAAHE); the Asia-Pacific Quality Network (APQN) and the ASEAN Quality Assurance Network (AQAN).

Introduction

This chapter is a study of quality assurance systems of higher education in the South-East Asian region. Higher education in this context means education at a college or university level and is divided into two levels: degree level, and level prior to or lower than that of degree level. This chapter identifies areas of similarity and difference of each country in terms of national quality assurance agencies; predominant modes of quality assurance agencies; scope of external quality assurance agencies; scope of quality assurance; voluntary/compulsory quality assurance; national qualifications frameworks; quality assurance practices; and existing international and regional networks. Finally, a comparative overview of quality assurance of higher education in the South-East Asian countries is highlighted.

Specific Issues and Challenges in Quality Assurance (QA)

It is the aim of the ASEAN (Association of Southeast Asian Nations) to put into place practices that allow free flow of education in the region by 2015. It is therefore urgent to build up mutual trust and degree recognition between nations by strengthening the quality of the QA systems in the region. There is a need for greater transparency of degree qualifications, recognition of accreditation, and the ability to facilitate student mobility and credit transfer.

Although QA development has improved over the years, there still are many issues and challenges that lie ahead. It is envisaged that some answers to these issues and challenges should include the following proposals: 1. emphasis on the QA system, i.e. both internal and external, to ensure improvement at programme and/or departmental level; 2. promotion of quality enhancement and benchmarking at every level from department through respective commissions on higher education; 3. improvement of the validity and reliability of both internal and external assessment results by basing enough qualified assessors and judgements on central educational statistical agencies, which must be upgraded or urgently established; 4. promotion of assessment results for improving quality of higher education institutions; 5. better alignment between higher education quality assessment results and government/institute budgetary allocations; 6. focusing external quality assurance on the integrity of the assessment process and findings (more in accordance with competitive economic and sustainable development).

Without real attention to these issues and challenges, the QA process may be another process which takes valuable time and resources away from the higher education community but bears no fruitful results. The following sections give an overview of the different quality assurance systems of the countries in the region.

Quality Assurance of Higher Education in Brunei Darussalam

There are a number of agencies that are responsible for determining QA in higher education institutions (HEIs) in Brunei Darussalam such as the Brunei Darussalam National Accreditation Council (BDNAC), the Ministry of Education, Brunei Darussalam Technical and Vocational Education Council as well as other statutory/professional bodies. BDNAC was established in 1990 and is assisted by 10 sub-committees whose responsibility is to assess and evaluate qualifications and to make recommendations to the Council in the following disciplines: Accountancy and Management, Communication, Education, Engineering and Architecture, Environmental Sciences, Islamic Religious Studies, Medicine, Law, Military and Security, and Information Communications Technology.

The vision of BDNAC is to establish a national and international reputable accrediting agency, while the mission is to ensure and maintain the quality and standard of educational credentials in accordance with the provisions set and required by the government (Salleh, 2009).

Although BDNAC adopts four main criteria for its accreditation and evaluation activities, in the context of course assessments offered by local private education institutions in Brunei Darussalam, the BDNAC Secretariat conducts continuous monitoring and evaluation of programmes/courses as well as the physical aspects of the institution.

The Ministry of Education of Brunei, through various departments such as the Department of Schools, Department of Technical and Vocational Education, Department of Examinations, the University Council/Senate and the Brunei Darussalam Technical Vocational Education Council, is responsible for determining the quality of educational awards, processes and products. In 2006, the Ministry set up the Quality Assurance Division, which was made responsible for the quality assurance aspects of administration, resources and academic issues in relation to the Department of Technical and Vocational Education and vocational and technical education institutions (Haji Ashri bin Haji Ahmad, 2007).

At present, Brunei Darussalam has three universities and due to this small number of institutions, all site visits and assessment are handled by BDNAC making external assessors unnecessary.

QA scope in the country includes both programme and institutional accreditation. Institutional accreditation is compulsory, however programme accreditation is voluntary. This means that a programme can operate without being accredited.

In order to get up-to-date and first-hand information and to obtain best practices, BDNAC implements cross-referencing and collaborates with overseas/international accreditation agencies such: the Australian Universities Quality Agency, the Malaysian Qualifications Agency, the New Zealand Qualifications Agency, and the Quality Assurance Agency for Higher Education of the United Kingdom (Akbar, 2008).

Brunei is also a member of both the Asia Pacific Quality Network and the ASEAN Quality Assurance Network; here it has been taking active steps to gain knowledge for the progressive development of BDNAC.

Quality Assurance of Higher Education in Cambodia

The Cambodian government throughout the 1980s started re-establishing its institutions of higher education. A network of nine public higher education institutions have been established which provide for instruction in areas such as agriculture, medicine, economics, industry, technology, teacher training, science, art and culture. A further 15 technical and professional training institutions (specialised secondary schools) also offer tertiary-level courses lasting for periods of two to three years for upper secondary school graduates. All higher education institutions providing degree programmes are public. Although Cambodia is economically weak, higher education is almost completely free of charge, as nominal payments may be made but the vast majority of payments are covered by the government (Southeast Asian Ministers of Education Organisation-Regional Institute of Higher Education and Development [SEAMEO-RIHED], 2009).

National reconciliation, peace keeping, human resource development and alleviation of poverty are the principal goals of the Cambodian government. To achieve these goals, the government makes an effort to enable people to obtain basic education, skills training and qualification in life skills. Formal and non-formal education are considered as an official education system of the country (Ministry of Education, Youth and Sport [MoEYS], 2008).

Education reform started in 2000 and its impact was immediate (Khorn, 2009a). There has been concern about quality in Cambodia's higher education since privatisation in higher education was introduced. Since the quick mushrooming of HEIs in Cambodia in early 2003, a concern over higher education quality has been expressed by the public and policy makers. Finally, the Accreditation Committee of Cambodia (ACC) was established in March 2003 with its main purpose, as stated in the Royal Kret, to establish a legal mechanism for administering the accreditation of higher education for all HEIs (Khorn, 2009b).

The quality of higher education was in the past supervised by government agencies, particularly MoEYS and other relevant ministries (Ministry of Health, Ministry of Agriculture, Ministry of Culture) (Xiongchunou et al, 2009).

ACC is the newest QA agency in the region. The mission and objectives of ACC are to:

- ensure and promote academic quality for greater effectiveness and quality consistent with international standards;
- determine the organisation of structure, roles, functions, and duties regarding the administration of the accreditation process of higher education for all HEIs which grant degrees in the Kingdom of Cambodia (ACC, 2009).

The main roles of ACC are to develop accreditation policies and measures to assure the quality of HEIs. To determine the accreditation status of HEIs as well as approve the curriculum of foundations courses, ACC publishes the results of accreditation to the public.

ACC makes site visits to all its HEIs in order to assess the quality of the institution as part of the accreditation process. Accreditation is compulsory in Cambodia. Full accreditation takes place at five-year intervals. Provisional accreditation is done at three-year intervals. Accreditation status is granted after the majority vote (50% + 1) of ACC's governing board in support of accreditation. ACC applies institutional accreditation (ACC, 2009).

ACC is funded by the Cambodian government, which includes the costs incurred for site visits and accreditation. At present Cambodia is working closely with other South-East Asian countries through its affiliation with the ASEAN Quality Assurance Network to help further its progress in implementing and evolving its QA systems. It has been working particularly closely with Thailand, which has similar cultural, religious, and political traits. Both countries have devout Theravada Buddhist beliefs and are both officially constitution monarchies with democratically elected governments. Both countries border each other and share much history. This proximity has also produced frequent exchanges of students between the two countries.

Unrelated to QA, but with a very heavy bearing on the government's investment in education, there have been recent discoveries of offshore oil and natural gas (Su, 2006). These will have a great socio-economic impact on the population of Cambodia, making education much more accessible, desirable, and attainable.

Quality Assurance of Higher Education in Indonesia

Based on the National Education System Act no. 20, 2003, there are at present three national external quality assurance agencies which provide mandatory accreditation in Indonesia. The government established the National Accreditation Agency for Higher Education or BAN-PT, as well as placed BAN-S/M in charge of accrediting schools and madrasahs (Islamic schools), and BAN-PNFI in charge of accrediting non-formal and informal educational programmes and institutions.

BAN-PT is an external QA institution in Indonesia. BAN-PT was established in 1994 as an independent body with authority to accredit programmes and institutions at tertiary education at all levels. It is located outside the Ministry of Education structure. The agency conducts the accreditation of study programmes and institutions of higher education. This accreditation takes place on a five-year cycle and is conducted by assessors who act as peer reviewers. Eligible study programmes and higher education institutions requesting accreditation submit their accreditation documents, which consist of a comprehensive self-evaluation report, among others. After the assessment reports are validated, the reports are sent directly to the applying programmes or units and published nationally through BAN-PT's website and directories, and reported to the Ministry of Education.

The accreditation instrument was developed and based on two groups of standards used for accreditation. Firstly, standards reflecting components of leadership and institutional development: integrity, vision, governance, human resources, facilities and infrastructure, funding, information system, and sustainability. Secondly, standards reflecting components of quality, efficiency, and effectiveness of the programme: students, curriculum, methods of learning, QA mechanism, management, and academic atmosphere. Scopes of accreditation include Quality Control (system and mechanism to assess compliance with performance indicators), Quality Audit (appraisal of internal quality control mechanisms), and Quality Assessment (system efficiency and effectiveness) (Yavaprabhas, 2009).

Currently, the QA system for higher education institutions consists of three activities, essentially aimed both independently and collectively at assuring the quality of higher education management: (a) an assessment programme based on self-evaluation; (b) accreditation of higher education, conducted by the national accreditation body for higher education institutions or BAN-PT; and (c) quality assurance.

Indonesia is a member of the Asia-Pacific Quality Network, the ASEAN Quality Assurance Network, University Mobility in Asia and the Pacific, the ASEAN University Network, the Association of Southeast Asian Institutions of Higher Learning, and the Association of Pacific Rim Universities.

Quality Assurance of Higher Education in Laos

The development of higher education institutions in Laos occurred in the years 1975-96. There are 31 private HEIs and five public HEIs. Higher education in the private sector began with the prime minister's Decree 64 in 1995, which aimed to increase the number of HEIs on a yearly basis.

Currently, there is no independent organisation responsible for quality assurance or accreditation in Laos but the Ministry of Education has played an important role in 'developing' quality. In 2008 the Ministry formed the Education Standard and Quality Assurance Centre (EQAC), which serves as the body for developing the standard, assessments and indicators for educational quality (Xiongchunou et al, 2009). This QA centre is also under the Ministry of Education.

EQAC controls and monitors the teaching and learning process in both public and private HEIs. The quality assurance scope of Laos focuses on both programme and institution level. However, Laos does not have the QA system to set up standards that control the quality of education (e.g. through curriculum assessment, student and teacher qualifications, among others).

Laos enhances cooperation with regional and international exchanges in the areas of accreditation and quality assurance through membership with the Asia-Pacific Quality Network, the ASEAN Quality Assurance Network, University Mobility in Asia and the Pacific, and the ASEAN University Network.

Quality Assurance of Higher Education in Malaysia

The Malaysian National Accreditation Board (Lembaga Akreditasi Negara, LAN) was officially established in 1996 to assure the quality of all programmes and qualifications offered by private higher education institutions. Subsequently, the Ministry of Education set up the Quality Assurance Division (QAD) in 2002 to conduct quality audit and establish internal quality assurance mechanisms for public universities. Through internationally benchmarked quality standards and quality assurance procedures, both agencies play a crucial role in facilitating the learning and institutionalisation of quality assurance in the Malaysian higher education system. This led to a dual quality assurance system within, perhaps, a dual qualifications framework structure in higher education – with a third one emerging from the skills sector.

Driven by other national needs and development, the government decided in 2005 that a new entity must be established taking over the role of LAN and QAD to implement the newly developed Malaysian Qualifications Framework (MQF) (Fahmi, 2009). On 1 November 2007, under the Malaysian Qualifications Agency Act 2007, the Malaysian Qualifications Agency (MQA) Act was established.

The Malaysian Qualifications Framework (http://www.mqa.gov.my/) is Malaysia's declaration about its qualifications and their quality in relation to its education system. MQF is an instrument that develops and classifies qualifications based on a set of criteria that are approved nationally and benchmarked against international best practices, and which clarifies the academic levels attained, learning outcomes of study areas and a credit system based on student academic load. These criteria are accepted and used for all qualifications awarded by recognised higher education providers. MQF has eight levels of qualifications in three national higher education sectors and is supported by lifelong education pathways. The sectors are (a) skills; (b) vocational and technical; and (c) academic. The levels are differentiated by learning outcomes, credit hours and student learning time. Lifelong education pathways cut across all levels of qualifications through accreditation of prior experiential learning (Malaysian Qualifications Framework, 2007).

MQA in the future seeks to create common training programmes for QA external auditors in the ASEAN region to enable recruiting assessors from the region – the exchanges are important for feedback, benchmarking practices and shared values. Such inputs will assist reviews of training modules and activities for ongoing QA improvement.

MQA and Malaysia have also taken a lead role in the development and organisation of international QA networks. Malaysia has been an executive member of the International Network for Quality Assurance Agencies in Higher Education, the Asia-Pacific Quality Network and the ASEAN Quality Assurance Network. MQA was the driving force in the foundation of the latter, and currently serves as its Chair.

Quality Assurance of Higher Education in Myanmar

Since Myanmar achieved independence in 1948, the higher education sub-sector has expanded tremendously. Higher education departments and institutions function in accordance with the policy directives of the Myanmar

Education Committee, the Universities Central Council, and the Council of University Academic Bodies.

The functions of the developments under higher education are coordinated by the Universities Central Council and the Council of University Academic Bodies. In addition, a committee is established with respect to each programme. In the university academic body, external experts (from different universities and different ministries) are included to assess the university course and syllabus for requirements in their specific field (Win et al, 2009).

In order to provide greater access and ensure equity, the education sector has undertaken far-reaching changes such as implementing new QA systems as well as launching new learning and research initiatives by investing in participation with international QA networks in order to learn from neighbouring countries with more developed QA systems.

At present, Myanmar is a member of the Asia-Pacific Quality Network, the ASEAN Quality Assurance Network, University Mobility in Asia and the Pacific, the ASEAN University Network, the Association of Southeast Asian Institutions of Higher Learning, and the Association of Pacific Rim Universities.

Myanmar is at its initial stages of developing an educational QA system. Certain problems however arise due to the lack of autonomy of its higher education institutions. The centralised government system of control slows down the implementation of progressive learning standards. With the SEAMEO-RIHED initiative on quality assurance in the region, it is foreseen that Myanmar will benefit from and eventually move forward to setting up a quality assurance system in the near future.

Quality Assurance of Higher Education in the Philippines

The Philippines passed the Higher Education Act of 1994, which established the Commission on Higher Education (CHED) as a separate and independent agency from the Department of Education, Culture and Sport (now known as the Department of Education). CHED is tasked with the primary objective of raising the quality of Philippine higher education through a system of grants and incentives that puts the premium on quality (Lagrada, 2009). The Commission is the agency mandated to provide policy directions for quality assurance at the national and regional levels. This effectively gives more autonomy and responsibility to the leaders of the HEIs. Quality is monitored and checked through a system of peer evaluation with the Commission providing the external pressure to assure adherence to the standards laid down (Padua, 1998). Most higher education institutions are licensed, controlled, and supervised by CHED, which is adopting an outcome-based approach to evaluation because of its great potential to increase both the effectiveness of the quality assurance system, and the quality and efficiency of higher education institutions.

Mechanisms for quality assurance in higher education are grouped into two sets, namely programme based and institution based (Lagarda, 2009).

There are five QA agencies in the Philippines (QA was first established in 1956); four of which are voluntary:

1. The Philippine Accrediting Association of Schools, Colleges and Universities (PAASCU) (http://www.paascu.org.ph/about%20us-introduction.htm) is a private, voluntary, non-profit and non-stock corporation. PAASCU is a private organisation which accredits academic programmes which meet commonly accepted standards of quality education. In November 1967, the Bureau of Education (now the Department of Education) officially recognised PAASCU and endorsed its work as an accrediting agency.
2. The Philippine Association of Colleges and Universities Commission on Accreditation traces its beginnings as an accrediting arm back to 1956.
3. The accreditation of curricular programs in the Philippines, particularly for state universities and colleges, is the main function of the Accrediting Agency of Chartered Colleges and Universities in the Philippines (http://www.aaccupqa.org.ph).
4. The Association of Local Colleges and Universities or ALCU is composed of 31 local colleges and universities of the Philippines. The primary thrust of ALCU is to improve the quality of instruction, research, and extension of its member schools and to provide high-value public tertiary education, especially to the poor and disadvantaged youth.

The fifth agency is CHED, which has a compulsory quality assurance system. In the Philippines, the scope of QA encapsulates both programme accreditation and institutional audit. Although the Philippines has the oldest QA bodies in the region, it suffers from problems associated with bureaucracy and limited resources.

The Philippines is an important member of multiple international quality assurance networks. In particular, it is a full member of the International Network for Quality Assurance Agencies in Higher Education, the Asia-Pacific Quality Network and the ASEAN Quality Assurance Network. It has taken a leading role in the two latter organisations and is currently a member of both executive boards.

Quality Assurance of Higher Education in Singapore

Singapore's higher education sector contains a mix of public and private institutions that provide degree courses, diplomas and certificates in technical and vocational areas, tertiary arts courses and other post-secondary qualifications. Quality assurance for tertiary education in Singapore is handled by the QA section of the Ministry of Education. Quality assurance utilises a system of institutional self-assessment by external assessors, and is compulsory for HEIs. The Ministry of Education is also responsible for institution and course accreditation.

In 2001, the Ministry of Education in Singapore put in place a quality assurance framework for its autonomous universities – the Quality Assurance Framework for Universities (QAFU). QAFU is modelled after quality assurance frameworks in Denmark, Sweden, the United States and Hong Kong. QAFU seeks to encourage institutions' continual self-learning, quality enhancement and development, and to ensure accountability for the use of public funds. The cycle takes place every five years and involves an institutional self-assessment, an external validation by an external review panel appointed by the Ministry, and follow-up initiatives by the institutions after the external validation. Similar frameworks modelled after QAFU have also been implemented for the polytechnics and the Institute of Technical Education (Ng, 2007).

Singapore uses examination results and conformance to the standards set out to measure the achievement of performance indicators. The country is currently in a process of decentralising government power in order to give HEIs more autonomy thereby giving the government a more remote supervisory role (Ng, 2007).

The Ministry of Education also initiates the establishment of the Council for Private Education as the entity to oversee the regulation of private education institutions which offer degree and diploma courses, amongst other types of non-higher education courses. A voluntary quality assurance framework is where private higher education institutions can apply for certification and are assessed on the level of their performance in areas such as corporate governance and administration, academic processes, and student welfare and support services (Naidu, 2009). Singapore's Ministry of Education is currently in the process of enhancing the regulation and quality assurance of privately funded HEIs.

Singapore is a member of both the International Network for Quality Assurance Agencies in Higher Education and more recently the ASEAN Quality Assurance Network. Although Singapore has arguably one of the most successful education systems in the region, it has taken a back seat with the development of international QA networks. Singapore has taken more of an observer's role and has not been a board member of any of the QA networks.

Quality Assurance of Higher Education in Thailand

Thailand's initiatives in quality assurance started in the late 1980s. It began a process of reform of higher education when the Ministry of University Affairs prepared the first 15-year Higher Education Plan covering the period 1990 to 2004. The Eighth National Higher Education Plan for the period 1997 to 2001 indicated that one of the six main policy directions would relate to quality and excellence. New quality assurance policies and guiding directions were announced in July 1996, and these stipulated that all universities need to improve and enhance their efforts for achieving quality of instruction and an appropriate academic learning environment. The Office for National Education Standards and Quality Assessment (ONESQA) was established in November 2000, serving as an independent body for compulsory accreditation and undertakes external assessments of education at all levels. The baseline for Thailand's quality assurance framework lies in the establishment of standards criteria and requirements for all levels of degree programmes offered in the country. The quality assurance system consists of both internal and external quality assurance. These aim at creating a system and mechanism to control, audit and assess operations of institutions to comply with each institution's policies, purposes and levels of quality established by the institution and/or governing authorities.

Internal quality assurance is a mandatory part of the education administration process and the Commission on Higher Education has focused on this. The internal QA system consists of quality control, quality audit and quality assessment. In 2009, the Thai Qualifications Framework for higher education was announced and consists of six domains of learning outcomes (e.g. ethical and moral development, knowledge, cognitive skills).

For external quality assurance, ONESQA assesses all educational institutions at least once every five years and requires these institutions to continuously enhance their educational quality and achieve efficient educational administration. External quality assurance can be classified at three levels: basic education, vocational education and higher education. For higher education, each institute is to submit data and a self-review report to ONESQA before being subject to an external assessment visit.

Quality Assurance of Higher Education in Timor-Leste

The higher education system in Timor-Leste consists of seven universities, six institutes, and three academies. A proposed classification system defines that universities confer degrees at Bachelor's, Master's, and doctoral levels with a minimum of four faculties (e.g. faculty of arts, science); institutes confer diplomas in applied/technical areas or academic degrees at Bachelor's or professional graduate degree levels with one to three faculties or departments (World Bank, 2009).

The higher education sector has grown without a legal framework for classification or a system of quality assurance and accreditation. However, in recent years the government has established quality assurance mechanisms. The National Commission for Academic Assessment and Accreditation was established in 2006 to take full responsibility for defining standards and criteria for academic accreditation and assessment and for accrediting higher education institutions and their programmes. A Basic Law on Education is expected to be finalised in the near future. The law is intended to establish authority for the Ministry of Education to determine which higher education institutions can be approved and licensed to confer diplomas or degrees and sets out general parameters for classification and accreditation.

At the present there is no curriculum or national qualifications framework. In addition, a process of professional certification or licensure does not exist. Most HEIs are operating without laboratories or libraries. In one of the quality issues, the government has mandated that all HEIs convert to the sole use of the Portuguese language in five years' time in order to provide a relative advantage to graduates since Portuguese is widely spoken as compared to Tetum. However, there is a paucity of Portuguese speakers in administrative and teaching positions.

Timor-Leste has started to join and cooperate with other countries; for example it is an observer of the International Network for Quality Assurance Agencies in Higher Education and the Asia-Pacific Quality Network.

Quality Assurance of Higher Education in Vietnam

Higher education institutions in Vietnam are classified into three categories: public, private and foreign-related universities that are branches of international universities from foreign countries. The Ministry of Education and Training (MOET) is responsible for the education system, and MOET directly controls one third of the institutions, with the other two thirds looked after by the associated government ministries and provincial People's Committees. All basic, and higher and professional education generally fall under MOET. Certain exceptions are for example the Hanoi Medical College, which falls under the Ministry of Health, and the Water Resource University, which falls under the Ministry of Agriculture and Rural Development (Runckel, 2009).

MOET has the main responsibility for planning and directing Vietnam's system of education and training as well as for many aspects of curriculum development and materials production. MOET has partial responsibility – shared with the Office of the Government, which is attached to the Prime Minister's Office with the Ministry of Finance and the Ministry of Planning and Investment – for broader decisions of policy formulation, target setting, and sectoral financing. The management and financing of education and training are becoming more decentralised in Vietnam. Higher education in Vietnam is similar to that of the former Soviet Union with a multiplicity of small mono-disciplinary institutions with limited linkage between teaching and research. The present structures and procedures have been inherited from the era of central planning when higher education was segmented by economic sectors with many specialised institutions, each with little autonomy of its own, reporting to a particular line ministry (Nguyen, 2009).

At present, accreditation is a relatively new topic in Vietnam. System-level accreditation was started when the Division for Educational Quality Accreditation was set up within the Department of Higher Education of

MOET in January 2002. Accreditation has been extended for other educational levels since the General Department of Education Testing and Accreditation (GDETA) was established in July 2003, which was supported in order to operate in December 2004 when the Temporary Standards for Accreditation of Universities were launched.

The influences of other countries on the Vietnamese quality assurance model are normally through bilateral cooperation and the support of international organisations, especially the World Bank, the Asia-Pacific Quality Network, SEAMEO and some other countries such as the USA, Australia, and the Netherlands. Although MOET wields significant power over higher education, many specialised institutions are supervised by other ministries and government agencies.

The Vietnamese quality assurance model has three sections: internal quality assurance system of the institution; external quality assurance system of the institution (including policy, procedure and evaluation instrument); and a system of quality assurance agencies (external review agencies and independent accreditation agencies) (Nguyen, 2009).

Quality assurance in Vietnam is currently voluntary. Vietnam makes use of self-assessment reports as part of its overall assessment. GDETA is fully responsible for the assessing, reporting, and accrediting of HEIs in Vietnam. This has led to much debate about whether a fully autonomous external QA agency would better benefit the objectivity of the QA assessment. In the past few years, MOET has carried out both quality assurance and institutional accreditation. However, MOET is currently in the process of moving the national body for education accreditation in Vietnam outside of MOET but it will remain directly under the control of the government (Cuong, 2009).

Vietnam is a member of the International Network for Quality Assurance Agencies in Higher Education, the Asia-Pacific Quality Network and the ASEAN Quality Assurance Network.

A Comparative Overview of Quality Assurance of Higher Education in the Countries of South-East Asia (Yavaprabhas, 2009)

1. National quality assurance agencies. In the South-East Asia region, every country except Myanmar and Timor-Leste has an agency responsible for QA, either within the Ministry of Education or outside.

2. Predominant modes of quality assurance agencies. There are three predominant modes of QA agencies in the region classified into three types of QA agencies as follows:

1. Centralised governmental QA agencies: QA in Brunei, Laos, Myanmar, Singapore and Timor-Leste falls under the Ministry of Education. In this case, the state ministers of education are responsible for overseeing national QA bodies.

2. Quasi-governmental QA agencies: national QA bodies are funded by national governments but allowed certain degrees of autonomy to manage their QA activities. These kinds of QA bodies can be seen in Cambodia, Indonesia, Malaysia, Thailand and Vietnam.
3. Non-governmental QA agencies: the third type of QA agencies in the South-East-Asia region is rarely seen except for some cases in the Philippines.

3. Scope of external quality assurance agencies. Only ONESQA in Thailand is responsible for assessing all educational institutions in basic, vocational and higher education. The external QA agencies in the other countries will assess only higher education institutions.

4. Scope of quality assurance. Programme and institutional accreditation can be seen in Brunei, Cambodia, Indonesia, Laos, Thailand and Vietnam. In Malaysia and the Philippines, QA consists of programme accreditation and institution audit. Institutional assessment is carried out in Myanmar and Singapore. In Thailand, disciplinary group and institutional audit is normally practised in external QA.

5. Voluntary/compulsory quality assurance. Voluntary/compulsory QA can be seen in Brunei, Malaysia and the Philippines. The rest of the countries in the South-East Asia region except Laos and Vietnam have compulsory QA.

6. National qualifications frameworks. Few countries in the region have developed a national qualifications framework; those that have are Malaysia, Singapore and Thailand. In Brunei, the initial stage of a national qualifications framework has been started.

7. Quality assurance practices. In South-East Asia, the common quality assurance practices are accreditation, self-assessment, quality audit, site visit and report. Peer reviews are practised in Indonesia, Malaysia, Singapore and Thailand. Quality control is practised in Laos and Thailand (see Table I).

8. Existing international and regional networks. The most popular international and regional networks in the region are the SEAMEO Regional Centre for Higher Education and Development (SEAMEO-RIHED), the ASEAN Quality Assurance Network (AQAN); the ASEAN University Network-Quality Assurance (AUN-QA); the Asia-Pacific Quality Network (APQN) and the International Network for Quality Assurance Agencies in Higher Education (INQAAHE). It is interesting to note that only Malaysia, Philippines and Thailand are members of all the networks listed.

There are three main international quality assurance networks that some or all of the South-East Asian countries are members of: INQAAHE,

APQN, and AQAN. Timor-Leste, despite being a non-member, is an active observer in such networks.

Countries	Self–Assessment	Accreditation	Quality audit
Brunei	?	✓	?
Cambodia	?	✓	?
Indonesia	✓	✓	?
Laos	?*	✓	✓
Malaysia	✓	✓	✓
Myanmar	?	?	?
Philippines	✓	✓	✓
Singapore	✓	?	✓
Thailand	✓	✓	✓
Timor-Leste	?	?	?
Vietnam	✓	✓	✓

Countries	Control	Peer review	Site visit	Report
Brunei	?	?	?	✓
Cambodia	?	?	✓	✓
Indonesia	?	✓	✓	✓
Laos	✓	?	?	?
Malaysia	?	✓	✓	✓
Myanmar	?	?	?	?
Philippines	?	?	✓	✓
Singapore	?	?	?	?
Thailand	✓	✓	✓	✓
Timor-Leste	?	?	?	?
Vietnam	?	?	?	?

* ? indicates membership under discussion or country as active observer.

Table I. Quality assurance practices.

INQAAHE is a world-wide association of some 200 organisations active in the theory and practice of quality assurance in higher education. The great majority of its members are quality assurance agencies that operate in many different ways, although the network also welcomes (as associate or institution members) other organisations that have an interest in QA in higher education.

APQN has been developed with the purpose of serving the needs of quality assurance agencies in higher education in a region that contains over half the world's population. APQN helps to build alliances between agencies, and assists countries/territories that do not have a quality assurance agency of their own.

AQAN is a network of quality assurance agencies made up of the South-East Asian countries set up with the desire to share best practices of quality assurance; to develop an ASEAN Quality Assurance Framework; to collaborate on capacity building; and to facilitate the recognition of qualifications and cross-border mobility.

Conclusion

Quality assurance in the quickly developing South-East Asian region is a diverse and multifaceted subject. Even though there are no two identical systems, they all have a similar focus on improving the knowledge and competitive ability of their human resources. The diversity in cultures, economic and social development, land and population size, as well as national resources, creates different challenges for individuals of the country to overcome. Through international alliances, particularly through quality assurance networks, specifically APQN and AQAN, the region has created a forum for the exchange of knowledge and experience to allow each country to share their quality assurance and accreditation systems as well as relevant and good practices to facilitate the development of all countries regardless of their state of development. It is hoped that this practice will improve transparency, as well as promote higher education credit transfer and thus improve cross-border mobility.

References

Accreditation Committee of Cambodia (2009) *QA in Cambodia: the information of ACC on organization structure/legal mandate and the number of personnel of ACC*. Phnom Penh: ACC.

Akbar, D.H. (2008) Brunei Darussalam National Accreditation Council, in *ASEAN Quality Assurance Agencies Roundtable Meeting, 6-8 July 2008*, pp. 29-37. Kuala Lumpur: Malaysian Qualifications Agency.

Cuong, N.H. (2009) *Higher Education Assessors*. Second Annual AQAN Annual Roundtable Meeting, 20-22 March. Bangkok: Office for National Education Standards and Quality Assessment (ONESQA).

Fahmi, Z.M. (2009) Malaysian Higher Education System, Quality Assurance System and Assessors, Second Annual AQAN Roundtable Meeting, Bangkok, Thailand, 20-22 March.

Haji Ashri bin Haji Ahmad (2007) Quality Assurance of the Assessment Process in Brunei Darussalam Vocational and Technical Education: stakeholders' perceptions and future challenges. Murdoch University.

Khorn, S. (2009a) ASEAN Quality Assessment Network (AQAN) Country Report/Guidelines: Cambodia, Second Annual AQAN Roundtable Meeting, Bangkok, Thailand, 20-22 March.

Khorn, S. (2009b) QA in Cambodia: the information of ACC on organization structure/legal mandate and the number of personnel of ACC. Bangkok.

Lagrada, H.D. (2009) History of Quality Assurance and its Structure in the Philippines, Second Annual AQAN Roundtable Meeting, Bangkok, Thailand, 20-22 March.

Ministry of Education, Youth and Sport, Cambodia (2008) *New Trend and Present Situation of Adult Learning and Education.* Phnom Penh: MoEYS.

Naidu, S.V. (2009) ASEAN Quality Assessment Network (AQAN): country report: Singapore, Second Annual AQAN Roundtable Meeting, Bangkok, Thailand, 20-22 March.

Ng, P.T. (2007) Quality Assurance in the Singapore Education System in an Era of Diversity and Innovation, *Education Research for Policy and Practice*, 6, 235-247.

Nguyen, H.C. (2009) Higher Education Assessors in Vietnam: current practices and the next step, Second Annual AQAN Roundtable Meeting, Bangkok, Thailand, 20-22 March.

Padua, R.N. (1998) *Quality Assurance in Philippine Higher Education.* Regional Workshop on Quality Assurance for Higher Education in Asia and the Pacific. Bangkok: SEAMEO-RIHED.

Runckel, C.W. (2009) The Education System in Vietnam. http://www.business-in-asia.com/vietnam/education_system_in_vietnam.html (accessed 8 December 2009).

Salleh, A.A.M. (2009) Higher Education Systems and Quality Assurance System practiced in Brunei Darussalam, Quality Assurance System and Assessors, Second Annual AQAN Roundtable Meeting, Bangkok, Thailand, 20-22 March.

SEAMEO-RIHED (Southeast Asian Ministers of Education Organisation-Regional Institute of Higher Education and Development) (2009) Cambodia Higher Education System. http://www.rihed.seameo.org/index.php?option=com_content&task=view&id=38&Itemid=41 (accessed 26 September 2009).

Xiongchunou, S., Chanthavong, P. & Keopanya, X. (2009) ASEAN Quality Assessment Network (AQAN): country report: Myanmar, Second Annual AQAN Roundtable Meeting, Bangkok, Thailand, 20-22 March.

Su, S. (2006) Cambodia Braces for Oil Boom, China May Profit from it, *Oil and Gas Industry Today*, 27 October. http://www.rigzone.com/news/article.asp?a_id=37532 (accessed 28 September 2009).

Win, S., Kaung, P. & Wai, K.M. (2009) ASEAN Quality Assessment Network (AQAN): Country Report: Myanmar, Second Annual AQAN Roundtable Meeting, Bangkok, Thailand, 20-22 March.

World Bank (2009) Timor-Leste Country Summary of Higher Education. http://www.worldbank.org/EDUCATION/Resources/278200-1121703274255/1439264-1193249163062/Timor-Leste_CountrySummary.pdf (accessed 26 September 2009).

Yavaprabhas, P.S. (2009) *Systems and Mechanisms for Accreditation and Quality Assurance in Asian Countries Higher Education: status comparison.* Bangkok: SEAMEO-RIHED.

APPENDIX
Acronyms Used in the Article

ACC	Accreditation Committee of Cambodia
ALCU	Association of Local Colleges and Universities in the Philippines
APQN	Asia-Pacific Quality Network
AQAN	ASEAN Quality Assurance Network
ASEAN	Association of Southeast Asian Nations
BAN-PT	Berkas Yang Harus Diserahkan Untuk Proses Akreditasi (National Accreditation Agency for Higher Education of Indonesia)
BDNAC	Brunei Darussalam National Accreditation Council
CHED	Commission on Higher Education in the Philippines
EQAC	Education Standard and Quality Assurance Centre in Laos
GDETA	General Department of Education Testing and Accreditation in Vietnam
HEI	Higher education institution
INQAAHE	International Network for Quality Assurance Agencies in Higher Education
LAN	Lembaga Akreditasi Negara (Malaysian National Accreditation Board)
MOET	Ministry of Education and Training in Vietnam
MoEYS	Ministry of Education, Youth and Sport in Cambodia
MQA	Malaysian Qualifications Agency
MQF	Malaysian Qualifications Framework
ONESQA	Office for National Education Standards and Quality Assessment in Thailand
PAASCU	Philippine Accrediting Association of Schools, Colleges and Universities
QA	Quality assurance
QAD	Malaysian Quality Assurance Division
QAFU	Quality Assurance Framework for Universities in Singapore
SEAMEO-RIHED	Southeast Asian Ministers of Education Organisation-Regional Institute of Higher Education and Development

CHAPTER 17

For Bulls and Bears Alike: education as investment in sustainable development

MIKKO CANTELL & DEREK ELIAS

SUMMARY Education is largely seen as a critical element in advancing sustainable development. The notions that investment in education can contribute to unsustainable patterns and may breed inefficiencies with limited returns have received far less attention. Education for sustainable development is an attempt to reorient the education sector fundamentally to address and prevent challenges to sustainability. Such a reorientation calls for emphasis on new skills in learners so that they are able to adapt to changing situations. While economic returns are important, it is not feasible to privilege these in education policy. Neither is it prudent to focus on injecting more resources into the education sector and to expect an increase in overall quality. The overarching objective of education will increasingly need to be values and behavioural change for sustainable development.

Some say a journey of a thousand miles begins with a broken fan belt and leaky tyre. In the deserts of Australia the acquisition of knowledge is not only the longest but the only road a person will ever travel.

Some commentators fear that education has lost its purpose and that it has all but become a thing of the past in terms of its relevance to driving development. As a World Bank publication recently put it in straightforward terms:

> Schooling has not delivered fully on its promise as the driver of economic success. Expanding school attainment, at the center of most development strategies, has not guaranteed better economic conditions. (Hanushek & Wößmann, 2007, p. 1)

In other words, economic wealth is simply no longer successfully correlated with increases in the quantity of education. Stevens & Weale (2003, p. 25) assert that it is difficult 'to be left completely satisfied by the wide range of studies looking at the effects of education on economic growth', and lament that there appears to have been selective studies in the field, validating commonly held assumptions.[1] Stevens & Weale do, however, find evidence to support the view that education is needed to increase productivity as a means to allow countries to make better use of available technology.

Even those education systems which are often perceived as internationally the best ones available do not appear to direct societies collectively to act wisely. On the contrary, these systems may simply encourage learners to perpetuate and repeat the same mistakes committed in the past, only more efficiently, perhaps. This can be exemplified by, for example, the findings of Coondoo & Dinda (2008, p. 363) who note in relation to emissions and economic growth that 'for the developed country groups of North America and Western Europe (and for that matter, Eastern Europe also) the causality seems to run from emission to income'.

In addition, educational policy and planning responses to accepted development challenges are typically disproportionate; education's share of OECD countries' Official Development Assistance (ODA) is a mere 8.25%, reflecting its priority rank among larger sectors. And yet, societies appear to have a thirst for education in the traditional sense, which meets neither twenty-first-century criteria for relevance, nor quality. UNESCO's former Assistant Director-General for Education Nicholas Burnett (2008, p. 2) described the paradigm shift in relevance as a 'need that development be sustainable. Currently characterized above all by need to deal with global warming, with, for the first time, natural environment issues caused by humans, not by external shocks. But sustainable development is not just about the physical environment, it has also to do with ... peace and poverty.' For quality, UNESCO's Education for All (EFA) Global Monitoring Report 2005, *The Quality Imperative* (UNESCO, 2004), speaks of the evolution of UNESCO's conceptualisation of quality by making reference to the International Commission on Education's report on education for the twenty-first century. The report described quality education throughout life as four types of learning: to know, to do, to live together, and to be (UNESCO, 2004, p. 30). These four types of learning remain a good starting point for quality education. Given the importance of initiating and responding to change, a fifth one dealing with learning to transform oneself and the surrounding world, is, however, sometimes suggested. These two elements – the notion of development's changing role with its implications for education and the relative novelty of the colour and depth of 'quality' – form jointly what we mean by twenty-first-century criteria for relevance and quality.

Education has all the potential to be treated as 'a permanent and complex series of organizational challenges, comparable to health, power, public sector management, business, legal and other sectors' (Heyneman, 2006, p. 20). Ultimately, there is no alternative to emerge and no real competition to the sector, which can only mean that education must be all the more ambitious and even brutal in its endeavour to improve itself.

UNESCO Bangkok organised in 2008 and 2009 a series of six workshops on Coordination and Capacity Building on Education for Sustainable Development (ESD) in the Asia-Pacific region, two of which had a specific geographic focus on South-East Asian countries. The discussions undertaken with government officials, researchers and NGO representatives showed that ESD in the region is reaching a new, more mature point from before. Member-states are increasingly beginning to engage in more coherent strategies for ESD by identifying clear thematic national sustainable development priorities, and linking such priorities to education and learning; education policy and planning; building inter-ministerial support; discussing financing; and, finally, engaging the right people at the national level.

The main social, economic and environmental challenges identified by the participants in the region ranged from HIV/AIDS, corporate responsibility and preserving biodiversity in Cambodia to improving education quality for the poor and ethnic communities, reproductive health and promoting local life skills in Laos. Other noteworthy sustainable development issues included challenges related to the impacts of school drop-outs and gender equality in Malaysia, conflict and political instability in the Philippines, and illiteracy and food security in Timor-Leste. In addition, representatives cited the pressures of being encouraged by their government to address several (more than nine) sustainable development issues at once, where an initial focus on three to four thematic priorities was seen to be ideal.

In terms of moving sustainable development forward through education, improved coordination of ESD was seen as crucial. Some of the main coordination issues in the region include developing a clear work plan on ESD, seen as necessary to enable coordination among other agencies and actors, and to bring other actors on board. Integrating ESD into wider national policies, plans and frameworks is also seen as crucial for engaging the donor community. As member-states which are newly engaged in ESD, Lao PDR and Singapore saw an essential need for inter-ministerial involvement in order to link ESD to existing programmes and prioritise and finance ESD. There is also the challenge of identifying non-ESD-branded activities, such as Thailand's concept of 'Sufficiency Economy'. Lao PDR in particular further identified the need to incorporate ESD into other agendas such as the Millennium Development Goals (MDGs) and EFA and to integrate ESD into different sectors and levels as opposed to creating a new committee for ESD.

While the country-specific chapters on the foregoing pages have discussed ways to tackle challenges in education at country level, this chapter provides a thematic (if critical) view on education and educational reform. The whole argument of the essay is just as applicable to South-East Asia as it is to anywhere else. Other thematic chapters in this volume touch upon various other issues such as gender, higher education, language policy, and quality assurance in higher education in South-East Asia. This particular thematic chapter shall complement these other contributions by offering a perspective on the promise of sustainable development and what role education can, and must, play in order to contribute strongly to an ambitious societal process needed to 'meet the needs of the present without compromising the ability of future generations to meet their own needs'.[2]

Rosalyn McKeown offers a concise explanation on sustainable development, which according to her is:

> generally thought to have three components: environment, society, and economy. The well-being of these three areas is intertwined, not separate. For example, a healthy, prosperous society relies on a healthy environment to provide food and resources, safe drinking water, and clean air for its citizens. The sustainability paradigm rejects the contention that casualties in the environmental and social realms are inevitable and acceptable consequences of economic development. [S]ustainability [is] a paradigm for thinking about a future in which environmental, societal, and economic considerations are balanced in the pursuit of development and improved quality of life. (McKeown, 2002, p. 8)

If education is one vehicle we have at our disposal then it may be in dire need of repair in the face of an arduous journey to play an important role in reaching a more sustainable future. Despite its shortcomings, the authors of this chapter are rather attached to it and advocate for careful revision and drastic repair measures rather than simple routine maintenance. Overall, we believe that without the promise of education, it would be wisest to abandon the whole idea of making a difference in the lives of those more unfortunate and relax right where one sits comfortably, without having to go to all the trouble of a thousand-mile journey. Yet it is not only about making it there any time. Unfortunately, the question for hundreds of millions of people going hungry, or fleeing conflict or disaster, is not if we make it, but whether or not we make it on time. Collectively, we need a potent medium for the voyage.

In terms of where we are at the moment as global citizens, it appears that issues such as democracy, human rights, the rule of law and a culture of peace – full and practised respect for human dignity in short – have generally been somewhat lost, forgotten and underrated, and that something resembling incurable ignorance has been driving 'development'. While most of us know the many things that are ailing us, we seem equally reluctant to change.

Education systems are, in principle, doing their best to improve this situation. Education has been shown to improve agricultural productivity, enhance the status of women, reduce population growth rates, enhance environmental protection, and generally raise the standard of living. However, as McKeown (2002, p. 11) notes, 'the relationship is not linear'. There is indeed a burning paradox in education in the twenty-first century – the more education is on offer, the better this is for an overcrowded planet as it tends to inhibit population growth. On the other hand, the more education, the larger the unsustainable footprint of an individual (McKeown, 2002).

Clearly, there is something wrong with the education we are offering – what national education systems have generally produced in terms of behaviour and values change is indeed not entirely convincing. The question then becomes how one induces systemic educational change that is able to transform whole societies. This is a difficult question, which we will approach from the angle of existing efforts and principles through ESD, and in highlighting the need for educational reform to incorporate the principles of sustainable development in educational policy and planning.

Education Sector in Development

It has been argued that the source of the validity problem education is facing in development is within the development education community itself. One underlying reason may be the sector's choice to focus heavily on one aspect of education in development, offering the overall development community only a partial picture of education. Heyneman (2006, p. 20) writes that treating '[EFA] as the single most important priority reduces the sector to being little more than one of humanitarian assistance. This one-dimensional view of the purpose of education diminishes the professional respect for the sector and makes it politically difficult to take an interest in any part other [than] basic education.' In his view, what started in the 1980s as being common sense in the sense that basic education is indeed critically important for development, has since turned into a restrictive *de facto* ideology predetermining the needs before actual analyses at country level.

It should be noted that, in direct contrast to Heyneman's assertions, however, Brannelly et al (2009) stress that their analysis of OECD countries' ODA and education aid's share to basic education reveals (in addition to the importance of increased prioritisation of education in aid budgets from the current average of 8.25%) the need for focus to be given to basic education. Interestingly, France, by volume the most generous donor to education, only addresses 10% of its education aid to basic education.

In general, however, the tendency to prioritise access to education and measure success primarily by quantity rather than quality or outcomes, has been criticised with a heavy hand. The development of qualitative indicators is notoriously difficult (see e.g. UNESCO, 2009, p. 108). The below listing represents one of the more neutral constructive criticisms and pinpoints four specific areas of concern which attribute to the tendency to assume that by simply raising the schooling level in a given population, productivity and 'development' graphs will sharply shoot upwards:

1. developed and developing countries differ in myriad ways other than schooling levels;
2. a number of countries and 'fragile states' in particular – both on their own and with the assistance of others – have expanded schooling opportunities without closing the gap in economic well-being;
3. poorly functioning countries with low-capacity infrastructures may not be able to mount effective education programmes;
4. even when schooling is a focus, many of the approaches do not seem very effective and do not produce the expected student outcomes (from Hanushek & Wößmann, 2007). We will discuss how ESD attempts to take these into account further below.

Educational Mandates for Development

In December 2002, the United Nations General Assembly (UNGA) adopted resolution 57/254 to put in place a United Nations Decade of Education for Sustainable Development (DESD), spanning from 2005 to 2014.[3] The primary goal for the DESD is laid out in the UNGA resolution 59/237, in which the General Assembly 'encourages Governments to consider the inclusion ... of measures to implement the Decade in their respective education systems and strategies and, where appropriate, into national development plans'. Furthermore, the General Assembly 'invites Governments to promote public awareness of and wider participation in the Decade inter alia, through cooperation with and initiatives engaging civil society and other relevant stakeholders, especially at the beginning of the Decade' (UNGA 57/254). The purpose of ESD is equally rather straightforward. It can be said to 'reorient education in order to contribute to a sustainable future for the common good of present and future generations' (*Gothenburg Recommendations*, 2008, p. 3). While all these definitions may instantly make sense, grounding them in reality or embedding them at appropriate junctures in educational planning, curriculum reviews, national sustainable development plans or any other of the many subsectors of education may often prove more difficult.

Friendly critics of the educational status quo – such as the authors of this chapter purport to be – are sometimes seen to equivocate and give ambiguous answers to blunt and direct questions on what needs to be done. In most cases, however, the key to answering the question becomes a question itself. More often than not, ESD advocates are expected to offer a blueprint for a 'ship'. It is clear that one cannot build similar ships for the Japanese commercial fleet and the indigenous Moken Sea Gypsies of Thailand, for the purpose of and requirements for these vessels are rather different. The same goes for furthering sustainable development in its intended local contexts. One needs to possess deep knowledge of the existing situation, challenges and stakeholders to get down to the solutions. In essence, education is indeed a vessel and sustainable development a journey, and as such not an attainable end goal or defined destination. In short, education that drives society in this direction is meant to build the capacities of individuals and societies alike to better respond to the larger needs of the surrounding world.

The World as Context

The inescapable economic principle, that a country's standard of living depends on how much it is able to produce goods and services, ought not to be overlooked in discourses on development.[4] We argue that sustainable development should not be primarily understood as reducing the quantity of goods and services produced, albeit this is being actively advocated for as a quick once and for all fix. Instead, one should be concerned with the quality of the end products and even more so with their social, economic and environmental impacts. Fixing a problem with urgency does mean, however, a rather radical approach, which in some respects resembles the extreme suggestion to cut down production (though our understanding is that this is being done without full comprehension of the ensuing economic implications).

The years 2008 and 2009 will no doubt long be remembered across the globe by the implosion of certain economic giants and the shockwaves that this created. Unsustainable and ethically suspect operations putting the whole world economy as we had come to know it in jeopardy is likely to appal economists and laymen for some time to come. When the dust finally settles, the expectation is that things will go back to normal so that ordinary people can live with security and free from fear. This is quite simply fallacious. First, the two years will be remembered much longer by those 55 to 90 million more people who are expected to fall into extreme poverty due to the economic crisis (United Nations, 2009, p. 6). Furthermore, taken as a whole, the global economic system is a perfect reflection of the world's myriad problems challenging sustainable development. Some of the largest profits are being made in the arms trade, which has grown rapidly over the past 10 years. Consider, for example, that the 'value of all arms transfer agreements with *developing nations* in 2007 was nearly $42.3 billion' (Grimmett, 2008, p. 6, italics omitted and added). To put the figure in perspective, this is roughly 65 times UNESCO's two-year budget with which it is tasked to advance peace and sound human development throughout the world through education, the sciences, culture, as well as communication and information. And so, '[w]hile stock markets gyrate and financial institutions (and even whole countries, like Iceland) teeter on bankruptcy, one global industry is still drawing plenty of high-end trades and profits: weapons' (*Time Magazine*, 2008). In a world where millions are living in extreme poverty or under $1.25 a day, military expenditure 'comprised approximately 2.4 per cent of global gross domestic product (GDP) in 2008, or $217 per capita' (Stockholm International Peace Research Institute, 2009, p. 179). That is quite an achievement and an interesting setting of priorities globally.

Education's Role in Development

It is understood that education plays a critical role in development. A recent survey of sustainability leaders' opinions (GlobeScan, 2009) shows that poverty reduction is overwhelmingly considered to be best addressed through investment in the education and healthcare sectors. A whole 93% of the responses to the questionnaire targeting experts from 90 countries around the world said that a 'great deal of effort' is needed in these sectors to reduce poverty. This oft-heard claim, that education is critical to sustainable development, holds true of course. We seem to know this almost intuitively and one hardly hears it contested in an intelligent conversation. Perhaps for this reason the contention is also surprisingly rarely scrutinised. Why education is so critical is a rather easy question to answer; normally the question would be approached from the angle of increased information, knowledge and abilities to tackle the problems we face in the world today. This, too, is almost innately understood and does not require formulation from an educational expert; development economists tend to argue along very similar lines (see e.g. Goldstein, 2008, p. 1) and assert, for example, that the broad 'consensus on the importance of education stems from extensive research on the macroeconomic, social, and private returns to education' (Amin & Chaudhury, 2008, p. 67).

One may logically wonder whether or not countries which have started to understand the consequences of unsustainable patterns are changing their behaviour for the better. This may be happening in some cases, but overall,

> one can argue that the values needed to achieve the Sustainability Transition are already in place, but it is the gap between attitudes and behavior, both individual and collective, that needs to be bridged. Such gaps are especially noteworthy in the persistence of hunger in Africa and the rapid growth in energy and materials consumption by developed countries and the megacities of newly industrializing countries. It is difficult to see how this can be reversed without some significant change, not only in the attitude-behavior gap, but also in individual lifestyles. (Leiserowitz et al, 2006, p. 435)

There is substantial work ahead in this regard.

Another claim which is consistently heard is that international aid for education needs to increase (see e.g. UNESCO, 2009). One should legitimately wonder why aid to education should remain stagnant in spite of this and is not rapidly increasing if it is almost universally agreed that it holds the key to (sustainable) development? Perhaps the answer partly lies in another often-heard claim according to which the education sector is in countless countries ridden with corruption and inefficiency at most levels, from ministries right down to the classroom where teachers may in effect teach little to nothing during normal class in an attempt to create enough demand for their private tuition lessons and tutoring taking place after the free 'education' classes. The reader will understand that education will in such cases lead to an inherent understanding of the power of money, the cold reality of poverty and the relative nature of right and wrong.

Nevertheless, anyone who has ever attended a large education and development seminar or workshop will know that there is a relatively large constituency of committed people who genuinely believe that the solution is simple: more resources in general to education to oil the machinery to run properly, and development will follow. This rational supposition is unfortunately not very well backed with evidence. What is rather well established, on the contrary, is that increased spending in education increases enrolment and traditionally used 'measures of education attainment' (Gupta et al, 2002, p. 732). Simply allocating more funds, however, will run the serious risk of compounding existing challenges of educational systems. Rajkumar & Swaroop (2008, p. 99), for example, have shown empirically that 'governance is central in determining the efficacy of public spending' and demonstrate significant differences in the performance of education and health sectors when studied together with good (or conversely bad) governance: 'a 1% point increase in the share of public education spending in GDP lowers the primary education failure rate by .70% in countries with good governance, and has no discernable impact in countries with weaker governance'. Funnelling more money into a broken system often only works to maintain the patterns that break and make the system inefficient in the first place. The authors' 'findings provide one possible explanation to the surprising result that public spending often does not yield the expected improvement in human development outcomes' (p. 99). As a result, the questions of where the extra money should be spent and how the existing system ought to reinvent itself, become critical.

Placing the emphasis on which interventions do yield positive measurable impacts is a more complicated question. Once this is done and potential leakages – such as those pertaining to the functioning and failure of markets, the composition of spending at education level, corruption, and the effectiveness of service delivery – are accounted for, analyses do reveal a correlation (see e.g. Goldstein, 2008). Yet even so, simple resource policies, as Hanushek & Wößmann (2007, p. 20) broadly call the typical measures to increase spending on schools, 'have little consistent impact on student performance when the institutional structure is not changed'.

Sound Investment in Education

Economically unforeseen or unimportant side effects related strictly to the transaction at hand are referred to as externalities in economics. 'An externality arises when a person engages in an activity that influences the well-being of a bystander and yet neither pays nor receives any compensation for that effect' (Mankiw, 2004, p. 204). Markets do not take into account externalities and market equilibrium is not efficient when externalities are involved. There are both positive and negative externalities and Mankiw in fact uses education as an example of an activity which yields positive externalities for society. Internalising this positive externality is, then, done by way of introducing incentives for the 'market' in the form of subsidies, or by affording education to citizens. Looking from within the education sector and bearing in mind the sustainability point of view, however, there are several negative externalities that follow from the more traditional formal education.

While an obvious viewpoint in terms of traditional development, which is by definition heavy on the economic dimension, the economists' emphasis is often on productivity and how that benefits society (Mankiw, 2004, p. 207). This is no different for education and regarding educational externalities. Externalities can be viewed from a different aspect, however. For example, if access to education in reality means access to a school with low-quality tuition, albeit free of charge, and where higher quality education is spared for later to be offered against a tutoring fee after normal school hours, as in the example given above, what kind of externalities are we then really talking about? These would logically include the informal yet effective lessons on corruption through offering good-quality education only for money when such education exists in parallel to a free education system. The major negative externality could here be labelled increased inefficiency of governance. Other potential negative externalities, especially in the context of South-East Asia, will include top-down communications maintaining rigid social relations which can be seen to stand in the way of social justice and just development, and, as an extension of strictly divided subject areas, a continued tendency to think in silos and failing to see systems-level challenges and solutions.

Mankiw concludes his discussion on externalities by noting how economists argue that some environmentalists hurt their own cause by not thinking in economic terms (Mankiw, 2004, p. 217). We believe this to be a true statement. Similarly, the obverse may yet be true for economists in the future, should sustainability thinking gain ground in learning in societies around the globe.

Spending more money on education wisely or at least spending more may then be a partial solution to advancing human welfare, yet the trouble remains that education in the traditional sense is not serving us well on average as measured against most large-scale sustainability indicators (take decoupling CO_2 emissions from economic growth and increased social cohesion as an example); education needs to transform itself. As part of wider development discourse, education is still largely considered part of poverty reduction efforts. This means that educational responses to social and economic problems are typically by default late and reactive rather than proactive. To contrast this more traditional thinking, Wade & Parker (2008, p. 6) have argued that education has an opportunity through ESD to be seen as poverty *prevention*, by way of turning unsustainable patterns around into something much more positive, reversing otherwise inevitable-seeming trends. The argument is that sustainability is not just a subject among others, but needs to be woven through curricula at all levels. Furthermore, as UNESCO's former regional director noted when explaining his vision for ESD in the Asia-Pacific, 'through ESD, education is taking a leadership role in not only seeing education as integral *for* development; ESD is also looking at education's role and potential contribution from different perspectives with*in* the broader context of development' (Shaeffer, 2008, p. 8, original emphasis).

To capture this possibility education policymakers and planners would be required to define what type of education is conducive to, or enabling for, sustainable development. As noted above, it is often the most unsustainable societies in the world that boast the best examples of what is regarded as the highest quality education. What appears common to all such societies are sufficient levels of wealth, and solid infrastructures driven and regulated by a high level of good governance within such a context. Quality education is, then, often conceived of as either a cornerstone of these positive attributes or an end result. Importantly, however, the context is not only negative; it is part and parcel of societies' mores, value systems and infrastructures. These create positive forces for development:

> Indeed, where applicable, indigenous and community knowledge of local contexts must be integrated into sustainable approaches – these types of knowledge are typically a more appropriate response to addressing local needs and opportunities ... than institutionalized knowledge or maximizing ... production on a larger scale. (Elias, 2009, p. 5)

Furthermore, as has been previously pointed out, while more traditional education

> focuses on the needs of all learners and their right to quality education, ESD ... moves sustainable, just and peaceful development for all to the forefront and uses this perspective to drive learning that enables every person to adapt behaviours and make informed decisions that can contribute to a [more] sustainable future. (Elias, 2009, p. 4)

Being reasonably resourced and localised seem consequently to be some of the necessary but insufficient conditions for quality education driving societies towards sustainable development. UNESCO has approached quality from a two-pronged perspective:

> the first identifies learners' cognitive development as the major explicit objective of all education systems. Accordingly, the success with which systems achieve this is one indicator of their quality. The second emphasizes education's role in promoting values and attitudes of responsible citizenship and in nurturing creative and emotional development. (UNESCO, 2004, p. 17)

In a similar vein, Hanushek & Wößmann (2007) imply that the quality of education may in fact be little more than a function of the value added to cognitive achievement. This is a useful definition as it leaves aside the age-old definition of quality as more or less an equation of materials, infrastructure and competent teachers (competency unfortunately often defined as being the number of years spent in teacher education and accreditation). Few things are further from an applicable indicator for good quality across nations and regions.

Overall, quality-related differences are observable and verifiable through levels of knowledge which are currently largely being neglected. Instead, literature on education and development (often euphemistically equated with 'growth') tenaciously promulgates the importance of measuring education and measuring it by years of schooling. Hanushek & Wößmann (2007, p. 4) hit the nail on the head with their final analysis summed up in the laconic statement: 'This misses the core of what education is all about.'

Education for Sustainable Development

Education's contribution to sustainable development as now widely understood under the heading ESD was first described by Chapter 36 of Agenda 21, a sustainable development programme adopted by 178 UN member-states at the 1992 Earth Summit. Chapter 36 identified four major thrusts to begin the work of ESD: 1. improve basic education, 2. reorient existing education to address sustainable development, 3. develop public understanding, awareness, and 4. training. These remain the commonly agreed-upon four thrusts in the implementation of the UN Decade of ESD for the years 2005-14 (cf. UNESCO, 2005).

One of ESD's challenges is, however, that it lacks the comparatively higher political profile of the six EFA goals. Of greater concern is the fact that perhaps the potency and potentials of education were not incorporated enough in the MDGs. This should not detract from the fact that the agreement of heads of state on a common global agenda for development was the greatest achievement of the UN system under the stewardship of Kofi Annan. One can argue for the omnipresence of ESD from multiple angles yet it remains absent politically until its relevance and contribution to the quality of education, which, in turn, contributes to broader access to education, are acknowledged. The lack of a noticeable validation for ESD in terms of systemic reform is not likely to be rectified very soon, for as Wade & Parker (2008, p. 22) note, the international agenda typically 'lags behind global imperatives and emerging issues'. Still, ESD should not be construed as an attempt to ride the latest wave of headlines. It does not pretend to offer a magical pathway to the latest scientific information on climate change for the classrooms. This is not what ESD is about. Plugging in information on sustainability issues is critically important. However, the struggle to open such spaces in education policy and planning has only just begun. ESD seeks to promote education that will foster skills in learners so that they are able to quickly adapt to new situations, face challenges with intelligent approaches without resorting to authoritative solutions and without remaining helpless in the face of major changes affecting their lives.

In many ways, the formulation of ASEAN's (Association of Southeast Asian Nations) Environmental Education Action Plan (AEEAP) for 2008-12 signifies such a commitment of ASEAN countries to further develop environmental education (EE) as a contribution to the Asia-Pacific Regional Strategy for Education for Sustainable Development. As a concrete shift away from purely EE, the plan adopted the theme of Environmental Education for Sustainable Development (EESD).

Framing the AEEAP 2008-12's overall direction are four target areas (formal sector, non-formal sector, human resource capacity building and networking, collaboration and communication) and their underpinning goals, which include creating a trained human resource pool on EE and ESD in ASEAN member countries. Partners of the various strategic actions include the respective ministries of the environment, education and higher education, as well as the Southeast Asian Ministers of Education Organisation and the ASEAN University Network. Universities and research institutions currently conducting EE/ESD research will also act as partners, supporting the advocacy of EE/ESD research at the national level.

If such a thing as quality education can drive sustainable development, consequentially one should clearly be keen on overcoming the challenges related to the means and opportunities to reform education systems accordingly. One major challenge in this logic is that education sectors are by definition, like any government bodies, highly conservative when it comes to territory, mandate and ways of the world. This serves the institutions well and as such they are right to institutionally resist sudden change. Education work in the context of post-conflict/post-disaster is one big challenge in itself, but provides an important externality: a window of opportunity for wider change. 'The "window of opportunity" approach refers to situations where quite dramatic changes are made to the education programming, not in direct response to need (although they are often marketed that way) but because of the flexibility provided by the situation (such as limited capacity and fragmented services) and a wish to improve the overall quality of education' (Baxter & Bethke, 2009, p. 29).

While it has been noted that it is exceedingly hard to convince donors of the need to provide educational services as a response to conflict and disaster situations (Penson & Tomlinson, 2009, p. 149), it is similarly clear that fundamental educational reform can only take place in conjunction with major societal developments, and usually very negative ones. It is this context where change, 'generally transitional (in the timeline and in scope) but with a view to being foundational', is being achieved (Baxter & Bethke, 2009, p. 29). Citing Mary-Joe Pigozzi's United Nations Children's Fund working paper from the 1990s, Nicolai (2009), too, notes that conflicts in all their human tragedy offer an exceptional opportunity for educational change, including even at system level. This is due to many reasons but perhaps most importantly because they commonly represent a time for seriously reviewing the weaknesses of the existing system and because there is likely to be a strong sentiment for reform across the board.

It should be stressed once more, however, that education reform in the aftermath of a disaster or a conflict is very demanding, in multiple ways. Only one example is that donor funding for education 'often dips after an initial emergency, with education programming falling into the gap between humanitarian assistance and long-term development programming' (Kirk, 2009, p. 113). Also, as Scott (2002, p. 106) argues, such advocates often 'walk a tightrope when they attempt guidance in such matters because of their need to stimulate without prescribing, and [the] need to see conceptual frameworks as scaffolding to build learning around, rather than as barriers to new ideas and creativity'. Given ESD's base in human rights, difficulties may at times be further compounded by the uneasy relationship between the disciplines of human rights and economics, which is, at theory level, 'often awkward and [at] times openly hostile' (Seymour & Pincus, 2008, p. 388), and not always unproblematic to reconcile in practice. In the development sector, education is sometimes crudely polarised to mean EFA for the poor and ESD for the rich, but contrary to common belief 'ESD is also vitally important for poor communities, especially those that depend directly on ecosystem goods and services' (Wade & Parker, 2008, p. 7).

With the Determination of a Bull and Insight of a Bear

ESD is about transforming societies to be more sustainable through changes in people's 'attitudes, values and actions' (Wade & Parker, 2008, p. 6) and should provide learners 'with skills and knowledge that they need for an active life in the democratic society of the future' (Gustafsson & Warner, 2008, p. 91). This is all well and good, but in reality, before this can even begin to gain ground in schools or, more appropriately, in all learning spaces formal or non-formal, a reform of its own needs to sweep across the education sector.

ESD is also about awareness raising; the education system must be able to send out the smoke signals about challenges ahead. Anything less would be immoral and would underestimate the learners' capacities. Given the complexities of the challenges, the awareness-raising function is, however, not the sole one. The messages conveyed to the learner are going to be markedly different depending on their consonance or dissonance with the true nature and sustainability of the system.

The awareness-raising function should be an active, transformative one. As an example, the concepts underscoring ESD can bring about a situation where the democratic process is embodied in education itself. ESD further provides potential 'to schools in terms of tackling several goals at once. It has potential for subject integration, given that scientific, social, economic and cultural issues are all relevant and interacting' (Gustafsson & Warner, 2008, p. 91). Such changes will in many societies initiate change and discussion from 'below' and light a spark for positive change. This process is a very important one and ought not to be underestimated.

Finally, as ESD attempts to induce fundamental change in what drives education and how it is assessed, its primary target in many cases becomes the system level. ESD can and should draw from past experiences in the field of education. As Abu-Duhou (1999, p. 20) has demonstrated, in the various attempts to induce School-based Management (SBM), ministries of education have found themselves having to strike a balance to 'ensure "good" and "equal" levels of educational performance without having to exert high levels of centralized control'. In SBM, too, it is indeed 'leadership at the most *senior* level [which] has succeeded in changing the culture of the system' (pp. 20-21, emphasis added).

Coming back to incorporating quality education across the sector, one only needs to connect with existing sacred texts of education:

> the Dakar Framework for Action declared that access to quality
> education was the right of every child. It affirmed that quality was
> 'at the heart of education' – a fundamental determinant of
> enrolment, retention and achievement. Its expanded definition of
> quality set out the desirable characteristics of learners (healthy,
> motivated students), processes (competent teachers using active
> pedagogies), content (relevant curricula) and systems (good
> governance and equitable resource allocation). (UNESCO, 2004,
> p. 29)

The challenge remains to operationalise the commitment.

Before closing and in an effort to shed some light on possible solutions for this challenge, it may be helpful to revisit the four characteristics of development discussed above. The listed four areas of concern will, if neglected, stand in the way of sound policies and policy advice but can be approached directly by existing ESD responses, namely a) that the policies should be tightly linked to the local context and national sustainable development priorities (with reference to our first concern as aforementioned: 1. 'countries differ in myriad ways'); b) development must be balanced in relation to the economic, social and environmental dimensions (ref. 2. 'schooling opportunities are expanded with no or little regard to the economic well-being gap'); c) ESD must not operate alone but be embedded in existing sustainable development priorities, including the UN Development Assistance Frameworks, where applicable (ref. 3. 'countries may not be able to mount effective programmes'); and d) policy should not be guided by what can be measured, but by what needs to be accomplished, i.e. values and behavioural change for sustainable development (ref. 4. 'ineffectiveness and expected student outcomes not achieved').

This is where we also come back to our previous assertion that fixing the broken fan belt and the leaky tyre requires something more or less radical. The radical claim – which has been done by others, including Hanushek & Wößmann – is that the solutions may be painful but rather simple, and that the answer to attaining quality education measured by competencies and achievements for sustainable development is not more resources for the old system, but reforming it fundamentally. It is going to have to make a world of a difference.

Notes

[1] To clarify for the use of the word 'assumption', Stevens & Weale (2003, pp. 25-26) assert that 'researchers tend to feel most comfortable with those macro-economic studies which provide estimates of rates of return similar to those found in micro-economic studies, in the range of 6-12% p.a.. Since results which suggested much higher or much lower returns would lack credibility, there has probably been an element of selection bias in the findings which are published. Thus the most that can be concluded from the various studies is that there has been no conclusive evidence suggesting that the returns to education are very different from this.'

[2] From the most used definition of sustainable development in *Our Common Future* (World Commission on Environment and Development, 1987).

[3] UNGA 57/254.

[4] For the principle see e.g. Mankiw (2004, pp. 11-12).

References

Abu-Duhou, I. (1999) *School-based Management*. Paris: UNESCO-International Institute for Educational Planning (IIEP).

Amin, S. & Chaudhury, N. (2008) An Introduction to Methodologies for Measuring Service Delivery in Education, in S. Amin, J. Das & M. Goldstein (Eds) *Are You Being Served? New Tools for Measuring Service Delivery*. Washington, DC: International Bank for Reconstruction and Development/World Bank.

Baxter, P. & Bethke, L. (2009) *Alternative Education. Filling the Gap in Emergency and Post-conflict Situations*. Draft report. Paris: UNESCO-IIEP.

Brannelly, L., Ndaruhutse, S. & Rigaud, C. (2009) *Donors' Engagement. Supporting Education in Fragile and Conflict-affected States.* Paris: UNESCO-IIEP.

Burnett, N. (2008) What Sort of UNESCO for What Sort of Education, Gaitskell lecture, University of Nottingham, UK, 22 May.

Coondoo, D. & Dinda, S. (2002) Causality Between Income and Emission: a country group-specific econometric analysis, *Ecological Economics*, 40, 351-367.

Elias, D. (2009) Food Security and Agriculture: applying ESD to global challenges for a sustainable future, *Journal of Developments in Sustainable Agriculture*, 4, 1-6.

GlobeScan (2009) *The Sustainability Survey 2009. Global Expert Insight.* Toronto: SustainAbility and GlobeScan.

Goldstein, M. (2008) Introduction. Why Measure Service Delivery? In S. Amin, J. Das & M. Goldstein (Eds) *Are You Being Served? New Tools for Measuring Service Delivery.* Washington, DC: International Bank for Reconstruction and Development/World Bank.

Gothenburg Recommendations on Education for Sustainable Development (2008) Gothenburg: The Centre for Environment and Sustainability, Chalmers University of Technology/University of Gothenburg.

Grimmett, R.F. (2008) *Conventional Arms Transfers to Developing Nations, 2000-2007.* Washington, DC: Congressional Research Service.

Gupta, S., Verhoeven, M. & Tiongson, E.R. (2002) The Effectiveness of Government Spending on Education and Health Care in Developing and Transition Economies, *European Journal of Political Economy*, 18, 717-737.

Gustafsson, B. & Warner, M. (2008) Participatory Learning and Deliberative Discussion within Education for Sustainable Development, in J. Öhman (Ed.) *Values and Democracy in Education for Sustainable Development.* Malmo: Liber.

Hanushek, E.A. & Wößmann, L. (2007) *Education Quality and Economic Growth.* Washington, DC: International Bank for Reconstruction and Development/World Bank.

Heyneman, S.P. (2006) The Effectiveness of Development Assistance in Education: an organizational analysis, *Journal of International Cooperation in Education*, 9(1), 7-25.

Kirk, J. (Ed.) (2009) *Certification Counts. Recognizing the Learning Attainments of Displaced and Refugee Students.* Paris: UNESCO-IIEP.

Leiserowitz, A.A., Kates, R.W. & Parris, T.M. (2006) Sustainability Values, Attitudes and Behaviors: a review of multinational and global trends, *Annual Review of Environmental Resources*, 31, 413-44.

Mankiw, G.N. (2004) *Principles of Economics*, 3rd edn. New York: Harcourt College Publishers.

McKeown, R. (2002) *Education for Sustainable Development Toolkit Version 2.* Knoxville: University of Tennessee. http://www.esdtoolkit.org.

Nicolai, S. (Ed.) (2009) *Opportunities for Change. Education Innovation and Reform During and After Conflict.* Paris: UNESCO-IIEP.

Penson, J. & Tomlinson, K. (2009) *Rapid Response. Programming for Education Needs in Emergencies.* Paris: UNESCO-IIEP.

Rajkumar, A.S. & Swaroop, V. (2008) Public Spending and Outcomes: does governance matter? *Journal of Development Economics*, 86, 96-111.

Scott, W. (2002) Education and Sustainable Development: challenges, responsibilities, and frames of mind, *The Trumpeter*, 18(1), 101-112.

Seymour, D. & Pincus, J. (2008) Human Rights and Economics: the conceptual basis for their complementarity, *Development Policy Review*, 26(4), 387-405.

Shaeffer, S.F. (2008) Of Concerns, Hope, and Legacies, keynote speech at the International ESD Forum in Tokyo, 2 December.

Stevens, P. & Weale, M. (2003) *Education and Economic Growth*. London: National Institute of Economic and Social Research.

Stockholm International Peace Research Institute (2009) *SIPRI Yearbook 2009: armaments, disarmament and international security*. Stockholm: SIPRI.

Time Magazine (2008) The Arms Trade Booms amid Global Woes. http://www.time.com/time/world/article/0,8599,1849972,00.html.

UNESCO (2004) *EFA Global Monitoring Report 2005. The Quality Imperative*. Paris: UNESCO.

UNESCO (2005) *United Nations Decade of Education for Sustainable Development (2005-2014): international implementation scheme*. Paris: UNESCO.

UNESCO (2009) *EFA Global Monitoring Report 2009. Overcoming Inequality: why governance matters*. Paris: UNESCO.

United Nations (2009) *The Millennium Development Goals Report 2009*. New York: United Nations. http://mdgs.un.org/unsd/mdg/Resources/Static/Products/Progress2009/MDG_Report_2009_En.pdf.

Wade, R. & Parker, J. (2008) *EFA-ESD Dialogue: educating for a sustainable world*. Paris: UNESCO.

World Commission on Environment and Development (1987) *Our Common Future*. Report of the World Commission on Environment and Development. Annex to document A/42/427 Development and International Cooperation: Environment. New York: United Nations.

Notes on Contributors

Colin Brock is UNESCO Chair in Education as a Humanitarian Response and Senior Research Fellow at the Department of Education, University of Oxford. A graduate in geography and anthropology from the University of Durham, he taught in high schools for a decade before becoming a lecturer in geography. On becoming Education Adviser in the Caribbean Development Division of ODA (now Department for International Development) he moved into international educational development at the universities of Leeds, Hull and then Oxford. He has worked on projects in Sub-Saharan Africa, South/South-East Asia, Latin America and all three tropical island zones for most of the main development agencies, with special reference to gender, teacher education and curriculum development. He has published widely in the field and is currently series editor of Education as a Humanitarian Response for Continuum Books and author of the core volume, *Education as a Global Concern* (2011).

Lorraine Pe Symaco is a visiting senior lecturer at the University of Malaya, Malaysia. She obtained her doctorate in education at the University of Oxford and has written and presented papers in various international conferences on education and development, higher education, and education in developing countries. She has also worked on research projects dealing with access and equity issues and serves as resource person for training school leaders in various regions in the Philippines.

Assad Baunto has worked on various research projects and served as consultant with multilateral agencies including the World Bank, the Food and Agriculture Organization and the Asian Development Bank. His research interests are in broad areas of human capital, growth and conflict. He holds an MPhil in development economics from the University of Oxford.

Bob Boughton is Associate Professor and coordinator of adult education studies in the School of Education at University of New England, Armidale, Australia. He has been undertaking research into the emerging adult education system in Timor-Leste since 2004, and recently completed a three-year study of the role of adult education in post-conflict development, funded by the Australian Research Council. Bob has had a long-term association with the independence movement in Timor-Leste, dating back to the period immediately prior to the Indonesian invasion in 1975. His other research interests include Indigenous adult education, learning in social movements, and the history and theory of popular education.

Mikko Cantell has worked at the UNESCO Regional Bureau for Education in Bangkok since 2008 when he joined the organisation as Associate Expert and is currently the Programme Specialist for Education for Sustainable Development (ESD) and acting Chief of the ESD Unit. Previously he worked at the International Department of the Finnish Ministry of Education and for the Finnish National Commission for UNESCO. His volunteer work includes board membership of the Finnish Section of Amnesty International as well as membership of the Crisis Management Initiative. Mikko holds a Master of Social Sciences from the University of Helsinki in international relations/world politics.

Chang Lee Hoon is a Professor and Deputy Dean (Post-graduate Studies and Research) in the Faculty of Human Sciences, Sultan Idris Education University, Malaysia. She received her BA Hons, DipEd and MEd from the University of Malaya and PhD from Macquarie University, Sydney, Australia. Her prior appointments were a secondary school teacher, teacher educator at a teacher education college and lecturer at the Faculty of Education, University of Malaya. Her area of specialisation and research is in moral and values education, and teacher education.

Derek Elias has been working for UNESCO since 2001 and was appointed in 2010 Head and Representative of UNESCO's Country Office in Bangladesh. UNESCO Dhaka strives to support human development in Bangladesh as part of the UN family and provide capacity development in all five of UNESCO's mandate areas – Education, Social and Human Sciences, Natural Sciences, Communication and Information, and Culture. Derek has a PhD in anthropology from the Australian National University following two Bachelor's degrees in anthropology from University of Queensland and Deakin University in Australia.

Gerald W. Fry is a Distinguished International Professor and Professor of International/Intercultural Education at the University of Minnesota and holds a doctorate in international development education from Stanford University, an MPA from the Woodrow Wilson School at Princeton and an honorary doctorate from Thailand in the field of Education for Local Development. He was also a Pew Faculty Fellow in International Affairs at the Kennedy School at Harvard. He has been doing research and development work on South-East Asia for five decades, with a major focus on Thailand, Vietnam, Laos, and Cambodia. He has spent approximately 12 years in the field in South-East Asia. He is the author of many books and articles on South-East Asia. Among his recent publications are the books *Association of Southeast Asian Studies* and *Thailand and its Neighbors:*

interdisciplinary perspectives. Recently he received the University of Minnesota's Award for Global Engagement.

Haji Omar Haji Khalid is Vice-Chancellor of the Technology University in Brunei. He holds a doctorate in educational studies from the University of Oxford, as well as a BSc in chemistry and physiology from the University of Salford, a Master's degree in educational administration from Simon Fraser University, Canada and a Postgraduate Certificate of Education from the University of Leeds. Before becoming Vice-Chancellor Dr Haji Omar was a Senior Officer in Higher Education at the Ministry of Education, having been involved in various aspects of the development of tertiary education. He has also been registrar and secretary of Universiti Brunei Darussalam. His Oxford doctorate was in special needs education, and today in his spare time Dr Haji Omar is involved in Pusat Ehsan, an organisation promoting special needs provision, and training of people with special educational needs. He is a member of the Board of Trustees of Pusat Ehsan.

Martin Hayden is Professor of Higher Education and a member of the Centre for Higher Education Policy and Practice at Southern Cross University in Australia, where he is also Head of the School of Education. He has published extensively on topics related to higher education policy. He has worked with ministries in Vietnam and Laos on projects funded by the World Bank, the Asian Development Bank and the United Nations Children's Fund concerning the development and implementation of legal and regulatory reforms in the education system. He is co-editor of a recent book on the higher education system in Vietnam, published by Springer, and he is the author of various chapters, articles and reports on issues in higher education in Vietnam.

Pei-Tseng Jenny Hsieh is a post-doctoral research fellow in the Department of Education, University of Oxford. With a background in language policy issues, her research interests are now in assessment and evaluation of educational policies and programmes in both developed and developing contexts. She has worked for major consultancies as well as for the World Bank and is currently engaged on large-scale assessments in developing countries and how they contribute to progress in education. She has worked on such issues in East and South Asia as well as Sub-Saharan Africa, and is currently involved in projects in India, Nigeria and The Gambia.

Richard Martin is an international education and employment consultant who was previously Education, Science and Training Counsellor at the Australian Embassy in Hanoi and Chief Technical Advisor on a World Bank project in Vietnam. He has worked with the United Nations Children's Fund on developing a plan of action for education legal reform in Lao PDR, and has written on the higher education system in Burma. He currently works for the Southern Cross University in Australia as the Director of International Cooperation and Development, South-East Asia and is recipient of a scholarship by the Australian government to work with the National University of Laos to suggest improvements to their operations.

Pham Lan Huong is Director of the International Educational Research Center in Ho Chi Minh City, Vietnam. She has published books and articles on education in Vietnam. Among her recent publications (with Gerald Fry) are *Education and Economic, Political, and Social Change in Vietnam, Universities in Vietnam: legacies, challenges, and prospects* and *The Emergence of Private Higher Education in Vietnam: challenges and opportunities*.

Richard Noonan is an education and training economist and planning specialist by profession. Beginning in mathematics and physics at Ohio University, he turned to comparative education and economics of education at Columbia University, where he earned a doctorate (EdD) in 1974. In 1976 he completed a doctorate at Stockholm University (PhD), where he taught education research methods. He began a consulting career in the early 1980s, and has extensive experience working in developing countries in Africa, Asia, and the Caribbean. Since the mid-1990s he has worked mainly in South-East Asia, especially Laos, where he has lived since 2002. He is also currently preparing a monograph on the history of education in Laos.

Siow Heng Loke is currently the Dean of the School of Graduate Studies and a Professor at the School of Education and Cognitive Science at Asia e University, an international university established with the support of 31 Asia Cooperation Dialogue member countries. Prior to joining Asia e University, he had served as a chemistry and physics teacher, curriculum officer and professor at the Faculty of Education, University of Malaya. He earned his doctorate in science education at Temple University, Philadelphia. His current research interests are in science education, curriculum and instruction, education and work. He has been a consultant on different occasions to local and international organisations such as the Ministry of Education Malaysia, INTEL, Sabah State Government, the World Bank, and Regional Centre for Education in Science and Mathematics (RECSAM).

Somwung Pitiyanuwat has been the Director of the Office for National Education Standards and Quality Assessment, Thailand since 2001. He has worked in the field of education since 1976. Previously, he was Dean of the Faculty of Education of Chulalongkorn University. He has been the Vice-President for research affairs for Chulalongkorn University since 2000. Dr Pitiyanuwat obtained his PhD in educational psychology at the University of Minnesota. He has been instrumental in shaping both Thai quality assessment and educational reform at all levels of educational institutions. He is a member of numerous national and international boards and committees concerned with educational development and quality assurance and served as host of the ASEAN Quality Assurance Network 2009 Roundtable Meeting and the Asia-Pacific Quality Assurance Network Annual Conference in Thailand.

Jason Tan completed his Master's degree in education and national development at the University of Hong Kong and his doctoral studies in comparative education at the State University of New York at Buffalo. He is currently Associate Professor in Policy and Leadership Studies at the National Institute of Education in Singapore. Jason is Executive Editor of the *Asia Pacific Journal of Education*. His most recent publications include *Globalization and Marketization of Education: a comparative analysis of Hong Kong and Singapore* and *Thinking Schools, Learning Nation*.

Natthapoj Vincent Trakulphadetkrai received his MSc in comparative and international education from the University of Oxford, and he is currently completing his PhD in education at the University of Cambridge with a focus on teacher education reform and educational equality in Thailand. He is also pursuing his second Master's degree in international public policy at University College London, University of London. Prior to this, Vincent received a scholarship to study for his BA (Hons) in primary education at Brunel University (London) where he graduated with first-class honours and a Qualified Teacher Status qualification. His interests, apart from education and international development, also include international relations. Vincent is also the Founder and Chairman of the Global Student Education Forum.

Keith Watson is Emeritus Professor of Comparative and International Education and a former Director of the Centre for International Studies in Education Management and Training at the University of Reading. He is a former Editor-in Chief of the *International Journal of Educational Development*, a past Chairman and President of the British Comparative and International Education Society, and Chair of the United Kingdom Forum for International Education and Training. He is author of *Educational Development in Thailand* and has written widely on comparative education, South-East Asia, education and language policies, and educational administration.

Anthony Welch is Professor of Education, University of Sydney. His numerous publications address reforms, principally within Australia, and the Asia-Pacific. He has consulted to international agencies, governments, institutions and foundations. Project experience includes East and South-East Asia, particularly in higher education. His work has been translated into numerous languages, and he has been Visiting Professor in the USA, UK,

Germany, France, Japan, and Hong Kong (China). A Fulbright New Century Scholar (2007-08), his most recent books are *The Professoriate: profile of a profession* (2005), *Education, Change and Society* (2007), and (in press) *ASEAN Industries and the Challenge from China*. His forthcoming book *Higher Education in Southeast Asia: blurring borders, changing balance* will appear in 2011. He is Director of the Australian Research Council project, *The Chinese Knowledge Diaspora*.